S0-BBD-964

Robert Slade's
GUIDE TO COMPUTER VIRUSES

Second Edition

Springer
New York
Berlin
Heidelberg
Barcelona
Budapest
Hong Kong
London
Milan
Paris
Santa Clara
Singapore
Tokyo

Robert Slade's

GUIDE TO COMPUTER VIRUSES

How to avoid them,
how to get rid of them,
and how to get help

Second Edition

With 19 Illustrations and a Diskette

 Springer

Robert Slade
Vancouver Institute for Research into User Security
3118 Baird Road
North Vancouver BC
Canada V7K 2G6
Email: roberts@decus.ca

Cover photo © Omikron, Science Source/Photo Researchers.

Library of Congress Cataloging-in-Publication Data
Slade, Robert.
    [Guide to computer viruses]
    Robert Slade's guide to computer viruses : how to avoid them, how
to get rid of them, and how to get help. — 2nd ed.
        p.   cm.
    Includes bibliographical references and index.
    ISBN 0-387-94663-2 (softcover : alk. paper)
    1. Computer viruses.   I. Title.
QA76.76.C68S55 1996
005.8—dc20   95-49098

Printed on acid-free paper.

© 1996, 1995 Springer-Verlag New York, Inc.
All rights reserved. This work may not be translated or copied in whole or in part without
the written permission of the publisher (Springer-Verlag New York, Inc., 175 Fifth Avenue, New York, NY 10010, USA), except for brief excerpts in connection with reviews or
scholarly analysis. Use in connection with any form of information storage and retrieval,
electronic adaptation, computer software, or by similar or dissimilar methodology now
known or hereafter developed is forbidden.
The use of general descriptive names, trade names, trademarks, etc., in this publication,
even if the former are not especially identified, is not to be taken as a sign that such
names, as understood by the Trade Marks and Merchandise Marks Act, may accordingly
be used freely by anyone.

Production coordinated by Impressions and managed by Bill Imbornoni; manufacturing
supervised by Jeffrey Taub.
Typeset by Impressions Book and Journal Services, Inc., Madison, WI.
Printed and bound by Hamilton Printing Co., Rensselaer, NY.
Printed in the United States of America.

9 8 7 6 5 4 3 2 1

ISBN 0-387-94663-2 Springer-Verlag New York Berlin Heidelberg SPIN 10524179

To Gloria

PREFACE TO THE SECOND EDITION

For those who didn't buy the first edition, welcome aboard. For those who did buy the first edition, welcome back, and thanks for making the second edition possible.

For those who bought the first edition and are standing in the bookstore wondering whether to buy the second, what's in it for you? Well, for one thing, it's smaller. (No, no! Don't leave!) I tried to make the first edition a kind of master reference for antiviral protection. That meant I included a lot of stuff that I thought might possibly be helpful, even if I had some doubts about it. This time I've tried to be a little more selective.

I've added a little more material to Chapter 4 (Computer Operations and Viral Operations) dealing with the question of computer viruses infecting data files and the new "macro" viruses. I've added two new sections to Chapter 7 (The Virus and Society). One looks at the increasing problem of false alarms while the other looks at the ethics of virus writing and exchange.

Appendices B and C, dealing with software reviews, have had a lot of changes. A number of outdated or less important products have been removed. New critiques of the latest products on the market are also included. A number of the original reviews have been rewritten to reflect the latest versions and technology. Some evaluations, however, have been left unchanged. Even in the rapidly changing world of antiviral software, many products remain essentially unchanged from release to release.

The Vendor and Contacts Listing in Appendix D has been updated to reflect the latest information, of course. I have also tried to give the listing more structure and I hope this makes it easier to use.

The Antiviral BBS Listing, which formerly made up most of Appendix F, has been removed. Maintenance of the BBS list became an enormous chore for very questionable return. The decline in overall quality of the Fidonet and VirNet virus discussion groups was another factor. Finally, the enormous growth in access to the Internet has made the list less important. I have included some pointers regarding sources of antiviral information online.

The disk included with the first edition held a variety of antiviral software for the MS-DOS platform and one program for the Mac.

However, I had forgotten to include Tim Martin's "special purpose" KILLMONK program, and guess what everyone needed? This time I have included virus information, as well, courtesy of the Virus Test Center of the University of Hamburg. Amiga, Atari, MVS, and UNIX users also get some goodies. Unfortunately, until overwhelming sales convince Springer-Verlag that the book rates a companion CD, something had to be removed to make room. This does *not* reflect on the quality of the Flu-Shot and Integrity Master programs: I still consider them to be the best in their respective categories and recommend you find and use them.

You learn an awful lot about the English language when you write a book, especially when you're an old science grad who grew up in the days of "Humanities" instead of English classes. It's very humbling to realize just how inconsistent you are in the use of the language, terms, and references, particularly when science is so dependent upon consistency. The first edition would have been even more of a disaster without the expert editing (copy, proof, and literary) of my-best-friend-who-is-also-my-wife, Gloria.

In this edition, the publisher (Springer-Verlag), the typesetting firm (Impressions Book and Journal Services, Inc.), and I have tried to improve the level of stylistic coherence. In addition, I've tried to reflect the changes in technical English that are a result of the influence of "online English." For example, "E-mail" is now "email," because techies aren't fond of shift keys and use the hypen only to identify command-line switches. "Trojan horse" is a common rather than proper noun in the data-security field and has nothing to do with Troy. (Those interested in the linguistic aspects of the online world are referred to *The New Hacker's Dictionary*. See the book review in Appendix E.)

In the course of preparing the second edition, we've identified a number of style issues that have not been addressed by the current style guides. Reviews of technical literature haven't helped an awful lot, since there don't seem to be any standards. We have tried to find the most common usage, although that is often hard to determine. (I must say that Laurie McGee, the copyeditor for this edition, has been able to find the most astonishing range of authorities for items that I thought were still in the realm of slang.) We hope the result is a more polished, lucid, and useful reference for you, the reader.

PREFACE TO THE FIRST EDITION

If you have bought this book in a panic because you suspect that your computer is already infected by a virus, please turn to Chapter 2—the "Beginner's Panic Guide to Viral Programs."

The only audience the book is *not* for is serious antiviral researchers—and those looking for a "how to write" cookbook. The CIO of a Fortune 1000 company needs to know the reality and scope of the problem, and how to "shortlist" the available resources. The technical manager needs product contact and assessment information. The technical support or help desk worker needs accurate information on how to deal with the problem. Small business owners need to know how to protect themselves and their business information. The computer retail and repair person needs to avoid infecting his or her customers. The home user needs all the help he or she can get.

The book is written to apply to all systems—micro, network, and mainframe. The concepts are the same in all cases. Examples are drawn from many systems, although MS-DOS predominates since the concepts are clearest when presented with MS-DOS examples. Technical experts working in other operating systems should be able to extrapolate from the examples given here—the average user shouldn't have to worry too much about the technical differences. Contacts are listed for Amiga, Atari, Macintosh, MS-DOS, OS/2, and UNIX systems.

The text of the book has been written with the average nontechnical computer user in mind. Jargon and assumptions about familiarity with technical concepts are kept to a minimum. At the same time, based upon experience in seminars, the material is sufficiently esoteric to be new and of interest to technical experts outside the virus research field. The material is based upon a weekly column that has been vetted for accuracy by the best of the international virus research community, as well as upon seven years of compilation. The contact and review information is the result of thousands of hours of compilation and testing over four years.

Not all parts of the book will appeal to all audiences. For example, even the "Beginner's Panic Guide" might be beyond the absolute neophyte who doesn't yet know how to get a directory listing. I'm sorry, but to write a step-by-step guide at that level would just make the book too big. By the same token, experienced technical people will find the description of basic computer functions to be quite elementary (although I hope not simple to the point of inaccuracy).

However, there should be something in the book for just about everyone. Even the executive or manager who can't read his or her own email should be able to understand the scope and concepts of the problem and appreciate the policies and procedures to minimize risk. In addition, given the wide range of viral activities and the scarcity of accurate information (not to mention the abundance of rumors and myths), even the most technically literate should find new information regarding defense and recovery. Hopefully for the vast majority of "intermediate" users, this should be a help, comfort, and resource.

I hope nobody who buys the book will ever need it. The odds, according to the best available studies, seem to indicate that a quarter of those who do will use it within two years. About 25 books have been published on this topic altogether. Many are over three years old, a lifetime in a field where software "generations" are measured in months. A number are written to promote a specific product. Those few remaining that are reasonably accurate are intended for the research, academic, or technical audience, and not for the average manager or user.

Most popular personal computer magazines have reviewed antiviral software from time to time. These reviews tend to cover the same few products each time and have been almost universally condemned by the research community. The reviews are technically suspect and subjective. Mediocre products are consistently given the highest reviews, tending to indicate that rankings are assigned on the basis of advertising budget.

It is difficult to decide a proper order for the presentation of this material. To a large extent, the chapters are independent from each other and can be read in almost any order. I think this order makes as much sense as any, but feel free to read as you please. Much of this is intended to be reference material, although I hope it is readable as well. Also, some material is covered in more than one place. For example, defining the terms "stealth" and "polymorphism" requires much technical detail, so you will find as much information on them in the definitions chapter as in the chapter on viral functions and operations, possibly more.

Chapter 1   Introduction: Definitions, Jargon, and Myths
What is a virus? What related problems are not viral? What are the
    other types of "malware"? Terminology of viral programs and virus
    research.

Chapter 2   Beginner's Panic Guide to Viral Programs
What to do if you (or a friend) is infected and have made no preparations.

Chapter 3   History and Examples of Viral Programs
Some cases and descriptions of major viral programs or attacks on MS-
DOS, Mac, and mainframes. The descriptions give some back-
ground and framework to the functions discussed in Chapter 4.

Chapter 4   Computer Operations and Viral Operations
Discussion of computer functions used by viral programs. Why a "perfect" defense isn't possible. How viral programs attack, and what
to look for.

Chapter 5   Antiviral-Protection Checklist
How to protect yourself and reduce the risk of virus infection. Policies,
procedures, and tools you already have to detect infections.

Chapter 6   Antiviral Software and Evaluation
What the types of antiviral software are, and their strengths and weaknesses. How to choose the best type for your situation.

Chapter 7   The Virus and Society
Opinion and social implications concerning:

- Hackers, crackers, phreaks, and virus writers
- The "no sharing" rule
- "Teaching" virus writing
- Trends in virus technology
- The scope of the problem
- Computer "Third World" hygiene

It may seem strange, but the appendices are longer than the book. They
include:

A   Frequently Asked Questions
B   Quick Reference Antiviral Review Chart
C   Reviews of Antiviral Products
D   Antiviral Vendors and Contacts Listing
E   Antiviral Bookshelf
F   Sources of Information On-Line
G   Glossary (terms used in antiviral research)

Included with this book is a disk with antiviral software for MS-DOS and Macintosh systems. All of the programs are functional and effective, and you are allowed to try any of them that you wish. Some are shareware, and if you continue to use the programs you should register them with the authors. Full details are included with the documentation in each archive file.

The disk is a 3½″ high-density (1.44 megabyte) MS-DOS formatted disk. I am in full sympathy with those who find this to be a problem and can only ask for your forbearance in what is, after all, a matter of practical constraint in production. This format has been chosen as the most accessible to the greatest number.

I became interested in the virus field following studies into the social aspects of computing and the risks of various types of technologies. In 1987 the first major virus infestations occurred, taking them out of the realm of academic curiosity and into the position of real security threats. Acting initially as the unofficial archivist for the budding research community, I eventually specialized in evaluating antiviral products, maintaining what have come to be termed "Mr. Slade's Lists" of antiviral contacts, products, and BBSes. Since 1991 I have written a weekly "tutorial" column for the on-line community. Most recently this has been augmented by a weekly "news and gossip" column.

In a very real sense I did not write this book, I only compiled it. The field of virus research is very small, but even so the level of technical detail is so wide-ranging that no one person can encompass it all. To a large extent, then, this is the work of the international virus research community, and primarily those who meet around the digital campfire known as *VIRUS-L* or *comp.virus*, moderated through the dedication of Ken van Wyk (as of January 1996, moderated by Nick FitzGerald). The attendees are too many to name here. Some get named in the body of the book someplace—most don't. All have my thanks.

William D. Knipe did the cartoons.

Thanks to Dr. Kinsey who observed that you can eventually get some interesting results out of any field of research, as long as you collect enough data.

Thanks to all those computer users who, in 1989 and 1990, kept asking which antiviral software was the best and who got me into this.

CONTENTS

RICHARDS' LAWS OF DATA SECURITY:

1. Don't buy a computer.

2. If you do buy a computer, don't turn it on.

MEMOIRS OF A (RELATIVE) VIRUS RESEARCHER

"Hi, Rob."

"Oh, hi, Larry."

"You busy?"

"Oh, reading through message logs for virus-related stuff like usual."

"Geez, every time I call you're always doing that! How much time do you put in on that every week, anyway?"

"Oh, about 60 hours altogether, I guess."

"Rob, you know you're wasting your time on that stuff. I mean, it may be interesting, and all that, but no one is ever going to care about it. How often do you see a virus on somebody's machine, anyway?"

"Oh, it happens."

"Yeah, well . . . anyway, you got a minute?"

"Always time for my favorite brother-in-law. You still setting stuff up on your friend's machine?"

"Yeah, and I need some more space. There's a directory in Windows called TEMP and it has a whole bunch of files with .TMP extensions. Do I need them?"

"Nope. Like it indicates, they're just temporary files that Windows hasn't cleaned up when it finished with them. As long as Windows isn't running, just dump 'em."

"OK, good. That'll get me about a dozen megs. What about these files all over the place with .BK! extensions?"

"They're WordPerfect backup files. If your friend doesn't want them, you can get rid of them, too."

"You mean I have to go through every directory and delete them?"

"No, you can do it more easily. Remember that SEEK program? Ask it to look for them and redirect the output to a file. That way you get a list of all the filenames with a full pathname, and you can edit the file into a batch file to delete them all."

"Oh, OK, yeah, I can see that. Oh, by the way, I saw something strange just a minute ago. When I was rebooting the machine, right at the beginning it said 'Your PC is now Stoned.' Do you know why it did that?"

"Yes, as a matter of fact I can tell you exactly what it means, Larry. Your friend's computer has a virus."

CHAPTER 1

INTRODUCTION: DEFINITIONS, JARGON, AND MYTHS

WHAT AND WHAT NOT

The "man on the street" is now often aware of the term "computer virus" even if he (or she) does not use a computer. However, it is often the case that those who are otherwise technically literate do not understand some of the implications of the phrase. This is not surprising in that the term is slang, and often misused, and that "hard" information is difficult to come by.

It is important to know what a computer virus is if you are going to defend yourself against the many that are "out there." It is also important to know what a computer virus is not. There are other types of programs and situations that can do damage to your computer or data, and many of these will not be caught by the same methods that trap viral programs.

We find a biological analogy in any dictionary. The *Oxford English Dictionary* speaks of a virus as: "a moral or intellectual poison, or poisonous influence."

While satisfying to the wounded ego of those who have been hit, it is not terribly helpful in a technical sense. *Webster's,* however, steers us in a more useful direction by stating that viruses are: "dependent on the host's living cells for their growth and reproduction."

By eliminating the biological references, we can come to the definition that a virus is an entity that uses the resources of the host to spread and reproduce itself without informed operator action. Let me

3

stress here the word "informed." A virus cannot run completely on its own. The computer user must always take some action, even if it is only to turn the computer on. This is the major strength of a virus: it uses *normal* computer operations to do its dirty work, and so there is no single identifying code that can be used to find a viral program.

Dr. Fred Cohen is generally held to have coined the term "computer virus" in his thesis (published in 1984). However, his original definition covers only those sections of code that, when active, attach themselves to other programs. This, however, neglects many of the programs that have been most successful "in the wild." Many researchers still insist on Cohen's definition and use other terms such as "worm" and "bacterium" for those viral programs that do not attack programs.

If one of those programs is a virus, what are two of them called? Given that the term is still in the realm of slang, this debate has been the longest, silliest, and most bitter debate in the whole field of computer virus research. Various linguistic "experts" have called for virae, virii, viren, and virides. The biological analogy would support viruses, and that is, in fact, the most common, although not universal, usage. Having listened to the entire debate, I think the strongest arguments support viri. My personal favorite, however, is the suggestion that it is one virus, two virii, three viriii, four viriv. . . .

Computer viral programs are not a "natural" occurrence. Viruses are programs written by programmers. They do not just appear through some kind of electronic evolution. Viral programs are written, deliberately, by people. (Having studied the beasts almost from their inception, I was rather startled when a young, intelligent, well-educated executive proposed to me that viruses had somehow "just grown" like their biological counterparts.)

The popular press has recently started to publicize the term computer virus, but without giving any details other than the fact that viral programs are to be feared. (Often the reports talk about "main storage destroyed" and other such phrases, which have very little meaning.) This has given most people the impression that anything that goes wrong with a computer is caused by a virus. From hardware failures to errors in use, everything is blamed on a virus. *A VIRUS IS NOT JUST ANY DAMAGING CONDITION.*

Similarly, it is now popularly believed that any program that may do damage to your data or your access to computing resources is a virus. We will speak further about trojan horse programs, logic bombs, and worms, but it is important to note that viral programs have common characteristics that other damaging or security-breaking programs may lack. Viral programs are not simply programs that do damage.

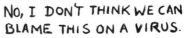

Indeed, viral programs are not always damaging, at least not in the sense of being deliberately designed to erase data or disrupt operations. Most viral programs seem to have been designed to be a kind of electronic graffiti: intended to make the writer's mark in the world, if not his or her name. In some cases a name is displayed, on occasion an address, phone number, company name, or political party (and in one case, a ham radio license number).

On the other hand, viral programs cannot be considered a joke. Often they may have been written as a prank, but even those that have been written so as not to do any damage have had bugs, in common with any poorly written program. The original author of Stoned virus knew nothing of certain drive specifications, and the virus conflicts with some disk formats. In fact, it appears that the trashing of data by the Ogre/Disk Killer virus, one of the most damaging viruses, was originally intended to be reversible, were it not for an error on the part of the programmer. Any program that makes changes to the computer system which are unknown to the operator can cause trouble, the more so when the program is designed to keep spreading those changes to more and more systems.

However, it is going too far to say (as some have) that the very existence of viral programs, and the fact that both viral strains and the numbers of individual infections are growing, means that computers are finished. At the present time, the general public is not well informed about the virus threat, and so more copies of viral programs are being produced than are being destroyed. As people become aware of the danger, this will change.

If we stick to a strictly "Cohenesque" definition of viral programs as only those that attach to specific programs, then there are some difficulties with defining other similar programs that reproduce themselves without being linked to a program file. Unfortunately, although attempts have been made to address this issue, there is as yet little agreement over terminology.

RELATED PROGRAMS

In early multitasking operating systems, programs often "broke the bounds" and would overwrite sections of other programs or data. Since this damage was generally random, the pattern of damage, when mapped, gave the appearance of twisting tracks, which appeared and disappeared. This closely resembled the patterns seen when cutting through a piece of worm-eaten wood, giving rise to the term "worm" for such rogue programs. A separate, and very interesting, derivation of worm is given by the experiments in distributed computing by John Shoch and Jon Hupp. They wrote programs that would transfer copies of themselves to other machines on a network while remaining under the control of the original program. They saw the entire matrix of copied programs as a "worm": a single entity with many program segments. The term "worm" has therefore come to be used to refer to viral programs that do not attach to specific programs and, more specifically, to those that use network communications as a vehicle for spreading and reproduction. Two examples of this usage are the famous Internet/Morris/UNIX Worm of late 1988, and the lesser known CHRISTMA EXEC mail worm of December 1987.

This still leaves a class of viral programs that do not attach specifically to programs. There are actually many subgroupings within this group and within viral programs generally. However, European researchers, particularly those from France, often refer to such programs as "bacteria," rather than viruses.

In these areas of terminology, there is often much debate about whether a given virus, or type of viral program, fits into a given class. Boot sector infectors (BSIs), for example, would not appear to fit the definition of a virus infecting another program, since BSIs can be spread by disks that do not contain any program files. However, the boot sector of a normal disk, whether or not it is a "system" or bootable disk, always contains a program (even if it only states that the disk is not bootable), and so it can be said that a BSI is a "true" virus.

Two other groups of security-breaking programs are very often confused with viral programs. The first is the "trojan horse," and the second, the "logic bomb." The confusion is understandable, as viral-type programs, trojan horses, and logic bombs make up the three largest distinct groups of security-breaking software, and often one may contain the code of another.

A trojan horse is a program that pretends to do one thing while performing another, unwanted action. The extent of the "pretense" may vary greatly. Many of the early PC trojans relied merely on the filename and a description on a bulletin board. "Login" trojans, popular among university student mainframe users, will mimic the screen display and the prompts of the normal login program and may, in fact, pass the username and password along to the valid login program at the same

Trojan horse

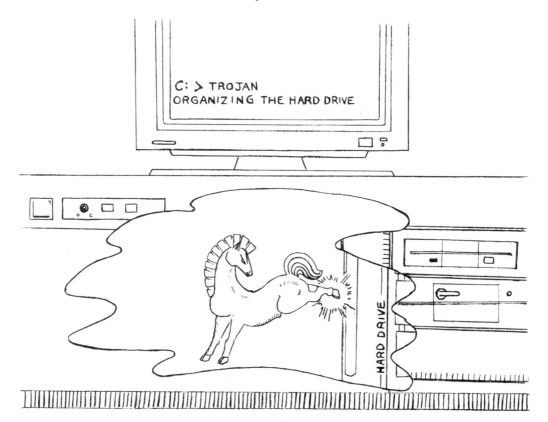

time as they steal the user data. Some trojans may contain actual code that does what it is supposed to be doing while performing additional nasty acts that it does not tell you about. (I make the distinction that trojans are always malicious, as opposed to "joke" or "prank" programs.)

A recent example of a trojan is the "AIDS Information Disk," often incorrectly identified in both the general and computer trade press as a virus. Not to be confused with the fairly rare AIDS I and II viruses, this program appears to have been part of a well-organized extortion attempt. The "evaluation disks" were shipped to medical organizations in England and Europe, with covers, documentation, and license agreements just like any real commercial product. When installed and run, the program did give information and an evaluation of the subject's risk of getting AIDS, but it also modified the boot sequence so that after 90 reboots of the computer, all files on the disk were encrypted. The user was informed that, in order to get the decryption key, a "license fee" had to be paid.

Some data security writers consider that a virus is simply a specific example of the class of trojan horse programs. There is some validity to this usage since a virus is an "unknown" quantity that is hidden and transmitted along with a legitimate disk or program. However, the term "virus" more properly refers to the added, infectious code rather than the virus/target combination. Therefore, the term trojan refers to a deliberately misleading or modified program that does not reproduce itself. Trojan horse programs are sometimes referred to as "Arf, Arf" or "Gotcha" programs, from the screen messages of one of the first examples.

A logic bomb is a malicious program that is triggered by a certain event or situation. Logic bomb code may be part of a regular program, or set of programs, and not activate when first run, thus having some of the features of a trojan. The trigger may be any event that can be detected by software, such as a date, username, CPU ID, account name, or the presence or absence of a certain file. Viral programs and trojans may contain logic bombs.

Peripherals, such as terminals and printers, can and have been used as the vectors for viral programs and the like. Two examples given were the "logoff" mail prank on Wyse 85 terminals and a purported Mac Laserwriter virus. "Terminal" viral programs usually take advantage of interpreter devices or programs. The ANSI.SYS program can be seen as a special case of this. It is a program used in the MS-DOS environment that provides standard screen control, generally used to emulate an ANSI terminal. It can also be used to redefine keys on the keyboard.

Logic bomb

This latter use is not as well known, although it is used by some to provide keyboard macros or to remap specialized keyboard layouts.

ANSI bombs are, however, not viral, in that they do not reproduce. They may be considered as trojans or logic bombs. An ANSI bomb is a sequence of characters that is interpreted by ANSI.SYS as redefining a key, or keys, on the keyboard. Thereafter, these keys will not send the normally assigned characters, but rather the redefined string. This string may contain any ASCII characters, including <RETURN> and multiple commands. Therefore, the space bar, for example, can be redefined to:

```
DEL *.* <cr>Y<cr>
```

This sequence would, in MS-DOS, delete all files in the current directory.

ANSI bombs are stored in normal text files or messages. They are triggered by sending the text to the "console" device while ANSI emulation is active. What this normally means is "TYPE"ing the text of a file so that the file can be read. (Reading a text file with a word processor generally does not "port" the data to the "console," since the text is interpreted by the word processor before it is displayed to the screen. Only a very few older word processors use the ANSI.SYS program for screen control.) However, reading an email message with a terminal program that uses ANSI.SYS will have the same effect, as will extracting an archived file that contains the ANSI sequence in the text comment header.

Reading all text files with an editor, lister, or word processor is a protection against ANSI bombs, but it still leaves the possibility of being affected. The best protection is to remove ANSI.SYS from the system and not to use terminal emulators or other programs that require it. You can also replace ANSI.SYS with the shareware FANSI, ZANSI, or NANSI programs. As a last resort, a technically competent person can remove the key-rebinding capability from the ANSI.SYS file itself.

Why are viral programs special? What is it about the simple fact that they reproduce that makes them a class by themselves? There is no shortage of malware (malicious software) out there: trojans and logic bombs abound and were known long before viral programs. Why can't we simply class viral programs as another form of trojan and be done with it?

A trojan program relies upon other programs to do the reproduction necessary to hit a target. The dangers (and the results) are self-limiting. If a "friend" gives you a trojan and it triggers, you lose trust in that friend. It is very seldom that you will get stuck from the same source twice. Trojan writers like to use bulletin boards, but even that method of transmission is limited. A posting of a trojan program will usually now get an individual barred from the BBS, perhaps even from all that are in the city. Logic bombs, of course, are even more limited. Generally they aren't meant to reproduce at all.

These types of malware, therefore, can generally present an attack from a single point. As any military strategist can tell you, defense against such an attack is fairly straightforward. Intelligence, in the form of advice from other users, can be used to eliminate the attack before it even starts.

In Greek mythology, Hercules had to kill the Hydra, a serpentlike monster. A rather simple task, which he approached in a straightforward manner—he cut off its head. The Hydra, however, had a special property. When its head was cut off, it immediately grew two new

The binary hydra

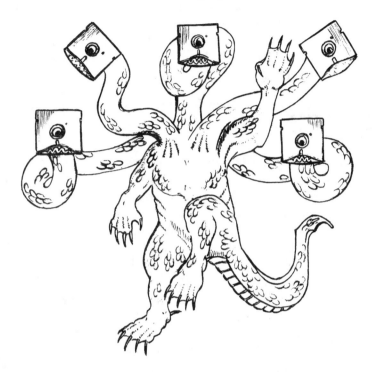

heads. In fact, each head Hercules severed quickly grew two new replacements. He was soon confronted with a beast armed with a great number of fang-filled maws, each capable of attacking from a different direction.

So it is with viral programs. Far from being limited to a single point, they can attack from any quarter. The enemy can attack in strength as well. You have no idea of the enemy strength because the individual "soldiers" can reproduce using systems around you—or your *own* system. When a trojan program is found, it is generally deleted, or at least quarantined. When a virus is detected, it has generally already had a chance to infect other targets on your system. In my experience at being called in to deal with them, by the time a boot sector infector (BSI) is caught, it has generally infected a third to a half of all the diskettes used around that system, making it almost certain that the system will be reinfected within a month.

Even without a damaging payload, the ability of viral programs to reproduce and spread can cause problems. The Internet Worm deleted no files, but its uncontrolled reproduction clogged machines and mail queues and denied service to legitimate users and programs. The concept of beneficial viral programs has been examined, but the reproductive capacity means that a single error in one such experimental program can shut down more than a hundred machines at one site. The growth of the personal workstation, with arbitrary characteristics, presents a very high risk that a "self-spreading" program can cause trouble.

SPECIAL TERMS

Most people think of viral programs in terms of a variation on Cohen's definition: that is, a virus is a program that always "attaches" to another program. This has given rise to a great many misconceptions about some of the most common viral programs, boot sector infectors.

Boot-sector-infecting viral programs *do*, in a sense, attach to another program. Most people are unaware of the fact that there is a program on every disk, even those that are blank. Every formatted disk has a boot sector, specified not by a filename, but simply by its location as the first physical (or logical, in the case of hard drives) sector. When the computer is booted, the ROM programming looks for a disk, then runs whatever happens to be in that sector as a program.

In most cases, with nonbootable disks, the "program" that is there simply prints a message reminding the user that the disk is nonbootable. The important thing, however, is that regardless of how small the actual program may be, the computer "expects" there to be a program in the boot sector and will run anything that happens to be there. Therefore, any viral program that places itself in that boot sector position on the disk will be the first thing, other than ROM programming, to run when the computer starts up. BSIs will copy themselves onto floppy disks and transfer to a new computer when the "target" machine is booted (usually inadvertently) with an infected floppy in the A: drive.

The terminology of BSIs comes from MS-DOS systems, and this leads to some additional confusion. The physical "first sector" on a hard drive is not the operating-system boot sector. On a hard drive, the boot sector is the first "logical" sector. The number one position on a hard drive is the master boot record (MBR). (This name gets slightly confused by the fact that the MBR contains the partition table—the data specifying the type of hard disk and the partitioning information. "Master boot record," "partition table," and "partition boot record" are often used interchangeably, although they are not identical entities.) Some viral programs, such as the Stoned virus, always attack the physical first sector: the boot sector on floppy disks and the master boot record on hard disks. Thus viral programs that always attack the boot sector might be termed "pure" BSIs, whereas programs like Stoned might be referred to as an "MBR type" of BSI. The term boot sector infector is used for all of them, though, since all of them infect the boot sector on floppy disks.

The term "link virus" will likely be familiar only to those using Atari and Amiga systems, but for others, this is simply the standard "file-infecting" virus. For most people, this is what is thought of as a virus. File-infecting viral programs "link," or attach, in many different ways. The largest number will place the bulk of the viral code toward the end of the program file, with a "jump" sequence at the beginning of the file that "points" to the main body of the virus. Some viral code attaches to the beginning of the file—simpler in concept, but actually more difficult in execution. These two techniques are known as "appending" and "prepending," respectively, but the terms are used less than in years past.

Some viral programs do not attach to the beginning or end of the file, but write their code into the target program itself. Most often this is done by simply overwriting whatever is there already. Most of the time, the virus will also make a modification to the beginning of the program, which points to the virus, but on occasion the virus will rely on chance for a computer operation to stumble on the code and run it. Of course, if a virus has overwritten existing code, the original "target" program is damaged, and there is little or no possibility of recovery other than by deleting the infected file and restoring from a clean backup copy. However, some overwriting viruses are known to look for strings of null characters. If such can be identified, the viral code can be removed and replaced with nulls again. (The Lehigh virus, for example, attaches "behind" the COMMAND.COM file, in a sense, but overwrites slack space at the end of the file so as not to change the file size.)

Some viral programs do not physically "touch" the target file at all. There are two ways to "infect" in this manner. One method is quite simple and takes advantage of "precedence" in the system. In MS-DOS, for example, when a command is given, the system checks first for internal commands, then COM, EXE, and BAT files in that order. EXE files can be "infected" by writing a COM file in the same directory with the same filename. This type of virus is most commonly known as a "companion" virus, although the term "spawning" virus is also used.

The second method is more difficult. "System" viral programs, such as DIR-II (often mistakenly referred to as "FAT" viruses), will not change the target program, but will change the directory entry for the program so as to point to the virus. The original file will not be changed, but when the target program is called, the virus will be run first instead.

BSIs are the most "successful" of viral programs in terms of the number of copies made and the number of systems infected. This is rather odd, given that BSIs can make, at most, one copy per disk. While it is sometimes possible for more than one "boot virus" to infect a disk, it is also the case that some combinations, such as Stoned and Michelangelo, conflict in their use of the same areas of the disk. This renders the system unbootable and alerts the user to a problem.

On the other hand, BSIs, once "installed" on a hard drive or boot disk, are almost always active, since they start at boot time. Unless the system is booted from a "clean" disk, the virus will continuously infect any and all disks that are "proper" targets for it. BSIs also have a strong psychological edge, since most users still do not understand how a virus can be carried on a "blank" disk. The *InformationWeek* survey of June 1993 shows that while Stoned was the highest reported virus, BBSes and networks are seen as the major vectors. The majority of computer users and managers still do not understand the concepts that prohibit BSIs from spreading via modems and networks, and allow them to spread on *any* disk.

At first glance, file infectors have many advantages. There are many more program files on a given system than boot sectors and, therefore, more opportunities or targets for infection. Multiple copies of a given virus can reside on a given system. While some viral programs may conflict in the use of memory or interrupts, most of the time multiple viral programs can quite happily infect a given program file. Files can be transferred via bulletin boards and communications links and can even be infected through a network.

On the other hand, a virus that has infected a file has to wait until that file is executed. The majority of "traded" information these days tends to be data, rather than programs. This provides a vector for a BSI (if passed on disk), but not for a file infector. Also, program files tend to be passed in "archived" form, and even if the program becomes infected on one system, the archive itself is unaffected. It is usually the "original" archive that is passed along, rather than a "re-archived" copy, which might have become infected. Therefore, unless the original archive was infected, it will likely not become a vector, even if it passes through an infected system.

BSIs, therefore, have certain advantages, while file infectors have others. To get the greatest "spread," one wants to build a virus that will infect both files and boot sectors—a "multipartite" virus. At first glance, this seems to be an obviously advantageous feature for a virus to have.

In practice, these programs have had some success, but have proven to be terribly dangerous to the user population at large.

Scanning software is, for all of its limitations, still the most widely used of antiviral software. The idea is to find the virus "signature string": a piece of code that appears in the virus and in no other program, thus giving a unique identification. There is an art to the choice of a signature string, as with anything else. You want a piece of code more than you want text that is easy to change. You want a piece of code integral to the operation of the virus. You want a string that may identify new mutations of this virus, as well as the current infection. However, once you have a suitable signature, you can identify the virus.

Unless the virus changes.

This is the idea behind polymorphism. There are a number of ways to change the "shape" of a virus. One way is to get a simple "random" number, such as the value of the "seconds" field of the system time when the infection occurs, and to perform a simple encryption on the value of each byte in the viral code. Only a short chunk is left at the beginning to decrypt the rest of the virus when the time comes to activate it. Encryption could be used in other ways: encrypting a regular, but arbitrary, number of bytes, or encrypting most of the code as a whole rather than on a byte basis.

In programming there are always at least half a dozen means to the same end. Many programming functions are commutative—it doesn't matter in what order certain operations are performed. This means that very small chunks of code, pieces too small to be of use as signatures, can be rearranged in different orders each time the virus infects a new file. This, as you can imagine, requires a more "intelligent" program than a simple encryption routine.

"Sequential" polymorphism

For opcodes defined as:

1 = increase the value of REGA by 1
2 = add the value of REGB to REGC
3 = read REGD from disk
4 = compare REGD to REGE

Equivalent polymorphic sequences for a program fragment sequence 1234 are:

1324	1342	2134	2314	2341
3124	3214	3241	3412	3421

'irus usually contains some kind of identifiable string or code
1 be used to identify it. Even if the virus is new or polymorphic,
lds its code to the infected program, thus adding to the size of
ram. Even if the virus overwrites original code so that it does
add to the length of the file and even if the virus tries to match a
"checksum" calculated on the code overwritten, a sophisticated CRC
(cyclic redundancy check) or other signature will still find a change.
So how to hide from all of these detection mechanisms?

Lie.

Or, rather, get the computer to lie for you.

"Stealth" technology, as applied to computer viral programs, most
broadly refers to all the various means that viral programs use to hide
themselves. Specifically, however, it refers to the trapping mechanisms
that viral programs use to circumvent detection. These mechanisms
are only effective once the virus is active in the computer ("active in
memory"). The virus will "trap" calls to read the data on the disk and
present back only the information of the original, uninfected program.

VIRAL MYTHS

The old saw "It ain't that folks is so ignorant, it's that they know so
much that ain't so" is true in the computer virus field as in no other I
have been involved with. For a variety of reasons, hard facts about
computer viral programs are extremely difficult to come by, while rumors, innuendo, and outright lies abound.

The terms "virus" and "damage" are so closely connected in the
minds of most computer users that "virus" is now being used to describe any situation in which a computer is damaged, unavailable, or
simply not doing what the user wants. (This leads to the "Hurricane
Hugo Virus," the "I-hit-*Exit*-and-the-word-processor-stopped Virus,"
and the favorite of all technical support people, the "Not-Plugged-In
Virus.") By the same token, many users fear *any* viral program, regarding all of them as if they carried the Black Death.

The truth is that relatively few viral programs perform any overt
damage to a system. Of the hundreds of viral strains, only a small number carry a "payload" intended to corrupt data or erase random files,
and these tend to be correspondingly rare in terms of number of infections. Those few viral variants that destroy their target files or disks
are, by definition, self-revealing and self-limiting.

Of course, all viral programs make some kind of change to the
system. Even those that are designed to be benign may cause unforseen

problems in new situations. It is quite certain that the author of the Stoned virus did not intend any kind of damage to result from its spread; he just did not know enough about certain kinds of disk controllers or formats. Most "header" or "integrity" checks in programs are intended only to trap bad copies or disk sectors, but they will stop programs from operating if a viral infection occurs. In these days of increasingly multilayered operating systems and background utility programs, the addition of a resident virus is increasingly likely to result in unforeseen interactions.

The myth of viral programs damaging hardware seems to be one of the more enduring. *No viral program yet found has been designed to damage hardware, and THERE HAS NEVER BEEN ANY CONFIRMED CASE OF A VIRAL PROGRAM DIRECTLY CAUSING PHYSICAL DAMAGE TO COMPUTER HARDWARE.* Is that plain enough?

It *is* possible for certain pieces of hardware to be damaged by software or programming. To the best knowledge of the international virus research community, no such programming (with the exception of low-level formatting) has ever been found on a virus existing in the wild.

Certain older types of display monitors (notably, early IBM monochrome graphics adapters) could be made to "freeze" the sweep of the

Stealth virus

electron beam and thus burn in a section of the screen phosphors. No one has ever burned a hole in a monitor, nor have they ever caused one to overheat and blow up because of software.

Power supplies are a favorite of the hardware-damage theorists, since power supplies obviously deal with electricity and power and, therefore, can be expected to provide fireworks. Except for some very specific and limited functions dealing with powering down in advanced computers, power supplies cannot be addressed by software. No one has ever "melted down" a power supply with software.

As with any physical or mechanical device, printers can be damaged by getting them to do any one thing for too long. This, of course, depends upon the machine running unattended for a long time.

Some disk drives can be damaged by "pushing" the heads beyond normal limits. For others, this is a good way to find more disk space. Certain drives can be damaged by having the heads seek back and forth at a resonant frequency. (Usually older drives, for mainframes, are more susceptible to this. There is also a story, likely apocryphal, that one computer company set up a "portable" computer, including banks of drum drives, in a semitrailer for demos. The first time the truck took a turn with all the drives running, it flipped over due to the enormous stored angular momentum of the spinning drums.)

Some IDE controllers and drives do not allow for the calls that were the normal way to generate a low-level format of the drive. If such a call is made on a system with an IDE controller, the results are uncertain. The drive will not be formatted, but it may not be left in a usable state. IDE drive manufacturers have not, in the past, shipped programs for low-level formatting, and so a call for a low-level format on an IDE drive appears, to the normal user, no different from hardware damage. As this has become known in the user community, more IDE manufacturers have been shipping the formatting programs.

Hardware damage by software is possible, but extremely rare.

Related to hardware damage is the topic of "write protection." Although this is a part of normal computer operation, the details are not necessarily well understood by the general public. In addition, certain procedures related to write protection often recommended as antiviral measures are of little or no use. They may, indeed, be "dangerous," in that they encourage users to think themselves safe and not to take further measures.

First, there is software write protection. Many user manuals for antiviral programs have suggested changing the file attributes of all program files to "read-only" and "hidden." A minor problem with this is that a number of programs write to themselves when making a change in configuration. However, the more major problem is that this action provides almost no real protection. What software (the operating system or protection program) can do, software (a virus) can undo. The overcoming of this protection in MS-DOS is so trivially simple that utility programs, asked to make a change to a protected program, simply remind the user that the file is protected and ask for permission to proceed. (At least, the better written ones ask. Such is the contempt for "read-only" flags, that some programs just "do it.")

There are, as well, programs that attempt to write-protect the hard disk either as a whole, or as individual files. Since these programs use methods other than the standard OS calls they are generally more successful in protecting against "outside intrusion." However, what software can prevent, software can circumvent.

Software write protection must, of course, be running to do any good. Thus BSIs and any other viruses that manage to start up before the software protection is invoked have little to fear from these programs. Some of the protection programs start themselves as replacements for the master or partition boot record in order to get around such "early" infectors. In testing, however, few have been able to prevent infection by the ubiquitous Stoned virus. (Regular readers of my reviews will note the trial of one such hard-disk security program that not only did not prevent the infection, but would not, thereafter, allow disinfection! In my reviewing, I have come to be much more afraid of antiviral programs than of viral programs themselves.)

(In talking of these MBR replacements, I must, however, make an exception for Padgett Peterson's excellent DISKSECURE, SafeMBR, and FixMBR programs. This simple but elegant concept in system-change detection should have been *the* antiviral product of 1991. Micro OS vendors, are you listening?)

Generally, in the microcomputer world, write protection is held to mean write protection implemented by hardware. Although it is a truism that "Whatever the hardware people can do, the software people can emulate, and whatever the software people can do, the hardware people can emulate," it is physically impossible to overcome "sufficient" hardware protection with software. Note, however, that not all hardware protection devices are as safe as they may seem at first glance.

First, the universal write-protect "tab" on floppy disks. It *is* possible to write to *some* write-protected drives. Certain systems (MS-DOS is not one) check for write protection in software rather than hardware. Thus, even though the write-protect device is hardware, the software checking can be circumvented by a virus. (In systems where the write protection *is* effective, it is still the case that the notification of an attempt to write to the drive is done through software, and so the warning that something may be going on may be trapped by the virus.)

However, even on some MS-DOS systems, write protection may not be reliable. Some manufacturers use an optical, rather than mechanical, sensor for the write-protect tab or notch. The "silvered" write-protect tabs, "translucent" floppy disks, or even the shiny black ones on 5¼" diskettes, may allow sufficient light to get through to the sensor to leave the disk unprotected. It is interesting to note that because of the two different protect-tab designs, the hardware write protection circuits for 5¼" diskettes generally "fail safe" in a write-disabled configuration, whereas 3½" diskette drives "fail" into a writable configuration.

(A pity. I prefer the ability to protect and enable repeatedly without building up gobs of tape adhesive around the notch. And when I did protect 5¼s, I used to use "magic" tape as it was easier to remove. These days I'm using Post-it notes, which have an annoying tendency to come off inside the drive.)

I deplore the failure of drive manufacturers to provide write-protect switches on "fixed-media" hard drives. Recently a manufacturer of drives and controllers spent a great deal of time and money promoting a complex, expensive, and ultimately unusable antiviral system, but has shown no interest at all in providing a simple, optional, write-protect switch and cable assembly. Tape and cartridge media do have tabs or switches. Those knowledgeable about hardware and drive cabling can "retrofit" switches, but recent tests at various sites with hardware write-protect switches have indicated problems with certain types of drives. No one procedure has been proposed that works for all types of drives.

I am indebted to Padgett Peterson for reminding me of the following additional "hardware" viral programs, which have occasionally been reported:

1. Lethal-Floppy-Eject, aka "Toaster" virus

I think this one belongs with the users who can't find "Any" keys, photocopy floppies, or can't see whether the screen is on (because the power is off).

2. BIOS virus
3. CMOS virus
4. Battery virus

These three are all variations on a similar theme and are regularly reported.

First of all, BIOS is ROM BIOS. The RO in ROM stands for "read only." The BIOS, therefore, cannot be infected by a virus. At least, not yet. Intel has already developed flash EEPROMs, which it is pushing as "upgradable" ROMs for the BIOS. It *is* possible to get "bad" ROMs, and it is even possible that a run of BIOS ROMs would be programmed such that they constantly release a virus. It hasn't yet happened, though, and it is extremely unlikely since it would be easy to trace.

The CMOS can be changed. The CMOS table, however, is stored in a very small piece of memory. It is highly unlikely that a virus could fit into the leftover space, even though the theoretical limit of the "minimal" family is about 31 bytes. More importantly, in normal operation the contents of the CMOS are never "run," but are referred to as data by the operating system.

We have had "joke" reports of electrical "metavirals" (e.g., "They cluster around the negative terminal, so if you cut off the negative post you should be safe . . ."; "They transmit over the 'third prong,' but occasionally leak over onto the others."). However, there are also a number of reports that changing the battery in a computer damages the CMOS. This is probably because no matter how fast you change the battery, there is a loss of power during that time, and, therefore, the data is lost. Some computers, but by no means all, have a backup system that gives you about ten minutes to change the battery.

5.   Modem virus

The first report I got of the modem virus in *VIRUS-L* 1, no. 42 (December 1988) came from the JPL (Jet Propulsion Laboratory, the NASA research institute) of all places. The original report was supposed to have come from a telecommunications firm in Seattle and contained all kinds of technical bafflegab, including the fact that the virus was transmitted via the "subcarrier" on 2400 bps modems, so you should use only 300 or 1200. The subcarrier was supposed to be some secret frequency that the modem manufacturers used for debugging. The virus was supposed to make all kinds of changes on the internal registers of the modem. That first report gave no indication of how the virus got from the modem into the computer.

As people started to raise objections to the possibility of this ridiculous scenario, the initial report was traced back to a posting on Fidonet (the earliest date I have in my records is October 6, 1988) by someone who gave his name as "Mike RoChenle." Ken van Wyk later suggested this might be read as "microchannel," the then-new bus for IBM's PS/2 machines.

Among serious researchers, these rumors were dealt with rather quickly, within about two weeks. We continued, however, to receive reports of the virus for most of 1989. The facts—that modem manufacturers use all the bandwidth available for transmission; that the internal registers are data rather than programs; that "unused" pins in an RS-232 cable are still "assigned" and can't be used for spurious transmissions; and that terminal emulation programs do not "call" incoming data as programs—only served to spur the reporters to greater flights of fancy in their descriptions of the "modem virus."

With the phenomenon being flat-out physically impossible, why did the rumor persist for such a long time?

One reason is that the rumor itself may have prompted a lot of interest in computer viral programs among computer and modem users. As these people joined virus discussion groups and saw that the modem virus was not being discussed, they continued to post reports of it. Also, the rumors contained enough "pseudotechnical" language to seem credible, while remaining essentially incomprehensible to those who, while using a modem, know little of the technology involved. One of the major likely reasons, however, is that people were primed to believe it. BBSes, and, by extension, modems have had a consistent (and unfair) bad press over the past few years. BBSes are seen as the ultimate source of all "evil" programs—viruses and trojans—and anything bad said about them is to be believed.

Which is another myth.

In early 1992, there were reports of a virus that shut down Iraq's air defense system during "Desert Shield/Storm." This seems to have started with *Triumph Without Victory: The Unreported History of the Persian Gulf War* and the serialization of the book by *U.S. News & World Report*. The articles were rerun in many papers (as well, apparently, as on CNN and ABC's "Nightline"), and the article on the virus that ran in my local paper is specifically credited to *U.S. News & World Report*. The bare bones of the article are that a French printer was to be smuggled into Iraq through Jordan; that U.S. agents intercepted the printer and replaced a microchip in the printer with one reprogrammed by the NSA; and that a virus on the reprogrammed chip invaded the air defense network to which the printer was connected and erased information on display screens when "windows" were opened for additional information on aircraft.

First question: Could a chip in a printer send a virus? Doesn't a printer just *accept* data?

Both parallel/Centronics and serial RS-232 ports are bidirectional. (Cabling is not always bidirectional and, in the early days of PCs, I well remember having to deal with serial ports that had been used as printer ports and could not be used as modem ports because the "return" pin had been sheared off, a common practice to "fix" balky printers.) However, the "information" that comes back over the line is concerned strictly with whether or not the printer is ready to accept more data. It is never accepted as a program by the "host."

The case of network printers is somewhat more complex. There are two possible cases—network print servers and network printers (such as the Mac Laserwriters)—and they are quite distinct. The print server (on, say, DECnet) is actually a networked computer acting as a print server, accepting files from other network sources and spooling them to a printer. True, this computer/printer combo is often referred to simply as a printer, but it would not, in any case, be able to submit programs to other hosts on the net. The Mac case is substantially different, since the Mac laser printers are attached as "peers." Mac Laserwriters, at least, do have the ability to submit programs to other computers on the network, and one Mac virus was at one time reported to use the Laserwriter as a vector. However, it is unlikely that the Iraqi air defense system was Mac-based, and few other systems see printers as peers.

Second question: If it *were* possible to send some kind of program from the printer to the computer system/network, could it have been a virus?

Given the scenario of a new printer coming into an existing system, any damaging program would pretty much have had to have been a virus. In general, the first thing to do when the system malfunctions after a new piece of equipment has been added is to take out the new part. Unless the "chip" could have sent out a program that could have survived by itself in the network or system, the removal of the printer would have solved the problem.

Third question: Could a virus, installed on a chip and entered into the air defense computer system, have done what it was credited with?

Coming from the popular press, "chip" could mean pretty much anything, so my initial reaction that the program couldn't have been large enough to do much damage means little. However, the programming task involved would have been substantial. The program would first have to run on the printer/server/peripheral in order to get itself transferred to the host. The article mentions that a peripheral was used in order to circumvent normal security measures, but all systems have internal security measures as well, in order to prevent a printer from bringing down the net. The program would have to be able to run/compile or be interpreted on the host and would thus have to know what the host was and how it was configured. The program would then have to know exactly what the air defense software was and how it was set up in order to display the information. It would also have to be sophisticated enough to masquerade as a bug in the software and persistent enough to avoid elimination by the reloading of software, which would immediately take place in such a situation.

There is, however, a much more telling piece of evidence supporting the mythical status of what came to be known as the Desert Storm virus. *Infoworld* (April 1991) carried an article reporting a computer virus that U.S. authorities had used to shut down Iraqi computer systems. The *Infoworld* article was, to careful readers, an obvious April Fool's joke (supported by the name of the virus: AF/91). The article ended with the warning that the virus was out of control and was now spreading through systems in the Western world. It was a spoof of the then-new Windows 3 program, the popularity of which was startling industry analysts.

Although the "Triumph Without Victory" story was confirmed by sources in the Pentagon, the similarities to the *Infoworld* AF/91 prank article are simply too great. This is obviously a case of official "sources" taking their own information from gossip that had mutated from reports of the joke. There had been, however, another article, quite seriously presented, in a French military aerospace magazine in February 1991 (which had possibly prompted the *Infoworld* joke). This earlier article stated that a virus had been developed that would prevent Exocet missiles, which the French had sold to Iraq, from hitting French ships in the area. The author used a mix of technobabble and unrelated facts, somehow inferring from the downloading of weather data at the last minute before launch, the programmability of targets on certain missiles, and the radio destruct sequences used in testing, that such a virus was possible.

It *is* true that at the time the U.S. military was calling for proposals regarding the use of computer viral programs as computer weapons. Three contracts giving $50,000 to develop further proposals were subsequently issued. Presumably at least one of those contracts has now entered the second phase, which allowed a half-million dollars for further refinement. It should be noted that the proposals were to have covered defense against viral programs as well.

If I had to choose one viral myth that contributed most to the unchecked spread of viral programs that exists today, it would be that of the "safety" of commercial software. Although there is little agreement as to actual numbers, most virus researchers would agree with the statement that the vast majority of viral infections are caused by viruses that are both easy to detect and easy to remove. Yet one recent survey of 600,000 PCs indicated that 63 percent had been hit with an infection. Why? Easy. Only 25 percent had any kind of protection against viral programs. (Note—even more disturbing—*at least* 38 percent *had been hit and STILL HAD NOT TAKEN PRECAUTIONS!*)

I am often faced with the assertion from computer users that, "Oh, I don't need to worry about viruses. *I* only use *commercial* software. If it doesn't have shrink-wrap, it doesn't go into *my* computer!" This statement, and the feeling of false security, relies on three assumptions:

1. That shareware is a major viral vector.
2. That commercial software is never infected (only shareware and pirate software are).
3. That there are no viral vectors other than software.

Although shareware has been involved in the spread of viral programs, it is difficult to say how much of a role it plays. In nine years of involvement with the local and extended communications community, I have not yet downloaded a file that I found to contain a viral program infection. (Except for the ones that were sent to me as such.) Note that I am not making any claims to superior knowledge or expertise here: my random sampling of interesting-looking files off the nets and boards has yet to pull in one that is infected. Many say otherwise, although it was interesting to note that in a recent conversation with someone having the opposing view, the person finally had to admit he'd never downloaded an infected file either. In fact, for many years, shareware antivirals, primarily available from bulletin boards, were the most widely used form of protection.

Every major microcomputer operating system except CP/M has had at least one instance of a major commercial software vendor distributing infected programs or media. Software vendors take precautions, of course, but apparently still don't give virus checking a high enough priority. More recently we have seen a great many reports of virus infections on CD-ROM products. Computer users seem to think that CD-ROMs are even safer than shrink-wrapped software, since they cannot have been written to since leaving the pressing plant. Unfortunately it is quite possible for the programs to have been infected "at source." While the publishers do take precautions, the sheer volume of material involved increases the chance of missing an infection.

Besides which, there are other possibilities for obtaining viral infections from commercial sources. Most commercial software is still distributed on writable media. Software retailers will often accept returned software, rewrap it (shrink-wrapping is easy to do) and resell it—often without checking for any incidental infection. Hardware or system retailers are all too often selling infected systems these days, not knowing (or perhaps not caring) that they do so. Repair shops and service technicians often spread virus infections without knowing it. None of these people are out to get you, but the general level of knowledge about viral programs is so low that there is no guarantee that they know enough to keep themselves, and you, clean.

I hear it from almost everyone I talk to about viral programs: "I'm in no danger, I don't use a modem."

Yes, there are pirates, crackers, and phreaks out there who inhabit bulletin boards. Yes, there are even pirates, crackers, and phreaks who run boards. Yes, if you hang around even the best BBSes, you will find lots of messages from ankies (a short form of "ankle-biter," the term used to describe young, enthusiastic, high-message-volume, and almost illiterate users), techno-weenies, nerds, geeks, and people to whom spelling and grammar are foreign concepts. But bulletin boards are not going to "auto-magically" infect you. Modems cannot infect you. Reading messages cannot infect you (albeit you might come across an ANSI bomb, but they can't "infect" you). Even downloading and running programs is not that dangerous.

Bulletin boards are not the major vector in the spread of computer viral infections. I can even go a fair way to proving that statement. The most successful viral programs have always been boot sector infectors. Every time I give a seminar I always ask what viral programs people have experience with, and every time there are more copies of Stoned out there than all other viral programs combined. And BSIs are not spread over bulletin boards. (I said "are not." I didn't say "can't." Yes, you *can* use programs such as TELEDISK or SENDDISK, which bundle up the whole disk, boot sector and all, into a file. Yes, "droppers," which are programs written to place a BSI onto a disk, are possible, and even known. But droppers are extremely rare, and most people don't even know what TELEDISK is.) Thus, the major vector *must* be disk swapping.

(Recently my use of the Stoned virus as an illustration of the success of BSI viruses has come under heavy criticism. In some parts of the world, Stoned never was that widespread, and in recent years Stoned has been losing its place to other infections such as Form, Michelangelo, and Monkey. Form, Michelangelo, and Monkey, however, are also BSIs, and Michelangelo and Monkey, in fact, are variants of Stoned. My assertion that BSIs are the most successful viral programs still holds true.)

Bulletin boards are not the enemy. In the computer-virus arena, bulletin boards may be your greatest friend. Where can you get information about computer viral programs? From newspapers, which sometimes state that backups are all the protection you need against Michelangelo? From magazines, which at times have stated that you need to disconnect the hard drive if you get an infection? Or from television stations, where it is possible to hear about BSIs and see the screen produced by the Cascade file infector? You can read a lot of nonsense on BBSes and networks about viral programs, but you *can* get good information, too. And the shareware programs are generally the best, cheapest, and most up-to-date.

After all, you can't even get DISKSECURE commercially.

MEMOIRS OF A (SLOPPY) VIRUS RESEARCHER

All right, it was my own fault. I only kept one copy of the master file, and I really shouldn't have had the habit of using the same filename when I wrote it out to what I thought was a different disk.

Even then, my trusty word processor would have saved my butt, if I hadn't immediately deleted the backup file it had created. ("Backups? We don' need no steenkeen' backups!")

Now, mind you, I still had a perfectly good file. There it was, the latest edition of the antivirus BBS list, one of Mr. Slade's infamous lists, shiny and gleaming and freshly scrubbed and edited, ready to be sent out to the nets. Perfectly good. Too good.

You see, the master file contains both antiviral and vx (virus exchange) board listings. That way the vx boards don't make the AV BBS list when it gets sent. Except that, having deleted all of the vx boards, I had saved the AV BBS list back over the master list. And deleted the backup. And didn't notice what I had done until enough activity had passed that the good ol' UNDELETE was not even going to think about trying to get it back.

Fortunately, as many of you will know, DOS is really insecure. (If you didn't know that, let me say it again: DOS is really insecure.) As I built the file, and edited it over time, bits and pieces of it were strewn all over the disk. Knowing this, I was able to use a sector editor to search for patterns that I knew existed in the file, and probably would have been able to recover better than 90 percent of what I had lost.

Think of that for a moment. Let me make it even more incredible, in security terms. My disk is quite small, and the majority of what is on it are programs and "stable" reference material. There is not a lot of room for lost bits of files to accumulate. About six months ago, I did a major "defragging," which bundled all of my "permanent" material together and left about three megs for files to wander around in. And yet, when I needed to, I found at least eight partial copies of this one file. Three of the "lost" copies were almost complete versions, at least as of that "editing."

So, you have some kind of security lock on your PC, right? And those who try to get at your PC will never be able to run it normally? You delete all sensitive files when you don't need them anymore?

If I can get at my stuff after a goof, they can get at your stuff, too.

CHAPTER 2

BEGINNER'S PANIC GUIDE TO VIRAL PROGRAMS

DON'T PANIC

If this were the *Hitchhiker's Guide to Viral Programs*, that warning would be in large, friendly red letters. Most books dealing with what to do about an infection tell you not to panic. Unfortunately, most of them seem to assume that you are reading at leisure, in advance, in time to prepare for the disaster to come. They don't tell you much of what to do when you actually *are* in trouble, unprepared, and have bought the book in a panic to find out what to do.

The following is far from perfect. Ideally, this should be a sort of hypertext situation where you could follow a flowchart and get help at any point. Given that this is text, the help will have to be included all the way along. As soon as you get the idea of one item, you can skip any remaining text and move to the bottom of the item to find out where to go next.

Again ideally, there should be a clear "If yes, go to 5.3; if no, go to 5.4" type of progression through the questions. Because it is impossible to foresee all of the many situations you might be in, the path may get a bit fuzzy at times. For starters, I don't even know what computer you have, or what operating system you are using. Therefore, this guide will have to be very generic. At many points, the direction is going to have to be, "If you don't understand this, get some extra help from your friends/user group/support staff."

In most cases—far and away the majority—dealing with a virus is a simple matter of running an antiviral scanner with a disinfecting feature. Two of the programs on the diskette included with this book are of the scanning type: F-PROT, for MS-DOS computers; and Disinfectant, for the Macintosh. (Integrity Master has a pretty good scanner, too.) However, there may be a problem if you do not have access to a "clean" computer or boot system in order to extract the antiviral programs. After all, if you extract the programs only to have them immediately infected, they may not work and may even do some harm.

You should, at a minimum, be able to boot your computer from a clean system disk. This is a bootable floppy disk that is known to have an uncontaminated version of the operating system. If you can do that, then you can extract the antiviral programs and start to work. Alternately, if you can extract the files on another computer, copy them to a diskette, and write-protect the floppy, then you can at least keep the antiviral software protected while you go to work.

There are still some other possible problems. Some viral programs make themselves a necessary part of the boot process. If your MS-DOS computer, for example, is infected with a virus called Monkey, then when you boot the computer from a clean system disk, it will appear that you cannot access the hard disk. On the other hand, if you try to run antiviral software from a protected floppy while a virus is active in memory, many antiviral programs will refuse to run, unless a specific command is given. (Please read the program documentation carefully to find these commands: they should *not* be used indiscriminately.) If, however, you do run antiviral software this way, you will likely need to shut the computer off after you disinfect the virus so that it does not immediately reinfect what you have just cleaned. Trying to disinfect a computer with a virus still active in memory is extremely dangerous: this is why antiviral software refuses to do it by default. If you try it, you may be *very* unhappy with the results.

There may be times when you cannot use antiviral software. There may also be times when antiviral software doesn't effectively clean up the problem. In those cases, there are some other actions you can take, which we will look at toward the end of this chapter.

If you are comfortable with getting, and using, utility software from BBSes, then you will probably be able to follow this guide all the way through. I don't mean to imply that you *will* be getting utility software with a modem, but that "comfort level" indicates the kind of technical level that people are at. You may need to use utility software at some point—it makes no difference whether this is shareware, commercial software, or software bundled with the operating system. However, just because you own a commercial utility package doesn't mean you always know what it does. If you have doubts, call someone you know who is comfortable at that level and have them go over the guide with you.

Please have them go through the guide with you. There are an awful lot of people out there who think they know a lot about computers. Trouble is, most of them do—but that doesn't guarantee that they know anything about viral programs. I once worked with a very capable technical support person. He was one of the first in the city to get a "dual boot" OS/2 and MS-DOS system working. He thought he was hot stuff—and, generally, he was. He thought my "expertise" in viral programs was interesting but a bit pointless . . . until the day he had to ask me to clean his system. He'd infected himself while trying to clean up someone else.

POWER

Let's assume the worst possible case. You have reason (maybe good, maybe bad, we'll cover that later) to believe you have a virus. What do you do first?

Most people would tell you to shut the power off immediately. That *might* be a good idea—but it might not. Shutting the power off will definitely keep a virus from operating. If the power already *is* off, don't turn it back on—at least not until you're a bit more comfortable with what might be going on. However, if the power is on and the virus is active, what is it going to do? Infect your computer? It's already done that. Erase files? Format your disk? Well, maybe. There are viral programs that will do that. You probably don't have to worry about that happening, though.

With some few, possibly debatable, exceptions, no virus is beneficial. You don't need anything randomly adding itself to programs, you don't need to lose the extra disk space, and you don't need to lose the memory and interrupts. Most common viral programs, though, are termed "benign." This means that they carry no overtly damaging code and that any damage they do is unintentional. "Malicious" code tends to draw attention to itself, and thus be destroyed, or to destroy itself when it formats the drive to erase everything else. Therefore, the odds are in your favor that if you do have a virus, it won't be doing any damage.

If you *do* happen to have an infection of one of the malicious viral breeds, you still might not be in trouble. Most malicious payloads require some sort of trigger event. Sometimes this can be a specific time of day, but not very often. The Michelangelo virus, for example, triggers on March 6—but only if the computer is booted on March 6. If you leave the computer on all day March 6, nothing will happen. (This is not to say that leaving the computer on all day on March 6 will avoid Michelangelo. There is too much risk of an accidental reset, and far better ways of dealing with the infection.) Therefore, your chance of any damage happening while the computer is on is reduced further.

If, of course, you have just seen, "Ha, ha! I, the Disk Head Crash Virus have just erased your disk," then you're in trouble. You probably won't, however, get into any more trouble by leaving the computer on. In fact, if you don't panic and calmly leave the machine on, there can be a better chance of recovering something. Some of the system information is still in memory, and if that can be written back to the disk, the chances of recovery may be improved.

To conclude, then: if it's off, leave it off. If it's on, leave it on. If, of course, the printer is going nuts, there is one too-bright dot in the middle of the monitor, and the disk drive is in a constant spin cycle while making rattling noises—turn it off.

BACKUPS

OK. Maybe we don't yet know what's wrong, but if the computer is still running, we can start salvage operations. Let's do a backup.

You did one just yesterday? Great! Let's just check it to make sure. Try to restore one of the files—a data file, for example—preferably to another computer, one that isn't infected. (Oh, but just in case it *does* happen to be infected, write-protect the backup disk/tape first. No sense in taking chances, and there is no reason to write to the backup media while you are trying to restore.) If the operation goes smoothly, and the file checks out OK once restored, then you can go on to the next section on how to get started with the recovery.

The reason for checking out the backup is that some viral programs, boot sector infectors especially, can ruin diskettes, or at least the data on them. Some backup programs, particularly the fancier, commercial ones, use a proprietary disk format to speed up the process and cram more stuff onto each disk. If those specially formatted disks get infected with a BSI that expects a standard DOS disk, the backup could be corrupted.

When we do our backup, then, let's not get fancy. Use a simple method, wherever possible—something as simple as copying each file, individually, if you can.

What? Copy each individual file for Windows and all your Windows apps? No. Don't bother with the programs. If it turns out that a bunch of your programs are infected, the best thing to do anyway is erase and reinstall them. Besides, the programs aren't the valuable parts. How much did that really extravagant database program cost you, anyway? $500? Even if you don't have the original disks to install it again, you can run down to the store and get another tomorrow. It's only money. Ah, but your client file. *That* you've been working on for *five* years—more, if you count all the time spent on it before you got the computer. How many hours would it take you to reenter all that data? Do you even *have* all the bits and pieces written down in other places? You can't go down to the store and buy another copy of that file, so that is what you should be backing up. It's your data that is really the valuable part of the system, not the programs. And, oddly enough, your data probably takes less time to back up.

If you are on a network, backing up can be as simple as copying all your data onto the server. This is especially true if the server is a different type of machine (e.g., you are working on a PC or Mac, and the server is a VAX). Don't worry if the system operators yell at you for exceeding quota: this is an emergency, and they are always yelling at somebody anyway.

Of course, the best solution is to back up both ways. Redundant backup, it's called. Poor choice of words. If something crashes, a backup is *never* redundant.

GETTING STARTED

You likely have more resources than you realize. First of all, you have your own observations. If you can keep cool and not panic, you can probably note and recall more than you think. Don't consider this as a potential loss of your accounts receivable, look at it as a detective story. Look for the clues.

Get some paper and a writing implement. (Pen, pencil, sharp piece of coal—in this situation, who's fussy?) You will want to be as accurate and as detailed as possible. Most crimes aren't solved by "Elementary, my dear Watson" cerebrations, but by "Just the facts, ma'am" deliberations. Start writing now. What type of computer is it? What operating system? What version of the operating system? What happened? In detail.

Now start to inventory your resources.

First, you want anything that can tell you about this machine. Do you have invoices with details of the machine, such as the name of the operating system and the version number? Invoices for the software? Was a file created for this machine? Have you got a file listing from the last time anything was added to it? What *was* the last thing added to it? Have you got a file listing from when it was first set up? Have you got a recent backup? (You do? Fortunate mortal!)

Next, look for software that can tell you things about the present state of the machine. You do have some. There is a fair amount the operating system itself can tell you. How much disk space is left? Has that changed a lot? Memory is a *very* important factor. The Mac system info will tell you what programs are using how much memory. The MS-DOS CHKDSK program will tell you not only about the disk space and other interesting things, but also about the "total memory," which can sometimes pinpoint specific viral programs. If you have MS-DOS 5 or higher, MEM/C can give you a *lot* of information. Even if you can't use this information, people you call on for help might be able to.

Do you have utility or disk tool programs? These can also give you valuable information. Both commercial and shareware utilities can help here. If the computer is still working reasonably well, look at the memory statistics. Look at the files. Are there a lot of hidden files? This is a possible sign of a companion virus, especially if they are all the same size. Are there a lot of new files? Or are there a lot of files with very close "creation dates"? This could be an indication that files had been modified recently, another indication of a virus. Look at the disk boot sector and the master boot record. There should be some common system error messages there about missing operating systems. This is a *good* sign. If you don't see them, or see some very odd messages, that's an indication, too. These messages may not mean an awful lot to you, but they should mean something if you need to go to someone else for help.

Are you writing all this down? Or, if the printer is still working, printing the screen to save all the data? (Starting to feel less panicked? Yes, you usually feel better when you have something to do.)

There are probably a number of things around you that you can use either to diagnose the problem or to aid in recovery. We've looked at some of the basic information, resources, and history that might help. Now, let's look for some tools that might be less obvious.

Another computer is a big help, particularly if you are pretty sure it hasn't been infected or affected. Having several computers can be a really big help. Another computer can be used to examine (carefully) floppy disks and files from the infected machine in order to try to determine what is being infected, and how. If you don't have a "clean system disk," that prerequisite for any virus disinfection, you can make one from the other computer. When it comes time to try to clean the infection off your computer, you will likely be told to reboot the computer with a "known clean system disk." That way, you know the computer at least *starts* out clean, so when you do get to erasing the virus from the disk, it does not immediately reinfect the disk from memory.

You may be able to confirm or deny a virus infection with the other machines. If you suspect a virus simply on the basis that "something weird is happening," then you probably don't have a virus at all. Computers do many strange and wonderful things, only very few of them at the behest of viral programs. In any event, swapping out bits and pieces of the computers may identify some malfunctioning hardware. You still have a problem, but at least it is an isolated and identifiable one.

Along with whatever system and utility software you can find, get several blank, formatted disks. Make some of them system disks. Copy a range of programs of different types and sizes onto them. These disks and files you will want to use as bait. (If the infected computer uses different types and sizes of disks, get examples of all the various formats.) Record the file sizes and dates of the "bait" files, as well as the "free space" remaining on the disk. (Viral programs may use various means to hide the fact that a file has grown. Few, however, bother to try to hide the fact that disk space has shrunk.) Take a look at the boot sectors of the disks so that you will be able to notice any changes.

Get a pot of coffee. Get a few friends, even if computer illiterate, for the moral support and the extra eyes. (Observations are key.) Get some lunch. Get some perspective. *Don't panic.*

Who do you turn to? Whom do you trust? Who can help?

This is *very* difficult.

Do not automatically trust your local repair shop. Computer retail, rental, and repair outfits have become significant vectors for viral spread. The technicians may very well have superlative skills in diagnosis and repair, but being able to put a computer together, or take it apart and find out why it isn't working, is not the same as study and research in the virus field. The number of experienced and knowledgeable virus researchers in the entire world is probably less than 100: the number of "instant experts" on the basis of possession of an out-of-date scanning program is in the hundreds of thousands.

The preceding may be seen as a slap at computer repair people. It is in no way intended to be so. The point that I am trying to make is that knowledge about viral programs is extremely specialized. Computer repair is highly skilled and specialized itself—but not in the virus area. Nor is this to say that help desk personnel, computer consultants, systems integrators, or even data security specialists have any advantage in dealing with viral programs, unless they have made specific study in the field.

Enough with the bad news. Where *can* you find help?

For most people, the only place to get accurate and timely information is from the virus discussion groups on computer networks. I am referring to the international networks—the Internet and Fidonet—rather than commercial systems, no matter how large. CompuServe has at least three "virus"-related forums: all are merely technical-support venues for specific commercial products. Of the various "virus" discussions on commercial systems, I am only aware of two with any substance. Therefore, whoever you call on for help should have access to, and read regularly, *VIRUS-L* on the Internet, *comp.virus* on Usenet and either *VIRUS, VIRUS_INFO* or *WARNINGS* on Fidonet or VirNet (which uses Fidonet technology).

It is, of course, very easy for someone to *say* that he or she keeps up with the latest research and not quite as easy for you to test the statement. Virus "experts" should, however, be contributing members. If they make regular contributions, they put their knowledge and expertise to regular testing, which is the only way to keep sharp in this field. Contributions can also be checked fairly readily. You should also check responses to their postings.

I may have overstated the case regarding the necessity for on-line information sources, but not by much. There are two monthly journals, *Virus Bulletin* and *Virus News International*. Both are for the very serious researcher and are academic in tone, with subscription prices in the $150 to $250 range. (My own *V.I.R.U.S. Monthly* and *V.I.R.U.S. Weekly*, unfortunately, also fall into a similar price range, although concentrating more on news and gossip.) Of the two, *VB* has somewhat the higher profile and promotes an annual conference, which also has a good name. Be aware, though, that both publications have links to product vendors, and thus product reviews may be slightly suspect.

Other vendors produce newsletters on a less ambitious scale. The ones I have seen here had very sporadic publication schedules and very little information of value, being confined to announcements of new product releases. In any case, you have to be a customer to get the mailings.

You will probably want information on the various specific viral programs. This is a constant battle, given the thousands of known viral programs and variants and the hundreds of new ones produced each month. In the MS-DOS world, the reference usually mentioned first is the *Virus Summary List*, maintained by Patricia Hoffman. This is a shareware database, which goes under the name VSUMXymm.ZIP, where *ymm* is the last digit of the year and a two-digit month. Thus, VSUMX309.ZIP is the file for September 1993. VSUM is probably the most extensive list of **MS-DOS** viral programs but has an unfortunate reputation for inaccuracy. A rival program, the *Virus Information Door*, is suspected of being linked to virus-exchange groups and is, in any case, almost unavailable apart from a direct call to the author's BBS. An alternate source of information is the good, but aging, list in *PC Viruses* by Alan Solomon (Springer-Verlag). An updated and more comprehensive version is contained in the documentation for Dr. Solomon's Anti-Virus Toolkit.

For Mac users, there is a hypertext virus encyclopedia that should be available on many boards. However, for any of the other microcomputer systems, or for the most accurate listings, the best source is the *Computer Virus Catalog* produced by staff associated with the Computer Antivirus Research Organization (CARO) and the Virus Test Center (VTC), and available from the ftp site at the University of Hamburg. This has had unfortunately limited distribution outside of the Internet and is quite restricted in the number of **MS-DOS** samples cataloged, but it is generally most reliable.

Assume You're Wrong

These days, almost every computer problem has people yelling, "Virus!" In fact, while viral programs are a constant and growing risk, computers have the most marvelous array of bugs, glitches, failures, and just plain bizarre happenings. There is every chance that you *don't* have a virus.

So it is probably time to start looking at the possibility. Go to various people and describe the problem. What may be a completely new quirk to you may be old hat to someone else. Some (very few) examples from a (very long) list of possibilities:

- A power surge or spike can make the monitor flash and/or go blank. Depending upon how the computer fails, various noises may result. This is very common in buildings with older electrical wiring and elevators or other large electric motors. Computers vary greatly in their tolerance for this. One may fry, while the next in line doesn't notice.
- BIOS machines (usually those running MS-DOS) can sometimes not "notice" the fact that a Shift, Control, or Alt key has been released. This may seem to make the keyboard, and computer, act in

a very strange manner. Susceptibility to this varies by computer, keyboard, and program.

■ We frequently receive queries about the "blem wit" virus, which appears in memory on computers running on a Novell LAN. The Novell driver has text, reading "problem with," in the location that DOS expects to find an identifying name.

■ Floppy disks can go bad. Suddenly, and without warning. For various reasons. You need not have done anything wrong. There are also factors such as the infamous "critical-error handler bug," which means that very innocent actions on your part can be damaging. Funny, they've never fixed that.

These examples are by no means meant as a troubleshooting guide. They are merely to show that some very odd things can happen around computers. Unfortunately, a book of telephone-directory size would likely be insufficient to cover all the bases. Still, try to find out what you can.

Swap out keyboards and monitors to check hardware. Note any recent changes or upgrades to the system or programs. Check other machines that have the same history. If you can call in someone to check, it's probably a good idea. If you are pretty sure that it is *not* a normal bug or hardware failure, then go on.

SCANNERS

OK. You suspect you have a virus. You have made what preparations you can. Let us look at what to do in light of the different ways this problem has come to your attention.

If you truly do have a virus, you probably have been alerted by a virus-signature scanning program. Scanners, for all their faults, still account for the vast majority of virus-infection alerts, as much as 90 percent, according to one study. Therefore, you probably even know the name of the virus. Thus you may be in a position to call for help with that specific virus. But be careful.

This type of request is made all the time on the nets, and the answer is always the same. Which scanner did you test it with? Which version of the scanner do you have (and is it up to date)? Have you confirmed this with another scanner? The reason behind these questions is that all scanners do not use the same name for the same virus. In particular, some of the very popular commercial programs feel no need to correspond to anyone else. Therefore, the names they assign may be very arbitrary and of no help to someone trying to assist you. Two of the

MS-DOS antivirals on the enclosed disk have scanners: F-PROT and Integrity Master; both have good records as far as accurate identification goes. The Mac program, Disinfectant, is pretty close to a standard in its environment.

Furthermore, all scanners are subject to "false-positive" results. This occurs when a virus signature used in the scanner matches a string in a noninfected file. Most viral scanning programs use signatures that are worked out independently, and, therefore, they each work slightly differently from any other. Therefore, it is a good idea to check the results of one scanner against another, or even against many others. Also, it is a good idea to ensure that you have the latest version of any given scanner, so that any problems previously noted may have been ironed out.

If you do a second test with an updated version of your scanner and it reports a different virus name, don't be alarmed—this is not unusual. Virus researchers and scanner authors have to give a virus *some* name when they receive it. They may later change the name when others are using a more suitable or standardized name.

In summary: if you are using scanning software, have more than one scanner around. In fact, it might be a very good idea *not* to standardize on a single product. If you have a very large company, you might license three different antiviral programs, each for a third of your computers. If the various scanners are distributed throughout the company, it's almost as good as having all three on each machine, since infections tend to occur in geographic clumps. Keep your scanners up to date, and when an alarm is raised, check the problem out with the other programs.

OTHER ANTIVIRALS

Scanners are still the most widely used of antiviral software and result in by far the highest number of infections detected. When an infection is detected, you usually get a virus name with the report of the infection. You may, however, have one of the other two types of antivirals, sometimes lumped together under the term "generic" antivirals, since they do not rely on a specific identification (and, indeed, cannot perform it). These two antivirals are activity-monitoring software and change-detection software.

If you have activity-monitoring software, you will likely have been told that a suspicious activity has been detected, or that a certain program has viruslike characteristics, or even simply that a certain program is infected with a virus. If a specific program is named, the easiest thing to do might be to get rid of it. Copy the program on to a disk first, so that someone qualified can study it. Then reinstall the program from the original (or original backup) disks. There is a chance, and a fairly good one, that you still have other infected programs somewhere on your disk, but at least you have dealt with the immediate problem.

I said that there is a good chance that other programs were infected: this is assuming that the alarm was valid and that the program named *was* infected. This is by no means always the case. Both activity monitors and change detectors are subject to false-positive alarms. This occurs when the antiviral detects something similar to a virus in a program that actually is not infected.

Activity monitors check programs for suspicious actions. Viral programs will try to change other programs, or change the boot sector on floppy disks, or do "direct" writes to the hard disk (bypassing the operating system). The trouble is that other programs sometimes have valid reasons for doing the same thing.

If, therefore, it is inconvenient to replace the program, you will have to do some more investigating. What were you doing just before the alert? Were you using one program to delete another? Were you trying to format a floppy disk? Both of these will trigger some activity monitors. Were you changing some settings in WordPerfect? (A number of settings in WordPerfect cause the program to rewrite its own code, an action that will trigger alarms. So will setting up a new program with SETVER, a part of DOS 5 and DOS 6. Utility programs also will often set off all kinds of alarms.)

To investigate:

Make a copy of the suspect program, and get it to a recognized researcher. Someone who knows the field can perform more sophisticated tests. One quick check, even if you don't replace the file, is to compare it with the original for size.

Or, just get a really good scanner, and check things out.

If your "generic" antiviral is a change-detection program, then you will probably have a much better idea of what is infected, although less idea of how. Change detectors will usually tell you that the boot sector, or MBR, or a specific file has been changed. Sometimes, in the case of a stealth virus, it will not be able to "see" any change on the disk, but will report a change in memory of the interrupts.

Activity monitors usually run all the time, so, in addition to sometimes telling you, specifically, what type of action is being done, they generally give you some clues by catching something as it happens.

Change detectors are usually run at set intervals, often at boot time, and so only report after the fact. However, because change-detection software identifies specific objects, you will generally get more information from them about BSIs than you will get from activity monitors, and BSIs are much more common.

As with activity monitors, if the antiviral identifies a file that you can easily replace, copy the file off your drive and replace it. If a change detector shows that only one file changed, then it is highly unlikely that any other files are infected. If a cluster of files are changed, particularly in one directory, then the chances are very good that you do have a real infection.

However, like activity monitors, change detectors are subject to false-positive alarms. If you have made changes to WordPerfect, SET-VER, or another program, these will generate alerts from change detectors. If you upgrade your DOS version, the boot sector will change. If you repartition the disk, the master boot record will change.

If, therefore, it is inconvenient to replace the modified program, or if the boot sector appears to be infected, then you may have to do the same types of investigations as were outlined for activity monitors. Since BSIs are more likely to be identified here, trying to trap an infection on a floppy disk is more important. If you have two different-sized floppy disks, then format two new disks, one for each. Label each as to whether it is drive *A:* or *B:* on the computer. Copy some files onto them, and take several directory listings. If you have utility software, try to look at the boot sectors of the floppy disks. The reason for all this activity is that one must try to force the virus to infect the disk, and this is not always as easy as it sounds.

Also, if a boot sector infector is identified, recovery is not quite as simple as replacing a file. Boot from a system disk that is known to be free from infection. If you cannot access the hard disk at this point, do not try anything further. Even if you can repair the boot sector, remember that you will also need to check *all* diskettes for infection.

LOCAL REPORTS

If you hear reports of a virus in your particular area, be cautious, but don't panic. A few years ago, there were a great many news reports of the formidably named SatanBug virus. This virus is perhaps more widespread than some because of the activity of virus-exchange bulletin boards, but got much more press than it warranted because of reports from Washington, D.C. In the same way, we have recently been inundated with reports of Stoned 3 and Stoned 4: these are the names given by a particularly widely distributed (though not particularly good) scanner to a wide variety of viral variants and even to false alarms.

However, it is true that virus infections tend to happen in clusters. Therefore, if there are a lot of validated reports of one particular infection in your area, then it is best to be careful. Make sure that you have a program that is able either to prevent effectively, or identify correctly, this specific virus. It is a good idea to get accurate information about the virus: What does it infect? What are the exact symptoms? How does it behave? Is there any information you can check to determine that you do *not* have the virus? In this latter category, during the months leading up to March 1992, we were able to advise people who were worried about the Michelangelo virus to use CHKDSK. This simple utility checks the files and space on the disk, but it also gives a report on the memory. For most machines (although not all) it should report "Total Memory" as being 655,360 bytes. If it does, then you do *not* have the Michelangelo virus. You may, of course, have something else.

Try to find out all you can about the distribution and spread of the virus, as well as any technical details. The more people that you know have been hit, the more risk there is to you and your system. If, on the other hand, only machines in lawyers' offices are being hit, and you don't know or deal with any lawyers, then you are probably at lower risk. Not no risk, but lower risk.

Try to assess the source of the reports. In 1994 the Clinton Administration's health plan was distributed to interested parties and the media on disk. Almost immediately a newswire report was issued, and got almost universal coverage, stating that the disks were infected with a virus. (The mythical but ubiquitous Stoned 3, as it happened.) When the dust cleared, it turned out that the *only* report was from one reporter—who happened to work for the newswire service. He had infected his machine and "decided" that the only source could have been the Clinton disk. (I must admit that this report caught me out, too. You can't be too careful.)

Most of the time you will *not* get accurate information about the level or type of computer virus infections in your area from the media. Computer virus infections are generally reported neither to the media nor by them. You will, from time to time, see reports of a disastrous new virus sweeping the city/country/world. These reports are almost inevitably overblown.

The reports may be due to the infection of a machine belonging to someone in a position to publicize it. Alternately, it could be a slow news day. On occasion, these are media campaigns by the vendors of antiviral software, in an attempt to boost sales. Past examples have been the Scores virus (reported by NASA), Stoned 3 and the Clinton health plan, and the Joshi virus (reported by McAfee Associates).

In 1994 two such reports arose. The first was the promotion, by an antiviral vendor, of the Junkie virus as a new "supervirus." The virus was said to be encrypted, polymorphic, and multipartite. The Junkie virus does have these features, if you use a fairly loose definition of the terms. Variable encryption *is* the simplest form of the polymorphism, the virus *does* have a very simple form of variable encryption, and the virus *does* infect both boot sectors and COM (but not EXE) files. The vendor further stated that Junkie can make the "anti-virus toolkits" actually spread the virus. This is common with viral programs that infect on "file open" calls and with virus scanners that don't check for viruses already present in memory. Finally, the vendor said that the "only known cure is reformatting the hard disk," which is simply false.

At the same time, the Internet was inundated with copies of a warning about a new virus placed in an archive at an ftp site. The archive, named CD-IT.ZIP, purported to be a utility to turn a CD-ROM reader into a CD-ROM recording device. (For those who are not electrical engineers, this is roughly similar to giving someone an old 45-rpm record and telling them that it will turn their LP turntable into a recording studio: it is flat-out physically impossible.) In an effort to add verisimilitude to the program, one of the documentation files stated that it came from a major CD-ROM reader manufacturer, and it is likely the efforts of the manufacturer that spread the "virus" reports so far.

The CD-IT archive did *not* contain a virus. The INSTALL program in the archive *did* contain a trojan. The trojan was identified by F-PROT as the Warpcom-2 trojan, originally written in 1990. (Flu-Shot, if active, will prevent the trojan from operating.) The Warpcom-2 program will overwrite the COMMAND.COM file with a short damaging program and a lot of garbage. The altered COMMAND.COM will attempt to overwrite system areas of the *D:* drive. (This may be a modification to the original Warpcom-2 and may be targeted at disk compression programs, which often create a logical *D:* drive as part of their operation. This last is only speculation, since we don't know what the intent of the author was, but an attack on a *D:* drive is rather odd.) In any case, nothing about any of the programs associated with CD-IT was in any way viral, and very few copies of CD-IT are known to exist.

WEIRD BEHAVIOR

As I have mentioned, there are a great many things that computers do that have nothing to do with viral programs. People are all too ready to cry virus for every oddity they see.

The truth is, most viral programs do not display any overt signs. The viral programs that do are self-limiting, because they alert the user to something wrong and therefore get destroyed before they have a chance to spread. The Stoned virus, for example, is said to display the message, "Your PC is now Stoned," on the screen. It does—very rarely. The only time it might display is when the computer is booted from an infected floppy disk. Even then, there is only a one-in-eight chance that it will display. Once the infection is resident on the hard drive, unless you boot from an infected floppy disk again, you will never see the message display.

The MacMag virus was said to display a "universal message of world peace." This, however, would only happen on the target date of March 2, 1988. At any time before that, there was no overt sign of any change. The Scores virus, on the other hand, did make some overt changes to both folders and icons. These changes, though, were not very spectacular, and unless you knew the virus and its effects, it was not something many users noticed.

Some changes are inevitable: that is the idea behind change-detection software. The Monkey virus affects the hard disk such that, when the computer is booted from a clean disk, the hard disk is inaccessible. Most security software does the same thing, however. Both Stoned and Michelangelo reduce the "total memory" reported by DOS. A lot of computers, though, do the same thing for other reasons. High-density disks infected by Stoned may become unreadable. On the other hand, lots of disks become unreadable for no apparent reason. Windows programs will often fail to run if infected by a virus. Of course, Windows seems to take random time-outs anyway.

If you suspect a virus simply on the basis of odd behavior, please get a scanner and check it out. Get a very new, very good scanner. If you still want to report odd behavior, please give all details of your computer, your operating system, your resident programs, any device drivers, and which specific antiviral programs you have used to assess the problem. Get the behavior to reproduce, and give specific details of how you get it to reproduce. (Reports of intermittent oddities are almost useless.)

CLEANUP

The easiest way to get rid of an infection in a program, file, or resource is to delete the program, file, or resource and to reinstall it from the original. Please be aware that this actually does not make the infection "disappear," it only means that it is (normally) no longer accessible. It is possible for some quirk to reactivate the virus, but unlikely. A more positive solution is to use an overwriting delete. Such things are available in many utility programs. If you don't have one, a possible, although less certain, method is to copy a much larger file onto the name of the infected file.

In MS-DOS, the SYS command will overwrite the boot sector of the disk, so a command of SYS *C:* should get rid of viral programs in the boot sector of the hard disk. Many BSIs, however, don't infect the boot sector of the hard disk, but rather, the master boot record. With MS-DOS versions 5.0 and later, the command FDISK /MBR will overwrite a portion of the master boot record. This is generally enough to disable the virus, although antiviral programs may find traces left over and falsely report an infection. There are dangers with FDISK /MBR: if used on a computer infected with Monkey or certain other viruses, it may make the hard disk inaccessible.

By this point I hope something has helped. Beyond this point, the activities become much more complex. For each rule in recovering a system, there is an opposing example that breaks it. The strongest rule in virus disinfection is that you mustn't try to clean up a system with a virus still active in memory. Everyone in the virus research community will tell you the same thing: "Start with a known clean boot disk." Unless you happen to have a virus that uses stealth programming. These viral programs have a self-cleaning property, which means that they are actually easier to get rid of if you start with the virus active. (You copy all the infected files to nonexecutable filenames, *then* boot with a clean system disk and rename the files back to executable names.)

In the majority of cases, something should have worked by now. Ninety-nine percent of what you are likely to see should be identified and fixed by a good scanner. If, however, nothing has yet worked, then your problem is harder than the run-of-the-mill virus. You will need more knowledge of how viral programs work and how to get rid of viruses. Which is what most of the rest of the book is about.

MEMOIRS OF A (MEDIA STAR) VIRUS RESEARCHER

I have been known, from time to time, to make rather unkind statements about the accuracy of virus reports in the mainstream media. Some of my antipathy arises simply from the fact that there is an awful lot of "mythology" surrounding viral programs, and most pieces that appear in the media simply perpetuate this. Some of my experience, however, is firsthand.

A reasonably prominent periodical devoted to security topics had been advertising for writers in, among other areas, the virus field, so I sent some sample materials off. I did not hear anything for about eight months, and then I got a call asking me to do an article. On groupware.

However, it was not enough to write the article. No, I had to contact the vendors and listen to what they had to say on the topic. This actually consumed the most time. Some research, and roughing out an outline, took up two hours. A rough draft took three. Polishing the final draft took about an hour. Lots of room for profit there. (Of course, when you consider the years it took to build the background to be able to do that, it tends to reduce the margin a bit. . . .) But contacting three consultants, two user-group representatives, and eleven representatives from seven major vendors took more than fourteen hours spread over a ten-day period. In the end it got me one very helpful vendor contact (Carol Smykowski from Fischer International), one returned message, one faxed spec sheet from a loosely related product, and a heavy parcel, which arrived postage due after the deadline. Needless to say, this was less than helpful to the project.

In the end, the article was rejected. Not enough "vendor quotes."

What is really important here is the fact that most of the articles being generated in the trade press are, by and large, "infomercials" on the printed page. Articles are being written by people who, if they have a technical background at all, are writing out of their field and are being judged on the acceptability of the content to vendors and advertisers. The vendors, quite happy with the situation, are in no hurry to be helpfully involved in the process (or even to return phone calls).

As two examples, I cite the releases of PKZip 2.04 and MS-DOS 6.0. For the first month after the release of the new PKZip, while the nets were stretched by the reports of the various bugs and the latest release by PKWare to try to correct them, PC Week blithely rhapsodized over "version 2" and advertised that it had version 2.04c (the real buggy one) on its own board. Meanwhile, in spite of the protests of the virus research community before MS-DOS 6 was released, and the almost immediate storm of reports of bugs and problems with various of the new features, the trade press only, after six weeks of ecstatically positive reviews of MS-DOS 6, started to report some of the potential problems.

CHAPTER 3

HISTORY AND EXAMPLES OF VIRAL PROGRAMS

EARLY HISTORY

Viral programs have a long, and sometimes honorable, history. (I do not intend, by this statement, to be involved in the current debate about whether or not viral programs serve a useful purpose outside research environments.)

In the earliest computers, it was vital that you knew the initial state of the computer. It was also important that no parts of other programs remained. (It is hard enough to debug programs now; you don't need extraneous "noise" to deal with.) An instruction was often implemented that had only one function: it would copy itself to the next memory location and then proceed on to that location. Thus, by starting this instruction at the beginning of memory, the entire memory space could be "filled" with a known value. This single instruction could be seen as the first viral-type program.

As computers progressed, it became possible to run more than one program at a time in a single machine. It was, of course, important that each program, and its associated data, be contained within certain bounds, or partitions. Inevitably, there were programs that "broke the bounds" and would either perform operations on the data or programs belonging to different procedures, or actually transferred control to random areas and tried to execute data as program instructions. Random operations and damage would result. Attempts to trace the "path" of damage or operation would show "random" patterns of memory locations. Plotting these on a printout map of the memory made a design very much like that of holes in worm-eaten wood: irregular curving traces, which began and ended suddenly. The model became known as

Wormhole damage pattern

```
00 00 00 00 00 00 00 00 00 xx 00 00 00 00 00 00 xx 00 00 xx 00 00 00 00 00 00
00 00 xx 00 00 00 00 00 00 00 00 xx 00 xx 00 00 xx 00 00 00 xx 00 00 00 00 00
00 00 00 00 xx 00 00 00 00 00 00 00 xx 00 xx 00 00 00 00 00 00 00 00 00 00 00
00 00 00 00 xx 00 00 00 xx 00 00 00 00 xx 00 00 00 xx 00 00 00 00 xx 00 00 00
00 00 00 00 00 xx 00 xx 00 00 00 xx 00 00 xx 00 00 00 00 00 00 00 00 00 00 xx
00 00 00 00 00 00 xx 00 00 00 00 00 00 00 00 00 00 00 00 xx 00 00 00 00 00 00
00 00 xx 00 xx 00 00 xx 00 00 00 00 00 00 00 00 00 00 00 00 00 xx 00 00 00 00
00 00 00 00 xx 00 00 00 00 00 00 00 00 xx 00 00 xx 00 00 00 00 00 00 00 00 xx
00 00 00 00 00 00 00 00 00 00 00 00 xx 00 00 00 00 00 xx 00 00 00 00 00 00 00
xx 00 xx 00 00 00 00 00 00 00 00 00 00 xx xx 00 00 00 00 00 00 00 00 00 00 00
00 00 00 00 xx xx 00 00 00 xx 00 00 00 00 00 00 00 00 00 00 00 00 00 00 00 xx
00 00 00 00 00 xx 00 00 00 00 00 00 00 00 00 00 xx 00 00 xx 00 00 00 00 00 00
00 00 xx 00 00 xx 00 00 00 00 00 00 00 00 00 00 xx 00 00 00 00 00 00 00 00 00
xx 00 00 00 00 00 00 00 00 xx 00 xx 00 00 00 00 00 00 00 xx 00 00 00 00 00 00
xx xx 00 00 00 00 00 00 00 00 00 00 00 00 xx 00 00 00 00 00 00 00 00 xx 00
00 00 xx 00 00 00 00 00 00 00 00 00 00 xx 00 00 00 00 00 00 xx 00 00 00 00 xx
00 00 00 00 00 00 00 00 xx 00 00 xx 00 00 00 00 00 xx 00 00 00 00 00 xx 00 00
00 00 xx 00 00 00 00 00 00 00 xx 00 xx 00 00 00 00 00 00 00 xx 00 00 00 00 xx
00 00 xx 00 xx 00 00 00 00 00 00 00 00 xx 00 00 00 00 00 00 xx 00 00 00 00 00
00 xx 00 00 00 00 00 00 xx 00 00 00 xx xx 00 00 00 xx 00 00 00 xx xx 00 00 00
00 00 00 xx 00 00 00 00 xx 00 00 00 xx 00 xx 00 00 00 00 00 00 00 00 00 xx 00
00 00 00 00 xx 00 00 00 xx 00 00 00 00 xx 00 00 00 xx 00 00 00 00 00 xx 00
00 00 00 00 xx 00 xx 00 00 00 00 00 00 xx 00 00 00 00 00 00 xx 00 xx
00 00 00 xx 00 00 00 00 00 xx 00 00 00 xx 00 00 xx 00 00 00 00 xx 00 00 00
```

a "wormhole" pattern, and the rogue programs became known as "worms." The term is sometimes used for viral programs that spread by some method other than attachment to, or association with, program files.

(Programmers being who they are, the development of such rogue programs became a sport. This is now enshrined in the game of "Core Wars." A program that "simulates" a computer environment is run. A standard set of instructions, known as "Redstone code," is used to build programs that battle each other within the simulated environment. The objective is survival. The use of such tactics as attack, avoidance, and replication is of interest to virus research, as is the trade-off between complexity of design and chance of destruction.)

I have given one derivation of the term "worm." There is another. It is interesting that two completely separate routes should give rise to the same term and that the meanings should complement so well. It is also interesting in that this story arises from an early attempt to use viral programming for beneficial purposes.

One of the very earliest examples of a local area network (LAN) was implemented at Xerox PARC (Palo Alto Research Center). As well as being useful for the types of business functions common on LANs today, it was a test bed for the development of those functions and experiments with others. John Shoch and Jon Hupp, two researchers there at the time, were interested in the concept of distributed processing—the ability of computers to work cooperatively on single or related tasks.

The specific experimental program they were testing was one that would examine other computers on the net to look for activity. If a computer was idle after normal working hours, for example, the program would submit a copy of itself to the idle machine. In this way the original program would spawn multiple copies of itself to idle machines in order to make use of the CPU time that would otherwise go to waste. The intention was to write programs that would be aimed at solving problems normally submitted to a supercomputer. By breaking the problem down into small chunks, each capable of solution on one of the machines on the network, you would, in effect, have a large

Shoch and Hupp segmented "worm" experiment

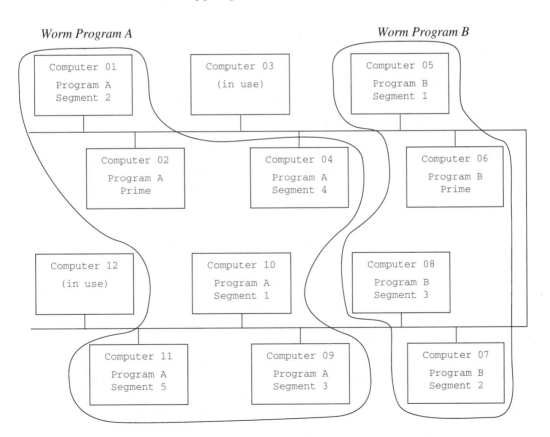

program consisting of small program segments working on individual machines. Since biological worms are defined by the fact that they have segmented bodies, they called this new type of program a "worm."

Alas, the experiment was not an unqualified success. One night, a programming error caused the computers to which the worm program had been submitted to "hang." Since the program had been submitted to a great many computers over the course of the night, the researchers arrived in the morning to find an institution full of dead computers. This program became known as the Xerox worm or, in many references, the "infamous Xerox worm."

PRANKS AND TROJANS

One of the factors involved in the success of viral programs is a study of the mind-set of the user—a study of the psychology or sociology of the computer community. Since the spread of viral programs generally requires some action, albeit unknowing, on the part of the operator, it is instructive to look at the security-breaking aspects of other historical programs.

"Password trojans" are extremely popular in the university and college environments (where most of the new security-breaking ideas and pranks tend to come from anyway). These programs can be extremely simple. An easy "painting" of the screen with a facsimile of the normal login screen will generally get the user to enter his or her name and password. It is quite simple to have a program write this information to a file, or even mail it to a specific account. Most of these programs will then send back a message to the user that the login has been denied; most users will accept this as an indication that they have either made a mistake in entering the login data or that there is some unknown fault in the system. Few question the message even after repeated refusals. Some programs are sophisticated enough to pass the login information on to another spawned process: few users even know enough to check the level of nesting of processes.

(A famous, if relatively harmless, prank in earlier computers was the "cookie" program, which ran on PDP series computers. This program would halt the operation that the victim was working on and present a message requesting a cookie. There were consistent reports of viral programs following this pattern, including a very detailed report of a "Spanish Cookie" virus; however, I have never seen any such program. In the absence of such data I had, regretfully in the case of the reported Spanish Cookie, come to the conclusion that this was another piece of computer folklore that had mutated into legend. I have, however, recently been assured by another researcher that it does, in fact, exist.)

Another lesser-known prank has a closer relationship to current viral programs. In the *RISKS-FORUM Digest* (March 1988; 6–42), there was a detailed outline of the use of the "intelligent" features of Wyse 75 terminals. This was a specific instance of a general case of the use of intelligent peripherals for security cracking. In this incident, the terminal had a feature that would allow keys to be remapped from the host system. Another feature allowed the keys to be called for from the host. This allowed email messages (actually only the subject line) to be composed that would remap a key to correspond to the "kill process and logout" command and then have the command submitted by the terminal. With only a little thought, an email virus could be written taking advantage of this fact. This is quite similar to the phenomena of ANSI bombs on MS-DOS machines, which, while not viral, use the ANSI.SYS key-remapping facility to assign deletion or formatting commands to specific keys.

Pranks are very much a part of the computer culture. So much so that you can now buy commercially produced joke packages that allow you to perform "Stupid Mac (or PC) Tricks." There are numberless pranks available as shareware. Some make the computer appear to insult the user; some use sound effects or voices; some use special visual effects. A fairly common thread running through most pranks is that the computer is, in some way, nonfunctional. Many pretend to have detected some kind of fault in the computer (and some pretend to rectify such faults, of course making things worse). One recent entry in our own field is PARASCAN, the paranoid scanner. It tends to find large numbers of very strange viral programs, none of which, oddly, have ever appeared in the VTC index. Aside from temporary aberrations of heart rate and blood pressure, pranks do no damage.

I would not say the same of trojans. I distinguish between a prank and a trojan on the basis of intent to damage. The trojan horse was a gift with betrayal inside; so a trojan horse program is an apparently valuable package with a hidden, and negative, agenda.

Trojans are sometimes also referred to (less so now than in the past) as "Arf, Arf" programs. One of the first was distributed as a program that would enable graphics on early TTL monitors. (That *should* have been a giveaway: Such an operation was impossible.) When run, it presented a message saying "Gotcha. Arf, arf." while the hard drive was being erased.

Trojan programs are spread almost entirely via public-access electronic bulletin boards. Obviously, a damaging program that can be identified is unlikely to be distributed through a medium in which the donor can be identified. There are, as well, BBSes that are definitely hangouts for software pirates and act as distribution points for security-breaking tips and utilities. These two factors have led to a confusion of trojan programs, viral programs, and "system crackers," which has proven extremely resistant to correction. It has also led to a view of BBSes as distribution points for viral programs. (Recently our local "tabloid" paper's computer columnist, normally better versed than this, dismissed the availability of antiviral software to combat Michelangelo by saying that no self-respecting company would ever use a BBS.) This, in spite of the fact that the most successful viral programs, BSIs, cannot be transmitted over BBS systems in normal use.

Pranks have, in odd ways, entered the realm of virus mythology. The PDP-series "cookie" prank has given rise to all manner of reports of a cookie virus. There is also the "crabs" program, which initially ran on the Xerox Star system and has subsequently been ported to the Mac and Atari systems. More of a screen saver than anything else, it is sometimes reported by careless authors as a class of viral programs that attack video displays. A similar program in the MS-DOS world is BUGRES, which is reported as a virus by a major commercial antiviral. This tends to be where pranks do the most damage: in addition to the time spent getting rid of a prank on a system, they tend to generate a lot of calls to researchers and waste not only time, but network bandwidth.

THE WORK OF DR. FRED COHEN

No historical overview of viral programs can be complete without mention of the work of Fred Cohen.

In the early 1980s, Fred Cohen did extensive theoretical research, as well as setting up and performing numerous practical experiments regarding viral-type programs. He first presented his ideas to a data-security seminar in 1983, and folklore credits his seminar advisor, Len Adleman, with the assignment of the term "virus" to Cohen's concept. Cohen's paper was published in 1984, and his dissertation was presented in 1986 as part of the requirements for a doctorate in electrical engineering from the University of Southern California. This work is foundational, and any serious student of viral programs disregards it at his or her own risk.

Dr. Cohen's definition of a computer virus as "a program that can 'infect' other programs by modifying them to include a . . . version of itself" is generally accepted as standard. On occasion it presents problems with the acceptance of, say, boot sector viral programs and entities such as the Internet/Morris/UNIX Worm. It is not, however, fair to Dr. Cohen to hold him responsible for the misuse of his work by others. The preceding definition given is not, as he has pointed out on many occasions, actually his. His definition is mathematical in nature, and the English version is only an approximation. His work did experimentally demonstrate and theoretically prove many vital issues.

For some reason Fred Cohen's work was never given the credit or value it deserved. From the very beginning, systems administrators and the security community have seen his work as either negative or as an academic curiosity. This situation is decidedly odd but has not, perhaps, been helped any by Cohen's manner when defending his work and position, or when presenting new concepts.

This overview is the merest introduction to his work and is not intended to be anything more. In my opinion, the most important aspects are the demonstration of the universality of risk and the limitations of protection. His practical work proved the technical feasibility of a viral attack in any computer-system environment. (This feat was achieved within a closed environment and could not, by its nature, have predicted the social and psychological factors that have contributed to the pandemic spread of viral programs "in the wild.") Equally important, his theoretical study proved that the "universal" detection of a virus is undecidable. Although monitoring and analytical programs have a place in the antiviral pantheon, this fact means that they, and all other antiviral software, can never give 100 percent guaranteed protection. Without this early work, it is likely that some toilers in the antiviral vineyards would still be laboring in vain.

THE "AIDS" TROJAN (NOT VIRUS)

I'll conclude the introductory history with the AIDS Information Disk trojan for two reasons:

1. It deserves a place in the history of "malware."
2. It was so widely—and incorrectly—reported as a virus.

In the fall of 1989, approximately 10,000 copies of an "AIDS Information" package were sent out from a company calling itself PC Cyborg. Some were received at medical establishments; a number were received at other types of businesses. The packages appeared to have been professionally produced. Accompanying letters usually referred to them as sample or review copies. However, the packages also contained a very interesting "license agreement":

> *In case of breach of license, PC Cyborg Corporation reserves the right to use program mechanisms to ensure termination of the use of these programs. These program mechanisms will adversely affect other program applications on microcomputers. You are hereby advised of the most serious consequences of your failure to abide by the terms of this license agreement.*

Farther in the license is the sentence: "Warning: Do not use these programs unless you are prepared to pay for them."

The disks contained an installation program and a very simplistic AIDS-information "page turner" and risk assessment. The installation program appeared only to copy the AIDS program onto the target hard disk, but in reality did much more. A hidden directory was created with a nonprinting character name, and a hidden program file with a nonprinting character in the name was installed. The AUTOEXEC.BAT file was renamed and replaced with one that called the hidden program and then the original AUTOEXEC. The hidden program kept track of the number of times the computer was rebooted, and, after a certain number, encrypted the hard disk. The user was then presented with an invoice and a demand to pay the license fee in return for the encryption key. Two major "versions" were found to have been shipped. One, which waited for 90 reboots, was thought to be the "real" attempt. An earlier version, which encrypted after one reboot, alerted authorities and was thought to be an error on the part of the principals of PC Cyborg.

The Panamanian address for PC Cyborg, thought by some to be fake, turned out to be real. Four principals were identified, as well as an American accomplice who seems to have had plans to send 200,000 copies to American firms if the European "test" worked. The trial of the American was suspended in Britain, as his bizarre behavior in court was seen as an indication that he was unfit to plead. An Italian court, however, found him guilty and sentenced him in absentia.

VIRAL EXAMPLES

APPLE 1, 2, 3

The earliest case of a virus that succeeded "in the wild" goes back to late 1981, even before the work of Fred Cohen. In fairness, this activity does not appear to have been noted by many until long after the fact. We have, indeed, reports of two very similar programs with startlingly similar features and histories. Here, for the sake of simplicity, I present only the one first related on the net.

The idea was sparked by a speculation regarding "evolution" and "natural selection" in pirated copies of games at Texas A&M: the "reproduction" of preferred games and the "extinction" of poor ones. This led to considerations of programs that reproduced on their own. (I see no reason to doubt the author's contention that there was no malice involved: this was, after all, the first case that we know of. Indeed, it was one author's contention that a virus had to be relatively "benign" in order to survive.)

Apple II computer diskettes of that time, when formatted in the normal way, always contained the disk operating system. The programmer attempted to find the minimum change that would make a version of DOS that was viral and then tried to find an "optimal" viral DOS. A group came up with version 1 of such a virus in early 1982, but quarantined it because of adverse effects. Version 2 seemed to have no negative impact and was allowed to "spread" through the disks of group members.

Eventually security was relaxed too far, and the virus escaped to the general Apple user population. It was only then that the negative impact of the virus was seen: the additional code length caused some programs, and one computer game in particular, to abort. A third version was written that made strenuous efforts to avoid the memory problems: parts of the coding involve bytes that are both data and opcode. Version 3 was subsequently found to have spread into disk populations previously felt to be uninfected, but no adverse reactions were ever reported.

(For those who have Apple DOS 3.3 disks, location B6E8 in memory, toward the end of track 0, sector 0 on disk, should be followed by 18 zero bytes. If, instead, the text "(GEN xxxxxxx TAMU)" appears, the digits represented by the "x"s should be a generation counter for virus version 3.)

The story has an interesting postscript. In 1984 a malicious virus was found to be spreading through the schools where all this took place. Some disks appeared to have immunity. All of these immune disks turned out to be infected with version 3.

LEHIGH

Autumn 1987 really seemed to get the ball rolling with regard to virus research. The first message to awaken interest was sent by one "LUKEN" of Lehigh University. For all the damage that the Lehigh virus caused, we should at least be grateful that it generated sufficient interest for Ken van Wyk to start the *VIRUS-L* mailing list (now also mirrored on Usenet news as *comp.virus*).

Not all students are minihackers; not all students are even semi–computer literate. Student consultants at universities and colleges are presented with a steady stream of disks from which files have "mysteriously" disappeared. In November 1987, however, it appeared that certain of the failed disks were due to something other than user carelessness.

The Lehigh virus overwrote the stack space at the end of the COM-MAND.COM file. This meant that there was no increase in the size of infected files. A later report of a 555-byte increase in file size was a confusion with the size of the overwriting code. When an infected COMMAND.COM was run (usually upon booting from an infected disk), the virus stayed resident in memory. When any access was made to another disk, via the TYPE, COPY, DIR, or other normal DOS commands, any (and only) uninfected COMMAND.COM files would be infected. A counter was kept of infections: after four infections, the virus would overwrite the boot and FAT areas of disks with contents from the BIOS.

The primary defense of the virus was that, at the time, no one would have been looking for it. The date of infected COMMAND.COM files was altered by the virus, and when attempting an infection on a write-protected disk, the virus would not trap the "WRITE PROTECT ER-ROR" message (a dead giveaway if all you were doing was a DIR).

The virus was limited in its "target population" to those disks that had a COMMAND.COM file, and, more particularly, those that contained a full operating system. Admittedly, in those heady bygone days, more users kept copies of the operating system on their disks. However, the virus was also self-limiting in that it would destroy itself once activated and would activate after only four reproductions. To the best of our knowledge, the Lehigh virus never did spread off the campus in that initial attack. (It is, however, found in a number of private virus collections and may be released into the wild from time to time. As noted, it has little chance of spreading today.)

JERUSALEM

In terms of the number of infections (copies or reproductions) that a virus produces, boot sector viral programs seem to have an advantage among microcomputer users. Among file-infecting viral programs, however, the Jerusalem virus is the clear winner. It has another claim to fame as well. It almost certainly has the largest number of variants of any virus program known to date.

Initially known as the "Israeli" virus, the version reported by Y. Radai in early 1988 (also sometimes referred to as "1813" or Jerusalem-B) tends to be seen as the central virus in the family. Although it was the first to be very widely disseminated and was the first to be "discovered" and publicized, internal examination suggests that it was, itself, the outcome of previous viral experiments. Although one of the oldest viral programs, the Jerusalem family still defies description, primarily because the number of variants makes it very difficult to say anything about the virus for sure. The "Jerusalem" that you have may not be the same as the "Jerusalem" of your neighbor.

A few things are common to pretty much all of the Jerusalem family. They are file- or program-infecting viral programs, generally adding themselves to both COM and EXE files. When an infected file is executed, the virus "goes resident" in memory, so that it remains active even after the original infected program is terminated. EXE programs run after the program is resident in memory are infected by addition of the virus code to the end of the file, with a manipulation of the file header at the beginning of the program. COM files are infected by prepending. Most of the family carry some kind of "date" logic bomb payload, often triggered on Friday the 13th. Sometimes the logic bomb is simply a message; often it deletes programs as they are invoked.

David Chess has noted that it is a minor wonder the program has spread as far as it has, given the number of bugs it contains. Although it tends to work well with COM files, the differing structure of EXE files has presented Jerusalem with a number of problems. The "original Jerusalem," not content with one infection, will reinfect EXE files again and again so that they continually grow in size. (This tends to nullify the advantage that the programmer built in when he ensured that the file creation date was "conserved" and unchanged in an infected file.) Also, EXE programs that use internal loaders or overlay files tend to be infected "in the wrong place" and have portions of the original program overwritten.

The history of the Jerusalem virus is every bit as convoluted as its functionality and family. The naming alone is a fairly bizarre tale. As mentioned before, it was originally called the Israeli virus. Although considered unfair by some, it was fairly natural, as the virus had both been discovered and reported from Israel. (Although the virus was reported to slow down systems that were infected, it seems to have been the "continual growth" of EXE files that led to the detection of the virus.) It was also referred to by its infective length of 1,813 bytes. For

COM files. For EXE files, it was 1,808 bytes. Sometimes. It varies because of the requirements of EXE file structures. (All quite clear?)

One of the early infections was found in an office belonging to the Israeli Defense Forces. This fact was reported in an Associated Press article and, of course, made much of. It also gave rise to another alias, the IDF virus. (This alias, however, was rarely used seriously and should not be confused with the more widespread use of the alias for the Frodo/4096 virus.)

Yet another alias is "sUMsDos," based on text found in the virus code itself. This was, on occasion, corrupted to "sumDOS."

The name "Jerusalem" has gained ascendancy, possibly due to the McAfee SCAN program identification. (He certainly must be responsible for the "B" designation for the "original" version.) Of course, the great number of variants have not helped any. Because a number of the variants are very closely based upon one another's code, the signatures for one variant will often match another, thus generating even more naming confusion. This confusion is not unique to the Jerusalem family, of course, and is an ongoing concern in the virus research community.

When the virus was first discovered, it was strongly felt that it had been circulating prior to November 1987. The "payload" of file deletion on Friday the 13th gave rise to conjecture as to why the logic bomb had not "gone off" on Friday, November 13, 1987. (Subsequent analysis has shown that the virus will activate the payload only if the year is not 1987.) The next following "Friday the 13th" was May 13, 1988. Since the last day that Palestine existed as a nation was May 13, 1948, it was felt that this might have been an act of political terrorism. This led to another alias, the PLO virus. (The fact that Israel celebrates its holidays according to the Jewish calendar and that the independence celebrations were slated for three weeks before May 13, 1988, were disregarded. The internal structure of the virus, and the existence of the sURIV viral programs seems to indicate that any political correspondence is merely coincidental.)

Although it is difficult to be absolutely certain about pronouncements as to the provenance and family history of viral programs, it is almost certain that the Jerusalem virus is, in fact, two viral programs combined. Among the Jerusalem "family" are three "sURIV" variants (again, named for text in the code). It is fairly easy to see where "virus" 1, 2, and 3 come from. Virus sURIV 1.01 is a COM-file infector, COM being the easier file structure and therefore the easier program to infect. Virus sURIV 2 is an EXE-only infector and is considerably longer and more complex code. Virus sURIV 3 infects both types of program files and has considerable duplication of code: it is, in fact, simply the first two versions "stuck" together.

Although the code in the sURIV programs and the 1813 version of Jerusalem is not absolutely identical, all the same features are present. The date of the payload is April 1 in the sURIV variants. There is also a year condition: some of the payload of the sURIV variants was not supposed to go off until after 1988.

Perhaps this explains the popularity of the Jerusalem virus as a template for variants. The code is reasonably straightforward and, for those with some familiarity with assembly programming, an excellent primer for the writing of viral programs affecting both COM and EXE files. (There is, of course, the fact that Jerusalem was both early and successful. There are many copies of Jerusalem "in the wild," and it may be availability that has made it so widely copied. Its value as a teaching tool may be an unfortunate coincidence.)

Of course, not every virus writer who used the Jerusalem as a template showed the same good taste and imagination in what they did with it. Not all of them even fixed the obvious flaws in the original. The variations tend to be quite simplistic: there are a number of "Thursday the 12th," "Saturday the 14th," and "Sunday the 15th" programs. (Some of the copycat virus authors added errors of their own. One of the "Sunday" variants is supposed to delete files on the seventh day of the week. Unfortunately, or perhaps fortunately for those of us in the user community, nobody ever bothered to tell the author that computers start counting from zero and Sunday is actually the "zeroth" day of the week. The file deletions never actually happen.)

(C) BRAIN

The "Brain" virus is probably the earliest MS-DOS virus. At one time it was the most widespread of PC viral programs (yet more support for the "superiority" of BSIs in terms of numbers of infections). Extensive study has been done on the Brain family, and those wishing further details should consult Alan Solomon's analyses (which, unfortunately, are too detailed for full inclusion in the Anti-Virus Toolkit). In spite of this, and in spite of the existence of address and phone number information for the supposed author, we still have only secondhand reports of the production of the virus, so little can be said with absolute certainty. (We do have a firsthand report from the author of the Den Zuk variant, for which I am grateful to Fridrik Skulason.)

The Brain family is prolific, although less so than Jerusalem. (Seemingly, any successful virus spawns a plague of copies as virus-

BRAIN disk map

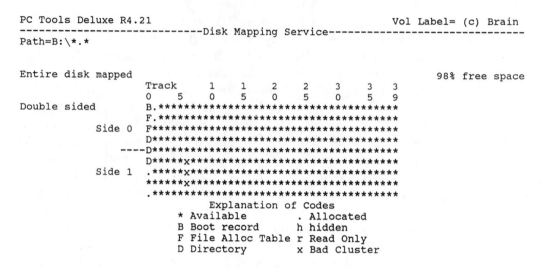

```
PC Tools Deluxe R4.21                              Vol Label= (c) Brain
-------------------------------Disk Mapping Service---------------------------
Path=B:\*.*


Entire disk mapped                                        98% free space
                 Track   1   1   2   2   3   3   3
                 0   5   0   5   0   5   0   5   9
Double sided     B.*************************************
                 F.*************************************
        Side 0   F*************************************
                 D*************************************
        ----D*************************************
                 D*****x*******************************
        Side 1   .*****x*******************************
                 ******x*******************************
                 .*************************************
                      Explanation of Codes
                 * Available      . Allocated
                 B Boot record    h hidden
                 F File Alloc Table r Read Only
                 D Directory       x Bad Cluster
```

writer-wannabes use it as a template.) Again, like the Jerusalem, it seems that one of the lesser variants might be the "original." The "ashar" version appears to be somewhat less sophisticated than the most common Brain, but Brain contains text that makes no sense unless Brain is "derived" from ashar. Brain contains other "timing" information: a "copyright" date of 1986 and an apparent "version" number of 9.0.

Brain is a boot sector infector, somewhat longer than some of the more recent BSIs. Brain occupies three sectors itself and, as is usual with BSIs, repositions the normal boot sector in order to "mimic" the boot process. As the boot sector is only a single sector, Brain, in infecting a disk, reserves two additional sectors on the disk for the remainder of itself, plus a third for the original boot sector. This is done by occupying unused space on the diskette and then marking those sectors as "bad" so that they will not be used and overwritten. The "original" Brain virus is relatively harmless. It does not infect hard disks, or disks with formats other than 360K. (Other variants are less careful and can overlay FAT and data areas.)

Brain is at once sly and brazen about its work. It is, in fact, the first stealth virus, in that a request to view the boot sector of an infected disk on an infected system will result in a display of the original boot sector. However, the Brain virus is designed *not* to hide its light under a bushel: the volume label of infected diskettes becomes "(c) Brain" (or "(c) ashar" or "Y.C.1.E.R.P" for different variants). Hence the name of the virus.

Who wrote the Brain virus?

BRAIN version with address text removed

```
61EB:0130 28 63 29 20 31 39 38 36-20 42 72 61 69 6E 17 26  (C) 1986 Brain.&
61EB:0140 20 41 6D 6A 61 64 73 20-28 70 76 74 29 20 4C 74  Amjads (pvt) Lt
61EB:0150 64 20 20 20 56 49 52 55-53 5F 53 48 4F 45 20 20  d VIRUS_SHOE
61EB:0160 52 45 43 4F 52 44 20 20-20 76 39 2E 30 20 20 20  RECORD v9.0
```

Well, it's quite simple really. In one of the most common Brain versions you will find text, unencrypted, giving the name, address, and telephone number of Brain Computer Services in Pakistan. The virus is copyrighted by "ashar and ashars" or "Brain & Amjads," so we have two brothers running a computer store who have written a virus. Simple, right?

Oh, the danger of simple answers.

First, Alan Solomon's analysis and contention that ashar is older than Brain is quite convincing. Also, in the *most* common version of Brain, the address text does not appear. Further, it would be a very simple matter to have overlaid the text in the ashar or Brain programs with the address text.

What motive would the owners of Brain Computer Services have for writing a virus? One story is that they sell pirated software, a practice that is legal in Pakistan, but not in the United States. Therefore, the infected disks were sold to Americans in punishment for their use of pirated software. Unconvincing. The moral attitude seems quite contrived: Brain would have no reason to "punish" the United States (its major source of software), and the Brain infection is not limited to the Western world. This story has, though, been confirmed by one researcher and is cited by him as an example of Islamic logic.

Another story is that Brain Computer Services wrote some software of their own and were incensed when others pirated *their* software. Unlikely. Infected disks would most likely be sold by Brain Computer Services, and this would tend to mean that a customer would be more likely to get a "clean" copy if it was pirated. (The hypothesis that Brain is some kind of copyright device is absurd: the virus would then be going around "legitimizing" bootleg copies.)

Given that Brain is relatively harmless, it is possible that the virus was seen as a form of advertising for the company. Remember that this is the earliest known **MS-DOS** virus and that the hardened attitude against viral programs had not yet arisen. Brain predates both Lehigh and Jerusalem, but even some time after those two "destructive" infections, viral programs were still seen as possibly neutral or even beneficial. In those early, innocent days, it was not impossible that the author saw a self-reproducing program that "lost," at most, 3k of disk space as simply a cute gimmick.

I have mentioned Alan Solomon's analysis of the Brain family with regard to the dating of the ashar variant. Fridrik Skulason performed a similar analysis of the Ohio and Den Zuk versions and has been proven 100 percent correct in his conclusions.

The Ohio and Den Zuk variants contain the Brain identification code, so they will not be infected or overlaid by Brain. However, Ohio and Den Zuk identify Brain infections and will replace Brain infections with themselves. Thus, Ohio and Den Zuk may be said to be agents acting against the Brain virus (at the expense, however, of having the Ohio and Den Zuk infections). Skulason also found that the Den Zuk version preferentially overlaid Ohio. (This "seeking" activity gives rise to one of Den Zuk's aliases: "Search." It was also suspected that "denzuko" might have referred to "the search" for Brain infections. There was, in fact, an extensive search for the meaning of the words "den zuk" and "denzuko" in a number of languages as an attempt to find clues to the identity of the virus author. This turned up closely related words meaning "sugar" and "knife" as well as search. As it turned out, none of these had the slightest relation to the origin of the virus.)

There is text in both strains that indicates a similarity of authorship. Ohio contains an address in Indonesia; both contain a ham radio license number issued in Indonesia. Both contain the identical bug that overlays FAT and data areas on non-360K format disks. Den Zuk has the more sophisticated touches in programming. From all of this, Skulason concluded that Ohio was, in fact, an earlier version of Den Zuk.

So it proved to be, in a message from the author. The author turns out to have been a college student in Indonesia who, to this day, sees nothing wrong with what he did. (On the contrary, he is inordinately proud of it and is somewhat peeved that his earlier creation is "misnamed" Ohio: he's never been there. The name of Ohio was given by McAfee in reference to the place of the first identification of the viral program, Ohio State University.) Den Zuko is his nickname, derived from John Travolta's character in the movie *Grease*.

Full details of Skulason's analysis and his contact with the author are available in Skulason's article in the *Virus Bulletin*.

Technically, the Brain family, although old, has a number of interesting points.

Brain itself is the first known MS-DOS virus, aside from those written by Fred Cohen for his thesis. In opposition to his virus, Brain is a boot sector infector. One wonders, given the fact that the two earliest viral programs (for the Apple II family) were "system" viral programs, whether there was not some influence from these earlier, similar programs.

Brain is the first example of stealth technology. Not, perhaps, as fully armored as other later programs, but impressive nonetheless. The intercepting and redirection of the system interrupts had to be limited in order for the virus to determine, itself, whether or not a target was infected. The use of stealth, especially given the volume name change, is probably not deliberate. As has been found by security systems and utilities, when you mess with the operating system at this level, you often need to mislead the system in order to function properly.

The Den Zuk and Ohio variants use the trapping technology, which can be used to allow a virus to survive a warm boot. Although they do not survive, the fact that the

```
<Ctrl><Alt><Del>
```

key sequence is trapped and that another piece of programming (in this case, the onscreen display) is substituted for the reboot code proves the point. The virus could be made to survive and to "fake" a reboot. (The recovery of the system would likely require a lot of programming and code. This has been pointed out before, and the "recovery mode" of Windows 3.1 probably proves it.)

Den Zuk and Ohio are also "virus-hunting viruses." This possibility has long been discussed, and these examples prove it can be done. They also indicate that it is not a good idea: Den Zuk and Ohio are far more dangerous than Brain ever was.

The Solomon and Skulason analyses are fascinating for tracking the trail of a virus mutation through the same, and different, authors. The evolution of programming sophistication, the hesitation to alter the length of text strings even while they are being replaced, and the retention and addition of bugs form an engrossing pattern.

MACMAG

On February 7, 1988, users of CompuServe's Hypercard Forum were greeted with an intriguing warning message. It told them that the NEWAPP.STK Hypercard stack file was no longer on the system. The notice suggested that if they had downloaded the file, they should not use it. If they had used it, they should isolate the system the file had run on.

The story, on CompuServe, had actually started the day before. A user had earlier downloaded the same Hypercard stack from the GEnie system and noticed, when he used it, that an INIT resource had been copied into his System Folder. (In the Mac world, this generally means that a program is executed upon start-up. Many of these programs are background utilities, which remain active during the course of the session.) The user, noticing that this same file was posted on CompuServe, had put up a warning that this file was not to be trusted.

The moderator of the Forum initially downplayed the warning. He stated that there was no danger of any such activity, since Hypercard "stacks" are data files, rather than programs. Fortunately, the moderator did check out the warning and found that everything happened as the user had said. Furthermore, the INIT resource was "viral": it spread to other systems that it came in contact with. (At that time "system" disks were common among Mac users, as "bootable" disks were among MS-DOS users.) The moderator apologized and posted the warning, and a number of people started looking into the structure of the virus.

The virus appeared to be benign. It attempted to reproduce until March 2, 1988. When an infected computer was booted on that date, the virus would activate a message that "RICHARD BRANDOW, publisher of MacMag, and its entire staff would like to take this opportunity to convey their UNIVERSAL MESSAGE OF PEACE to all Macintosh users around the world." A laudable sentiment, perhaps, although the means of distribution was unlikely to promote a "peaceful, easy feeling" among the targeted community. Fortunately, on March 3 the message would appear once, and then the virus would erase itself.

Richard Brandow was the publisher and editor of the *MacMag* computer magazine. Based out of Montreal, it was reported at the time to have a circulation of about 40,000. An electronic bulletin board was also run in conjunction with the magazine.

Brandow at one point said that he had been thinking about the "message" for two years prior to releasing it. (Interesting, in view of the fact that the date selected as a trigger, March 2, 1988, was the first anniversary of the introduction of the Macintosh II line. It is also interesting that a "bug" in the virus that caused system crashes affected only the Mac II.) Confronted by users upset by the virus, Brandow never denied it. Indeed, he was proud to claim "authorship" (see *Chicago Tribune*, 14 February 1988, section 7), in spite of the fact that he did not, himself, write the virus. (Brandow had apparently commissioned the programming of the virus, and the internal structure contains the name "Drew Davidson.")

Brandow gave various reasons at various times for the writing of the virus. He once said that he wanted to make a statement about piracy and the copying of computer programs. (As stated before in association with the Brain virus, a viral program can have little to do with piracy per se, since the virus will spread on its own.) However, most often he simply indicated that the virus was a "message" and seemed to imply that somehow it would promote world peace. When challenged by those who had found and disassembled the virus that this was not an impressively friendly action, Brandow tended to fall back on rather irrational arguments concerning the excessive level of handgun ownership in the United States.

(It is interesting, in view of the "Dutch Crackers" group, the Chaos Computer Club, and the Bulgarian "virus factory," that Brandow apparently felt he had a lot of support from those who had seen the virus in Europe. The level of social acceptance of cracking and virus writing shows an intriguing cultural difference between the European states and the United States.)

My suspicion, once again, is that the MacMag virus was written primarily with advertising in mind. Although it backfired almost immediately, Richard Brandow seems to have milked it for all it was worth in terms of notoriety. For a time, in fact, he was the "computer commentator" for the CBC's national midmorning radio show, "Morningside" (somewhat of an institution in Canada). While I never heard of *MacMag* before the virus, I've never seen a copy since, either. According to the recent news reports, Richard Brandow more recently wrote for "Star Trek: The New Generation."

Brandow claims to have infected two computers in *MacMag's* offices in December 1987 in order to "seed" the infection. It probably isn't beyond the bounds of possibility that a few deliberately infected disks were distributed as well.

A resource (named DREW in the Hypercard stack and DR in its viral form) was copied into the System Folder on Mac systems. The System Folder, as the name implies, is the "residence" of the operating system files. With the resource-based structure of the Mac OS, the operating system can be configured and customized by "dropping" resources into the System Folder. (MS-DOS users, tired of fiddling with entries in CONFIG.SYS, conflicting TSRs, and the like, might be warned that this does not always work as easily as it sounds.)

Bootable Mac disks contained a System Folder, in the same way that bootable MS-DOS disks contain the hidden system files and COMMAND.COM. In addition to boot disks for computers with no hard drive, Mac users would often create system disks with specialized configurations. (I well remember, at the time, a number of Macintosh programs that would work with only one specific version of the Finder.

This would put the user in the position of having to "downgrade" the computer each time he or she desired to run these programs.) The Mac OS "opens" each disk inserted into the machine. Therefore, on an infected machine, any diskette that was inserted into the drive would have put the MacMag virus into the System Folder.

The MacMag viral resource was placed into the folder as an "INIT." This meant that it would be one of the "initial" programs automatically run on system start-up. Many, if not most, INITs are background or resident programs that either monitor or support different functions all of the time. Therefore, this was a perfect position for a virus. On an ongoing basis, the virus would be able to watch for opportunities to spread.

The MacMag virus was not a sophisticated piece of programming. As one of the earliest (one of the, rarely used, names for it was the "Macinvirus") Mac viral programs, it didn't have to be sophisticated. (Some would say that Mac viral programs don't have to be sophisticated anyway. Although the Mac world has far fewer viral strains than does the MS-DOS world, infection rates of a given virus have tended to be far higher in Mac populations.) There is no particular secrecy to the MacMag virus. Anyone who looked could find it. Few, however, looked.

The most widely distributed early reports of the MacMag virus were undoubtedly those relating to its appearance on the CompuServe system. In a sense this notoriety is unfair: even those reports from CompuServe were prompted by the notice to CompuServe from someone who had first downloaded the file from GEnie. CompuServe had nothing to do with the production of the file, and it was uploaded and distributed through other systems as well. However, the fact remains that the MacMag virus did get some distribution via a Hypercard stack that was for a time posted on CompuServe.

Hypercard was the first widely available implementation of the "hypertext" or "hypermedia" concept. The basic idea is that related information is "linked" so that associated data can be seen together, or at least accessed quickly. An example might be that in reading email you might come across an unfamiliar term and be able to get a definition of it. At a higher level, when reading a news report of some conflict, you would be able to quickly "pull up" a map of the area, political history, studies of the ethnic groups involved, and economic data about the products and exports of the area. Hypercard was also seen as a development tool.

In any case, Hypercard stacks are essentially databases with internal link information. As such, the initial report of the fact that "NEW-

APP.STK," supposedly a file of information on new Apple products, actually altered system data met with skepticism. Even then, it was "known" that viral programs could not spread via data files. When this "fact" was confirmed, it was erroneously reported that MacMag was an example of a virus that could. In fact, the NEWAPP.STK might better be described as a "dropper."

Semantics aside, how could a data file affect the system at all?

Well, more and more programs have "macro," "script," or interpreter capability. Thus the distinction between data and program blurs. Hypercard stacks have commands as well as data associated with them. Generally, these commands only govern the ability to "flip" from one "card" to another. However, an extended command set, XCMD, allowed for additional functions beyond those normally available in Hypercard. This was used to effect the system changes.

Other systems, such as Lotus 1-2-3, have macro capabilities associated with data files. In theory, it is possible for a virus to be able to switch forms from "object" to macro in the same way that multipartite viral programs switch from file to boot sector format. However, the viral code would be of considerable size. To date no such virus has been seen.

Surely the most renowned aspect of the MacMag/Brandow/DREW/ CompuServe/Macinvirus virus was that it holds the dubious distinction of having been the first virus to infect commercial software.

The president of a company producing educational material for computer training visited Canada. He was given a copy of the "Mr. Potatohead" program. (At a party, by one report.) It was infected.

At home, he ran the program. Once. In his office. Thus infecting his computer.

The training company, MacroMind, some time later delivered some training software to Aldus Corporation. Aldus was, at that time, preparing the release of its then-new "Freehand" drawing product. Computers at Aldus were infected with the virus, and it eventually spread to the production copy of the Freehand program. Three days' production of the program were infected (by one report 7,000 copies; by another 10,000). An unknown, but fairly large, number had already been distributed by the time the infection was discovered.

At the time, MacroMind's customers included Microsoft, Lotus, Apple, and Ashton-Tate. Ashton-Tate consistently refused comment; the others all, at various times, denied any infection; and none was ever found coming out of those four companies.

Some other historical notes:

John Markoff, with far less accuracy than he has shown of late, reported that the virus was a product of the Church of the SubGenius, "an ill-defined group of sometime pranksters." He also reported some amazingly inaccurate information about the SubGenii themselves (see *RISKS-FORUM Digest*, 17 March 1988). The problem is that the Church of the SubGenius is apparently entirely a work of fiction. It does have a "cult" following, but so does *Monty Python*.

We also have, in some of the reports of the virus, the first of what has come to be standard in media reports of viral programs—the warning to avoid shareware and only use commercial software. Very interesting that this particular canard should have started with this particular virus.

With the furor from the CompuServe reports and the media attention to the Aldus infection, it is unlikely that the virus was ever triggered other than by those who wanted to see the display.

SCORES

The Scores Mac virus is very interesting for a number of reasons. I would, however, like to concentrate on two. Scores is the first virus that has a definite company and application as a target, and of Mac viral programs, it definitely has the most interesting programming.

I haven't kept the very earliest reports of the Scores virus, but I believe it was detected in 1988, if not in late 1987. It baffled researchers, however, since, aside from reproducing, it did not seem to carry any payload. It was not until disassemblies and studies of the actual code were done that it was found to be looking for Mac "resources" identified as VULT or ERIC. At the time, no such applications were known to the general public.

(The first detailed account of the virus, including instructions for disinfecting a system, was posted by John Norstad. It is interesting, going back over it, to see that at first he decided not to write a disinfection program for it, since two others had already been produced. However, his reviews of the then-current disinfection programs turned up serious shortcomings in them. This may have reawakened his interest in producing the now widely acclaimed Disinfectant.)

It wasn't until May 1988 that EDS of Dallas finally spoke up. ERIC and VULT were identifiers of resources that were internal to the company. The company never did say whether the resources were associated with a strictly internal utility, or if they had been part of a project that never got released, at least not in that form. Whether utility or ill-fated application, it is clear that the Scores virus was "aimed" at EDS.

It may be that the virus was supposed to spread "into" the company and then interfere with vital internal applications. Or, it may be that the virus was simply supposed to lie in wait until a certain application was released for general use. Infected Macs would "misbehave," leading to complaints, bug reports, or a bad name for the company generally.

One of the early copies of Scores studied was recovered from the NASA HQ in Washington. This led to reports of the "NASA" virus. Indeed, as late as 1991, I still saw reports in major IS trade papers of how NASA had recently been devastated by the Scores virus as it swept through, trashing hard disks and so forth. (For those who do not know, this appears to be error on the part of the journals.)

In July 1988, a Texas man was charged with computer-related sabotage and burglary, and it was reported, in error, that he was the author of Scores. In December 1988, Apple sources were saying that they knew who the author was, and the matter was in the hands of the lawyers. In December 1990, it was reported that the Dallas prosecutor's office would be proceeding with charges and that reports of damage were being solicited. This was the last message relating to the trial that I ever saw.

The Scores virus has a complicated structure and operation. There are time delays, and both the system and application files are used for reproduction.

Scores starts simply enough. When an infected application is run on a new system, the System Folder is infected. Two invisible folders are created, one named Desktop and the other, Scores (hence the name). Thus the Scores infection gets to start early and go "resident." (INITs of 6, 10, and 17 are created. This led to later problems with other INITs numbered the same way that were mistakenly thought to be infected.)

The Note Pad and Scrapbook files, if not already present, are created. The file types for these files are changed, as are the normal icons.

The virus waits two days before it starts to infect applications. Thus the Scores might almost seem to be an early form of the multipartite virus, since it "toggles" between system and application files. However, it is only after the infection has entered the System Folder that the other activities take place.

Four days after the infection of the System Folder, the second part of the virus starts up. At this point, it looks for applications which, when run, identify themselves as ERIC or VULT. If such an application is run, the application will be terminated after 25 minutes of operation.

Seven days after the infection of the System Folder, the final part of the payload comes into play. Again operating on applications with the VULT resource, it will force errors and termination on a complicated series of timings and operations.

The timing sequences and complicated arrangements for triggering errors and program termination would seem to indicate that the author saw this program interfering with an application in a normal environment and generating "normal" problems. An intermittent bug would be difficult to trace and less likely to be effectively attended to as a virus. This would tend to support the idea that the author thought to cause trouble for ERIC and VULT as a released application. It does not, however, rule out the possibility of creating trouble for an in-house utility.

CHRISTMA EXEC

In December 1987, IBM mainframe computers in Europe, connected via the EARN network, experienced a "mailstorm." Such events are fairly common on the "internetworks," caused by mailer problems, incompatibilities, or even "autoanswer" daemons replying to messages from unmoderated "distribution lists." This particular mailstorm, however, was of unprecedented severity. It shut down whole sections of the net, at least as far as effective work was concerned.

For many, probably for most, users, email is simply text. A select group are involved with the exchange of programs or other binary files, often UU- or XX-encoded and sent through email systems, often "embedded" within messages as a greater or lesser portion. Some users have these facilities provided for them through systems that are configured with these functions. (NeXT users have these functions in automated form, for example, and also have a reputation for not knowing how they work, cross-posting incomprehensible garbage to distribution lists and newsgroups.) IBM mainframe users often have such functions provided through PROFS and an interpreter language called REXX. Programs in REXX are called EXECs.

The CHRISTMA EXEC was a message that contained such a program. "Christmas card" messages with this system can be more than just the usual "ASCII tree." (Perhaps, since this deals with IBM mainframes, I should use the more generic "typewriter picture." Anybody remember what a typewriter was?) These messages could include forms of animation such as asterisk snowflakes falling on a winter scene, or a crackling fire from a Yule log. The message header contained a note that "Browsing this message is no fun at all. Just type Christmas . . ." which was intended to stop people from trying to read the "source code" of the message, but it is unlikely that few would even think to do so.

Typing either "Christmas" or "Christma" would generate the "card." It really wasn't anything special—a very simplistic conifer shape made out of Xs. (Mine is *way* better.) At least on the surface. However, at the same time that it was displaying the tree on the screen, it was also searching for the NAMES and NETLOG files associated with the user's account. This provided a list of other users that either sent mail to, or received mail from, this account. The important thing was that it was a list of valid email addresses. The CHRISTMA EXEC would then mail copies of itself to all these accounts.

The important point, technically, was that all the accounts were valid. As a side benefit, all those accounts would be used to receiving mail from the account that had just read it. And they would tell 40 friends, and they would tell. . . .

The exact number of copies made by any one reading of the CHRISTMA EXEC would depend upon the number of listings in the NAMES file and the messages received by the NETLOG file. However, for all intents, any nuclear physicist knows that it only needs to be, on average, "greater than one." The CHRISTMA EXEC would destroy itself after having been read, but more copies would be created than destroyed.

Some of the newly spawned messages would "die" a natural net death, being sent to outdated accounts, or directed at those who were on holiday (or, perhaps, executives and managers, who, of course, never read their email). Most, however, would reach a working account and a mildly (but likely not sufficiently) curious user. The user would type "Christmas," see the tree, shrug, and dismiss the message while a number of new messages would be created and head off in all directions.

Eventually, a large number of users would be reading and inadvertently sending copies of the message. Therefore, a large volume of mail would be being generated, using up a large chunk of bandwidth. Eventually, in some cases, all the available bandwidth. Some machines were essentially cut off from the net—with the exception of the CHRISTMA "cards."

In addition to bandwidth, CHRISTMA consumed disk space. The individual messages would not be large, but the numbers of them would start to consume significant amounts of disk drive real estate. Mail spool entries would also be used up. Not only would they be used up on the system itself, but users' mail directories would start to show repeating listings for the CHRISTMA EXEC, crowding out other more important messages. (Most of this crowding would be psychological, but occasionally it would be physical, as system limits were reached.)

The general "disinfecting" action taken was to shut down the system and purge all copies of the message from the mail spool. However, since the transmission was "cross-system," users would have to be warned to be on the alert for the message when received from an outside source. The major impact was mostly confined to the period of December 9 to December 14, 1987. IBM's internal network, VNET, was more heavily hit than either EARN or BITNET. (VNETers seemed to be more severely affected because of larger NAMES files.)

Once again, the CHRISTMA EXEC demonstrates a virus (or, more exactly, a worm) in an area that is generally thought to belong to data. Although IBM mainframe systems can use mail to transfer files (mail is, in fact, simply a specialized case of file transfer), the CHRISTMA message was contained in text. REXX source code, to be exact.

It is often said, when answering the frequent question about whether a virus can be transmitted via a data file or a message, that the line between data and programming is very blurred. This is quite true. In fact the MAKEBOO program, a utility for converting binary files into printable characters suitable for transmitting across email systems, itself contains only printable characters. The MAKEBOO program, then, can be sent as a message over normal email systems.

The CHRISTMA EXEC, however, was not a program in this sense. An EXEC is a source code program, which is then run by interpreter. REXX is an interpreted, rather than a compiled, language, much the same as most BASIC interpreters. No object code is ever produced in this kind of situation. In that case, what is the source code? A program to be run, or a data file to be edited? The answer, of course, is both.

Interpreters are making a resurgence. While interpreted programs are much slower than compiled ones, modern computers are fast enough to deal with the speed problem. In addition, interpreted languages allow the programs to be run on multiple platforms without object-code compatibility problems. There is no need to adjust, or even recompile, the code. Simply run what you are given. REXX interpreters are available on a wide variety of platforms. Many other similar languages are available.

Indeed, application programs are tending to become such interpreters. "Programs" are being written in 1-2-3 and WordPerfect. Terminal emulators, as well, have "scripting" languages that are being used to automate any function that users might have the slightest difficulty with.

"Groupware" is the current buzzword. Groupware will rely heavily on the configuration, automation, and presentation of functions through exactly these kinds of systems. "Open systems" and cross-platform compatibility, both desperately desired by users and corporations, will also present opportunities to the authors of viral programs.

Commentary prompted by the CHRISTMA EXEC ranged over many topics. One subject was the "trusted source." That is, you only run a program when you "know where it's been." This is a good principle for data security in general, but it is interesting that it came up in discussion of this particular outbreak, since the messages, after the initial spread, would have all come from "known," and presumably trusted, sources.

Also interesting, in view of the fact that the EXEC actually contained the source code, was the opinion piece that suggested that only source code should be trusted. This posting seems to have been written by someone firmly settled, not only into the UNIX community, but also into UNIX culture. It states that there is no reason not to have the source code for everything you run. The author further asserts that there is no reason for software producers and publishers not to give you the source code for every program you buy. (One can only surmise that he was a tad frustrated at having to deal with some piece of commercial software and that he wasn't, himself, a software producer or publisher.)

However, this author had included an error in his posting, and thus killed his own argument almost as soon as he made it.

The first article appeared in *RISKS-FORUM Digest* (January 1988, 6–2) and included the year 1987 in the masthead. The posting is not exactly fanatical, but certainly strident, and includes the adage, "IF YOU CAN'T READ IT, DON'T RUN IT." It also contains the statement that testing unknown programs on "write-only harddisks" is useless.

Well, I'd agree. In fact, I'd say a "write-only harddisk" was a pretty useless piece of equipment. However, two further respondents, the next day, quoted that exact passage (one defending the thesis, one attacking it), without commenting on the error. It wasn't until a few days later that another posting pointed this out.

It also pointed out that the original poster did not catch this error in the three-paragraph "source," that two further authors quoted the error without noting it, and that the moderator, known for his love of pun-laden editorial comment, missed it all three times. Obviously, the ability to catch a loophole hidden in several thousand lines of source code is not a defense.

The CHRISTMA EXEC was extremely prolific, not only in terms of the number of copies produced during the 1987 infestation, but also with respect to the number of its "descendants." Many worms owe their "spiritual" origin, at least, to this program. The code, of course, was widely distributed by the action of the worm itself. Anyone who received a copy, and who knew what it was and didn't run it, could have kept a copy, since it carried its own source code. (A number of those who received it would have been able to keep copies even if they didn't know what it was and tried to run it. The mailings were not confined to IBM VM systems.) The code was also published in Burger's virus book (see book review section).

In October 1988, a program called MOIN EXEC was reported to be "loose" on the "net(s)." Although the wording of the warning seems to indicate a viral type of activity, the description of MOIN appears to be more consistent with a trojan horse program. It purported to be a type of CHAT program and to provide the user who ran it with an email "answering machine" capability (answering mail while the user was away), but also allowed an outside "caller" to submit commands to be run on the user's account.

The most famous network worm of recent times is, of course, the Internet/UNIX Worm created and released by Robert Tappan Morris in November 1988. Although the Internet Worm was considerably more sophisticated, involved much greater coding, and ran on the Internet protocols and UNIX operating systems, a number of conceptual features from the CHRISTMA EXEC were also found in the Internet Worm.

In December 1988, another infestation of the CHRISTMA EXEC occurred, although with greatly reduced impact. By this time there were filters in place at major BITNET backbone sites "watching" for the CHRISTMA file and preventing its spread. Thus, although the EXEC was able to post itself, on any invocation, it would tend to be restricted in distribution to "local" sites. One noteworthy occurrence, though, was the fact that the operation of CHRISTMA on this run posted itself to the *GAMES-L* distribution list.

In December 1988, VMS systems on DECnet networks were hit by a worm based on a file called HI.COM. On VMS systems COM files are similar to the REXX exec files and MS-DOS batch files. They are programs in VMS DCL source code. HI.COM used the fact that DECnet nodes had, by default, a standard "anonymous" account that could be used by the network and other machines to gain limited access to a machine. This account was able to start processes running. The process that HI.COM started replicated, submitted itself to other machines, informed a specific account at a specific site, and waited until midnight on December 24, 1988, when it began mailing Christmas greetings to all users. The content of the message and the notification address seemed to indicate a German author with access to an account in France. The first notifications of this infestation came from the NASA SPAN network and the U.S. Department of Energy's HEPNET.

HI.COM owed a number of features to the Internet Worm. One was a stealth technique, whereby the file was copied into memory and then erased from the disk. Another stealth procedure used by HI.COM was the use of a process name suggestive of normal mail routines.

The spring of 1989 saw a resurgence of interest in mutating the original CHRISTMA on VM systems. A modified version (BUL EXEC) was released from the EARN backbone site in Turkey on March 8. ORGASM EXEC was released from Pennsylvania State University on April 4 and HEADACH EXEC found at the University of Ottawa on April 8. DIR EXEC, discovered November 1989, purported to be a version of the MS-DOS DIR command for VM systems, but was a dropper for CHRISTMA. There was a Turkish version EXEC in November 1990 called TERM MODULE, and a reposting of CHRISTMA EXEC to *alt.hackers* in December of 1990. The latest reported sighting was as GAME2 MODULE in January 1991.

The WANK/W.COM worm of October 1989, and its successor, owed most of its inspiration (if you can call plagiarism inspiration) to the Internet Worm and HI.COM.

Finally, there was the XA1 Christmas Tree PC virus in March 1990. Although it owed no technical or programming detail to any of the network worms, it seems to have been written "in memorium." It contains (in German) the message, "And still it is alive : The Christmas Tree !"

During the summer of 1988 there was considerable confusion regarding the CHRISTMA EXEC. These were the early days for the virus field as a whole, of course, and so there were the usual media reports confusing microcomputers with mainframes, talking on the one hand about international networks and on the other about disks being erased. One story describes the symptoms of the CHRISTMA EXEC while at the same time talking about computerized medical systems being sabotaged. There was also a rumor among Mac users that CHRISTMA was a Mac virus. (I mean, it had to be IBM, right? Who else uses eight-character filenames?)

The author of the CHRISTMA EXEC was fairly quickly traced back to a university computer in Germany. The culprit's account was lifted. The NETLOG file that the EXEC used to obtain account and system names is a transaction file that lists all mail sent and received. Therefore, while the file could be suppressed by some users, in most cases an entry would show where the message had come from and confirm where it had been sent to. Backtracking the infestation was therefore relatively easy, even though the author had left no clues in the program, and eventually the paths converged. (This was a good thing: this particular type of mail system does not carry the same amount of header and "received from" information that others may be used to.)

In fact, the author had not intended to cause any problems: he had thought to send the greetings to his friends. A second student used the EXEC created by the first, with some slight modifications, and didn't realize the havoc he was about to cause. Fortunately, his lack of programming expertise showed up in other areas: the "parsing" of account info from the NETLOG file was faulty and reduced the traffic to only 5 percent of what it could have been.

Also, some copies never did get to reproduce because they ended up on incompatible systems. One VMS user received six copies of CHRISTMA. Obviously, he never sent any on.

One of the frequently asked questions in the virus world is "Has there ever been a virus in a mainframe, and can I get a scanner for mine?" CHRISTMA and the Internet Worm are often used as examples of viral programs on mainframes and networks (with the obligatory "It's not a virus, it's a worm" pedantry), but the answer about scanners is always "No." This is not correct. All major BITNET backbone or "core" sites run a selective file filter to catch any of the known variants of CHRISTMA EXEC. A scanner by any other name. . .

THE INTERNET WORM

By the fall of 1988, *VIRUS-L* had been established and was very active. At that time it was still an "exploder" mailer, rather than a digest, but postings were coming out pretty much on a daily basis, so I was quite surprised when I didn't receive any on November 3. I didn't get one on November 4 either. It wasn't until November 5, actually, that I found out why.

Most machines on the net were not of the type that would have been affected. The nuisance was only able to run and propagate on machines running the UNIX operating system, and then only those with specific versions and specific CPUs. However, given that the machines that are connected to the Internet also comprise the transport mechanism for the Internet, a "minority group" of machines, thus affected, had an impact on the performance of the net as a whole.

I learned of the specific problem, initially, from a newspaper report. However, by November 5 I was also starting to get mailings across the net again. During the run of the mailstorm, a sufficient number of machines had been affected that both email and distribution-list mailings were impaired. Some mail was lost, either by mailers that could not handle the large volumes that "backed up," or by mail queues being dumped in an effort to disinfect systems.

Most mail was not lost, but substantially delayed. The delay could have been caused by a number, or combination, of factors. In some cases mail would have been rerouted via a possibly less efficient path after a certain time. In other cases backbone machines, affected by the problem, were simply much slower at processing mail. In still others, mail routers would either crash or be stopped, with a consequent delay in mail delivery. Ironically, electronic mail was the primary means that the various parties attempting to deal with the trouble were trying to use to contact each other.

By Sunday, November 6, things were pretty much back to normal. Mail was flowing, distribution lists and electronic "periodicals" were running, and the news was getting around. The one difference was the enormous volume of traffic given over to one topic—the Internet Worm.

The Internet Worm is still the preeminent case of a viral program in our time. Even today, no virus story in the popular media is complete without some reference to it. It rates a mention in *The Cuckoo's Egg*, by Clifford Stoll. Each school term brings fresh requests for bibliographic material on it (sparked, one suspects, either by choice or assignment of essay topics). As late as December 1992, there was a "thread" running through *comp.security.misc* on "Fun things to do with RTM" (the author), which occupied about half the total bandwidth.

In many ways this fame (or infamy) is deserved: the Internet Worm is the story of data security in miniature. The Worm used "trusted" links, password cracking, security "holes" in standard programs, standard and default operations, and, of course, the power of viral replication.

The Internet Worm has been analyzed in great depth by those far more competent than I. As no purpose would be served in my trying to duplicate that effort, I will only try to give the most superficial coverage to it here. I hope this description will not be so simplistic as to be inaccurate.

Some general background may be helpful to those without specific background in mainframes, UNIX, or the Internet protocols.

Unlike microcomputers, mainframes, and particularly those on the networks, are generally designed to run constantly—to be ready for "action" at all times. They are, indeed, specifically set up to run various types of programs and procedures in the absence of operator intervention. Again, unlike microcomputers, many hundreds of functions and processes may be running at all times, expressly designed neither to require nor report to an operator. Some such processes cooperate with each other; some run independently. In the UNIX world, such small utility programs are referred to as "daemons," after the supposedly subordinate entities that take over mundane tasks and extend the "power" of the "wizard," or skilled operator. Many of these utility programs deal with the communications between systems. "Mail," in the network sense, covers much more than the delivery of text messages between users. Network mail, mail between systems, may deal with file transfers, data on the best routing to reach remote systems, or even upgrades to system software. This kind of mail is often dealt with by the machine and the utility programs, generally without informing or asking permission from an operator.

When the Worm was well established on a machine, it would try to infect another. On many systems, this attempt was all too easy, since computers on the Internet are meant to generate activity on each other, and some had no protection in terms of the type of activity allowed. If a straightforward request was not sufficient, a couple of tricks were tried.

One such utility program, was "fingerd." The "finger" program allows a user to obtain information about another user. The server program, fingerd, is the daemon that listens for calls from finger. The client program, finger, will, of course, send a certain amount of data indicating which user to obtain information on. The version of fingerd common at the time of the Internet Worm had a minor problem: it didn't check how much information it was given. It would take as much as it could hold and leave the rest. "The rest," unfortunately, could be used to start a process on the computer that fingerd was running on, and this was used as part of the attack.

The program, "sendmail," is the "engine" of most mail-oriented processes on UNIX systems on the Internet. In most cases it only allows data received from another system to be passed to a user address. However, there is a debug mode, which allows commands to be passed to the system. Some versions of UNIX were shipped with the debug mode enabled; some, with it off. The greatest weakness, however, seems to have been that regardless of the default, debug mode was often enabled during installation of sendmail for testing and then never turned off.

However the Worm managed to get into a system, it then was supplied with the main program from the "previous" site. Two programs were used, one for each CPU that could be infected. If neither of the two would work, the Worm would erase itself and stop. If the new host was suitable, the Worm looked for further hosts and connections to try out.

The program also tried to break into user accounts on the infected machine. Given the information in the account and password file, it first tried simple variations on the name of the account and the user. It carried a dictionary of passwords that it would try and would also look for a dictionary on the new machine and attempt to use words from that as well.

If an account was "cracked," the Worm would look for accounts that this user had on other computers. Since the accounts and requests thus found were valid, it was easier to start new processes, and the new infection had a greater chance of success.

The Worm did have a means of checking to see whether there were multiple copies running on a given computer. However, the mechanism delayed the termination of a program for a significant time. Also, the Worm regularly produced copies that would not respond to the request for termination. The copies of the Worm would, regularly, destroy themselves—having first made a new copy. In this way the identifying process ID number would continually change.

Note that there is nothing in the Worm that is specifically or intentionally destructive. However, as with the CHRISTMA EXEC, the mere existence of the entity had implications for the infected systems and for those associated with them. The multiple copies of the program that ran on the host machines meant that processing was significantly affected. In addition, communications links and processes were being used for propagating the Worm rather than for the work they were intended to support.

Media coverage of viral programs and major infestations has been consistently, and depressingly, inaccurate. An enduring mystery remains from the Internet Worm: how did the media do so well at reporting it?

Highly accurate newspaper reports on the Worm were appearing even in regional newspapers as early as November 5. Although some errors appeared in some stories, the errors tended to be minor. Some very erroneous reports appeared, but the ones that got printed tended to be the more correct. How did the information get out so quickly, and how was the media able to discriminate between the stories so well?

(Even the erroneous stories that were carried contained exceptional information. A story from the *New York Times* on Sunday, November 6, stated that Robert Morris was able to track the progress of the Worm because "[e]ach second each virus broadcast its location to a computer named Ernie at the University of California." While this was not correct, it *was* true that the Worm was designed to have packets sent to ernie.berkeley.edu. The code that was to have done this was faulty, but, had certain programming been in place at Berkeley, it would have been possible to get rough estimates of progress.)

John Markoff has come to be widely recognized for the excellence of his reportage in technical matters. An examination of his article of November 8, 1988, is very instructive. While the technical details of his report could not possibly rival that of the papers prepared by Gene Spafford ("Crisis and Aftermath") or Mark Eichin and Jon Rochlis ("With Microscope and Tweezers"), the general concepts are present, clear, and well explained. Experts could quibble over some of the details (he describes the sendmail debug option as a "trapdoor" and is rather free with assignment of motivation), but I suspect they would have to admit that the important points are all there. (For those wanting more details, both papers mentioned here can be found in the book *Computers under Attack*; see the review section.)

Still, what contributed to this unprecedented, and so far apparently unequaled, media accuracy? One of the factors is undoubtedly the number of researchers who were involved. Across the country, dozens and perhaps hundreds of people were involved in a detailed examination of the Worm. Very little other work was being done until the problem was resolved. (Let's face it, for many people, little work *could* be done until it was resolved.) Even those who were not actually engaged in research as to what the bug did were following the developments closely so as to be able to disinfect the systems that they were responsible for. At the same time, there was not as much time for misinformation to spread via "friends of friends" who had once seen a copy. For most reporters, however, Markoff's articles at least served as a template, and his initial articles contributed greatly to the accuracy of the reports of the Worm.

The attempts to secure systems and the attempts to circumvent that security form a never-ending cycle of escalating programs, features, and procedures. There are two seemingly mutually contradictory factors at work. First, security by and large works. Second, there is no useful security system that cannot be circumvented.

Two philosophically opposed camps tend to form around this issue. The first states that security information should be restricted. This restriction will limit the information available to those who would try to break security systems. The second philosophy often refers to this first position as "security by obscurity" and proposes that restriction of information only serves to keep it out of the hands of those who need it. The "crackers," so this second theory goes, already have it.

(Of course, most people find themselves somewhere in between the two positions. The dividing line in the argument over what information should be in the public domain is constantly moving.)

The experience with the Internet Worm must be said to favor the latter position more than the former. The fixes, "work-arounds," and patches that enabled systems to recover and prevent reinfection were developed by an informal "network" of individual researchers who freely broadcast their results. (This "free broadcast" was somewhat hampered by the fact that the primary means of communication was the same system that was under attack. The important factor is that the information was not being censored as it was discovered, nor was it being provided by a central authority or clearinghouse.)

The authority in this case is generally conceded to be the National Security Agency (NSA) of the United States. It is quite fashionable, and likely unfairly so, to speculate that the NSA actually attempts to cripple, or at least limit, the security of systems in order to have access to them if need be.

I suspect that the NSA is comprised of well-meaning, and generally hardworking, public servants. I further suspect they are more effective than most. However, it is well established that the weaknesses in system security that the Internet Worm exploited were well known to the NSA. It is also well established that the system managers who should have been made aware of those holes had not been sufficiently warned.

Robert Tappan Morris. Son of Bob Morris (of the NSA). (Hence often referred to as Robert Tappan Morris Junior, in spite of the fact that Bob Morris' middle name is not Tappan.) Since the "birth" of the Worm, of sufficient fame to be known simply by his initials: RTM.

Robert Tappan Morris was a student of data security at Cornell University when he wrote the Worm. The Worm is often referred to as a part of his research, although it was neither an assigned project, nor had it been discussed with his advisor.

The release of the Worm, at the time that it was released, seems to have been accidental. Whatever the motivations for its creation and whatever the intentions for its future use, both internal evidence of incomplete coding and the early generation of "alerts" from the author would seem to support the theory of accidental release.

At the same time, RTM was not exactly immediately forthcoming in warning the net. The first recorded warning was one generated by a friend (and anonymously at that) about ten hours after the first release.

In reading various documents studying the Worm, there is a division of opinion regarding the quality of the program itself. However, an "averaging" of the comments might yield the following: the Worm shows a lot of knowledge of security "holes," and competent, occasionally flawed, but not brilliant coding. The Worm might be considered to be a "proof of concept," except that it contains too many concepts at once. There is no evidence that Bob Morris Senior had any part in, or knowledge of, the Worm under construction. Nevertheless, it is unreasonable to expect that there was never any shoptalk around the dinner table.

RTM was convicted of violating the computer Fraud and Abuse Act on May 16, 1990. In March 1991, an appeal was denied. He was sentenced to three years probation, a $10,000 fine, and 400 hours of community service.

Debate over the sentence started even before the last copy of the Worm was shut down. It ranged from "Hanging's too good for him," to "He's done us all a great favor." This range of opinion still exists today. Estimates of the damage done range from $100,000 to $97 million. It is very instructive to read the appeal court's decision. The arguments all hinge on very fine interpretations of the law and matters of intentionality. The decision also examines the question of whether permission to use a certain computer confers permission to use the network that the computer is attached to.

In October 1989, another network worm was found to be making the rounds—on VMS machines connected through DECnet. While even to this day there is considerable debate as to Morris' intentions with regard to the Internet Worm, there is no such ambiguity concerning the "WANK worm," as it is known. WANK was intended for propaganda, plain and simple.

WANK used a number of features similar to those of the Internet Worm. Mail functions were used to spread the worm from system to system, and "standard defaults" (in this case "system" and "field service" accounts and passwords) were used to get the worm running on new machines.

In addition to guessing system passwords, the WANK worm also attempted to change them. As the program would have no further use for passwords, once started, this would appear to have been directed at inconveniencing the system operator.

The message carried by the worm spoke of "Worms Against Nuclear Killers" and announced that the infected system had been "WANKed," as well as displaying a "text graphic" of WANK. It also contained the quotation, "You talk of times of peace for all, and then prepare for war." Obviously the author had believed the reports of the Internet Worm that had spoken of massive numbers of military computers being affected. Ironically, few, if any, of the people who saw the WANK worm's message would have had anything to do with the military.

Some aspects of the worm were just plain obnoxious, such as appearing to delete all of a user's files and paging users with the PHONE program.

A few weeks later, a second VMS/DECnet worm with very few changes from the original WANK was released. This "knockoff of a knockoff of a knockoff" tends to be more the rule than the exception in virus research. Of the thousands of MS-DOS viral programs, the vast majority result from "bit twiddling" in an attempt (often less than entirely successful) to fool scanners. In the end this often means nothing except more, and more boring, work for the authors of scanning programs.

MICHELANGELO, MONKEY, AND OTHER STONED VARIANTS

Michelangelo is generally believed by researchers to have been built on, or "mutated" from, the Stoned virus. The identity of the replication code, down to the inclusion of the same bugs, puts this beyond any reasonable doubt. Any successful virus inspires (if such a term can be used for the unimaginative copying that tends to go on) knockoffs: Michelangelo is unusual only in the extent of the renovations to the payload.

The Stoned virus was originally written by a high school student in New Zealand. All evidence suggests that he wrote it only for study and that he took precautions against its spread. Insufficient precautions, as it turned out: it is reported that his brother stole a copy and decided that it would be fun to infect the machines of friends.

Reporting on the "original" state of a virus with as many variants as Stoned is difficult. For example, the "original" Stoned is said to have been restricted to infecting floppy disks. The current most common version of Stoned, however, infects *all* disks. It is an example of a second "class" of boot-sector-infecting viral programs, in that it places itself in the master boot record, or partition boot record, of a hard disk instead of in the boot sector itself. In common with most BSIs, Stoned "repositions" the original sector in a new location on the disk. On hard disks and double-density floppies, this generally works out: On high (quad)-density floppies, system information can be overwritten, resulting in a loss of data. One version of Stoned (which I do not have) is reported not to infect 3½″ diskettes: this is undoubtedly the template for Michelangelo since it doesn't infect 720K disks either.

Stoned has spawned a large number of mutations ranging from minor variations in the spelling of the payload message to the somewhat functionally different Empire, Monkey, and No-Int variations. Interestingly, only Michelangelo appears to have been as successful in reproducing, although the recent rise in Monkey reports is somewhat alarming.

Michelangelo is widely reported (even by the CARO *Computer Virus Catalog*) to have been discovered in Europe in the spring or summer of 1991. Roger Riordan, however, had reported and named the virus in Australia in February of 1991. He suspected that the virus had been received by the affected company on disks of software from Taiwan, but this could not be finally determined.

The date in February 1991 is very telling. This indicates the existence of the virus prior to March 6, 1991 (the "trigger" date). This further indicates that the virus can survive, even though it destroys itself along with the system tracks of disks overwritten on that date. This is not really surprising: few computer users understand that BSIs can both infect from and infect any disk, whether or not the disk is bootable, contains any programs, or, indeed, contains any files at all.

Riordan determined that March 6 was the trigger date. He mentioned this to a friend who remarked that it was his birthday and that it was also the birthday of the Renaissance painter, sculptor, and engineer Michelangelo Buonarotti, born March 6, 1475, in Caprese, Italy. Riordan named the virus from this coincidence of dates. There is no text in the body of the virus and no reference to Michelangelo. There is also no evidence that the author of the virus knew anything of this connection.

(As a piece of trivia, March 6 is also Ed McMahon's birthday, leading to jokes about viral messages stating, "Congratulations! Your computer may already be infected!")

(Interestingly, in Taiwan the virus is widely known as the "Ninja Turtle" virus. Obviously, in the young and not highly cultured world of "teenage mutant ninja hackers," comic-book characters are more familiar than Renaissance artists, even though all of the "Teenage Mutant Ninja Turtles" (TM, probably) are named after painters of that period. However the cartoon/comic/toy characters have no known association with March 6, and this reference is obviously a mistaken extension of the Michelangelo name. It is also interesting that when I first mentioned this in a network posting, I got a very irate message from someone in Taiwan who claimed, without substantiation, to have been the first to *discover* the virus. The poster violently objected to the name, Michelangelo, claiming the virus should be called "Stoned II," and stated that he knew nothing about Michelangelo the artist. Given that this person is completely unknown otherwise and that there are strong indications that Michelangelo may have started in Taiwan, it makes you wonder.)

Looking at reports of the virus in the summer 1991, Michelangelo was very rare in the first half of the year. (Likely even rarer on March 7 than it had been on March 5.) However, it spread extremely rapidly, and by the fall of 1991 was sufficiently widespread that by the beginning of 1992, companies were beginning to ship out products infected with the Michelangelo virus. By the time the public became generally aware of the need to check, in late February 1992, it is likely that the number of copies was in the millions. Luckily, almost all of those actually on computer hard disks were caught before March 6.

The replication mechanism of Michelangelo is basically identical to that of Stoned. A BSI, it replaces the original boot sector on a floppy disk with itself. The original boot sector, whatever it may be, is placed in a new position on sector 3 or 14 of the disk, and the virus contains a "loader," which points to this location. After the virus loads itself into memory, the original boot sector is run, and to the user, the boot process appears to proceed normally.

When a computer is booted from an infected disk, the virus first checks to see if a hard disk is present. If it is, the virus infects the hard disk in much the same way as a floppy, except that the master boot record, or partition boot record (the first sector "physically" present on the hard disk) is replaced and moved to sector 7 (instead of the boot sector). In a sense, this method of replication is simpler than that of other BSIs. It is always the "physical" first sector that is affected. This also takes place at a very low level, not requiring MS-DOS to be fully loaded to operate.

As with Stoned, there is no stealth involved. Examination of the boot blocks with a sector-editing utility will clearly show the difference between a "valid" sector and one that is infected. (Stoned is easier to spot, with the text message within the sector, but the absence of the normal system messages should be a tip-off.) In addition, Michelangelo reserves itself 2K at the "top" of memory: a simple run of the CHKDSK utility will show total memory on the system, and if a 640K machine shows 655,360 bytes, then you do *not* have Michelangelo. (If the number is less, there may still be other reasons than a virus.) Removal is a simple matter of placing the original sector back where it belongs, thus wiping out the infection. This can be done with sector-editing utilities, or even with DEBUG. (There are cases where a computer has been infected with both Stoned and Michelangelo. In this situation, the boot sector cannot be recovered, since both Stoned and Michelangelo use the same "landing zone" for the original sector, and the infection by the second virus overwrites the original boot sector with the contents of the first virus.)

When an infected computer boots up, Michelangelo checks the date via interrupt 1Ah. If the date is March 6, the virus then overwrites the first several cylinders of the disk with the contents of memory (generally speaking, not much). There are two limitations of this damage. Interrupt 1Ah is not available on the earliest PCs and XTs. This is not to say that only ATs and up are vulnerable: "turbo" XTs have this interrupt as well. However, the disk that is overwritten is the disk booted from: A hard disk can be saved by the simple expedient of booting from a floppy. Also, the damage is only triggered at boot time.

A number of suggestions were made in early 1992 as to how to deal with Michelangelo. Since so very many antiviral programs—commercial, shareware, and freeware—identified the virus, it was odd the lengths that people were willing to go to in order to avoid the obvious step of using a scanning program to find the virus. The "computer expert" in one of our local papers wrote an article on Michelangelo for his weekly column. It was packed with errors, and he was roundly chastised by many people. A large contingent of his detractors were local BBS sysops who urged him simply to get one of the shareware scanners and make certain. His response, the next week, was to publish a column stating that no self-respecting business would be caught dead with a modem. Among the other recommendations of the high and mighty were:

Backups. *Always* a good idea. And, given that Michelangelo is a boot sector infector, it wouldn't be able to "store" on a tape backup. But on diskettes it would. Even worse, many popular backup programs use proprietary non-DOS disk formats for reasons of speed and additional storage. These, if infected by Michelangelo, would become unusable.

Change computer clock. Since Michelangelo was set to go off on March 6, just make sure March 6 never happened. Part of the trouble with this was that many people did not understand the difference between the MS-DOS clock and the system clock read by interrupt 1Ah. The MS-DOS DATE command did not always alter the system clock. Certain network-connected machines also have "time server" functions, so that the date would be reset to conform to the network. Finally, 1992 was a leap year, and many "clocks" did not deal with it properly. Thus, for many computers, March 6 came on the Thursday, not Friday. (An even sillier suggestion was to test for Michelangelo by setting the date to March 6 and then rebooting the computer. This became known as "Michelangelo roulette.")

OS/2, Novell, or UNIX boxes.   Michelangelo is widely perceived as an MS-DOS virus. This is not quite correct. It is, rather, a BIOS virus. It can infect Intel CPU BIOS/ISA-compatible machines, although many will no longer boot after the infection.

Stay off modems.   Neither the master/partition boot record nor the boot sector are identifiable files under MS-DOS. Therefore, neither can be transmitted as files over a modem or bulletin board by the average user. Although dropper programs are theoretically possible, they are extremely rare. The danger of getting a Michelangelo infection from a BBS is therefore so small that for all practical purposes it does not exist. The prohibition against bulletin boards merely cuts you off from a major source of advice and utility software.

In the fall of 1989, there was a large amount of media attention given to Datacrime and "Columbus Day" (actually different names for roughly the same virus). The promotion appeared to be instigated by a particular antiviral service vendor. It turned out that these viruses had far less distribution than was being claimed. I suspect that the media has had a distrust of virus hype stemming from this date.

However, the epidemic of Michelangelo in the spring of 1992 could not be denied. Vendors were making unsubstantiated claims for the numbers of infections, which, in retrospect, turned out to have been surprisingly accurate. More importantly, the research community as a whole was seeing large numbers of infections. The public was seeing them as well, since no less than 15 companies shipped commercial products that turned out to be infected with the Michelangelo virus.

Instant experts arose to fill the need for press releases, confusing Michelangelo with every other virus that had ever put a message on a screen. (One such "consultant" called a researcher for a "professional courtesy consultation"—to ask what a "boot sector" was.) Accounting firms (why are accountants supposed to be so "computerate"?) trumpeted the injunction not to call bulletin boards, heedless of the fact that BSIs don't *spread* via modem. The media darlings, of course, took full advantage, and even I had 20 seconds of my 15 minutes of fame used up on the tube. (But who got his picture in the paper? My brother. Who did not *believe* in viral programs—to whom I had given a copy of a scanner. And who found the computer in his church to be infected, at 11:50 p.m. on March 5.)

(Two producers of commercial antiviral programs released crippled freeware versions of their scanners. These I view with some disfavor. The programs *did* briefly mention that they checked only for Michelangelo, but certainly gave users the impression that they were checking the whole system.)

Because of the media attention, a number of checks were made that would not have been done otherwise. Hundreds, even thousands, of copies of Michelangelo were found within single institutions. Infection rates ranged from 1 per 1,000 to 25 percent or more in some parts of Europe. Some reports, such as the infection of an entire network of pharmacy computers in South Africa, were later found to be spurious, but estimates of millions of copies had a sound basis. (There were no reports of Michelangelo detected in Japan beforehand, but a small number of computers were wiped out on that Friday. This is particularly interesting in view of the fact that MITI, the Ministry of Trade and Industry, had been loudly proclaiming that Michelangelo would not be a problem in Japan.)

Because a great many copies had been found and removed, the number of "hits" on March 6 was not spectacular. Hundreds, perhaps thousands, of machines were struck, but the damage was nothing as great as it might have been. Predictably, perhaps, media reports on March 6 started to dismiss the Michelangelo scare as another overhyped rumor, completely missing the reality of what had transpired.

Michelangelo is a variant of Stoned. The original Stoned virus was, of course, not intentionally destructive, although it did cause some corruption and loss of data due to design flaws or lack of foresight. Stoned, however, has a major place in the viral pantheon since it was so phenomenally successful in its reproduction. (Some researchers in Britain dispute this. I am not sure how Britain avoided a plague of Stoned. If indeed it did: the reports may be confused, given that the major researchers in Britain refer to Stoned as "New Zealand." If so, however, this is the exception that proves the rule of the prevalence of boot sector infectors. The reported major infection in Britain is Form—a BSI.)

Michelangelo has followed hard in its predecessor's footsteps. In spite of the destruction of the virus when it is triggered, Michelangelo managed to survive not only March 1991 but also the widely publicized trigger date of March 6, 1992. It continues to survive and, by most accounts, is growing faster than it is being found and destroyed. In some countries, Michelangelo is the most widely reported virus.

A further Stoned variant, unrelated to Michelangelo, is Monkey. As of the beginning of 1994, this strain was becoming very commonly reported. It is even more widespread than most realize because Central Point/Microsoft Antivirus program misidentifies it as Stoned 3. Monkey adds a further twist: the common "generic" forms of boot sector/MBR eradication don't work well against it. If your computer is infected with Monkey and you boot from a clean system floppy disk, you will find that you cannot access the hard drive. In addition to repositioning the MBR, Monkey also encrypts it. Not seriously: the encryption is a simple XOR function with the 2Eh byte. What that does mean, though, is that you do not have valid partition-table data anywhere on your hard disk, and that you will have to go through an extra step to get rid of the virus. Many single-virus detectors and disinfectors have been developed, and few are considered to be important. Monkey, though, is both sufficiently prevalent and difficult enough to get rid of that I not only recommend Tim Martin's KILLMONK but also, with his gracious permission, have included it with this edition of the book.

MEMOIRS OF AN (INFECTED) VIRUS RESEARCHER

I've just finished reviewing another antiviral program. During the testing, I found out something interesting.

My primary test machine was infected.

Now, this, one would think, is not necessarily remarkable. But, you see, I have a grave shortage of equipment. The test machine is also the communications machine. And, it wasn't supposed to be infected.

Still, it happens from time to time.

There was the time, rushing the Michelangelo deadline, that I had made the world's only copy of Michelangelo on a 720K diskette. And then booted from it. Just after midnight on the evening of March 5. (Well, it was late, and all . . .) Took me another 20 minutes to put it together again.

That's another thing. The primary test machine is a laptop. Dual 3½" floppies. No hard drive. Safer that way. When I'm using it for communications, I simply use another diskette. Bootable. Write-protected. Except when I have to make corrections. But I do that on the desktop machine. No chance of infection if I never put it into the test machine unprotected.

But I must have. Sometime. And that sometime had to be more than three weeks ago, because that was the last time I did any live testing.

And what was it I was infected with? DIR-II. Stealth to the max. Fast infector with a vengeance. I must have infected everything in sight.

Except I didn't.

First, communications generally deals with either text files or archives. Unless the archives are self-extracting, they are not targets for infection, and neither are the test files. So for over three weeks, I was shuttling files from one machine to another, and the virus never had a chance to transfer. Must have been frustrating for it.

A couple of points about the DIR-II. It does infect text files. At least, it infected one of mine. The filename was SIGBLOCK.NTE, for those who are wondering. Only 340 bytes, so only the first chunk of the viral code shows.

Second, the business of renaming your programs to nonexecutable extensions, with the virus active, works like a hot darn for disinfection. Remember to do a CHKDSK /F, after you have finished and booted clean, in order to reclaim lost disk space. I got everything back fine. Except SIGBLOCK.NTE.

CHAPTER 4

COMPUTER OPERATIONS AND VIRAL OPERATIONS

This chapter has two purposes. The first is to outline the specific actions and functions of viral programs in the two major classes: boot sector infectors and file infectors. However, the bulk of the chapter looks at computer operations in general and how viral programs use them. One of the main points to keep in mind here is that viral programs don't use any radically different operations from other computer applications. This is vitally important to keep in mind when trying to set up an impregnable defense. Quite simply, such defense isn't possible.

BOOT SECTOR INFECTORS

Every disk has a boot sector. Most disks are not "bootable" because they do not contain the necessary system files, but all disks have a boot sector. The boot sector is simply that place in which the computer, by default, looks for the starting point of the boot sequence.

In saying that every disk has a boot sector, I am using the term "boot sector" in its most generic sense, this initial starting point. In the MS-DOS environment, "boot sector" has a more limited technical definition, and hard disks actually start with a master boot record rather than a boot sector. In either case, however, there is one spot that gives the computer some definition of the disk and information about the next step in the boot sequence.

In most cases, the boot sector does not point to a boot sequence, because system files are not available on the disk. In the case of a bootable disk, the "bootable" sector points to the location of files containing the programming necessary for input and output activity and a pro-

Boot sector infector flowchart

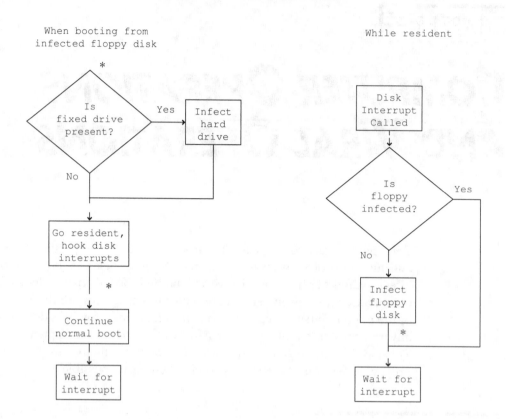

* = Payload may be triggered at these points

gram for the interpretation of operating-system commands. A "data," or nonbootable, disk, however, may simply contain information on the disk specification, and a small program informing the system, or operator, that the disk is "nonsystem."

The important point, however, is that a program is in the boot sector, in every case. (The other important point is that the boot sector doesn't show up in normal operation. There is no entry for it in the directory listing of the disk, and therefore most people assume it doesn't exist.)

The existence of a boot sector on every disk is the major strength of boot-sector-infecting viral programs, and it is a psychological, rather than technical, advantage. Because a "data disk" does not contain any recognizable "programming," it is often seen as "safe." If there is no program, then there is no program to infect, right? However, since there is, in fact, a "hidden" program on the disk, it *can* be infected. (I

Normal and Stoned disk sectors

Normal boot sector

```
c30d 0a4e 6f6e 2d53 7973 7465 6d20 6469 736b 206f 7220    Non-System disk or
6469 736b 2065 7272 6f72 0d0a 5265 706c 6163 6520 616e    disk error  Replace an
6420 7374 7269 6b65 2061 6e79 206b 6579 2077 6865 6e20    d strike any key when
7265 6164 790d 0a00 0d0a 4469 736b 2042 6f6f 7420 6661    ready      Disk Boot fa
696c 7572 650d 0a00 4942 4d42 494f 2020 434f 4d49 424d    ilure   IBMBIO  COMIBM
444f 5320 2043 4f4d 0000 0000 0000 0000 0000 0000 0000    DOS   COM
0000 0000 55aa                                                U
```

Stoned boot sector

```
b0b0 01b0 4202 03a0 b001 0303 db0e c0cd 130b c507 506f    B    3        Yo
7572 2050 4320 6973 206e 6f77 2053 746f 6e65 6421 070d    ur PC is now Stoned!
0a0a 004c 4547 414c 4953 4520 4d41 5249 4a55 414e 4121       LEGALISE MARIJUANA!
0000 0000 0000 0000 0000 0000 0000 0000 0000 0000 0000
0000 0000 0000 0000 0000 0000 0000 0000 0000 0000 0000
0000 0000 0000 0000 0000 0000 0000 0000 0000 0000 0000
0000 0000 0000
```

use "hidden" here in its generic sense. In the MS-DOS world "hidden" also has a technical meaning as a file attribute.)

By and large, boot sector infectors "displace" the existing boot sector and move it to another location on the disk. This means that the viral program gets "first crack." It installs itself in memory and then passes control to the original boot sector. Thus the disk appears to behave normally, unless the virus carries some visible payload.

In addition to the psychological advantage, BSIs have some technical values as well. For one thing, they get the first chance at the system, before most "protection" has started. For another, a BSI, to be effective at all, must be memory-resident. For a third, because BSIs make changes to system areas that are not normally seen, their changes are often undetected in normal operation.

In order to point out the areas of possible viral program attack, it is helpful to outline the sequence of operations in the boot process.

When the machine is first powered up, there is a certain amount of programming contained in boot ROM. The amount varies greatly between different types of machines, but basically this programming describes the most central devices, such as the screen and keyboard, and "points" to the disk drives. A very basic location on the disk is addressed for further information. This is the generic "boot sector": as mentioned previously, on MS-DOS hard disks, it is the master boot record that is accessed first.

The boot record or sector contains further information about the structure of the disk. It, or a subsequent linked sector, also describes the location of further operating system files. This description is in the form of a program, rather than simply data. Because this outline is in the form of a program, and because this sector is "writable" in order to allow for different structures, the boot record or sector is vulnerable to attack or change. BSIs may overwrite either the boot record or the boot sector and may or may not move the original boot sector or record to another location on disk. The repositioning of the original sector's program allows the viral program to "pretend" that everything is as it was.

This pretense is not absolute. A computer with an active viral program resident will, of necessity, be different in some way from the normal environment. The original sector position will, of course, have different information in it. The viral program will need to "hook" certain vectors for its own use in order to monitor activity in the computer and in order to function. The viral program will have to occupy a certain portion of memory and may be identified by a memory map, or, in the case of the Stoned virus, may try to hide by "telling" the computer that it has less memory than is actually the case.

These telltale indicators are not absolute either. There may be various reasons why the "top of memory" marker is set to less than 640K on a DOS machine. Each different type of disk drive and each drive of the same type that is partitioned differently will have a different boot record. As operating systems or versions change, so will the boot sector. Therefore, the environment of newly booted machines cannot, in isolation, be examined and said to be infected or free from infection.

It is possible, however, to compare any machine with itself in a "known clean" state. By saving information on the environment after a minimal clean boot, and comparing this with subsequent boots, changes can be detected, and the user alerted to a potential problem. It is possible to replace the boot record with a program that will check the state of the disk, memory, and interrupt table in order to detect the changes that a virus must make. (A program starting at this level can also function as the foundation of a security system that cannot be avoided by "escaping" out of the boot sequence.)

Obtaining the state of the environment immediately after the boot sector has been run is not as easy as it might sound at first. The computer, while functional, does not have all parts of the operating system installed at this point, and it is the "higher" levels of the operating system that users generally interact with.

The last section of the boot sector program points to the files or areas on the disk in which to find the next step of the operating system. At this point, of course, the specific files and subsequent steps start to diverge greatly from one operating system to another. However, it is fairly common for all operating systems to have "hidden" files along this route, which may be subject to viral attack. Given that these files are not evident to the user, they are more vulnerable, not to attack, but to an undetected change.

When setting up antiviral defenses, it is important to know the sequence of events in the boot process in order to know which programs will protect to which level. The MS-DOS sequence provides the clearest example, and those knowledgeable in other systems can use the illustrations it provides to analyze the specific details of their own systems.

After the master boot record and boot sector proper have been run, MS-DOS normally runs two additional programs that set up input/output routines and the most basic operating system. (As these programs are called by the boot sector, it is possible to reroute this process to call specialized driver programs first, or along with them. Some esoteric disk drives use such a process.) Traditionally, these files have "hidden" attributes and are not visible to the user on the disk. After they have run, the system has sufficient programming to interpret a text file that contains listings of various additional programming that the user wishes to have in order to run specialized hardware. This file, CONFIG.SYS, is the first point at which the intermediate user may normally affect the boot process, and is the first point at which antiviral software may be easily installed. As can be seen, however, there are a number of prior points at which viral programs may gain control of the computer.

After the programs listed in CONFIG.SYS are run, the command interpreter is invoked. The standard MS-DOS interpreter is COMMAND.COM, but this may be changed by an entry in the CONFIG.SYS file. After COMMAND.COM is run, the AUTOEXEC.BAT batch file is run, if it exists. AUTOEXEC.BAT is the most commonly created and modified "boot file," and many users, and antiviral program authors, see this as the point at which to intervene. It should be clear by now, however, that many possible points of intervention are open before the AUTOEXEC.BAT is run.

In spite of the greater number of entry points, viral programs that attack the programs of the boot sequence are rare, and not greatly successful. For one thing, while every disk has a boot sector, not every disk has a full boot sequence. For another, different versions of a given operating system may have different files in this sequence. (For example, the "hidden" files have different names in MS-DOS, PC-DOS, and DR-DOS.) Finally, viral programs that can infect ordinary program files may not work on boot sequence files, and vice versa.

There are some interesting variations in the boot process that can have implications for security.

On pre–System 7 Macintosh computers, each floppy disk that was inserted in the computer was "booted," in a sense. The Desktop information and the description of how it would appear on the screen were in program format, and so any program identified as WDEF would run automatically. This was used quite successfully by one Mac virus.

The Atari computer may reserve up to six sectors for the "boot sector": only one is ever used in the normal course of events. This, of course, provides an excellent "hiding place" for a virus. The additional five sectors can contain a reasonably capable virus, and there is no danger of overwriting, or any need to try to avoid detection in changing file sizes. In fact, however, most Atari programs do not use executables in the boot sector. Start-up files, including system accessories, are placed in a standard directory, and all such files found in the directory are run at boot time. Many Atari antivirals do nothing more than overwrite executable boot sectors. Since Atari computers are able to read MS-DOS formatted disks, a number of these antiviral utilities may corrupt DOS disks.

In terms of hiding places, the variations in the size of system areas and tables has caused some viral programs to be unintentionally destructive. Stoned, for example, places the original boot sector "out of harm's way" in a sector that, on a normal 360K disk, was generally redundant. That area would only be used if more than 95 files were placed on the disk; a highly unlikely occurrence. With high-density disks, however, that section of the disk is more important to the file allocation table, and this displacement to that section led to the loss of access to data on some diskettes. A similar situation occurred with hard disks.

On MS-DOS computers with extended partitioning of the hard disk, the master boot record may be read while accessing a different logical drive. It is therefore possible, even if the computer has been booted from a clean floppy disk, for an "infection" on a drive to show up in memory. Although there is almost no chance of a virus becoming active in this way, such partitioning will often trigger a "virus in memory" alert from scanning programs.

Recently, various BIOS systems will allow you to specify whether the computer is to be booted from the floppy or the hard disk, and from which disk. This is a handy safety feature (and equally handy for virus research). Some computers, Zeniths and Rainbows among others, would change the boot sector on every start-up. This was sometimes used as a pseudo "clock backup." The fact that the boot sector was changing at all times, however, conflicted with change-detection software that checked the boot sector.

FILE INFECTORS

File- or program-infecting viral programs, while possibly not as numerous as BSIs in terms of actual infections, represent the greatest number of known viral strains, at least in the MS-DOS world. This may be due to the fact that file infectors are not as constrained in size as BSIs, or that file infectors do not require the detailed knowledge of system "internals" that may be necessary for effective boot sector viral programs.

File-infecting viruses spread by adding or associating code to existing executable files. They have the potential to become active when an infected program is run. Whereas BSIs must be memory-resident in order to spread, file-infecting programs have more options in terms of infection. This means that there is greater scope for writing file-infecting viral programs, but it also means that there may be fewer opportunities for a given virus to reproduce itself.

With two exceptions, file-infecting viral programs must, of necessity, make some kind of change in the target file. If normal DOS calls are used to write to it, the file creation date will be changed. If code is added to it, the file size will change. Even if areas of the file are overwritten in such a way that the file length remains unchanged, a parity, checksum, cyclic redundancy, or Hamming code check should be able to detect the fact that there has been some change. The Lehigh and Jerusalem viral programs, the first to become widely known to the research community on the Internet, were both initially identified by changes they made to target files (the Jerusalem being widely known by its length—"1813"). Change detection, therefore, remains one of the most popular means of virus detection on the part of antiviral software producers.

Because change detection is a means of virus detection that requires no sophisticated programming (in some cases, no programming at all), virus writers have attempted to camouflage changes where they can. It is not a difficult task to avoid making changes to the file creation date, or to return the date to its original value. It is possible to "overlay" the original code of the program so that the file is not increased in size. Most recently, virus authors have been using stealth programming: a means of shortcutting the operating system and returning only the original, unchanged, values at any request for information.

There are four ways to attach code to an existing program: overwrite existing program code, add code to the beginning or the end of the program, or not add code to the existing program. (I will explain the logic of this Zen-like statement shortly.)

OVERWRITERS

Viral programs that overwrite existing code are a very simplistic answer to the problem of how to add code to an existing program without changing the file size. By simply overlaying code that is already on the disk, the original size remains unchanged. There are a few problems with this approach.

The first is the problem of how to get the virus "called" when the infected program is run. If the code is just inserted anywhere, it may not be in a part of the program that gets used every time the program is run. (Every programmer is aware of the Pareto Principle's application here: 20 percent of the code does 80 percent of the work. Some code never gets called at all.) It is possible, by an analysis of the code of the target program, to find an "entry point" that is used extensively. It is also possible, and a lot easier, to place a jump at the beginning of the program that points to the viral code.

The second problem is much more difficult to deal with. If the virus code overwrites existing portions of the program code, how do you know the loss of that program code is not fatal to the target program? Analysis of this type, on the original code, would be very difficult indeed. "Successful" overwriting viral programs tend to be short, and to look for extensive strings of NUL characters to replace. (The NUL characters tend to be used to "reserve" stack space and thus are not vital to the program.) Even if the original code is not vital to the program, it may, if replaced, cause the program to exhibit strange behaviors and thus lead to detection of the viral infection.

Overwriter diagram

| Original Program Code |

| Ori | Viral Code | Code |

While overwriting viral programs solve the problem of file size, they bring with them some inherent problems, which appear, at this time, to severely limit their effectiveness. To this date, while many overwriting viruses have been written, none have enjoyed great success, or become a widespread and major problem.

PREPENDERS AND APPENDERS

In order to avoid damage to the original program, which might lead to detection of the infection, the viral code can be added to the beginning or end of the program. (Or not attached at all.)

Adding code at the beginning of the original program ensures that the viral code is run whenever the program is run. (This also ensures that the virus is run before the program runs. The virus thus has priority in terms of operation, possible conflicts, and detection.) With the addition of code to the beginning of the program, it is possible to avoid any change to the original code. It *is* necessary to alter the file/disk allocation table, at least, in order to ensure that the program call starts with the viral code, and that the viral code is not overwritten by other changes to the disk or files. While the original code may be left unchanged, the file will be, essentially, altered and, unless techniques are used to disguise this, will show a different creation date, size, and image.

It is also, however, possible to add viral code to the end of the original program, and still ensure that the viral code is run before that of the original program. All that is necessary is to alter the file header information to reflect the fact that you want to start executing the file toward the end, rather than at the normal location. At the end of the viral code, another jump returns operation to the original program.

(This kind of operation is not as odd as it may sound. It is not even uncommon. A legacy from the days of mainframe "paging" of memory, it is used in a great many MS-DOS executables, either in single EXE files or in overlays. It is, therefore, not a coding indication that can be used to identify viral type programs or infected files.)

Prepender diagram

| Original Program Code |

| Viral Code | Original Program Code |

Appender diagram

| Original Program Code |

| JUMP | Original Program Code | Viral Code |

Appending, or prepending, viral code to an existing program therefore avoids the problems of damage and potential failure to run, which plague overwriting viral programs. Even these viral programs, however, are not foolproof. Programs that load in very nonstandard ways use the header information that the viral programs alter. Although not originally designed for virus detection, the "Program abort—invalid file header" message thus generated is an indication of viral infection. Sometimes the first indication that users have.

COMPANION

The simplest way for a viral program to avoid the detection that results from modifying the code of an existing program is not to modify the original program. This is an elementary solution, but would seem to have the drawback that, unless you change the file in some way, the virus will never be called.

There is a solution to this problem, and (if I may be allowed some enthusiasm for the concept, if not the reprehensible act), a rather elegant one at that.

Operating systems will identify files that are executable and distinguish between these and files that either do not contain executable code or that may be executed only in special ways. On the Atari, only files with a PRG extension can be run, although "accessory" files can set up "resident" utilities and functions at start-up. MS-DOS, on the other hand, has three possible executable file types, denoted by COM, EXE, and BAT extensions. AOS/VS has many more: I once saw a list of 150 executable filename extensions.

Because the different extensions provide an additional means to distinguish a file, three different executable files under MS-DOS can all have the same filename. You can have a WP.COM, WP.EXE, and WP.BAT. Normally, a program is only invoked by calling the filename; the extension is "filled in" by the operating system. How, then, does the computer decide which of these three to run?

The answer is built into the operating system. There are actually four levels of programming to check for. First, a search is made for an "internal" command of the command interpreter. If that succeeds, the command is run. Thus, under MS-DOS, when you give the command "DIR," the system generally runs the directory listing subroutine provided by COMMAND.COM, even if a file named DIR.COM exists. (When I first published a column on the net explaining companion viral programs, I said that no program named DIR.COM would ever be run. Boy, did I get an insight into the inner workings and weirdnesses of various DOS versions. But we won't go into that right now.) If the search for an internal command does not succeed, the computer looks for a file with that filename and a COM extension, then an EXE extension, then a BAT extension. At each stage, if the search succeeds, the file is run; if it fails, it goes to the next level. Thus, in MS-DOS, COM takes precedence over EXE, which takes precedence over BAT. (Again, in the specific case of MS-DOS, you can modify this order of precedence. The important point here is not the specific order, but the fact that the precedence concept exists.)

A companion virus can thus "infect" a STARTUP.BAT file by making a copy of itself called STARTUP.EXE. It can infect CPAV.EXE by creating CPAV.COM. (In fact, it is probably easiest simply to stick to COM files, whether you are infecting EXEs or BATs.) The COM file will take precedence, and typing "CPAV" will always call the virus first. The original file remains unchanged, and no manner of change-detection programs, except those that check not only the individual files but also the total files, will tell you any different. (In order to further avoid detection, the viral file will generally end with a very specific "call" to the original program, and the viral program has the "hidden" attribute set. In GUI operating systems, it is possible for a virus to take precedence by "overlaying" an existing icon with another that is either transparent, or identical to the first.)

Fortunately, companion viral programs are by no means perfect. For one thing, they are limited to those programs that are "lower" in the order of precedence. For another, the "hidden" attribute is relatively easy to overcome (particularly in MS-DOS), and an alphabetical listing of files will quickly turn up the anomaly of identical names. (The antiviral packages tested so far generally do little to alert the user to duplicate names. Often the user will be asked to validate a file, without any suggestion that if the file has not just been added to the system, something might be amiss.)

There is a valid argument that says that "companion" (or "spawning") viral programs are not viral at all. Companion viral programs certainly do not link to existing program code, at least not in a physical way. They use a certain provision of the operation system to trick you into running them rather than the program you meant to. Thus they might be said to be closer in definition to a trojan.

On the other hand, companion programs do reproduce. They also form, in a sense, a logical link with existing programs. Even though they are very different technically from "viruses," from the average user's perspective, they certainly behave in a viral fashion.

VARIATIONS

Unfortunately the overwriters, prependers, appenders, and companions mentioned do not exhaust the possibilities.

(By the way, much of this is basically courtesy of Vesselin Bontchev, who did all the research.)

In discussing overwriting viral programs I mentioned, by concept although not by name, the Zerohunt virus, which looks for a string of NUL characters of sufficient length to accommodate it. However, there is also the Nina virus, which overwrites the beginning of a file, and the Phoenix family, which overwrites a random section of a file. Both Nina and Phoenix append the overwritten part to the end. The Number of the Beast/512 virus and 1963 both overwrite the beginning of the file and then move the contents of the overwritten section beyond the *physical* end of the file into a portion of the last cluster that the file occupies. Because the clusters are always of a fixed size and because it is very unusual for a file to exactly match a "multiple" of cluster size, there is generally some space past the "end" of the file that is, essentially, invisible to the operating system.

In the world of prependers, a similar consideration is used by the Rat virus. EXE file headers are always a multiple of 512 bytes, so there is often an unused block of space in the header itself that the Rat assumes. The SURIV 2.01 works a bit harder: it moves the body of the file and inserts itself between the header and original file, and then changes the relocation information in the header.

Then there is the DIR-II. The viral code is written to one section of the disk . . ., and then the directory and file allocation information is altered in such a way that all programs seem to start in that one section of the disk. Because of the convoluted way this virus works, it is possible to "lose" all the programs on the disk by attempting to "repair" them.

At this point in my seminar, there is an overhead foil marked, "This page intentionally left blank." The point being that there are all kinds of subtle variations on the themes covered here—and quite a few not so subtle means—that will only become obvious after the techniques have been used. However, it is important to note that the most successful viral programs in terms of numbers of infections are not necessarily the "new models," but the older and often less-sophisticated versions. On the one hand, this indicates that novelty is not a "viral survival factor." On the other hand, it points out, in rather depressing manner, that most computer users are still not employing even the most basic forms of antiviral protection.

THE VIRAL USE OF COMPUTER OPERATIONS AND FUNCTIONS

Having looked at specific viral functions in terms of infection, let's look at what computers are and what they do—briefly. The functions that we ask of computers tend to fall into a few general categories.

Computers are great at copying. This makes them useful for storing and communicating data, and for much of the "information processing" that we ask them to do, such as word processing. Computers are also great for the automation of repetitive tasks. Programming allows computers to perform the same tasks, in the same way, with only one initiating call. Indeed, we can, on occasion, eliminate the need for the call, as programs can be designed to make "decisions" on the basis of data available. Finally, computer processors need not be specially built for each task assigned to them: computers are multipurpose tools that can do as many jobs as the programs available to them.

All computer operations and programs are comprised of these three components: copying, automatic operation, and "decision" making. All computer operations and programs, in various combinations, can also fulfill many functions. It is no coincidence that it is these same functions that allow computer viral programs to operate.

The first function of a viral program is to reproduce. In other words, to copy. This copying operation must be automatic, since the operator is not an actively informed party to the function. In most cases, the viral program must come to some decision about when and whether to infect a program or disk, or when to deliver a "payload." All of these operations must be performed regardless of the purpose for which the specific computer is intended.

It should thus be clear that computer viral programs use the most basic of computer functions and operations. It should also be clear that no additional functions are necessary for the operation of viral programs. Taking these two facts together, no one should be surprised at the conclusion reached a number of years ago that not only is it extremely difficult to differentiate computer viral programs from valid programs, but that there can be no single identifying feature that can be used for such distinction. Without running the program, or simulating its operation, there is no way to say that this program is viral and that one is valid.

The fact that computer viral operations are, in fact, the most basic of computer operations means that it is very difficult to defend against intrusion by viral programs. In terms of "guaranteed protection," we are left again with Jeff Richards' Laws of Data Security:

1.   Don't buy a computer.
2.   If you do buy a computer, don't turn it on.

On the other hand, to quote from John Parks, "A ship in a harbor is safe, but that is not what ships are built for." A computer completely protected is safe, but it is not useful. A computer in operation is a useful device, but it is vulnerable. The prudent operator will learn the reality and extent of the dangers and will take appropriate precautions, while still taking advantage of the uses of the machine.

VIRUS FUNCTIONS AND PAYLOADS

Although the most widely used definitions of computer viral programs refer to reproduction by attaching to other programs, viruses that act in this manner are less successful than those that use other means. In the microcomputer world, BSIs have been much more effective.

In larger systems, mini- and mainframe computers, network and mail viral programs have, so far, had the greatest impact. The Internet/Morris/UNIX Worm managed to spread and reproduce using the facility of networked machines to submit programs to each other. (A VMS program, WANK, used many of the same techniques.) The CHRISTMA EXEC used mainframe mail commands and the ability to submit programs by mail in order to reproduce copies that eventually flooded the network.

Network and mail viral programs carry, in a sense, their own payload. The reproduction of the programs themselves uses the resources of the hosts affected and, in the cases of both the Internet and CHRISTMA worms, went so far as to deny service by using all available computing or communications resources.

Most other viral programs seem to be written "for their own sake." A kind of electronic graffiti that writes itself on further walls. However, even these can do damage, as does the Stoned virus, which overwrites sections of the FAT with the original boot sector. Some appear to be written as pranks, and others as a kind of advertising, although the potential for damage from even benign viral programs cannot be considered funny, and the "advertising" viruses probably don't engender much goodwill.

Relatively few viral programs carry a deliberately damaging payload. Those that *do* attempt to erase infected programs or disks are, fortunately, self-limiting.

The last payload, or function, that a viral program may carry is some kind of intelligence to enable it to evade detection. So far the various kinds of evasive action—self-modification, multiple encryption, and stealth activity—have not proven to have any advantageous survival characteristics. In one sense, this is to be regretted, as it again demonstrates that the majority of computer users are not taking the most elementary precautions to defend against viral programs.

Viral programs use basic computer functions in more ways than one. It is easier to use standard system calls for purposes such as accessing disks and writing files or formatting. Most programs use the standard operating-system calls, rather than write their own system functions when "using" the hardware. For one thing, it's more "polite" to do this with application programs, which programs, if they follow "the rules," will be better "behaved" when interacting with other programs, particularly resident programs and drivers. But it is also easier to use system functions than to write your own.

Operating-system functions are generally accessible if you know the memory address at which the function starts, or the specific interrupt that invokes it. Viral programs can use this fact in two possible ways.

The first is to use the standard system calls in order to perform the copying, writing, or destructive actions. This, however, has unfortunate consequences for the viral author (and fortunate for the computer community) in that it is easy to identify these system calls in program code. Therefore, if viral programs used only this method of operation, it would be possible to write a universal virus scanner that would be able to identify any potentially damaging code. It would also be possible to write programs that "trapped" all such system calls and allowed the user to decide whether a particular operation should proceed. (In fact, in the MS-DOS world, two such programs, BOMBSQAD and WORMCHEK, are available and were used to check for early trojan programs.)

Operating systems are, however, programs, and therefore it is possible for any program, including any viral program, to implement a completely different piece of code that writes directly to the hardware. The Stoned virus has used this very successfully.

Stealth

Unfortunately, viral programs have even more options, one of which is to perform the same trapping functions themselves. Viral programs can trap all functions that perform disk access in order to hide the fact that the virus is copying itself to the disk under the "cover" of a directory listing. Viral programs can also trap system calls in order to evade detection. Some viral programs will "sense" an effort to "read" the section of memory that they occupy and will cause the system to hang. Others trap all reading of disk information and will return only the "original" information for a file or disk, an example of stealth viral technology.

A virus is able to do this because very few programs bother to read or write directly to the disk hardware. Because of possible differences in hardware and also because these functions are generally fairly standard, manipulation of the disk is left to the operating system and underlying software and hardware. The operating system provides standard system calls and "hooks" to the required functions. When a program wishes to read data from the disk, it asks the operating system to do it by calling the function from a standard, known address.

However, since the address is known, virus writers know it as well. Code inserted at the standard address can redirect the "call" to code provided by the virus. This stealth code may indeed use the original programming provided by the operating system, but it filters the data returned to the calling program. If an infected file is being read, the "infection" simply does not appear in the information that the "calling" program receives. Thus no trace of the virus infection can be found—at least not on disk.

Stealth is a technology, not a virus per se. There is no one stealth virus: there are a lot of viral programs that implement stealth in one form or another. Stealth is not, in fact, limited to viral programs. Antiviral software, and even utilities, use similar means to avoid compatibility problems with the wide range of computers and programs now operating.

One ironic aspect of stealth, in viral programs, is "self-cleaning."

Stealth virus flowchart

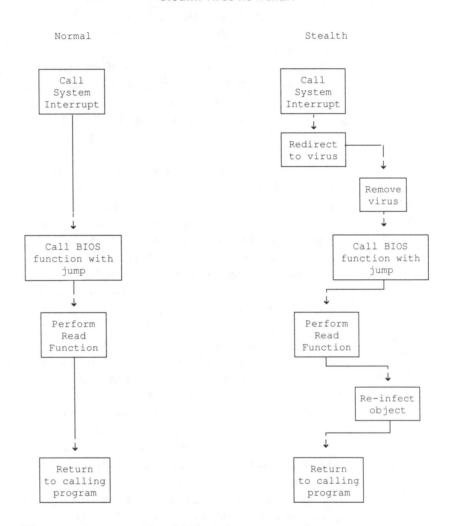

When copies are made of infected programs, the copy program runs the data through the stealth filter as well. This means that copies of an infected program, made while the virus is active, are clean. At least initially.

Tunneling

Somewhat related to stealth technology is the concept of "tunneling." Again, this is a technology, not a virus per se, and one that is used in both viral and antiviral programs.

To examine the concept of tunneling, let me go back a bit in computer history. Before there were viral programs, there were trojans.

Antitrojan software was generally of the activity-monitoring and operation-restricting variety, similar to a number of antiviral programs
today. Activity monitors do not really monitor activity. They place traps
and interrupts at certain points in the operating system. Certain system
calls are either potentially dangerous themselves (such as the function
that formats a disk) or are precursors to dangerous activities. Therefore, when a program calls one of these functions, the activity monitor
is triggered. Again, this relies upon the fact that operating-system functions *must* be made available in a known location so that valid programs can use them.

Activity monitors place traps at the location of potentially dangerous system calls. These traps are generally pieces of code that run the
activity monitor program, rather than the original operating-system
code. The activity monitor can then alert the user, and the user can
choose to stop the action or to allow the action, in which case the
original operating-system code is run.

This means that the activity monitor has performed a very viruslike
action. It has made a change in the original state of the system. Since
the state of the system is generally well known, a virus can be written to
examine these system entry points. The virus can "tunnel" or trace back
along the programming associated with the system call. If an activity-
monitoring program is found (and this generally means anything other
than the original operating-system code), the trap can be reset to point
to the original system call. The activity-monitoring program is now bypassed and will *not* trigger—at least not for that particular function.

This same type of activity can be used against viral programs. Viruses often trap certain system calls in order to trigger infection activities. Antiviral software can tunnel along the various interrupts, looking
for changes. Viral programs can thus be disarmed.

Tunneling may seem like a lot of work to go to in order for a virus
to defend itself. Indeed it is. One particularly well-known, and widely
marketed, antiviral has a resident component. Only seven bytes of code
are required to disable it. Not to tunnel around it, but to disable it
completely. (Viral programs are also becoming more aggressive. One
has been found that takes action to disable or cripple no less than 14
antiviral systems.)

Other Deception

One additional use that viral programs can make of operating systems
is as a source of hiding places.

Anyone who has ever tried to manage accounts on mainframes or
local area networks (LANs) will recognize that there is a constant battle

between the aspects of security and "user-friendliness" in computer use. This tension arises from the definition of the two functions. If a computer is easy to use, it is easy to misuse. If a password is hard to guess, it is hard to remember. If access to information is simple for the owner, it is simple for the "cracker."

(This axiom often gives rise to two false corollaries. First, the reverse—that those systems that are difficult to use must therefore be more secure—does not hold. Second, many assume that restricting the availability of information about a system will make that system secure. While this strategy will work in the short term, its effectiveness as protection is limited. Indeed, it often has the unfortunate side effect of restricting information to those who should have it, such as systems managers, while slowing the attackers only marginally.)

User-friendly programs and operating systems tend to hide information from the user. There are two reasons for this. In order to reduce clutter, and the amount of information that a user needs to operate a given system, it is necessary to remove options and, to a certain extent, functionality. A user-friendly system is also more complex in terms of its own programming. In order for the computer to behave "intuitively," it must be able to provide for the many "counterintuitive" ways that people work. Therefore, the most basic levels of a GUI (graphical user interface) system tend to be more complex than the corresponding levels of a command-line interface system, and these levels are hidden from the user by additional intervening layers (which also tend to add more complexity).

The additional layers in an operating system, and the fact that a great deal of management takes place automatically without the user's awareness, is an ideal situation for a viral program. Since many legitimate and necessary operations and changes are performed without the user being aware of it, viral operations can also proceed at a level completely hidden from the user. Also, because the user is basically unaware of the structure and operations of the computer, changes to that structure and operation are difficult to detect.

POLYMORPHISM

A distinction tends to be made between the early, and limited, self-encrypting viral programs, and the latter, more sophisticated, polymorphs. Earlier self-encrypting viral programs had limited numbers of variants: even the enormous Whale virus had less than 40 distinct forms. (Some of the earliest were the V2Px family written by Mark Washburn. He stated that he wrote them to prove that scanners were

Multilayered polymorph

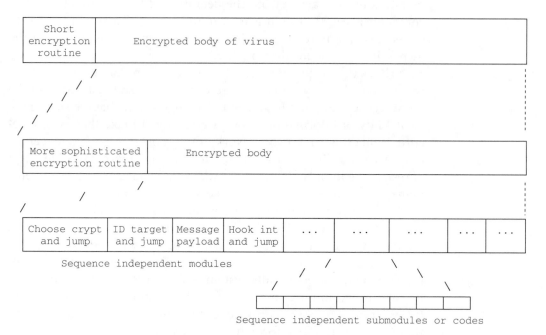

unworkable, and then he wrote his own activity-monitoring program. He is one of the very few people to have written and released a virus, and also to have written antiviral software. His release of "live" code into the wild would tend to deny him status as an antivirus researcher. Lest some say this is arbitrary bias, please note that his thesis was rather ineffectual: all his variants are fairly easily detectable.) More recent polymorphs are more prolific: tremor is calculated to have almost 6,000,000,000 forms.

The latest development is the polymorphic "engine." This is not a virus as such, but code that can be added to *any* virus in order to make it polymorphic. The most widely known of these is the Mutating Engine, known as MtE, written by a virus writer who identifies himself or herself as the Dark Avenger. There *is* no MtE (or DAME: Dark Avenger's Mutating Engine) virus; only other viral programs that have had the code attached. MtE is not the only such program around; many others have been developed, such as the more recent model known as TPE (Trident Polymorphic Engine). (Virus-writing and sharing groups, referred to as the vx community, tend to have as little imagination in naming as in programming.)

The polymorphic engines are sometimes confused with "virus kits."

The polymorphic engine, if properly attached to the original virus, will "re-form" the viral code on each new infection. A virus kit is a program to automate the actual writing of a virus. The user picks characteristics from a menu of choices, and the kit program sticks together preprogrammed pieces of code to make a virus for you. A polymorphic engine, then, is code added to a virus to make the same virus change its appearance each time it reproduces. A virus kit is a nonreplicating, nonviral program that automates the process of generating viral programs, each with different characteristics. Unless polymorphism is one of the options chosen, viral programs produced by a kit will retain their signatures from that point on.

Fortunately, polymorphism in any form and at any level has not been a significant threat. Polymorphs are still easily detected by change-detection and activity-monitoring software. Even scanners have not had great difficulty dealing with polymorphic programs. The early self-encrypting programs generally left readily identifiable signatures since the decryption code had to be left "en clair." Even those programs that performed significant encryption or used different encryption routines generally had only a few forms, which could all be readily identified. The latter polymorphs are marginally more difficult to identify, but algorithmic, as opposed to pure signature, scanning is having reasonable success. Indeed, in the case of the polymorphic engines, these codes have sometimes been a boon to the antiviral researcher. When you can identify the MtE code, you can also identify, at least as a virus, every new virus to which it is attached.

Infection Periods and Triggers

In attempting to protect against viral infection, and particularly when trying to disinfect systems, it is important to bear in mind the times that the virus is actively "infectious." The viral activation is not the same as the activation of the payload that a virus may carry. For example, the payload of the original Stoned virus was a message, which appeared on the screen saying "Your PC is now Stoned!" This message only appears at boot time, and on only one-eighth of the times the computer is rebooted. The virus, however, is infectious at all times— once it has infected the hard disk.

There are basically three possibilities for the infectious period: now ("one-shot"), during program run ("while-called"), or from now on (resident). These periods may be modified by other circumstances. A resident virus may remain in memory, but be actively infecting only when a disk is accessed. A while-called virus may infect a new program only when a directory is changed.

File-infecting virus flowchart

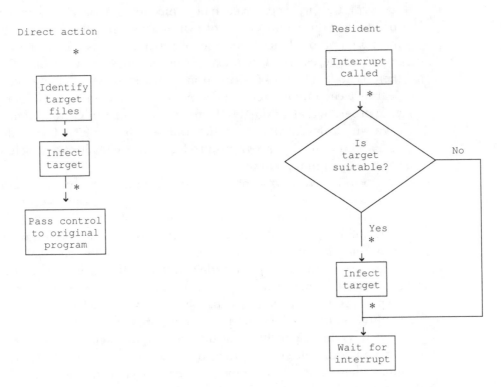

* = Payload may be triggered at these points

    One-shot (technically referred to as direct-action) viral programs only get one chance on each run of the infected program. The viral code will seek out and infect a target program. The viruses then pass control to the original program and perform no further functions. These are, of course, the simplest of the viral programs. Mainframe mail viruses are generally of this type.

    The second class (while-called) will activate when the infected program is called and will then pass partial control to the original program. The virus, however, will remain operational during the time that the infected program is running. Once this is accomplished, it is only a slight jump to a fully memory-resident virus.

    Resident viral programs are the most successful, and the most dangerous, of viral programs. A resident virus will become active when an infected program is run (or at boot time for BSIs) and remain active until the computer is rebooted or turned off. (Some viral programs are even able to trap the rebooting sequence, which is normally called when you press Ctrl-Alt-Del on an MS-DOS PC and, thus, are able to survive a warm boot.) The most successful of the file infectors, the Jerusalem virus, is resident, as are all BSIs. (For fairly obvious reasons, the boot sector is never called in normal operation.)

If a virus is active in memory, it is a waste of time trying to disinfect a file or disk. No sooner is the file cleaned than it becomes a suitable target for reinfection. You may try to disinfect a hard disk right down to performing a low-level format: as soon as the disk is reformatted, it may be infected all over again. This is why all directions for disinfection stress the necessity of cold-booting from a disk that is known to be free of infection before attempting any cleanup.

Multipartite

Multipartite, or dual-infection, viral programs have the potential to infect both program files and boot sectors. This expands the range of possible vectors. Multipartite infections can theoretically travel on any disk, and multiple copies may travel on a disk if program files are present. Dual infectors can also travel on networks, and via files passed over bulletin board systems and other communications channels.

Are multipartite infectors a terrible new threat? Well, no. They've been around for a few years now. Why haven't they taken over the world?

There are disadvantages as well as advantages to multipartite viral programs. One of the major disadvantages is complexity. In file infectors, one sees a number of viral programs that infect only one type of program file, an MS-DOS COM file, for example. A virus that infects both COM and EXE files generally has more than twice the code of one that infects COM files alone. The virus must not only know how to deal with both file types, but also how to distinguish between the target files. The same logic holds true for multipartite infectors. The virus must carry with it the means to infect two radically different types of targets, as well as the means to identify two very different types of potential hosts. The potential size of the program is much larger, as is the requirement for processing. The multipartite virus can be reduced in size, but this generally means a reduction in function as well.

The choice of targets might seem to be an easy matter, but the reality is slightly more complex. The most effective means of spreading would be a "get-everything" policy, but this might also lead to conflicts and detection. Some programs might choose to alternate: a program infector would infect boot sectors, and a boot sector infector would infect program files. Seems reasonable, until you realize that this merely makes the virus sequentially a BSI *or* a file infector in alternating generations. Statistically, this means that it will be slightly less effective than a boot sector virus, rather than more.

Ultimately, the failure (perhaps nonsuccess would be more accurate) of multipartite viral programs points out a very interesting fact. None of the new viral technologies—stealth, polymorphism, spawning, and others—seem to have much "survival value." The successful infectors tend to be the older ones, simple and basic. This is not to say that the virus threat is dying. Stoned has been around since 1988 and is still infecting more systems each year. Simple. But effective.

DETECTION

A virus, to be effective, has to change *something*.

This fact is absolutely fundamental to the operation of computer viral programs and, therefore, in a sense provides a guaranteed form of virus prevention or detection. If we make a machine that cannot change anything (and the disadvantages of this have been thoroughly discussed), we can prevent infection. If any change made can be detected, then any infection can be detected, although discriminating between an infection and a valid change remains problematic.

It is interesting to note that the early antiviral programs, at least the most widely used ones, relied first upon activity monitoring and then signature scanning. Nowadays almost all antiviral programs implement some version of automated change detection. The detection of the first viral programs and the ongoing research into new strains relies almost entirely on "manual" methods of change detection.

Manual Detection

The manual method of detection is available to anyone who has a computer and the most basic tools of the operating system. It is, of course, made somewhat easier with the more advanced utility programs available on the market, but the best defense remains a thorough knowledge of your computer and what it is supposed to be doing.

A knowledge of the programs on the computer and of the file sizes and creation dates is a simple piece of protection requiring no special programs whatsoever. This one simple tool, however, can provide detection of most file-infecting viral programs. It will even detect stealth viruses, if the computer is booted from a clean system disk before the check is made.

DEBUG is provided with every copy of MS-DOS and can be used to view and make a copy of the boot record of every disk. (Partition boot records of hard disks are beyond the easy reach of DEBUG, but within the reach of F-PBR, from 1.xx versions of F-PROT.)

Memory maps (and hex dumps of boot sectors) are not easy to read, even for experienced, but nonprogramming, users. However, it is not necessary that the user understand all the entries in a boot sector or memory map. It is only necessary that the user have a printout of a run of, say, MEM/C in an initially clean state, and then be able to spot a difference in a subsequent run of the program.

In reality, of course, most users will not take the time and trouble to check for changes in the system. Most users want a program that will do it for them, and preferably one that will do the checking automatically, alerting them to anything wrong.

Most file-infecting viral programs can be checked for quite simply, without any special programs or equipment. Provided, that is, that the computer user will pay the most minimal attention to the system and take the most basic precautions.

The simplest form of antivirus detection equipment is a list of all the programs to be run on the computer, with the size and last-changed date for each. (The list for resource-based systems, such as the Macintosh, will, of necessity, be somewhat larger and must include all code resources on the disk.) With some few (albeit important) exceptions, programs should never change their size or file date. Any changes that are made should be at the request of the user and easy enough to spot as exceptions.

While stealth technology of various types has been applied to viral programs, the most common (and successful) viral programs, to the date of this writing, have not used it. Most change the size of the file and generally do it in such a standardized fashion that the infective length of the virus is often used as an identification of the specific viral program. The file date is changed less often, but is sometimes deliberately used by the virus as an indicator to prevent reinfection. (One used the value of "31" in the seconds field, which is presumably why the later 1.xx versions of F-PROT all had dates ending in 31.)

Even when stealth techniques are used, they generally require that the virus itself be running for the measures to be effective. We thus come to the second piece of antiviral equipment—the often-cited "known clean boot disk." This is a bootable system (floppy) disk, created under sterile conditions, known to be free of any viral program infection, and write-protected so as to be free from possible future contamination. When the computer is booted from this disk, the hard-disk boot sector and system areas can be bypassed so as to prevent stealth programs from passing false data about the state of the system.

Antiviral protection can thus start with these simple, nontechnical provisions. Starting with a known clean system, the list can be checked regularly for any discrepancies. For added security, the clean disk can be used to cold-boot the system before these checks.

Checks should be performed before and after any changes made to software, such as upgrades or new programs.

Antiviral Software

Security does not, of course, end here. This is only a very simple first line of defense.

Historically, it is interesting to note that initially operation-monitoring and -restricting software was the preferred means of antiviral protection. Subsequently, signature-scanning software became more prevalent and currently holds dominance in terms of number of programs in use. Change-detection software, however, has recently become very popular and, from my reviews of software, now leads in terms of number of different programs implementing the technique.

The most basic type of change-detection program could simply automate the process of manual file checking. However, this would not catch overwriting viral programs, as long as they did not change the file date. Therefore, most change-detection software performs some type of "image checking" as well.

"Image," "numerical," or "statistical" file checking is based on calculations performed on the data making up the file. At its most rudimentary, this is based on the checksum. As the name suggests, this is nothing more than a check of the summing of all data in the file, or sometimes the modulus of that sum. The CRC (cyclic redundancy check) is preferred, since it performs sophisticated calculations on matrices of the data. (This is done in a fashion similar to the Hamming encoding used for error detection and correction.)

It would be fairly simple for an overwriting virus to calculate the checksum for a given file, and then to modify the code of the infected file in such a way that the checksum would still match. This is the reason for some of the more complex calculations that are implemented.

While the initial checking of files is fairly standard, there are a wide variety of implementations for the subsequent checking of files. The original information must, of course, be stored somewhere. Some programs create a single file for this; others attach the information to the program to be protected. Each means has advantages and disadvantages. A single file means a single entity, which virus authors may find out about and target. Attaching of data to programs that may be altered means that the calculated codes may be altered or erased as well. Sometimes small modules of code are attached to the programs in order to allow the programs to check themselves. Unfortunately, adding such modules to programs that already check themselves for changes may prevent the programs from running. (Norton AntiVirus stored the information in a number of hidden, 77-byte files, with names similar to that of the protected file. This has caused a number of users to suspect that the results of Norton's protection were actually the results of a virus. One fairly unique ploy is used by "Victor Charlie," which, in its earliest incarnation, simply offered itself as bait to viral programs—and then checked itself.)

These measures described will detect file-infecting viral programs (within limits). However, a very large class, or perhaps a number of subclasses, of viral programs do not make any changes to program files on the disk.

Boot sector infectors replace or move the boot program resident on almost every disk. Although these viral programs are extremely common, surprisingly few change detectors bother to make any check of this area at all. One reason may be that a number of computers make regular changes to the boot sector for "legitimate" purposes.

Companion viral programs, while they are associated with certain programs, do not make any changes to existing program files at all. Similar claims can be made for system viruses, such as the DIR-II virus, which leaves the file intact, but changes the directory entry so that the virus, which "officially" does not exist on the disk, gets called first.

It is, therefore, necessary to check much more than the size and image of the individual program files on the disk in order to detect viral infections. The boot sector (and master/partition boot record) should be checked (although it is possible that a certain area should be excluded from checking in the case of certain computers). A check on the total number of programs and names should also be kept separate from the system directory. A copy of the directory and file allocation table should also be kept, especially in regard to program files.

System memory and the allocation of system interrupts should also be checked. This is problematic during normal operations, as programs tend to use, and sometimes not fully release, areas of memory and interrupts as they work. Therefore, the best time to do such checking is at boot time, even before drivers and programs have loaded from the start-up files. (DISKSECURE does this to great effect. So did F-PROT's original F-DRIVER.SYS—which led to unfortunate conflicts with MS-DOS 5.0. The security programmer's lot is not an easy one, with virus writers, legitimate programs, and even operating systems continually finding new and "interesting" ways to do things.) It is also possible and quite desirable, however, to take a "snapshot" of memory immediately after the start-up sequence. This would make it possible to detect any changes made to programs involved in the boot sequence, as well as any other changes. (It may also catch program traps that redirect a warm boot in order to avoid disk security devices.)

Viral programs have almost no defense at all against disinfection. Ninety-nine percent of viral programs are almost trivially simple to get rid of— simply replace the infected file (or boot sector) with an original copy. (Some more recent boot sector and system viruses require slightly more knowledge in order to perform effective disinfection; but none requires drastic measures.) Far from their image as the predators of the computer world, viral programs behave much more like prey. Their survival is dependent upon two primary factors: reproductive ability and avoidance of detection.

Using the standard system calls to modify a file leaves very definite traces. The change in a file "creation" or "last modified" date is probably more noticeable than a growth in file size. File size is rather meaning-less, whereas dates and times do have significance for users. Changing the date back to its original value, however, is not a major program-ming challenge.

Adding code while avoiding a change in file size is more difficult, but not impossible. Overwriting existing code and adding code to "un-used" portions of the file or disk are some possible means. (The fictional rogue program p1, in Thomas Ryan's *The Adolescence of P-1*, avoided problems of detection by analyzing and rewriting existing code in such a manner that the programs were more compact and ran more effi-ciently. Such activity has not yet, alas, been discovered in any existing virus. Recently two viral programs seem to have been written with the intent of performing useful functions. Unfortunately, both have signif-icant problems.)

Some viral programs, or rather, virus authors, rely on psychologi-cal factors. There are a number of examples of viral programs that will not infect program files under a certain minimum size, knowing that an additional 2K is much more noticeable on a 5K utility than on a 300K spreadsheet.

In a sense these are all stealth technologies, but this term is most often used for programs that attempt to avoid detection by trapping calls to read the disk and "lying" to the interrogating program. By so doing, they avoid any kind of detection that relies on perusal of the disk. The disk gives back only that information regarding file dates, sizes, and makeup appropriate to the original situation, providing, of course, that the virus is active at the time of checking. Although this stealth method avoids any kind of "disk" detection, including check-summing and signature scanning, it leaves traces in the computer's memory that can be detected. (Some viral programs also try to "cover their tracks" by watching for any analysis of the area they occupy in memory and crashing the system if it occurs, but this tends to be rather noticeable behavior.)

Although the majority of current viral programs spread via disk boot sectors or the infection of programs, it is possible to use other means for replication and spread. The important factor is the ability of a system unit to submit information, which is then "run" as a program. It is, therefore, possible for terminals, peripherals, and network devices to operate as viral vectors.

This sounds very much like the "Iraqi/Desert Storm/printer" and "modem carrier" viral myths that we have already covered. And, indeed, these rumors used scenarios that seemed very plausible, as long as they were not closely examined. As previously stated, it *is*, in fact, possible for a printer subsystem in a network situation to "submit" information to other components in the network. Depending upon the network, configuration, and levels of privilege allowed, printer subsystems can even submit programs to other computers. However, in order for this vector to become a major threat, network printing will have to become much more standardized than is currently the case.

In order to function as a viral vector, a peripheral needs three features (or components). First, the user computers must be able to submit information or programs to the peripheral. Second, the peripheral must be capable of a certain minimum amount of memory or storage and must be able to perform certain levels of automated processing. Finally, the peripheral must be able to communicate with other user computers, and the information communicated must be accepted by those computers as programming with access to at least a minimum level of resources. However, once those conditions are met, any peripheral, be it printer, modem, disk pack, terminal, or otherwise, can act as a means of replication and spread.

In March 1988, a thread began in the *RISKS-FORUM Digest*, detailing problems with terminals that had programmable function keys. The specific examples given dealt with pranks and trojans, but the concepts and functions could have easily been used to generate, for example, mail viruses.

However, this example again points out a major weakness in the use of peripherals as viral vectors. Peripheral command sets, particularly those dealing with the more powerful functions, tend to be very hardware-specific. In the "programmable function keys" mentioned above, one example given used Teleray terminals while another referred to Wyse terminals. The commands for these terminals are not interchangeable, although the functions are almost identical. This is an advantage of the current "incoherent" computing environment. However, as open-systems initiatives gain strength, many new viral vectors may become possible.

Peripherals are not the only unusual vectors for viral programs. Consider the common boot sector. Although a knowledge of the structure of the boot (and master boot) sectors and boot sequence is practically a prerequisite for any serious viral study, *VIRUS-L*, no less than the Fidonet discussion echoes, is still inundated with postings by users who state they have contracted Stoned (or Michelangelo, or Monkey, or . . .), have deleted all the files on the disk, and are still infected! To the vast majority of users the fact that a program can be located at a *physical* position on the disk but *not* be referenced by the file directory list is a foreign concept. This confusion may contribute to the enormous success of boot sector viral programs.

The boot sector, and even the partition boot record on a hard disk, is accessible to dedicated amateurs armed with utility software. However, there are other places to *hide* on a disk that are not as easily examined. It is quite possible to format an additional track outside the normal range. In order to avoid problems between drives with variations in tolerance, the software does not "push" the limits of the hardware. I recall special programs for the Apple II computer that provided 38 tracks rather than the normal 35. There are various programs for MS-DOS, as well, which provide greater storage on the same-sized disks.

In addition to tracks outside of and between normal formats, there is substantial space between the sectors on a disk. There are programs that can increase the number of sectors so as to increase the space on disk. However, it is also possible to use the additional space without formatting additional sectors, simply by writing information to the space between. This fact has occasionally been used by commercial software for the purposes of copy protection.

Both of these hiding places are so well concealed that viral programs infecting them would never have a chance to become active. Therefore viruses using them would have to "start" with normally infected files or boot sectors. The initial viral code would have to provide the means to access the extra tracks or extra-sector space and then use the hiding space in order to store additional code. (This is, in fact,

Physical space diagram

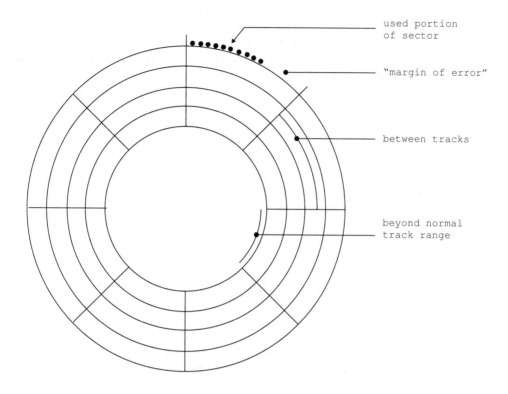

used portion
of sector

"margin of error"

between tracks

beyond normal
track range

already happening to a limited extent. The Joshi virus stores part of itself and the original boot sector on an "additional" track.)

Some hiding places are definitely a part of the system, while not being necessarily obvious. The Mac system, for example, associates at least 14 "resources" with each program and data file. Most of these resources can have code associated with them and therefore provide a number of additional "hooks" for viral access.

DATA VERSUS PROGRAMS

A major problem with the definition of a computer virus is the definition of a program. To the average user, this would appear to be merely an academic argument with no real world significance. Not so. The idea of what makes a program, as opposed to mere data, is quite important in deciding what can, or can't, work as a virus.

One of the most frequently asked questions regarding viral programs is whether you can get them from email, text files, graphics files, and other forms of data. The answer to this, unfortunately, is not, and cannot be, brief. It turns on the idea of what a program is. As I will point out in Chapter 7, a great number of false alerts are being generated nowadays, so an understanding of this issue can help you separate the wheat from the chaff.

In the first place, the computers we currently use are all built on what is known as von Neumann architecture. Part of what this means is that programs and data share the same disk and memory space. Programs are simply data files that have been identified to the computer as instructions.

But program files and data files are different, aren't they? Internet, BBS, and on-line service users are told that program files must be transferred in a different way than text. This is generally true, but the difference that is referred to in data communications is between those files containing only "printable" characters, which can be sent via email, and "binary" files, which can contain any data bytes. In fact, graphical data files also contain "binary" data, as do compressed files and even word-processing documents. (This is why you have to convert word-processing documents to "text" or "ASCII" before you post them as messages.)

In fact, programs can be written using only printable characters. Most processors have enough redundancy in the instruction set that you can eliminate more than half the instructions and still write just about any program you want. The program may not be quite as efficient as one written without such limitations, but it will work.

Let us, therefore, examine in more detail some of the specific questions about the possibility of viruses in data files.

Email and Text Files

Whether or not plain text can act as a viral vector depends to a great extent on what you do with it. There is, for example, the ANSI bomb, which was discussed in some detail in Chapter 1. A text file with an ANSI bomb in it will do you no harm at all unless you both have ANSI.SYS installed and running and perform some action that uses ANSI.SYS and feeds the text through it. Reading such a file with your word processor will do nothing unless your word processor uses ANSI.SYS (the last one I saw that did that was a special edition of version 3.3 of WordStar in 1985). Getting an ANSI bomb in an email message will do nothing unless your terminal emulation program uses ANSI.SYS, and I can't even recall using one that did. In any case, an ANSI bomb is very limited, and it is unlikely that you could make one that would reproduce itself. Although it could do damage, it couldn't be a virus.

Well, what about the printable character programs that I just mentioned? Yes, they could be used to make a virus, and, yes, they could be sent as an email message or text file. They wouldn't, however, fool anyone. Look at the two sample programs in the following figure. The text, although composed only of letters, numbers, and symbols, doesn't look anything like a message: it just looks like garbage. Even if you got this kind of program in an email message, it wouldn't do anything to you. Reading it on-screen, TYPEing a file with this text in it, or saving or copying such a file wouldn't activate it. What you would have to do is save the relevant part (and *only* the relevant part) to a file, name the file as an executable (.COM) file, and then type the filename as a command at the DOS prompt. This is not something you are likely to do by mistake, so printable character programs would not be a good choice for trying to spread viral programs. (Of course, if someone sends you a virus all packaged up like this, with directions for turning it into an executable program, and you extract and run it, you probably deserve whatever happens to you.)

The MAKEBOO programs

The following are two actual working programs composed entirely of printable characters. You can type in the two program chunks below with a word processor, save them as text (or ASCII) files called MAKEBOO.COM and UNBOO.COM, and then run them. (Yes, these are the same files mentioned in Chapter 3.)

MAKEBOO.COM

```
XPHPD[0GG0G,0G51G31GB'(G+(G:u'0g?(G>(GE1G@arwIV_F*=US@<1|_,5wXNg-7muTu(4
0\Rtsssssssssssssssssssssssssssssssssssssssssssssssssssssssssssssssssss
ssssssssssssssssssssssssssssssssssssssssssssssssssssssssss3@=2@3t2>85BB3S2Ta
3S283'2@T\_TU_X3S2@F3'27BF3S26B@3S2Y\_X3S@=S2HfX3S2gb3S2VbaiXeg3S2cebZeT
'f3S2TaW3S2jbeW3S2cebVXff\aZ3S2Y\_Xf3S2\agb3Sa25BB3S2Y\_Xf3@=@=S253t2F87
3S2BA3S2@F@>53S2IXef\ba3SdadS@=S28K83S2gb3S25BB3S2Y\_X3S2VbaiXegXe3a@=[2
V3\SdlkkS2J3a263aS2CTe^X3@=@=W2HfTZX3m@=SS2@3t2>85BB3S2Y\_XaT'X3a2Xkg3@=
W26baiXeg\aZ3SWS2gb3SWSaaaSWS2T_eXTWl3S2Xk\fgf3aS2BiXeje\gX3S2\g3rSW@=28
eebe3S2\a3S2Y\_X3SW2bcXa3W2VeXTg\ba3W2V_bfX3W2eXTW3W2je\gX3Wa@=Wa25BB0ss
3@=27baX3aS@=W0sssss1g3<1m09t@3T1q2s0s1_3e0W3V1s2h360\15351r2C0t3s1>0;1_
3o@2g3@oS2g3:o2Te35W2R1]0Ua3e1s]2B1k2C0t1>0B3^0;1<3AZ6tt0p1c2O0e1a0o2::1
>0j1rW0t3f0<1_3tU1s]2g350^j2<1<3A\61qW0t1ri0t1l3;0sf1Xm2C0t1g3p0@3T2f360
\1'0s1V2?0t1rW0t1>3A\66012J0p3t1c3a0e1a0oV362:KJQ1>0q1q3H611360sf1XmW0t3
f0<1g2A0@3T2e3Z1qW0t[3Z51g3<1mt350@3T1k0t3?0@3T2C1g351e3@0@3T1e3=0@3T2K3
W2R3o2Lg360\3U0t1mW0t1g3of0<@3T2eG1VS0t1g3<1m]350@3T1q2C0t[^t1g3<1mi350@
3T1qW0t[Qt1g3<1mn350@3T1qi0t3f1s>0[1V0P371V2W381r392Y1l3C0s1_3U1s2g3:_c0
[3b0tUg[3C0t1q3990^2>1Cm0e351c350\1;0t1m0j351c360\2s0t1m0s361c3:0\2k0t1=
0K3e0r^3m0[2i0s3U1s2h0f160p2>e360[Ps1c2A0[es112@0s1n2A0s[200s3U1s0T12C3^
0L1>06[Ps2K0^360[2=0s3U1s2g0@1=0S[3t0s1>0K[3o0s1=0[1>06D[D[190S160p2<e36
0[1P0s[1g0s1907C[C[[1^0s1=0V2s0W3B1=08DSDS190S[1N0s1=07C[C[[1E0s^1i0ss36
163q0P370s2g391_0r3A0P3706[3e0s2f0hi39Y60r2g3A0q3A0R372s3q0R370s2g3:1cC0
62K0\<s2K0[1N0s2f360\280r1g3<1m3N60@3T1k0s2?0@3T016i39Y60r2h0j2CFDE1>3Q2
?0t1m3991g3r1l0s2S0@3T1q3992MLNe3:1V0P37V1s2g352K06q39Y62K0163f0'2C1c0P[
```

```
3E0s1cOM[3@0s2K3f0'6ss[3M0s2e3G0^3;2t3q2W380s2Sf0d37c1]280r392W380k62K0^
2E1C2CFDE1>3Q1S0t1g3s1m392Y11os2S0@3T2MLNe3Ap0s2Sh3<0:392W380ss1r392YK06
[1Y0r1>3Q1S0t1g3s1m392Y1>3A2W380@3T1g3q0@3T061m<351g3<0@3T1k0t2?0@3T1m39
61c370^381m3>61c390[3B0s2C1g3<0@3T1m3D60@3T2K1g2?0@3T2CE1m0T351g3<0@3T2M
K061Cg351_3U1s2g391=0C@3T0^h64
```

UNBOO.COM

```
XPHPD[0GG0G,0G51G31GB'(G+(G:u'0g?(G>(GE1G@arwIV_F*=US@<1|_,5wXNg-7muTu(4
1m0T352t0osr2e3K1q2s0s3e0W1_F0:sss1@2G0t1k0s3p0@3T1m3>52f3>1k0t3<2C0@3T2
K1g2?0@3T1Fmj351g3<1q0s3:0@3T1g3r11Ots1>0I@3T1m0>352e0O2;h0L1_Eg352s0m3S
2j0W1g3of0<1;2?0r1m0s3:1>0m@3T2e0R1FH2E1m0s3:1>0B3^0=2g3=1g3s0@3T2e0@3^1
t2e0<1>0m1m0s361>0e11Os371g3r1:0P@3T1:0P2e1hDk0s3q0V1F2M1_3_c2o3Z1=0Y1=0
c2s0o2Ag3H0CSCS1:0=F[1:0=2s0]352k0t1]2s0U390^3<1KL2D1Dc0sf1]2L0UE^1T3@=2
G[\f3S2\f3S2Ta3S283'2@T\_TU_X3S2@F3'27BF3S26B@3S2Y\_X3@=2HfX3S2\g3S2gb3S
2VbaiXeg3Sa25BB3S2Y\_Xf3S2gb3S2g[X\e3S2Be\Z\aT_3S2Ybe'3@=25TfXW3S2ba3S2@
F5C6G3S2U13S27Ta3S2AbefgXWg3_S2FgbV^[b_'3_S2FjXWXa3@=@=2HfTZX3mS2HA5BB3S
2Y\_X3a25BB3@=W2HacTV^\aZ3S2gb3S2Y\_X3mSW28eebe3S2Whe\aZ3S2Y\_X3S2<3b2B3
W2Abg3S2XabhZ[3S2'X'be13W4
```

MAKEBOO will convert a binary file to printable characters for transmission over email systems, while UNBOO will convert it back. For more directions, run the files.

At your own risk, that is. No warranties, express or implied, are provided, particularly if you mistype something.

There is, however, yet a third type of text program. Source code for programs is written in text. It even looks like text, with words and some kind of structure. It doesn't look very much like a message, and you should be able to tell right away what it is, even if you are not a programmer. Even source code, though, is not immediately active. The text of source code must be turned into machine instructions with either a compiler or an interpreter. Compilers take the source and turn it into a separate file of machine program code. Interpreters turn the source code into machine code on the fly, without creating a separate file. In both cases, however, you have to invoke the language program to get the text of the program to become executable.

On the surface, therefore, it is unlikely that you could be hurt by receiving any kind of source code. But appearances, as should be obvious by now, can be deceiving. It is quite possible to work in an environment where an interpreter language is already active. Certain email systems, for example, have Perl or Rexx loaded and ready to go. Automated groupware systems have many useful functions built in, possibly including the capability to take advantage of any program that you may be sent.

In fact, many popular office systems can work perfectly well without source code interpreters. Most such systems allow any type of file to be sent as an attachment and automatically run whatever is necessary. Does the message contain a word-processing file? Load it up with a word processor. Budget figures? Fire up the spreadsheet. Is it a program? Execute it. This is all very much easier for the user, who doesn't have to gather the tools and learn how to use them, but it opens loopholes for the entry of malicious software.

Programs in Data Files

Leaving aside the problem of special types of text, can a program be buried inside a data file and still be a possible source of infection or malicious activity? The most common fear in this regard involves graphics files, which are very large and could hide any number of tiny viral programs within the data. It is true that program code would produce "snow" in a part of the picture, but that could be disguised in any number of ways. The major barrier to the use of graphics files as a viral vector is that the data will always be treated as just that: data. No known graphical file format allows any part of the data to be used to give instructions to the system yet. Therefore, nothing can ever be used to start a program. New developments emerge all the time, however, and it is likely that eventually some graphics system will want to start adding "features" by allowing program code. Watch out for this, and be aware of the dangers.

What about other types of files? Well, spreadsheets, word processors, and other programs almost all treat data like data. Therefore, programs hidden inside such files wouldn't (with one notable exception, covered in a few pages) get started. Since word-processing and spreadsheet files are much smaller and more open than graphics files, any programs would be much more obvious and easier to spot.

There is, though, one very easy way to put an active virus or trojan into a data file, and that is to use the Microsoft Windows OLE (Object Linking and Embedding) function. All good Windows applications provide this capability, and it can be used to create a data file with an active program inside.

This point is rather controversial and poorly understood, so I need to go into a bit of detail. OLE actually has two separate and quite distinct features. Object linking simply creates a pointer within the data file being worked on. The pointer may link to an outside program, or to another data file and the application needed to display that file. Only the pointer is contained within the file you are working on. This creates no particular problem. If the pointer points at an infected program, that program must be copied with the data file when it is transferred somewhere else in order to be of any potential danger. Even then, because the infected file is transferred as a separate object, it would be subject to scanning and detection.

The second feature of OLE is embedding, and herein is the concern for virus transfer. Embedding actually copies the object into the data file. Thus, an infected program can actually be buried, in an active and infectious form, within a normal word-processing, spreadsheet, graphics, or any other data file. It can't be invoked from outside the file, and even when the file is opened it needs to be activated by the user. A simple "double click," though, is all it takes. And who thinks to scan for viral programs inside word-processing files?

There is one other possible danger with data files. Modern applications have added the ability to create increasingly powerful macros or scripts to automate (there's that word again) tedious processes. These are, essentially, small programming languages and can therefore produce programs. In the academic circles studying viruses it has long been known that it was possible to create items that reproduced themselves in some ways using macros or scripts in various commercial programs. Microsoft Word and Lotus 1-2-3 even had the capability to start a certain macro automatically when the data file was loaded in. (This function is a vital one for viral activation and spread.) Macro viruses were, though, considered to be unlikely candidates for successful replication in a normal and diverse computing environment. They have been known, created, tested, and dismissed. The research community has its hands full with all the viral programs in the wild and, while trying to convince developers not to get too insecure, hoped that such scripts wouldn't become a major problem too soon.

That hope has ended.

MICROSOFT WORD MACRO

The message subject was "Nightmare has arrived." The report, from Sarah Gordon, gave some detail from her examination of the beast. Infected files (data files, remember) contained a number of macros that worked in concert to enable reproduction and spread. Other reports were fairly quick to arrive. Word Macro viruses are quite definitely widespread and plainly able to replicate.

This original, and unfortunately first of many, viral program will probably get an "official" name of WordMacro.Concept. At the heart of the system are two macros named "AutoOpen" and "FileSaveAs." These names are important, since the name itself contributes to the function. A macro named AutoOpen contained in a Microsoft Word word-processing file will, by default, load itself and execute when the data file is opened. In this case, it was used to load itself and the other macros into what is known as the global document template, stored in a file named NORMAL.DOT. Once in the global template, these macros become available during the processing of any file. (Two preventive measures can be taken to keep this from happening in your Word system. You can either program or reprogram an AutoExec macro in Word's global document template to include the command "DisableAutoMacros". Under TOOLS/OPTIONS, you can open the Save folder and select "Prompt to save Normal." This will prevent the NORMAL.DOT file from being modified without your being informed. As a final resort, if you do not want to make regular changes to the global template, you can flag NORMAL.DOT as a "read-only" file under MS-DOS.)

The macro named FileSaveAs, when installed in the global document template, modifies the "Save As" item in the "File" menu. Thereafter, any file "saved as" a different filename would also be stored as a document template, containing the macros required by the virus. This completed the replication cycle. An infected document would infect the Word system, and an infected Word system would infect any file saved under a different name.

It is fairly obvious that this first variant was a "proof of concept," leading to some of the alternatively proposed names such as Macro.Concept, WinWord.Concept, and just plain Concept. One of the macros is named "PayLoad" and contains only the remark "That's enough to prove my point." The PayLoad macro is, in fact, never called, but it could have been, and just about anything could have been put in it. Checking for a macro called PayLoad is one possible way to detect the infection, but since the AutoOpen macro also checks for it, writing an empty macro called PayLoad is also a means of prevention. (Writing a macro called FileSaveAs is another.)

(According to MS-Word documentation, holding down the shift key while the program loads, or while a document is being opened, should prevent the operation of AutoOpen macros. In tests by a major antiviral research group, it was found that this does *not* provide reliable protection against the Word Macro virus. Do *not* depend upon it.)

The proposed name of WinWord or WinWord.Concept is unfortunately misleading. The macros will operate under other compatible versions of Word, even on the Macintosh. The Word Macro virus is therefore one of the first (possibly the very first, depending on how you define it) viral programs to successfully cross platforms.

Microsoft, as could be expected, is none too happy to have one of their products associated with a virus. At first the company tried referring to it as the "Macro Prank," thus avoiding both the product name and the deadly "virus" appellation. (Microsoft itself, however, has inadvertently spread the virus. A British paper has reported that a Windows 95 promotional disk for vendors had the macro in one of the documents.) It is unlikely that mere marketing can avoid the issue: this entity definitely has all the required characteristics of a virus. The first version may have been relatively harmless, but the idea is so simple that new versions appeared within weeks.

In fact, within a month after the initial report of the original Word Macro in the wild, the first malicious and damaging variation appeared. It was openly posted on the Netcom system, which has a policy of allowing free availability to malicious software. In a rather cruel jest, the "Nuclear" virus, as it has been called, was contained in a document describing the prototype WordMacro.Concept. Nuclear attempts to turn off preventive measures, adds a political message to the bottom of random documents, attempts to inject a more mundane file-infecting virus into MS-DOS systems, and will delete the operating-system files on April 5.

Other Word Macro viruses arrived in fairly short order. Some used various functions within Word to further hide themselves, creating a new kind of viral stealth technology. Others used new ways to reproduce and spread, avoiding the telltale AutoOpen macro name. Some were mere variations of earlier versions, but others can only be seen as completely new viruses. Most of the preventive and detective measures that worked with the original Concept version can be bypassed in one way or another.

If a virus is easy to write (and it is), a Word Macro virus is even easier. Word Basic is a high-level language and meant to be used by people who have no programming training. A knowledge of the less frequently used functions might be necessary to reproduce some of the stealth tricks, but anyone with a copy of Word and a little time can write a working virus. It isn't even necessary to have a prior macro virus to show you how it's done.

Since nobody checks data files for infection, the viruses spread widely and rapidly. There are at least three instances of the original Concept virus being distributed on CD-ROMs (inside documents on the disk). Perhaps the novelty of the virus has caused more than the usual number of reports. On the other hand, I did see one warning from someone who worked for a large corporation. He estimated that as many as 200,000 documents within the company could be infected.

As far as sole identification with Word goes, that may change. The current versions (this is being written only months after the first one was seen) have been written in Word Basic. I have recently read in a number of books that Microsoft plans to replace the various macro and scripting languages in its assorted products with Visual Basic for Applications. This will mean that a macro virus written in Word will work equally well in Excel, Access, and a wide range of other products. The same reports state that Microsoft is eager to license VBA to other developers for use in non-Microsoft products. At which point the virus would work in licensed and compatible products from a variety of vendors.

As details of the Word Macro virus began to come out, we also saw a fresh spate of reports of an email virus tied to Microsoft. Although these reports are very short on fact, they appear to relate to both the Word Macro virus and the email file attachment and automatic setup capability discussed earlier. The new Microsoft Network makes this type of activity particularly easy. By default, one mouse click is all it takes to download the attached file, invoke Word, read in the file, and infect your system.

MEMOIRS OF AN (UNTRUSTWORTHY) VIRUS RESEARCHER

I had been involved with a three-day data-communications course. At the end of the third day, the other instructor and I were winding down, when one of the hotel pages showed up with a message for me.

One of the financial institutions in town had been hit by a virus. In a panic, they had phoned the sysop of a board that I supported. The sysop, at the insistence of the bank, phoned my home. My wife, at the insistence of the bank, called the hotel.

Those of you who have been in this position know that "virus attacks" usually don't involve viral programs. They are far more likely to involve things like power cords, diskettes that have been stapled to folders, and disk caching programs. To my surprise, the contact was fairly knowledgeable about computers. Even better, careful note had been taken of all the untoward activity. It certainly sounded viruslike. What was more, it was a completely unknown virus behavior, seemingly circumventing the security of a certain LAN OS (whom we know but do not name). All of this took only about ten minutes to ascertain.

Having discussed all this at length, I stated that I agreed that this was a viral occurrence. However, given that it was unknown, I could not proceed any further until I actually got to their site and ran tests.

At this point, we hit a snag.

"Oh, no" she said. "You can't come down here. It would violate our security."

I must have misheard. Their security was already compromised, was it not? Yes, it was, she confirmed. To a sufficient degree that she had pestered my friends, colleagues, and family until she got me? Yes. And we had determined that this beast was exhibiting viral behavior, but was an unknown quantity. Yes. Yet the bank, having determined that it had a significant, yet unknown, virus loose in their LAN, would not allow into the data center the expert they had called upon for the purpose of dealing with said problem because the entry of the security consultant would constitute a security risk? Yes.

In other words, their security was broken, but they wouldn't let me fix it because that would violate their security? Exactly.

There was, of course, only one thing to say.

"Good luck."

CHAPTER 5

ANTIVIRAL-PROTECTION CHECKLIST

Having meandered around various academic and technical aspects of viral programs for a while, it's now time to get down to brass tacks and direct some attention to how the average user, or office, can detect the presence of computer viral programs and deal with them when detected. In this section I'll be laying out a guideline blueprint that any user can follow, even without specialized software. In the next chapter, I'll be dealing with the various types of antiviral software and how to evaluate them.

First, though, a few strategies and attitudes to give you a better chance of success in your defense.

Assume you are going to fail.

Or rather, not to be too fatalistic about it, *don't* assume you are going to succeed. Any program that claims that it will be able to deal with all future viral programs is flat-out lying, and the software byways are littered with the corpses of those programs that figured they knew it all. Make redundant provision for checking, and don't trust any one antiviral program or system. Keep testing it, and keep up-to-date.

Which brings us to the second point: inform yourself and inform others. Not every computer user needs to read the *VIRUS-L Digest* (or *comp.virus* on Usenet) or the Fidonet VIRUS_INFO, VIRUS, and WARNINGS echoes. But every computer user should know of someone who does read these sources. You can't trust CNN for the latest virus bulletin: they still think the NSA shut down Iraq's air defense with a printer.

By the same token, let the word out a bit more if *you* find out something. If you get hit, make sure you send a copy of the infection to a researcher. (It's terribly frustrating to try to deal with the aftermath of a bad disinfection when you don't have a copy of the virus to work with. ("Oh, we just reformatted the drive.") If you get hit, admit it. Don't imagine that you can ignore it and it will go away. (We are continually asked how bad the problem is . . . by the same people who will not answer surveys so that we can find out how bad the problem is.) This last is a bit of a touchy issue with those who feel that we should not say anything for fear of giving virus writers ideas. Never fear. Virus writers don't need any help. *The Cuckoo's Egg* proves the only result of keeping information to yourself is that the people who really *need* the data won't have it.

Antiviral Checklist

This section is going to outline and explain a checklist of steps that any computer user can take to reduce the risk of computer viral program infection and to increase the chances of detecting an infection early—ideally before the virus has much chance to do any damage. Please note that I am not going to deal with specific, or even generic, antiviral software at this point. That has a place of its own.

This checklist is intended first as a conceptual guide and is, as far as possible, also intended for the nonspecialist user of any system. Second, the checklist is intended to show that virus protection is possible without specialized software (although antiviral software can ease the burden tremendously). Third, the most important aspect of virus protection is that the user know his or her system. That cannot happen if the user is relying on some "magic bullet": there never will be a magic bullet that will give 100 percent protection.

FOR EACH COMPUTER

I really feel that the following list is reasonable, achievable, and necessary for each individual computer. All of the items, with one exception, can be obtained by any intermediate user with only the software supplied with the computer. Most of the items should be done in any case, as they are good technical-support practice.

Directory List of All Program Files, Date, and Size
This, of course, is completely straightforward, and yet it is so seldom done. The vast majority of file-infecting viral programs would be

instantly detected by a comparison between the original "clean" list and a directory listing taken after an infection. For best results, of course, other factors are needed and will be covered in due course.

List of Programs Run at Start-up

With the number of background and resident programs running on computers today, it's a wonder *anything* can operate at all. If you don't know what your computer is supposed to be running, how on earth do you know when something unusual creeps in?

For the MS-DOS world, this list can be obtained simply by printing a copy of the CONFIG.SYS and AUTOEXEC.BAT files. It may be felt that because these files are present on the computer anyway, it is redundant to print them out. A fair point, but a booklet of this information at each computer would save time and trouble all round.

"Source Code" for Menus

These days the computer vendor/reseller or a technical-support person installs the computer hardware and software and then installs a simple menu system for the user. It is not always obvious, from the disk structure, which program the user may be using on a regular basis.

The previous checklist items are, I am sure, unchallenged by anyone. They are things that the most naive user can find and that any reasonably intelligent person can understand. The following may not be as readily accepted. However, I stand by them as items that every computer should have. In fact, they may be even more important than the foregoing.

Description of Boot Sector

By a description I mean something as simple as a copy on a separate diskette or a "hex dump" listing. But even this is a formidable object for a novice user to understand, let alone produce.

The technical difficulty is, however, not an insurmountable objection. The user does *not* have to understand what the listing means, only to notice if a change occurs. As for generating the listing, that can be done by the qualified people who installed the system. With DEBUG on the system, batch files can be written to show the user the first few lines of the current boot sector. It might also be a good idea to have printouts of the most common boot sectors and to have batch files to check the boot sectors of floppy disks.

Description of Partition Boot Record

Similar objections will be raised to this item, and similar arguments defeat them. With the prevalence of Stoned and Michelangelo, the master/

partition record is even more important than the boot sector. For MS-DOS machines, FixMBR allows capture and F-PBR from the 1.xx versions of F-PROT allows examination of the relevant sector. (FixMBR, by the way, should be a part of any BIOS DOS, and all users should be part of a massive letter-writing campaign to Microsoft and Digital Research, demanding to know why they haven't licensed it yet.)

Description of Memory Map and Interrupts at Start-up

These two can really be handled together, both in concept and in execution. Again, while the novice user can't be expected to know what all the numbers mean, anyone of sound mind can see whether or not they change. The one problem here is that during the normal running of programs, some of these numbers do change. Therefore, it should be stressed that if any change is noted, it should be checked again after a reboot of the system. At this point, some of the benefit is lost, as the novice user may not be able to differentiate between a valid program that is sloppy in its use of memory and a viral infection. Having this item on the checklist, however, will give the experienced support person an immediate baseline.

From the esoteric, we move back into the mundane, and some uncontroversial measures.

As we progress through the list, it will be noted that a number of the measures proposed are no more than those proposed for good computer management and support without regard to viral programs. This should not be surprising. The operations of viral programs are not different in kind from normal computer operations. (This is why it is impossible to identify a viral, as opposed to a valid, program by examination of the code alone.) Therefore, any operation of a viral program could just as easily be done by the proverbial "ingenious idiot," who has, historically, been far more deadly than any kind of malware.

Backup "Originals" of Software

I recommend that all software be installed from "backup originals." These disks, or copies made after installation, should there be any customization involved, should be kept with the computer. This serves two purposes. It allows for quick access to known clean software for reinstallation, if necessary. (These "originals" may reduce or eliminate the need for full backups of the system, as the software is often the larger portion of material on the user's disk, and generally the most stable.) It also provides a baseline for a quick check for any changes to the software.

Backup of Hard Disk Directory Structure

Backups are a part of good procedure. However, while provisions are often made for the programs and data to be backed up, the directory structure itself is often forgotten. Rebuilding the directory structure may, in fact, be the most time-consuming part of a recovery.

Keeping a copy of the directory may help in other ways. Some malware, the AIDS Information trojan being a notable example, build extra directories in order to escape detection. Having a baseline copy of the valid directories gives you another means to detect viral programs, rather than another means (and place) for them to hide.

FOR EACH OFFICE

"Each computer" is pretty easy to define. An office is less so.

For the purposes of this checklist, an office is defined as a group of people who interact on a regular basis. "Regular," for this purpose, need be no more than once per week.

An office is, therefore, defined less in terms of locale and walls than in terms of communication. For this definition, an office may consist more of those working on a common project in far-flung cities than of those in the next cubicle to whom we never speak. However, it need not follow "official" reporting lines either. An office is defined more in terms of how fast you can find information when you need it. The items in this next section of the checklist are those that may not be referred to for long periods of time as long as things are going well, but that may need to be found quickly, once an anomaly has been identified.

Description of Current Common Viral Programs

This may be a prepared list, or it may be maintained in the office. For all systems, the major list must be the *Computer Virus Catalog* prepared by the Virus Test Center. This list is not complete, but it does cover all platforms and the most widely distributed viruses.

In the MS-DOS world, another possible source is the shareware summary list collated by Patricia Hoffman. While this list is more complete in covering the 2,000 (3,000? 5,000? By the time you read this, who knows?) MS-DOS viral programs, it is, of necessity, less accurate at times.

Antiviral software, especially that which incorporates scanning, often includes listings of viral programs, their symptoms, and features. Some of these are good; some, less so.

All of these lists must be kept up-to-date, and it is probably a good idea to have someone in the organization who is supporting the prepared lists with additional information from sources such as *VIRUS-L.*

List of Local Virus Information Contacts

Who ya gonna call?

This is a very difficult section to advise anyone on. For my part, I can think of perhaps 20 people in the world of whom I could state, with confidence, that they are competent in the field. This is not to say that there are not more, but it is an esoteric field, with few standards to judge by.

The information is hard to find, for one thing. The popular and even the technology trade media has very little appreciation for the difficulties and traps of virus hunting. The recent experience with Michelangelo points this out sharply. Almost all the articles in advance of the March 6 date stressed that this virus could be defeated by making backups or resetting the date. None mentioned that a BSI could corrupt nonstandard disk formats used by many backup programs, and none pointed out the difference between the DOS date and the system or clock date.

Virus experts, in common with most system-level hackers, tend to be charter members of "Egos-R-Us." This is bad enough. However, what is worse is that everyone with an outdated copy of SCAN thinks he or she is a virus expert and assumes the arrogance without necessarily having the expertise to back it up. (Given that the general population, even of advanced computer users, has very little background in the subject, the problem of proving credentials is often moot.)

So, how can you find a local expert? The following indications will help.

Points for

- Is a "member" of *VIRUS-L* and has been for a least a year
- If no Internet access, reads all three Fidonet echoes
- Is a contributing member

Points against

- "One antiviral fits all"
- Boasts of the size of his/her virus collection
- Warns against BBSes and on-line services

List of all Hardware and Software Purchased, Supplier, and Serial Number

This is one of the items that should be a part of any office computer "kit," simply on the basis of good management. The reason for its inclusion on the virus-fighting side is partly to track where a virus might have come from. (As I have mentioned before, originals should be protected and copied, and those copies protected before installation.) More and more companies are becoming aware of the need for software auditing, and this may become very helpful here. (It is less helpful in those companies that take a "righteously indignant" stance against shareware.) The hardware list is also valuable, because certain pieces of hardware will affect the operation of the computer, particularly in regard to memory utilization.

Designated Machine for Receiving/Testing New Disks/Software

Now *this* recommendation I *know* is going to stir up a storm. It always does. Why spend good money on a machine that is going to be used for nothing except testing software?

This appears to be based in the deeply rooted prejudice that says that the only important part of a computer system is the part you can see, feel, and throw through windows at times of stress. Let's look at the picture in real financial terms. If you buy two copies of a commercial antiviral program (for an office of, say, 20 computers), plus the upgrade fees for a year, you've spent about $400. Three hundred dollars will easily get you a bare-bones used machine for testing, and, in addition to antiviral testing you can also detect trojans, which relatively few antiviral programs do. (An AT-level machine should only be $500; even low-end Macs can now be had for about $1500.) A designated machine also allows you proactive rather than reactive protection.

Besides, very likely you already have a computer that no one in the office will use because of its age and "obsolescence." However, a word of warning is in order here: we have seen cases, most recently with Michelangelo, where older machines will not detect the full range of functions of the viral program. There are also a number of viruses that are version-specific in terms of the operating system, but it is relatively easy to set up a situation that allows for quick changing of the operating system.

One point I also stress in regard to testing is to make sure that the hard disk is not empty. There are some prima donna viral programs that refuse to operate unless it is "worth their while" in terms of the amount of file space used. Keep the drive about 80 percent full.

Log of Disks/Programs Received

Many large companies think they already have this. Many small companies see this measure as far too draconian. As usual, the truth lies somewhere in between.

Corporations, both large and small, and government departments often have policies restricting the use of software. Usually these schemes make some statement regarding bringing disks and software into the office. These policies are, of course, universally disregarded, even by those who drafted them. Such procedures are unnecessarily restrictive and unworkable, and they fail to address the issues that prompted them in the first place.

The intent is good. The institution wishes to protect the copyright of authors and other companies (or at least wishes to avoid being sued for failing to do so). The policy is also supposed to prevent the intrusion of viral and trojan software into the company, and, in some cases, the extraction of sensitive data from company files.

Unfortunately, I have yet to see such a policy actually achieve what is intended. In most cases, the procedures are both insufficient for the intended outcome and are damaging to normal business practice. I will use some examples from the federal government in Canada. (Anyone gloating over the foolishness of this institution does not know the policies in their own company.)

The Treasury Board is the governing body in financial matters and therefore publishes directives covering pretty much all aspects of Canadian federal government practice. Several years ago, it published a circular stating that all computer-related software or hardware had to have an associated purchase order (PO) before it entered government premises. At first glance, this would appear to be sound, and even an advantage for software companies. Not so. If you are reviewing software, a local government office cannot afford to purchase the necessary variety of software and still keep within its budget. Of course, it *is* possible to cut a PO for the software for no money. This takes about as long as the review process itself, as well as potentially putting the software company at risk (there being other policies regarding minimum and maximum pricing). Even if you intend to purchase the software the next fiscal year, you cannot review it in this fiscal year if you have no funding left for that line item or cannot afford to "lose" that funding this year.

This policy was, of course, intended to keep pirated software out of the organization and to ensure that software publishers were paid for their efforts. In practice, however, the policy was ignored, and evaluation software was obtained "under the table." In the end, all this policy did was prevent publishers who had standardized policies for review software from competing in reviews by local offices.

Canadian government policy also provides for tracking all inventory through accession numbers. The system works well for desks and cars, but not so well for computers and software. (I had a hard time convincing the "matériel management" people in one office that it did not make sense to issue one accession number to 12 video cards, but it did make sense to issue one number to one card, three disks of setup software, and one manual—for the same card.) Because of the difficulty involved in putting items into inventory (obtain the inventory coding for the item, obtain an accession number, affix a label—you ever try to find space for a 2 × 6 cm label on a video card?—and enter up to 46 fields of data into the inventory database by paper form, since only two people in the local office have access to the database itself), very few software-related items were ever entered into inventory. Data disks were never labeled: after all, what do you do with a carton of 100 blank disks, which are probably headed for 30 different offices?

In order to effectively track infections, however, even data diskettes and customer data diskettes have to be identifiable. The system for doing so must be easy, must not interfere with normal work, and must be *rigorously enforced—by the users.*

The trouble with most policies of this type is that these considerations are not *designed in* from the beginning. Trying to make transitory computer materials fit an inventory system designed for permanent fixtures, or forbidding the entry of disks into the company, simply means that people will ignore the policies in favor of greater productivity. The specifics of recording and tracking will have to vary with the corporate climate and culture. If an intent, and some relevant background (rather than a mandated procedure) is presented to employees, the users will come up with a solution . . . and one that is far more effective than those imposed by head office.

Memory and Disk Mapping Utilities

Earlier I mentioned the need for memory and disk lists for each computer. In most situations, these areas do not need to be checked constantly, so there is no need for a copy of these utilities with each computer. The utilities should, however, be available quickly and easily, should anything prompt a check. Checks should also be done on a regular basis, and these tools can be used on each computer in turn.

Having said that, many of the utilities needed are already a part of the operating system. In the MS-DOS world, CHKDSK, while it will not show you a graphic map of the disk, *will* provide information on the number of bad sectors or hidden files. As of MS-DOS 5, the MEM program provides needed information regarding memory and interrupt usage. The Mac world, and the GUI OSs in general, tend to provide fewer of these tools, but I believe that ResEdit is now part of the Mac OS.

In any case, these utilities are widely available both commercially and as shareware. Commercial utility packages often do double duty: PCTOOLS probably is sold most often for its backup capability, but it can provide helpful information in other areas as well. Shareware tools sometimes lack the interface compatibility of the commercial tools and more often are dedicated to a single task, but they frequently have useful features not found in their commercial counterparts. (Neither PCTOOLS nor Norton have the ease of access to specific sectors that the shareware SHOWFAT has.)

REGULARLY

What is "regularly"? The definition will depend on your situation, but, in general, "regularly" will mean "more often than you do now." The items under this section of the list are particularly those that should be going on regularly for good maintenance and support anyway.

Back Up Data

Our good old friend, the backup. Why stress data? Three reasons. First, programs and structure should be backed up at installation and at every change in configuration. They need not be backed up between times. Second, backing up only data reduces backup time and increases the frequency with which people are willing to do a backup. Third, you can buy another copy of Perfect Writer tomorrow. Can you buy another copy of your last month's receivables?

Monitor Disk Space, Map, Memory Map

Especially if you partition programs from data, checking the free space can give you a quick indication of many problems. On a disk map, check for increasing numbers of bad sectors showing up, or programs that insist on moving to the end of the disk. Again, the memory map should be checked primarily at boot time. You need not understand what all the numbers and interrupts mean, but if they change, you might have a serious problem.

Monitor Program File Sizes

If programs are partitioned from data (and data should here include any configuration files that change frequently), a reading of disk space should give a quick check for prepending or appending file-infecting viral programs. A listing of the files themselves would indicate specific infections. Generally speaking, a check of the sizes of program files takes less time than might be realized at first. Modern commercial programs take up a lot of space, but the number of individual files is not excessive. (Except for those of us who have to have all the very latest in freeware utils . . . All right, except for Windows . . .)

AT SOFTWARE INSTALL/CHANGE

This area should not require any definition. I should, however, mention one thing in regard to "change." There are, unfortunately, still a number of programs that modify their own code when a change is made in the configuration. I am not including these minor amendments in this section's definition of "change." When changes have been made that affect the size or composition of a program file, that program should be backed up (either by itself or as part of a full system backup), and the printout list of program file sizes should be redone. The following items, however, are recommended more in the case of installation of new software or a major upgrade.

Protect Original

I feel commercial software vendors are negligent in the face of an obvious and present danger in continuing to ship software on disks that are not only writable, but not even protected. Always protect the original disk immediately after you remove it from the package. Following this procedure will ensure that you know whether the new software infected your machine, or the machine infected the new software.

Install from Protected Backup

With the original disk protected, make a backup copy. Then protect the backup copy, and perform the installation from the protected backup. You are allowed to make an archival backup, and this procedure allows you to store the "original" original off-site, and the "backup" original near the computer, in case you need it for disaster recovery.

Unfortunately, software manufacturers still insist on various types of copy-protection schemes. Recently, the most popular have involved writing changes to the program based on a registration of your name and company—on the original disk. The practice of using a backup original will allow you, in this case, to keep the manufacturer's software disk protected. However, there are still some schemes that require reading from and writing to the manufacturer's disk. Whenever possible this practice should be avoided.

As with previous items in this antiviral checklist, I am sure that some will object that it is far easier simply to scan the disks for viral programs and "have done with it." I do, in fact, recommend scanning all disks. Note that both original and backup original should be scanned *after they have been protected*. As for my previous reasons regarding not stressing the use of scanners, may I add the fact that scanners, by their nature, will never be able to protect you against all viruses, although they should protect you against most.

Trial Run on Isolated System

Once again, this should be a part of general practice, regardless of the existence of viral programs. A trial run allows you to find any bugs in the program and to review the program's usefulness. At one time, a trojan version of SCAN was uploaded to a local bulletin board. It created all kinds of havoc because it was "approved" by the board—on the basis, of course, of having passed a virus scan. A single run on an isolated system would have detected the problem.

There will be, of course, complaints that this measure is too expensive for the normal office. However, one might compare the cost of a commercial virus detection program (or even, say, a full set of the VIRUSCAN suite) against the cost of a used machine, or one that no one will use in the office anymore because it is "old." As has already been noted, the test machine need not be sophisticated.

Map Memory Before and After Run

With the mapping of memory for all machines, it was not important to understand any of the entries. When testing new software, this understanding becomes more vital. However, the one significant part of this test is quite simple: has anything new been left behind, active, in memory?

Offer "Bait" Files and Disks

Some antiviral programs are starting to do this to trap viral programs. However, I am more concerned here with the variety of bait to be offered. As with the level of disk usage, remember that some viral programs will only infect certain types of files, others will only infect files of a certain size, and yet others look for specific internal characteristics (such as long strings of NUL characters). Offer a number of different files for which you know the sizes and can quickly check.

IF INFECTION FOUND

Once you find an infection, what do you do about it?

First, don't panic. Remember that a lot of viral programs don't do any damage—at least not intentionally. While you should not go blithely on as if nothing has happened when you find a virus, don't overreact either. Instead of focusing on the immediately obvious problem of the infection itself, try to take a few steps for future protection.

Send Copy to Recognized Researcher

This step is vitally important, and all too often neglected. Get a copy of the virus. Copy an infected program to a disk, or infect a floppy disk with a boot sector infector. The instant reaction is to sweep it under the rug: that helps no one. Many people are afraid to report viral programs because of their reputation of being related to pirate software. However, if we never try to find out how viruses spread, how can we determine how to stop them from spreading? New variants spring up all the time, and we need to track and trace these mutations.

Isolate Machine and Disks

Do not simply carry on as before. The floppy disks used in the machine are often neglected in the panic. Remember that the most successful viral programs have always been boot sector viruses, and these are *always* spread by diskettes.

Perform Minimal Disinfection

Please let me stress "minimal." Do the *least* that you can do and still ensure security. While there is some doubt as to the wisdom of disinfecting program files, it is surely better to delete one file than to restore the whole directory. It is better to delete and restore one directory than to restore the whole disk.

AND. No one. Ever. (Yet.) Has found a virus that requires a low-level format. NO LLFs. Got that?

However, *do* perform a thorough disinfection. Many people, while going far too far in gouging an infection out of their workstation, will fail to check out their floppy diskettes and backups. One of the most Frequently Asked Questions on *VIRUS-L* is "I cleaned off Stoned, but now it's back. How come?" Easy answer: "You didn't check your disks."

Also, with few exceptions, when disinfecting, power down cold and start fresh. If you have a virus in memory, none of your disinfection methods can be guaranteed, and some may even harm.

Memoirs of a ("Gifted") Virus Researcher

And it came to pass that a certain Manufacturer said unto itself, Let me make unto myself a system controller, that many may buy it, and that I may become wealthy. And it took of its gurus and said, Now that the controller is complete, make unto us a sexy application for this new controller, that we may hype it in the marketplace. And the one said, Let me, for I shall use the controller to smite the slime that infests the machines. And the Manufacturer saw that what had been made was good.

And when the app was completed (or almost completed, which was as good), then did the Manufacturer say unto the elders of AV, Look now, upon this app that is completed, is it not fair? And lo, it shall control the slime that ye revile.

And lo, among the elders was one (rather short, whose disks and CPUs were but few, but the others did put up with him) who spake and said, Well, I kinda specialize in looking at apps, so I could give it a crack, if you want.

And the Manufacturer did rejoice and did promise unto the small elder many things. And after many trials did the app, in a box, appear before the elder, wherefore the elder brought forth his tools and looked into the box. And he spake and said unto himself, This app is odd. And he looked some more and spake and said unto himself, This app is an absolute mess! And perchance could I make some observations, but they would be as like as apples unto oranges unto other apps. Therefore shall I clean this, that I might have a baseline to measure against.

And he strove mightily against the mess, and also (truth must be told) against the app. And after many days (or what seemed like many days) the box was again calm. But there had arisen during the strife certain lost clusters, which were now made into the form of files. And the small elder gazed upon them, that he might determine if they were, indeed, needful to the app.

And one file was very large, and as the small elder gazed upon it, he beheld its data structure, like unto a ZIP file. And he said, I shall extract these files. And forth did come AIDS and Ambulance and Anti-Pascal and BADBOYS and Name of the Beast and Burger and many others, so that they filled the directory, and their number was like unto 875.

And the small elder pondered all these things. And on the third day, the small elder returned unto the Manufacturer the box with the app, saying, And if thou art so keen to combat slime, why hast thou not yet come up with a dip switch that can be used to write-protect the hard disk, and wouldst cost but half a shekel?

But before he returned the box, he overwrote the whole hard disk.

CHAPTER 6

ANTIVIRAL SOFTWARE AND EVALUATION

STANDARDS AND MEASURES

We have already looked at general guidelines and procedures for keeping your system as safe as possible. In this section we will be dealing with software specifically designed to detect, protect, or disinfect viral attacks.

When I speak to user groups, the most common question is "What is the best protection program I can get?" Indeed, many people are interested only in the answer to this question and do not want to have to endure any talk about what a virus is or how it works. They want to buy something and then forget about the whole virus situation.

This attitude ignores three vitally important points. The first is that "the best" may not be good enough by itself. No security force would ever pick "the best" guard and then leave him to guard an entire refinery by himself. There is a trade-off between security and cost, but I always recommend that more than one antiviral be used (and hopefully different types as well).

The second point is that, even within the limited realm of antiviral programs, data-security software operates in many different ways. Thus, one type of security may be better in one situation, while another variety may be better in a different environment. (Which make better guards—dogs or men? Wise security firms use both.) There are basically three "classes" of antiviral packages: activity monitors, change-detection software, and scanners. Each type has its own strengths and weaknesses, and one type of software that works perfectly in the word-processing pool may be worse than useless in the development shop.

(By the way, I am not adamant about the number of classes listed

145

above. I used to say 5. Some say there are only 3 types of antiviral software. Some add the various types of implementation and say there are 14 or more.)

The final point is that security, of every type, is always a "moving target," and the virus world moves faster than most. Not only are new viral programs being written every day, but new types of viral functions are being coded all the time (albeit at a much slower rate than the run-of-the-mill copycat virals). Any antiviral program developer that promises to "guarantee" protection against "all known and unknown" viral programs simply does not comprehend the reality of the situation.

Before going into detail on the specific types of programs, I would like to address certain issues that apply to reviewing any antiviral software. Aside from the specific efficacy against large numbers and certain types of viral programs, there are considerations of user aspects of the system in question. This does not relate solely to the chimera of user-friendliness, but to the fact that a given system is intended not only to be somehow effective against viral programs, but must also be run by a "user population" in a given work, social, and technical environment.

It is very easy to "rank" antiviral software on the basis of how many viral programs or strains it will identify. It is not quite as easy to assess many other, more important, features. (Note, as well, that it is easy to rank only scanning software in this regard. Activity monitors and change-detection software have to be tested in completely different ways.) Although there may be more than 5,000 different strains of viral programs in the MS-DOS world (fewer in the other environments), it is likely that only 1 percent of that number is responsible for 99 percent of infections. Thus it is of far greater importance that, for example, one particular antiviral program does not prevent infection by the Stoned virus, than that it protects against literally thousands of others.

Thus the choice of a "test suite," sometimes called a "zoo," is made more difficult than it might be otherwise. Certain programs are very significant in terms of danger of attack and therefore must hold higher ranking than others. It is not possible to say that any collection of 80 viral programs is better than any collection of 10. If the 80 happen to be all "basement variants" of Jerusalem, that test suite is virtually useless. First, a decent antiviral program should deal with variants. Second, basement variants have a generally low survival rate in the wild and are not likely to be a threat. Third, basement variants tend to mutate nonfunctional aspects of viral programs through the insertion of NOP codes and the changing of text.

The test suite should, however, contain a range of viral programs that are functionally distinct. A good test suite should contain programs from different categories of viruses, such as BSIs versus file infectors and MBR infectors versus BSIs. Self-encrypting, polymorphic, stealth, tunneling, multipartite, and companion viral programs should all be represented. Some of these programs are very rare in the wild, and so the value of their inclusion may be questionable. (Indeed, there is some evidence that the more sophisticated a virus is, the less likely it is to be successful.) However, it would be well to test antiviral programs against the known possible viral technologies.

If at all possible, some rare, or even unknown viral programs should be included in the test suite. The assertion by some software producers that they can catch all "known and unknown" viral programs should never be left unchallenged. The only way to get completely unknown viral programs is to make them up. This is beyond the scope of most users, of course, and so it is not a realistic suggestion in most cases. In addition, there is the danger of letting another beast loose in an already overcrowded environment. If you do write new virals, please leave them crippled in some way, or take extreme care that they are not released.

The analysis of virus type and function may even be beyond the capabilities of some reviewers. Many of the problems of "numbers" reviews are much more basic than that.

The test suites for most numeric reviews now generally contain in excess of 1,000 items. Each of those items *should* have gone through a screening process. At a minimum, one should know certain things about it, such as, is it actually a virus? Does it reproduce? Under what conditions does it reproduce? Is it the same for each type of object it infects? Is it the same for each succeeding copy? When invoked, does it infect memory?

It is unlikely that each of the 1,000 or more items has been tested for all these criteria. Reviewers are much more likely to take shortcuts. One of the shortcuts is to obtain a test suite from someone who has already done the work. The most obvious candidate here is a developer of an antiviral scanner. Scanner developers have to do all of this anyway.

Unfortunately, there are two inherent problems in this. One is that if you get a test suite from only one developer, the test suite will exactly match the capabilities of the one product. Viral programs that this one scanner does not catch, but that others do, will not be factored into the review. The other problem is that it is quite possible that the developer has been careless. There may be nonviral items in the zoo. The one scanner will detect them, whereas nobody else will (correctly, since they are not viral). Thus, both factors will tend to boost the rating of the one product.

An untested zoo may also contain duplicate files. Particularly if one scanner catches them while others don't, duplicates may skew the results. Of course, in some cases you should have duplicate files. If this virus infects more than one type of object, you should have an infected copy of the different types of things it will infect.

All of this may give the impression that I think numeric rankings against a test suite are of no use. This is not the case. Ranking tests have a strong place in the evaluation of scanners. Bill Lambdin at one time posted a monthly test of the major MS-DOS scanning programs. He came under attack for doing so. He freely admitted that his tests are not perfect. I note that only one of those who complained about his tests has tried to do anything on a scale remotely similar to what he did, never mind any better.

Patricia Hoffman, in the VSUM list, also has a ranking test. Unfortunately, the list was so long tied to McAfee Associates that many simply ignored it. Recently, however, the ranking has become much more realistic. Ironically, some suspect this is because scanner developers are refusing to pay her so they can be tested.

In passing, I recommend to everyone the "Reader's Guide to Antiviral Reviews," an article by Sarah Tanner in the November 1993 issue of the *Virus Bulletin*. Each of the 26 points she discusses is a way to skew the results to favor one product or denigrate another. Some of these strain credulity, but each is known to have been used in major published antiviral reviews.

This begins to point out some of the difficulties in choosing antiviral software. There are, of course, matters of the type of viral program, the test suite against which the system is effective, the user interface, and the style of the program. Still, surely there must be *some* standard by which to measure antiviral software?

In the computer world, the nice thing about standards is that there are so many to choose from.

However you divide the different types of software, it is extremely difficult to apply the same standards to various categories. Besides the problems of the "numbers game" in testing a given program against a given suite of viral programs, the importance of the test results are of different significance to a scanner, a change detector, and an operation restrictor. For operation-restricting software, it may be of no consequence whatsoever that the program does not "catch" infections; so long as the restricting software is 100 percent effective in preventing the spread of infection, it does not matter whether it ever identifies any viral programs. Change-detection software may catch all infections, and yet be less effective than a scanner that catches only 90 percent, but effectively identifies them as well. (Unfortunately, one must also factor in the reality that change detectors will generate a *lot* of false positives, particularly because software vendors continue to insist on writing programs that modify themselves.) Therefore, a single "numeric" standard, based upon the use of a test suite, would be of little utility in assessing the overall effectiveness of antiviral software.

In addition, the environment is constantly changing. The number, specific strains, and types of viral programs are increasing all the time. The companion, spawning, or "precedence" virus does not change the files on disk at all, but rather takes advantage of the order in which programs are "called for." Thus those operation-restricting programs that prevent changes to program files become useless, as do change detectors that peruse only those files in the database at the previous run. Standards, therefore, that are based upon the currently existing viral environment will be very quickly outdated, and mostly useless.

A single, or even multiple, numeric measure simply does not have sufficient flexibility to gauge antiviral software. It may be possible to construct one that could, after considerable work. However, even if a criterion reference could be made broad enough to cover the various types of antiviral software, the gauge would have to be a moving one. Thus, antiviral software tested at one point would have to be retested each time the standard was renewed: at a minimum, that retest would likely need to be done on a yearly basis.

As viral programs are constantly developing new methods of attacking files and avoiding detection, so too antiviral software is constantly developing new detection methods, or at least new twists on old methods.

The problem here is the application of a single standard to diverse, and changing, types of antiviral software. It is, however, complicated by the fact that we do not know what the new features of antiviral software may be until they appear. Thus, while it might be possible to gather a series of criteria broadly applicable to the wide variety of antiviral software, and to balance and weight the various gauges in order to come up with a "fair" assessment, it is impossible to so judge some feature that you have never considered.

As examples, let us consider the recent rise of three new forms of "generic" antiviral software: "heuristic" scanning, checksum "generic" disinfection, and "heuristic" "generic" disinfection (these terms will be defined in more detail later in the chapter).

Heuristic scanning, an analysis of suspect code or files based upon possible activities rather than specific patterns, is nowhere near being a dependable form of viral detection. A great many programs, including antiviral software and other powerful utilities, are all accused (falsely) of being "suspicious" when scanned in this manner. At the same time, a number of viral and trojan programs are not caught. Thus, heuristic scanning would fail miserably at criteria set up to judge signature-scanning software.

It would, though, be a great pity to inhibit the development of heuristic-scanning software. This field is really the application of "expert systems" to antiviral software: an "expert" antiviral disassembler is checking the code for you. Along with hoped-for advances in change detection, this bodes well for the future of antiviral software. Indeed, not only will it identify suspect viral programs, but, with only minor additions, trojans and other malware as well.

If you know that you have a virus infection, don't bother purchasing a "checksum" disinfector. This type of software uses checksum, CRC, hamming, or image calculations that *must* be done while the software is clean, since this software only tries to return the disk, drive, or program files to an "original" state. Even then, checksum disinfectors have a very low success rate with disinfection and would undoubtedly fail any test set up to measure a set of "cleaning" programs. Heuristic disinfectors are even worse: they sometimes harm "good" programs. While disinfection is often recommended against, there are situations where you want to keep an existing program rather than replace it with an original copy, which may not contain setup information. In this case, you may need the services of a disinfection program that does not rely on a database of known viral programs. The chance of this situation happening is slight, but "generic" disinfectors could be useful where ordinary disinfectors fail.

USER REACTION AND INTERFACE

Also of very high importance in testing antiviral systems is the fact that the proportion of computer users who have a thorough understanding of viral operations, in comparison to the total user population, is so small that it is statistically insignificant. Therefore, it is vital that any antiviral program be judged on the basis of installation and use by "naive" users. A naive user in this case may be one with significant technical skills, but little background in regard to viral programs.

(I realize that my statement regarding the naïveté of computer users may be extremely controversial. Recall, however, that there are about one hundred million users of MS-DOS, and then compare that with the number of people who take an active interest in prevention of computer viral programs. Note that a very low proportion of computers have any defense against viral attack. Note that my "clipping file," covering 30 general computer industry periodicals over a period of two years, has only 11 articles on computer viral programs. Note also the very high sales of some highly publicized programs known by the virus research community to have very definite shortcomings.)

It is critical, therefore, to judge the interaction of the program with the user. Again, this interaction is not simply the presence or absence of a menu, but the total intercourse between the program and the user, by way of the documentation, installation, user interface, and messages. It is important to note how the total package "comes to" the user. Given that the user's system may already be infected, what can the package do to remedy the situation? Also, while the package may have significant strengths if installed correctly, is the "normal" user likely to be able to do the setup and installation properly?

Remember that for all the seeming simplicity of some programs, antiviral software is still a part of computer security. Security is not now, has never been, and never will be obvious to the majority of the population.

Part of the assessment of the user is the user environment. This aspect covers not only the "corporate culture" (e.g., home user, user in a large corporation with internal support staff, etc.), but also the operating-system environment. For example, the MS-DOS environment has a very large number of viral strains, with more being produced every day. The Macintosh environment has relatively few viral programs. Therefore, generic identification of new and unknown viral programs is more important to MS-DOS users than to Macintosh. (Interestingly, while Macintosh antivirals are quite mature, and protected Macintosh systems have a negligible infection rate, the infection rate on unprotected Macs is astronomical. This, too, should be taken into account.)

Related to the interaction of the user and the program is the potential negative impact of the security program. Antiviral programs consume time and disk space and may also interfere with the normal operation of the computer system. As Jeff Richards' first law of data security has it, you can guarantee security only if you don't buy a computer. This is just not a very useful alternative. Computer systems can be secured more and more by restricting the operations more and more, but restriction of "dangerous" operations also restricts useful ones. There comes a point at which the trade-off for greater security becomes more than users want to pay.

An antiviral program, therefore, must be matched to the environment in which it is to be used. In a "low-risk, low-change" situation, such as a word-processing office, change-detection software provides very effective protection, without too much interference with operations. In a "high-change" milieu, such as a software development team, change-detection software is less useful against viral programs, although it has other helpful features. In a "high-risk, multirisk" environment such as a college computer lab, operation-restricting software not only may prevent viral infection but may help to "idiotproof" the computers as well.

We come, though, full circle back to the corporate climate. It is important also to match the type of program to the type of support provided within the company. Sadly, in many cases, this assessment may go against the use of a superior product. However, note that even the best product is of little use if improperly installed or supported. If routine maintenance is not performed on computers, then a scanner will be of little use, since it needs to be updated from time to time. (Of course, if a company is not doing regular maintenance and support, it is in danger of acquiring more than viral programs . . .)

TYPES OF ANTIVIRALS

I am not suggesting that a standard for the judging of antiviral software cannot be achieved. It is, however, an extremely difficult task and one that we may not be able to accomplish at this time. One of the consistent barriers to judging software is that antiviral software comes in so many types. I would now like to elucidate upon *my* list of what those types are.

As we proceed in more depth through the various categories of antiviral systems, you will note that almost endless permutations can be made by a combination of the various features. I hope the following will allow you to build your own categories and to judge the software best for your situation.

The first commercial antiviral systems to appear, interestingly enough, relied upon encryption. This was likely a holdover from the fact that most "serious" security types come from a mainframe or communications environment. Encryption is, of course, a good way to ensure that people cannot gain unauthorized access to your information. While it does have some potential for protection of existing software, few systems primarily targeted at viral infections now use encryption at all.

Those early encryption systems were often paired with operation-restricting software. Restrictive software has continued to be a reasonably popular means of defense, probably because it *does* defend systems and prevent the infection of programs and disks.

Both of these two, however, are special cases of activity-monitoring software. This software, as the name implies, oversees the operation of the computer and alerts the user when suspicious activity takes place. I differentiate it from operation-restricting software because control is left in the hands of the user. (Interestingly, a number of these programs are named "Vaccines," even though their actual method of operation has little in common with a biological vaccine.)

Change-detection software, also known as integrity-checking software, determines whether the program, file, or system has changed, as compared against a previously established database. If a sufficiently broad overview of the system is taken, this will provide 100 percent effective detection of a viral infection, but it also may raise a number of false alarms.

Scanners, particularly signature scanners, are currently the most popular of antiviral software. This is likely to be due to three factors: the fact that viral programs are specifically identified; the inclusion of disinfecting software with most scanners; and the fact that it's easy to play numbers games with signature-scanning programs.

ACTIVITY MONITORS

Although the analogy should not be stretched too far, activity monitors do share some characteristics, though not functions, of medical vaccines, being memory-resident and preventive in nature. An activity monitor watches for suspicious activity. It may, for example, check for any calls to format a disk or attempts to alter or delete a program file while a program other than the operating system is in control. It may be more sophisticated, and check for any program that performs "direct" activities with hardware, without using the standard system calls.

Activity monitors represent some of the oldest examples of antiviral software. Generally speaking, such programs followed in the footsteps of the earlier antitrojan software, such as BOMBSQAD and WORM-CHEK in the MS-DOS arena, which used the same "check what the program tries to do" approach. This tactic can be startlingly effective, particularly given the fact that so much malware is slavishly derivative and tends to use the same functions over and over again.

It is, however, very hard to tell the difference between a word processor updating a file and a virus infecting a file. Activity-monitoring programs may be more trouble than they are worth because they can continually ask for confirmation of valid activities. The annals of computer virus research are littered with suggestions for virusproof computers and systems that basically all boil down to the same thing: if you restrict the operations that a computer can perform, you can eliminate viral programs. Unfortunately, you also can eliminate most of the usefulness of the computer.

Activity monitors may also be bypassed by viral programs that do low-level programming rather than using the standard operating-system calls, or those that actually replace the standard system calls with viral triggers. In addition, while new viral technologies, such as stealth and polymorphism, have little effect on activity monitoring, new concepts in viral spread, such as companion or spawning viruses require new checks to be added to monitors. (The novelty of an idea does not have to be all that radical. One previously very popular vaccine, very effective against early boot sector infectors such as BRAIN, turned out to be completely useless against Stoned.)

I would like to cover, under the topic of activity-monitoring software, two variations on the theme. The first variation is very minor: that of operation-restricting software. Operation-restricting software is similar to activity-monitoring software, except that instead of watching for suspicious activities, it automatically prevents them. In the past I have tended to class operation-restricting software as a separate type of antiviral, even though the difference between a "monitor" and a "restrictor" is really only one of degree in the information given to the user. The reason that I have done so is that the degree is not a continuum, and there tends to be a definite gap between those programs that inform the user and those that do not.

As with mainframe security "permission" systems, these operation-restricting packages allow you to restrict the activities that programs can perform, sometimes on a file-by-file basis. However, the more options these programs allow, the more time they will take to set up. Again, the program must be modified each time you make a valid change to the system, and, as with activity monitors, some viral programs may be able to evade the protection by using low-level programming. Most general microcomputer security programs use operation restriction.

It is important, when evaluating both activity-monitoring and operation-restricting software, to judge the extent to which the operator is given the option of "allowing" an operation. It is also important, therefore, that the operator be informed, not only that a particular program or operation should be halted, but also why. There should not be too many false alarms generated by the software, and it would be helpful to have the option of "tuning" the software to be less, or more, sensitive to a given type of activity.

The second variant on activity monitoring may at first seem to be wildly divergent: heuristic scanning. However, please note that heuristic scanners attempt to do the same thing that an activity monitor does, if in a slightly different way. Instead of waiting for a program to perform a suspicious activity, a heuristic scanner examines the *code* of a program for suspicious calls (supposedly before the program is even run). Although such scanners may now (in their current, natal state) be limited to checking for very generic sections of code, eventually they will require a good deal more "intelligence" to justify the analytical nature implied by the name "heuristic." Heuristic scanners are currently tools best used by those with some background in virus identification and prevention, but they hold promise to become very useful tools, even for the novice, with future development.

As I mentioned earlier, the first commercially released antiviral software was primarily dependent upon encryption. I suspect that this is because much of the security world is concerned with confidentiality of data. The earliest companies to release commercial antiviral programs probably had strong backgrounds in mainframe and corporate security systems. Therefore, they automatically turned to encryption for an answer to this new security problem.

(I deliberately stress "commercial" here. A number of good shareware and even freeware antiviral programs were available as early as the summer of 1988. Many of those were far superior to the commercial products, as evidenced by the fact that some of the shareware programs still exist, while few of the commercial products do.)

Beyond the general bias toward encryption of the corporate security types, there were some indications that encryption might do a good job. For one thing, viral programs require a "stable" computing environment as much as any other program—perhaps more so. Any change to the environment might stop a virus from functioning properly. The primary expectation was that if all programs were run through a decrypting filter before control was passed to them, then any virus that did attach to them would be "decrypted" into garbage at best, and therefore the worst that could happen was that an infected program would fail, rather than causing further infections.

This theory still gets voiced from time to time. The most recent version of it suggests using PKLite or other such programs, which create "compressed executables" to protect your programs.

Unfortunately, this theory has a number of problems. For one thing, it doesn't address the issue of BSIs. For another, if an infection is "allowed" into the system, it is possible for it to use the encryption mechanism itself in order to infect the encrypted files. Also, if an infected file is introduced into the system and encrypted, it may escape detection by other antivirals, such as signature scanners. (Compressed executables, for example, may be infected either "internally" or "externally," and internal infections can be very difficult to detect.) Finally, encryption adds another layer of operation to the system, with all the attendant problems of computer speed and power, as well as all the possibilities of conflicts and crashes.

It is very difficult to specify in advance what you should check for in activity-monitoring software, since the developers are loath to state, in detail, what the program will be checking for. (This reluctance is understandable: if a developer "advertises" exactly what the product checks for, virus or trojan writers will simply use another route.) In addition, the work or computing environment must be considered, as well as, in certain cases, the corporate climate. Activity monitors, more than scanners or change detectors, are subject to review on the basis of political rather than technical grounds.

Activity-monitoring software should be thoroughly tested in a real working environment (one that uses all the programs you normally use, in the ways you normally use them) for some time in order to ensure that the vaccine does not conflict with normal operation. This "real" environment includes the "real" people who will be using the software: choose your sample population carefully and avoid simply giving it to the tech-support office to test. Two important factors to check for are the number of false positives (or false alarms) that the software generates and the level of information given to the user when an anomalous condition is detected. This last is difficult to judge: user populations that tend to remain at the novice level will not have more confidence in the system, regardless of how much information it gives them.

Activity monitors have a good chance to detect viral activity of new and unknown viral strains, but it would be very difficult to agree with those that claim to be able to detect "all current and future" viral programs. While it might generally be held to be a good thing to prevent changes to the file directory, it is unlikely that system viral programs could have been foreseen prior to the existence of the DIR family. Activity monitors are also unlikely to work well against companion-type viral programs without specific safeguards in place.

Monitoring programs should be tested against a battery of viral programs, but the test suite should be collected on the basis of function rather than simply diversity. If the activity monitor is effective against

Stoned, then Empire, Michelangelo, and Monkey variants are unlikely to trouble it.

Unfortunately, activity monitors tend to encourage a set-and-forget mentality toward viral protection. This should be avoided at all costs. If activity-monitoring software is your protection method of choice, continue to keep up-to-date with viral methods and to test your software regularly.

CHANGE-DETECTION SOFTWARE

Change-detection software, also often referred to as integrity-checking software, examines system and/or program files and configuration, stores the information, and compares it against the actual configuration at a later time. Most of these programs perform a checksum or cyclic redundancy check (CRC) that will detect changes to a file even if the length is unchanged. Some programs will use sophisticated encryption techniques to generate a signature that is, if not absolutely immune to malicious attack, prohibitively expensive, in processing terms, from the point of view of a virus.

A sufficiently advanced change-detection system, which takes all factors including system areas of the disk and the computer memory into account, has the best chance of detecting all current and future viral strains. However, change detection also has the highest probability of false alarms, since it will not know whether a change is viral or valid. (Additional thought put into the installation of change-detection software will go a long way to reducing the level of false-positive results. As always with security systems, there is a trade-off between the easy and the effective.) The addition of intelligent analysis of the changes detected may assist with this failing.

There are three major shortcomings of change-detection software. First, it provides no protection, but only after-the-fact notification of an infection. It is, therefore, quite possible to install an infected program on your system and have it continue to infect other programs. The subsequent infections will (or should) be detected, but the change-detection software will not identify the original culprit. (Deductive reasoning, along with the software's assistance, though, may.)

Second, you must inform the software of any changes *you* make in the system, otherwise the change-detection software will generate a false alarm. This means you must have sufficient knowledge of the system to know *when* you are making changes. Each invocation of SETVER, for example, changes the program file, whereas setup changes made to

WordPerfect sometimes alter the program file and/or change an external data file.

Third, as with scanning software, change-detection software may not see changes made, and hidden, by stealth viral programs. However, even with the most esoteric stealth technology, a virus must change *something* in the system. Therefore, sufficiently broadly based change detection is the best bet for absolute detection of all viral programs— if you can put up with the false alarms.

There are numerous implementations of change-detection software. Some versions of this software run only at boot time; others check each program as it is run. Some of these programs attach a small piece of code to the programs they are protecting, and this may cause programs that have their own change-detection features, or nonstandard internal structures, to fail. Some programs only protect system software; others only protect program files. Some change detectors keep the signature file in the root directory; some in the "local" directories. Some allow you the option of keeping the file on a diskette off-line and out of the reach of viral programs that might try to damage it.

A major factor in judging change-detection systems is installation and operation time. Since the system will be calculating signatures of all (or all selected) programs on your system (sometimes with very sophisticated algorithms), it may take some time to install and to update each time you make a change to your system. It may also take an unacceptable amount of time to boot or to check out a program before allowing software to run. You may find that a change-detection system with a "weaker" calculation algorithm is more effective for your situation given the time savings.

The answers to these questions should be available to you in the documentation. You shouldn't need to run the program to test it out. Unlike activity-monitoring software, there is no need for the producer of change-detection software to hide anything from either you or virus writers. A truly complete change-detection package is unbeatable (dependent, of course, on a "clean start") and does not require any hidden "tricks." A package with documentation that does *not* answer all your questions suggests lack of confidence on the part of the author, and possible weakness in the program.

Note that the preceding presumes that you are protecting a single computer or a local office. Change detection has other uses, including authentication of material sent via email or retrieved from an archive site. The calculation algorithms used in those situations must be much stronger. Delays of mere seconds caused by trying to "crack" protection will be detectable locally: it would be no problem to spend three days cracking the security of an archived file.

SCANNERS

Scanning software is, paradoxically, the least protective and historically most useful of antiviral software. These programs examine files, boot sectors, and/or memory for evidence of viral infection. They generally look for viral signatures, sections of program code that are known to be in specific viral programs but not in most other programs. Because of this, scanning software will generally detect only known viruses and must be updated regularly. Some scanning software has resident versions that check each file as it is run, but most require that you run the software "manually." It is also the classic case of "bolting the door after the horse is gone," since scanners only find out if an object *is* already infected. They do not perform preventive functions.

Why then, with all the disadvantages of scanning software, are they the most successful of antiviral packages? Generally speaking, it may be because they force the user to pay attention to the system. Again, when a user relies on one particular method of protection, he or she is most vulnerable.

I have stated that scanners can only find infections after they occur, but that does not mean that scanners cannot play a preventive role in protecting the system. If scanning software is used consistently to check each disk or file that enters a system (and is kept up to date), the chance of a viral infection being allowed to enter is greatly reduced. Unfortunately, the use of scanners tends to be less than effective in many cases. My own experience suggests that the most widely used scanning software, generally updated every month or two by the developer, is, on average, 11 months out of date on most user systems. In one case I was assured that a computer was protected because the vendor had installed antiviral software. On examination, this turned out to be a manually invoked scanner, long out of date, in an archived (and therefore nonexecutable) file, with no provision for either automated invocation or instructions for the users.

A recent addition to scanners is intelligent analysis of unknown code, currently referred to as heuristic scanning. More closely akin to activity-monitoring functions than traditional signature scanning, this looks for "suspicious" sections of code that are generally found in viral programs. While it is possible for normal programs to want to "go resident," look for other program files, or even modify their own code, such activities are telltale signs that can help an informed user come to some decision about the advisability of running or installing a given new and unknown program. Heuristics, however, may generate a lot of false alarms, and may either scare novice users, or give them a false sense of security after "wolf" has been cried too often.

Scanning software should be able to identify the largest possible number of viral programs and should be able to identify variations on the more important sections of code (that is, it should be able to "accept" the removal of text strings and other simple modifications that bush-league hackers might make). Note, however, the proviso that it is more important to identify some viral programs than others. For ease and speed of updating, the signatures should be stored in a separate file, and there should be a means to add new viral signatures to the file. For security, both scanning software programs and signature files should be renameable.

Areas scanned should include not only the identifiable program files, but all files, if necessary. (This has become much more important recently with the advent of successful Windows viral programs coincident with the new Windows "embedding" function. "Embedding" can allow infected viral programs to be contained, in an executable form, within document and data files, which are normally ignored by scanners.) Scanners should have the ability to search the more common archiving formats as well, particularly those that support self-extraction functions. Disk boot sector and hard-disk partition boot records should be scanned, as well as (in this day of stealth viruses) memory.

Scanners, as noted before, are the easiest antiviral programs to "rank." It is much more difficult to determine the utility of those types of programs that purport to protect against unknown and "future" viral programs. It is, indeed, impossible to judge these programs against any absolute standard: they will be judged by future events, and the future isn't here yet.

Many future viral programs will follow the patterns of those from the past. Most "new" viral programs are very simple modifications of existing ones. However, while it may be possible to foresee some of the potential loopholes that viral programs might use, it is impossible to know which ones will actually be used. It would also be excessively difficult to protect against all of the myriad potential means of attack.

A strong, albeit nontechnical, reason why scanners are so popular is the specific identification of the particular virus responsible for an infection. Rather than telling you merely that something is amiss, a scanner gives you a name. More than that, scanner authors, given the necessity of knowing the specifics of a virus in order to identify it, had an advantage in finding out how a virus infected a file, and therefore how it could be removed. Scanning software was, therefore, the first to offer disinfection of viral infections, either as a feature or in an adjunct program.

This would seem to be, and likely is, another reason to prefer scanning antiviral software. However, beware. Disinfection is by no means the optimal way to deal with viral infections. The best solution is to delete (and, preferably, overwrite) the affected file or area and restore programs from original sources. BSIs affect a whole disk and therefore present greater problems, but in most cases material can be recovered from infected disks, and the disks themselves "cleansed" in various ways. There comes a point at which the trade-off between security and convenience tips the scales in favor of disinfection, but be aware of the dangers.

In many cases, disinfection is simply not possible. An overwriting virus, for example, will not keep any track of the material it destroys when it dumps itself into a file. Many viruses contain bugs that prevent the recovery of the original file. Also, sadly, disinfection software has been known to contain bugs that left the situation worse after the attempted cleanup than after the infection.

Generally speaking, disinfecting software will contain a description of the specific viral operation of a given viral program, so that the infection process can be reversed. However, virus removal is no longer the exclusive province of scanning software. Two types of generic disinfection now exist. Some change-detection programs store sufficient information about the file to make an attempt to restore it if the damage is not too severe or complicated. Also, heuristic scanning is being used to trace and remove viral infections. So far testing has revealed serious drawbacks to both these applications, but the technology is still in its infancy and shows promise for the future.

OTHER CONSIDERATIONS

McAfee Associates SCAN program is probably the most widely used antiviral in the world and has been for a number of years. (Note that I have not said it was the first, or the best, or the most purchased.) It should, therefore, come as no surprise that SCAN has been the subject of many malicious software attacks. The easiest, of course, is simply to write a trojan and release it under the SCAN name. There have been a number of such trojan versions, so many that there is no point in keeping track of the pseudo-SCAN version numbers. Certain specific viral programs attempt to delete the SCAN program file itself.

SCAN isn't the only program to have had this problem. Indeed, it's almost an indication that you have "made it" in antiviral shareware to have been hit by a trojan version. (Commercial software houses, of course, do suffer from the release of "shareware" pirated copies of their software. And then there are those individuals who decide that they are national agents for a particular piece of software—without telling the authors.)

Some of the attacks are slightly more insidious, such as those that take a working antiviral version and try to "trojanize" it by removing the internal integrity checks and infecting it with a virus. A number of viral programs try to defeat specific antiviral software, not only by erasing the program files themselves, but by erasing ancillary files, such as change-detection image-calculation databases, or scanner virus-signature files. Thunderbyte's heuristic cleaning mode was targeted for a time: one program used it as a "trigger" to infect all files specified to be cleaned. (This didn't last long: within months, at most, Thunderbyte had eliminated the problem.)

Shareware is definitely not the only target here. As soon as an antiviral is released, virus writers notice apparent weaknesses that can be exploited. This is one reason to choose more than one antiviral product. Another is the fact that the weaknesses of one product should be covered by another: the attacks made against one product will likely not work against another. There are, it is true, viral programs that target more than one antiviral. One, in fact, tries to disable no less than 14 different protective programs.

One commercial antiviral has apparently had a lot more promotion than development. It is very widely sold and frequently included with other packages that give it a distribution in the millions. According to all independent tests, it is a mediocre product at best. However, it has some measure of success. It is targeted by a lot of viral programs. Some erase its files; some disable its resident portions. Some viral programs even contain portions of code from the main programs, probably just to confuse things. High praise indeed.

Price is always a consideration when purchasing anything, and antiviral software is no exception. However, in the case of antiviral software, there is an additional consideration: how much is charged to other people, not just yourself. Some antiviral software is free to individuals, or provides or sponsors free versions for the general public. These should be supported.

Well, you may say, that is all very well, and it's nice to see public-spirited companies and all that, but I have my own troubles. It's great that they are altruistic, but why should I be altruistic, too?

Ah, you misunderstand me. I am *not* asking you to support free software out of the goodness of your heart. I am telling you to support it out of self-defense.

The current situation with regard to computer "hygiene" is terrible. Thousands of people are "carriers" of computer viral infections—and don't know it. This is not through any malice on their part, it is simply that too few people understand the problem. During the months leading up to March 1992, no less than 15 different companies, all reputable (some major), sent out products infected with the Michelangelo virus. Computer retail and repair stores are, as of this writing, a major vector for the spread of computer viral programs. Just because you know how to put a computer together, or take it apart and fix it, does not mean you know how to keep yourself, and your customers, virus-free.

Anything, therefore, that helps to eliminate any viral programs will help the "hygiene" of the computer environment as a whole. If a company, or individual, provides materials that help keep the numbers of viral infections down, then regardless of whether you or your company actually use that service or product, that company, or individual, is helping to keep you safe. It is, therefore, in your own interest to support all such services.

F-PROT, in the MS-DOS world, is currently free for individual, noncommercial use. This means that you can legitimately give it to all employees for their home computers. (The fact that it is also arguably the cheapest and most accurate scanner is interesting.) For the Macintosh, Disinfectant always has been free. Padgett Peterson, author of DISKSECURE, also provides the free FixUTIL package. Thunderbyte Scan and VIRx used to be free promotional packages for their respective commercial products; unfortunately, both are now shareware instead. Two very widely promoted commercial antiviral packages brought out free "special editions" prior to March 1992 to search for Michelangelo. I do *not* consider these to have been beneficial since, while they *appeared* to check the whole disk, they only searched for that one specific virus (and, in one case, for "Maltese Amoeba"). The Norton AntiVirus did release a free NAVSCAN at one point; to the best of my knowledge, it has never been updated.

IBM's AntiVirus product is, in most cases and for most people, easy to use. The developers have made intelligent and informed choices in terms of the default operations. In the majority of cases—far and away, the majority of cases—the program will install easily and automatically and will protect the system from most viral infections that the normal user will see. I do not hesitate to recommend it: the existence of the IBM AntiVirus/DOS is, in my view, one of the compelling reasons to prefer PC-DOS over the recent Microsoft versions.

Discerning readers, however, will notice a lack of enthusiasm in this review of the IBM product. Why am I so cautious in praise of a product that is easy to use, technically competent, and reasonably priced?

Ease of use, actually, has a lot to do with it. Experienced computer users will know that user-friendly is a chimera. While some interfaces are very clumsy, after a certain point ease of use comes at the expense of functionality. That is what has happened in the case of the IBM AntiVirus. It is not that the program has been crippled—far from it. The jump from VIRSCAN to the AntiVirus has added significant new programming, which makes the protection more secure than before. Users who are not "virus literate" will not notice the changes, as they have been incorporated into, and integrated with, the scanning process. The trouble is, advanced users will not be able to take advantage of the new functions.

Personally, I do not like GUIs. In my opinion, the addition of a GUI to the IBM AntiVirus adds nothing to the protection provided and, in fact, slows the operation of the program. In this, however, I am in the minority. Millions (more than ten million, to quote the gospel according to Microsoft) prefer pictures to speed. It is not always a question of one or the other, though. An option can be built into the program to allow access to the more advanced functions.

(There are those who will take issue with my statement that a GUI does not add protection to the system. After all, a program is only as good as its use. A GUI, the promoters will say, encourages use. That is only true in situations where the GUI aids in the interaction between the program and the user. In the case of the IBM AntiVirus, the program has been very well designed to work with as little interaction as possible. In this situation, a GUI has little purpose. I do not perceive, in this particular case, that the GUI actually does anything to assist the user to increase the level of security. In fact, it is my opinion that the inclusion of the GUI may be responsible for certain problems in design and documentation. In that case, the user may be given a false sense of security, thinking that the system is using a variety of protection methods, when, in fact, the user may have failed to invoke some of them because their use is not intuitive or obvious.)

The new product indicates that IBM is committing serious resources to the project. It is a far cry from the VIRSCAN program with its dot matrix labels. IBM deserves some commercial success with this, and, I suspect, future developments in the program will add some "expert system" intelligence to other antiviral types that have been problematic in the past. I look forward to it.

I just wish it weren't a case of either/or.

LAN SECURITY

Back when LANs and viral programs were both fairly esoteric phenomena, people used to ask me if viral programs would work on a network. "Why should they?" I used to reply, "Nothing else does."

Well, times and technologies have changed. Incompatibility is no longer an issue, and therefore no longer any protection. Within limits, viral programs will work, and infect, on networks as well as stand-alone machines.

LANs do have certain advantages. Boot sector infectors, for one thing, will *not* infect across networks. And since LANs cut down on disk exchange and "sneakernet," the risk of the most successful infections is reduced. Reduced, mind, not eliminated.

Novell has been the target of a number of accusations in regard to antiviral security. Understandably, they have been a bit touchy in response. Let it be said, then, that no known virus has successfully been able to subvert Novell's security attributes—when properly implemented.

That said, it must be admitted that very few LAN administrators know how to set up proper security. The establishment of appropriate rights, privileges, and attributes is a task that not all mainframe systems operators understand, and few network managers take the time to ground themselves thoroughly in security concepts.

Network security, over the years, has also received some knocks from deliberate attacks. A group of Dutch hackers wrote a program that would look for passwords on the network traffic. Another program exploited an unusual bug in the LOGIN program in an attempt to gain SUPERVISOR access. Both of these programs, however, required physical access to a node on the network for a length of time. Neither was in any way viral.

One Novell-specific virus has, in fact, been written. The GP-1 virus is rather old. It does *not* manage to break Novell's security and infect properly protected programs. It is designed, however, to go resident on workstations and to collect passwords as logins are done on the net. These passwords are then broadcast on the net, supposedly to a receiver program. The receiver program has never been found. (This seems to be an unnecessary bit of overkill: it is quite easy to make a program to obtain any passwords transmitted over an Ethernet backbone.)

A significant proportion of all microcomputers in the business environment are connected to some form of LAN. You may have noted that the discussion of antiviral software has not addressed this area.

There are two reasons for this. The first is, basically, that any antiviral program can work in a micro attached to a LAN almost as easily as a micro that is not so attached. The second is that LAN-specific antivirals are still in their infancy.

This is not to say that such products do not exist. You will see mention of such products in my reviews and in the list of vendor contacts. Indeed, the LAN antiviral seems to be something of a growth market, at the time of this writing, with almost everyone bringing out an NLM version of their product.

Which is one of the problems. NLM stands for NetWare Loadable Module. Novell NetWare, in other words. Regardless of what you may think of Novell, their product, or their market share, these programs will not work with any other LAN operating system. Since antiviral software has to be system-specific (it must be, since it has to work so intimately with the operating system), it is also *network* operating system–specific.

There is, for example, a major technical division in network systems, between peer-to-peer and client-server networks. Client-server is the traditional style, with servers (usually dedicated) that you have to have an account on and sign in to. These systems are in a position to enforce certain measures onto the client at login. Peer networks, on the other hand, allow basically any node on the network to grant access to any resource it controls. However, once access is granted, the connection can be made without further activity. Note that this is not to say that peer-to-peer networks are inherently less secure than client-server architectures. In fact, some would argue just that point. The real issue, though, is that the security concerns and procedures are different.

Many of the functions of LANs, however, are the same. For example, email is almost universal these days. Email is used by some of the specialized LAN antivirals to alert the administrator to a security breach or possible infection. This is an admirable feature—and one that, with a minimum of time and "batch" or "script" programming skills, can be duplicated on almost any network. The same can be said of "centralized" logging of scanning and audit reports, updating of scanners, and a number of other supposedly advanced features. One need not accept an inferior antiviral product simply because it has LAN capabilities.

There are a number of uses you can make of LAN features and functions. These do not require specialized programs for LAN antiviral protection, although some may be assisted by small utility programs. All of these functions will need some level of programming skills, and some may tax the limits of intermediate computer users. However, LAN administration is not for the faint of heart, anyway.

So you want to make sure that all copies of your antiviral programs are kept up-to-date? Well, why not just have one copy? If your work is heavily involved with the LAN, simply call the antiviral program from the server. If you really do need copies on each machine, there are a number of ways to ensure regular updates. This could be as simple as having a copying process invoked when a user signs on to a client-server LAN. Small utility programs could compare file dates, or you could simply use a copy program that will only copy a source to a destination if the destination is older than the source.

If you want to collect all audit or report logs to one location, nothing could be simpler. Invoke the antiviral from a batch file. The batch file will also create a file noting the workstation, date, and time. Both the identification file and the report file can easily be appended to a master report file in a central location or server. Generally, this is a simple copy function. If there is any problem with the creation of a master file, separate files can be collected in one directory, or in sub-directories for each workstation.

Most antiviral programs will return one code if they find something and another if they don't. These codes can be used to decide whether or not to send a mail message. Voilà! We have an automated virus-alert reporting system that can send a warning to the LAN administrator or to the security specialist. The message can be a simple, "Come look at Larry's machine." Alternately, the report log generated by the antiviral could be written to disk and sent as well. Most LAN email systems write messages as a text file in the first place. The log file can simply be sent as a message every time it is run (similar to the collecting of reports at a central location), or since you really only want the exception reports, sent only if the "found something" code has been set.

It may be desirable to check for the presence or activity of resident activity monitors or scanners. The better antiviral packages, which contain resident program components, also contain programs that will check for the background program. These checking programs can be run during login on a client-server network—and the login can be logged out if the checks fail.

MEMOIRS OF A (REM DEPRIVED) VIRUS RESEARCHER

I talk in my sleep.

I suppose a lot of people do that, but my wife assures me that I talk unusually clearly and forcefully, if no more coherently. (She has to assure me: I, of course, am sound asleep and in no position to validate this for myself.) Although what dreams I can recall (and they are not many) do not feature computers, the ones I "report on" must.

There was, for example, the time that I declaimed, according to Gloria, in ringing, authoritative, and unassailable tones, that "The system is using five point zero!"

All previous "dream state"ments, however, were surpassed last night. My wife, having returned from a nocturnal visit to "the facilities," had just snuggled down under the covers. (This was written during the winter.) I suddenly turned to her and threw back the covers.

Gloria (very reasonably, in view of the fact that we were exposed to a somewhat chilly environment): Why did you do that?

Me (very decidedly): The!

Gloria: (This must be important!) . . .

Me (in best James T. Kirk style): The!

Gloria: (A very definite, definite article!) . . .

Me: The! Attack!

Gloria (becoming concerned): (!!!!?!?!) . . .

Me: Prevention!

Gloria (becoming less concerned): (Must be to do with computer-virus stuff.)

Me: System!

Gloria (relaxing): (Definitely virus stuff.)

Me (much, much less decidedly): And all that stuff . . .

Gloria (attempting to stifle hysterical laughter): . . .

Me (with some return to my earlier certitude): . . . has no more information.

After which, she got the blankets back.

CHAPTER 7

THE VIRUS AND SOCIETY

This chapter is going to deal with less technical material, possibly even less factual material, more opinion, and, of course, my opportunity to indulge myself in speculation. (There are probably those who feel I've been too self-indulgent already.) It is almost obligatory to have a chapter on social or future speculations in technical books these days, but social discussions have a very solid position in the study of viral programs.

In the first place, viral programs rely much more on sociology and psychology than technology to operate. This is not to say that virus writers are social psychologists of any skill; after all, most of them can barely get a virus to work, let alone successfully get it to spread very far in the wild. The programming of a virus, though, does not really require much skill beyond that of any minor utility program. Viral programs, if successful, are successful because of their manipulation of user actions and understanding. Programs are shared; therefore, some viral programs attach directly to other programs in order to be "shared" to other systems. Disks are shared; therefore, some viral programs attach themselves to disks in order to be "shared" to other systems.

A great many people feel that viral programs are a problem limited only to the MS-DOS operating system. PCs, so the theory goes, have no real security provisions and therefore are subject to virus attacks. The implication is that more sophisticated operating systems, usually those for mainframes, are not subject to the same types of attacks. This hypothesis is usually extended to say that future operating systems will be even more secure, and that the virus threat will soon be a historical footnote.

There is a lot to be said for this argument. Researchers are well aware that some relatively simple changes to, for example, the MS-DOS operating-system boot sequence would eliminate the most widespread and successful of the current crop of viral programs. To the developer of the best of these systems, it is particularly galling that the three major operating-system vendors refuse to incorporate such protection, and that the largest of these vendors has turned to a very ineffective after-the-fact solution.

Those who have studied the problem, however, and know best the weaknesses of the current systems also know that the virus problem will not go away. Viral programs use the same functions that useful programs use. The only way to reduce the possibility of a virus is to reduce the utility of the computer. Current viral programs may "die" as new computers and operating systems take over from the present ones, but new viral programs will take over—in new ways.

It is also important to note that, although there may be some debate over precise definitions, viral programs *have* successfully attacked mainframe systems. And no micro virus has ever infected over 3,000 systems—within hours of its release—as the Internet Worm did.

Those who postulate that new, or more secure, operating systems or computers can completely eliminate the risk of viral programs profoundly misunderstand the importance of the nontechnical aspects of security. Viral programs depend primarily upon people acting like people. A virus cannot attack a computer system without help from the user. The real trick lies in finding a way to make the user help the attacking program without realizing it.

Although I have stressed the importance of defining the difference between a reproductive viral program and a static trojan horse program, in this sense all malicious programs are examples of trojans. The logic bomb hidden in an accounting package is only activated because the user assumes the program is only an accounting package. The disk-reformatting trojan is only run because the user believes the BBS description that this program adds graphics to the system. The user is careless about having the disk in the A: drive when powering on the computer because the user believes the disk is blank. It is—except for the boot sector, which is infected.

The original Trojan horse was not an advance in military technology, or even in strategy: it was a trick. A pretty stupid trick, when you think of it. The Trojan horse was of absolutely no danger to Troy—as long as it was left outside the walls. Had the people of Troy left it there, the Greeks would either have starved to death, or, more likely, given up after a few days and shamefacedly slunk off home. However, the Trojans behaved as you would expect people to behave when "acquiring" a gift or prize—they gave it a place of honor . . . thus becoming the authors of their own downfall.

This is the reason that new operating systems will not, ultimately, be able to avoid the virus issue. Technology changes, but human nature doesn't. People will still use the ease and convenience of common procedures and beliefs. A brief survey of viral variants tends to indicate that they bear no relationship to the sophistication of operating systems, but only to systems in use. As new "standards" take hold, they will become subject to viral attacks of some (probably new) description.

The final argument comes from an interesting observation made by David Chess. This statement is that, far from being insecure, a stand-alone PC is *very* secure. The only way to subvert it is if I am able to sneak in and use your keyboard—or if I can convince you to run a malicious program I have written, or one of its descendants. And that has worked, very well indeed.

THE VIRUS COMMUNITY: TWO SOLITUDES

As with most specialized fields of study there is a subculture involved in the study of viral programs. Several subcultures, in fact. There are those who study to protect against viral programs, those who study to write viral programs, and a few, somewhat bemused, in the middle. Then, within each major grouping, there are a number of smaller, and sometimes competing, associations.

Which came first is a bit of a chicken-and-egg situation, but most of the early viral programs were written by isolated individuals, so I suppose that gives antiviral researchers, as a community, some precedence. Fairly soon after the first viral programs started to be seen in the wild (as opposed to being academic research toys in the lab) those primarily interested in studying and protecting against them coalesced around the *VIRUS-L* Internet distribution list, run by Ken van Wyk. This, with its *comp.virus* Usenet newsgroup mirror, has remained the major meeting place for serious antiviral researchers.

Numerous other organizations have sprung up over the years. One of the most widely known, and somewhat aggravating at times, is the Computer Virus Industry Association (CVIA). Started by John McAfee, it claimed to have 90 percent of the "antiviral market" at a time when those who truly did represent the most widely used antivirals had never heard of him or it. The CVIA has been seen primarily as a marketing tool for McAfee's own software (and must, in that light, be said to have been successful). Some time later, the organizer and promoter of one of the major antiviral conferences decided to start the Antiviral Methods Congress (AMC). Unfortunately, the AMC dissolved within months, and the conference is now basically history, too. Another start-up was the International/National Computer Security Association (ICSA/NCSA). An employee of the original Washington office started a rival NCSA in Philadelphia. The original office is now defunct, and the second office issues press releases from time to time selling books and courses.

In Europe, there is the European Institute for Computer Antivirus Research (EICAR), the Computer Antivirus Research Organization (CARO), and the Virus Test Center (VTC), which all seem to have interlocking memberships. CARO and EICAR are probably the preeminent antiviral organizations at present. An encouraging development is that CARO, particularly, has become much more active in North America in the past year.

Mention should be made of two virus-related (VIRUS and VIRUS_INFO), and a third more general (WARNINGS), Fidonet discussion echoes on bulletin boards. There is also a separate VirNet, which uses Fidonet technology and so may sometimes appear on the same boards. For a long time, very few people frequented both Internet and Fidonet, but now, more cross-posting is occurring, particularly with *VIRUS-L* issues being posted as files to Fidonet. Unfortunately, in the past year the VIRUS and VIRUS_INFO echoes were subjected to an attack by the virus-exchange groups, which consisted of floods of postings of virus source code and pornographic material. At the same time, VirNet distribution in North America appears to have broken down.

Why so many different groups in a community whose major players number less than a full football roster? Well, to a large extent, the antivirus research community represents "Egos-R-Us." Ray Kaplan theorizes that antivirus workers are picked from the ranks of "systems" programmers; in the computer world, the best of the best. None of them have any problems with self-esteem.

The antivirus community, while fragmented, is fairly simple. From the protective standpoint, virus research requires dedication, patience, and long years of very long hours of work. The pro-virus side is a bit more complex.

We will start with a bit of background. The hacker, in computer parlance, was originally someone who was very good with the technology: someone who could do what the majority of others could not. There is some precedent in the nontechnical world for this use of the word. Most hackers would broaden the definition to include other fields: an author with a superlative command of the language might be termed a literary hacker. (Being insufficiently skilled technically to make it as an antiviral hacker, I have hopes in this regard—interestingly, in view of the fact that others might view me as a "hack," a very pedestrian writer.) Hackers are often frustrated by arbitrary restrictions imposed by authorities (restrictions that they often are asked to circumvent—by the same authorities). Combine this frustration with the fact that the view of the computer nerd as socially inept has some validity, and you come up with a group of skilled people who have little time for social or diplomatic niceties. They tend to be much more interested in the possible than with the legal. Their concept of morality also tends to be . . . flexible.

Those who use information with a somewhat restricted circulation to break into computer systems call themselves hackers. For purposes of distinction, many data-security people would refer to them as "crackers." They tend to form small cliques and share information among themselves. (In the popular literature, it tends to be assumed that crackers, generally misidentified as hackers, can also manipulate the telephone systems. Breaking into, or controlling, a telephone switch requires a set of skills completely different from those involved in breaking into a government office's VAX or a college's UNIX machine. Those who play with the telephone switches are called phone phreaks. Although there may be some grudging admiration on both sides, the two groups do not have many members in common.)

(As I was writing this bit, my wife called my attention to a newspaper article discussing a debate regarding the use of the term "nerd." Some regard it as an accolade: a nerd is someone familiar with the technology, or dedicated to its use. Others view it as an insult, seeing only the stigma of the socially inept. There will, therefore, be a wide range of meaning for these terms, particularly in regard to self-reporting.)

In all of these fields there are those who aspire to become part of the elect, but don't have either the skills or the dedication required. These are referred to as "wannabes." Crackers tend to wannabe hackers. There is much less skill involved, however, in breaking into a computer than there is in writing a useful system utility or patch. As one Fidonet tag line has it, "Want to show you're a good programmer? Write a compiler. *Anybody* can write a virus."

Both cracking and phone phreak communities tend to hold virus writers in contempt. There are extremely few virus writers who program with any semblance of skill or imagination. The vast majority of "new" viral strains are simply copies of existing programs, with extremely minor variations made to them. It is, therefore, quite interesting to note that the virus-writing and virus-exchange ("vx") communities seem to want such a high profile.

For one thing, there are at least two books, available in some bookstores, that give sample code and instructions on how to write a virus. (Not necessarily very good instructions or code, but still . . .) One of these books is self-published, but the other comes from an established commercial house.

Then, there are the electronic newsletters. These are perhaps more understandable. After all, it is relatively easy and inexpensive to cobble together the latest virus samples and some self-indulgent whines about how everyone is out to get you, or long harangues directed at various individuals, and call it a newsletter. A lot cheaper, too.

Perhaps a quarter of the total text of these newsletters comprises articles trying to justify the existence of the virus-writing community. The usual argument tends to lean heavily on the right to free speech. The condemnation of virus writing is seen as a form of censorship—or at least, so the articles say. The books, as well, state that you cannot understand a virus unless you are allowed to write one. This is arrant nonsense.

You can explain the principles and operation of a virus perfectly well without giving samples of code to write one. Any competent programmer is able to write a virus: it simply is not that complicated a task. The only people that source code helps are those who are really not fully competent at programming.

In fact, if education were truly the aim of these publications, they are going about it in a very strange way. In one of the books, and the bulk of the magazines, the virus samples are not legible source code, which programmers could read, but "hex dumps." These are completely illegible to the user—but very easy to turn into "live" samples.

This is the final argument against these publications. It is not illegal to write and study such programs. If, however, you publish them, you put them into the hands of . . . well, who knows? Maybe other researchers. Maybe students. Maybe kids with too much time on their hands and a grudge against a local BBS sysop. As one writer succinctly put it, "Do you get guns with your gun magazines? No. Do you get viruses with your virus magazines? Yes."

Whenever I give a full-length seminar, I get a question that, quite frankly, astounds me. Someone always asks, "Isn't it true that the same people who write the antiviral software also write the virus programs?"

My astonishment arises, I suppose, from having been on the "inside" almost since the beginning. Most of these people would no more write, or release, viral programs than they would sprout wings and fly. The members of the antivirus community generally consider virus writers to be unimaginative time wasters, for one thing. For another, producers of antiviral software are far too busy sorting, cataloging, and analyzing the piles of new viral samples that come in each week to do much else. (Which may be why they are so vitriolic when speaking of virus writers.)

Having said that, I must admit that there is some truth to the rumor. At least two "researchers" have written and released viral programs as well. In at least one case, this was said to be a "proof" of the inadequacy of current antiviral software. (The proof didn't work: the software has proven itself against far more sophisticated attacks than that one.) This is part of the reason that the antivirus research community now uses the label "AV" to distinguish themselves from those "virus researchers" who are only interested in writing and trading samples. This is also the reason that AV researchers are so very protective of their own virus samples: not because they want to hoard them, but because of the damaged reputation(s) that could result.

There is another related issue. At least two Very Large Software Companies, with very highly marketed antiviral software, have offered rewards for "new" viral samples. Not just a new copy of the program, updated to include the new samples, but actual rewards of $1,000 (cash money). Given that there is almost no money to be made in virus research of any type, I must admit that I've toyed with the idea of writing samples, myself. For those who are doing it anyway, this must be a wonderful source of income for more and faster computers, software tools, and so forth. And, of course, as long as they are sending in the samples to _____ and _____, they might as well release them into the wild . . . just to prove that they are there, you understand.

More recently, one book publisher and one PC security hardware vendor have offered prizes for virus-writing contests in order to publicize new security product releases. The vendor offered $5,000. Of course, the limitations imposed on the contest proved that they didn't know what a virus was . . .

Antivirus researchers do not give out samples. Although infected files are not treated with quite the same fuss as the infected disk one company showed up at Comdex with one year (locked in a safe, with an armed guard handcuffed to the safe), the restrictions on samples have grown with each passing year. Those who are not part of the AV community view this attitude as either unreasoning paranoia or a form of hoarding.

The charge of paranoia is easily dealt with. Those who are suspicious of requests for virus samples have no lack of evidence. A researcher working on analysis of a new virus is asked for samples. He makes a nonfunctional but unusual change to the code before he releases it. Within a few months this "new version" appears in the wild.

Researchers tag samples with identifying numbers or even their own names. In spite of precautions, either the samples themselves, or fragments of the tagging code, show up in the wild.

Some producers of antiviral programs *do* hoard their samples. After all, it is to your advantage if you can say that your product detects the XYZ virus and that no other product does. On the other hand, that kind of attitude and action is not of much benefit, since, if the XYZ virus were common enough to worry about, it would be easy to get samples. In any case, this is not done within the AV community, as such. The main cries of "hoarder" come from the vx community, who want access to the sample libraries. The vx people steadfastly deny this. Not the fact that they are the only ones whining about the situation: that is only too obvious. However, in true "fox and grapes" fashion, they point to the large libraries of virus samples that they already have. I have no doubt that they have large sample libraries. And they are probably even more disorganized than my own.

Why, then, all the furor over trying to restrict virus sample libraries? For very good reason. Most new "variant" viral strains are simply modifications of existing programs. They are, for the most part, not the product of any programming thought or expertise but simply "cookbook" procedures performed on whatever samples you can find. The more samples you can get, the more variants you can turn out. Thus, any distribution of samples, whether from poor security on the part of the AV community or deliberate efforts on the part of the vx side, will increase the number of new variants seen in the wild. This creates more work for antiviral producers. The vx community, of course, says that it is keeping the AV community in business, and that AV should be grateful. Speaking strictly for myself, I'd be grateful for the chance to sit down and rest for a few months.

(There will be those who say that the additional workload only applies to the producers of scanning programs. True, that *is* the area where new variants produce the greatest workload. However, producers of other types of antivirals are affected as well. In addition, while there is a definite place for generic antivirals, scanners still account for the most popular programs, and the largest number of infections detected.)

In light of the reluctance of antiviral researchers to give out virus samples, a number of individuals have raised the question of how you can become a virus researcher without access to live code. Very often the question is highly suspect, as it is most often put forth by those known to be involved in virus-exchange activities. Still, it deserves to be addressed, both for those who sincerely want to become involved in the research, and in order to reduce its rhetorical value for the vx community.

It isn't easy. As a missionary friend of mine once said, the only people who should do it are those who can't do anything else. In other words, the commitment to the cause has to override almost all other concerns in life. The field moves so rapidly that it is a full-time occupation just to keep up with it. The traffic generated on the nets totals approximately 500 typed pages per week.

So, where do you start? There are no regular courses in the subject, either at academic institutions or through the various technical training companies. (At least two commercial training outfits started such seminars, and then canceled them for lack of business.) A handful of universities have faculty sufficiently interested and experienced to direct your studies, should you wish to do graduate work in the field.

You can, however, do what pretty much all the rest of us did. Study the traffic on the net. The volume may be overwhelming, but that simply means that you have that much more source material. Certainly, if you think you need virus samples, they are far easier to come by today than they were in 1986. If you do develop some background knowledge and help your circle of friends with protection, you are bound to come across a virus sooner or later: these days, probably much sooner. Any university or college micro lab is a fertile source of infections, and probably school labs as well.

The truth of the matter, though, is that you have no real need of live viral code or samples in order to study the issue. In the same way that viral programs use the same functions as normal programs, viral programming uses the same functions as any other programming. Learn about operating systems. Learn assembly-language programming. Learn the internals of the operating system. Learn the programming of peripherals and device drivers. By the time you know enough to take on viral programs, you will not need samples. You will be able to grow your own.

But please, don't release them. Thanks.

VIRAL MORALITY

Most computer users have no problem with the question of whether computer viral activity is good or bad. The only good virus is a dead virus. Period. Thus, it may come as a shock to find that the vx community sees nothing wrong with writing and spreading viruses. One problem with current discussions and literature regarding the ethics of virus writing and distribution is the lack of dialogue between the two opposing camps. There is little real debate on the topic: articles that do get written about it don't have much rigor of thought behind them and usually only "preach to the converted."

For those of traditional moral stance, the current situation is discouraging. Peter Denning's *Computers under Attack* has a very thorough survey of the field, but it provides little in the way of answers or hope. Deborah Johnson's work *Computer Ethics* (for both these texts, see the book review section) is preeminent in the field, but serves only to clarify the problem. Sarah Gordon's interviews with computer students show responses typical of almost all such studies. The base attitude appears to be, "If I find it interesting, and I can do it, why do you say I shouldn't?"

The proponents of security-breaking activities often question the traditional ethical position by asking, "Where's the harm?" This query is directly relevant to discussions of the morality of virus writing.

The AV community is not really opposed to the writing of viral programs. It is seen as a trivial, and therefore pointless, exercise; but not necessarily evil, in itself. The communication of viral program code is also a normal professional and academic activity, as long as it is limited, done for a stated purpose, and the recipients are known. It is the unregulated exchange of virus code and source, providing open access to anyone with a computer and a modem, that is upsetting. Remember that the opposing group is described as the virus-*exchange* community. For the purposes of this section, therefore, references to "virus writing," "virus exchange," or "vx" will mean the uncontrolled or unregulated exchange or provision of access to virus source and object code.

(This does not necessarily mean deliberate distribution of infected programs by such means as infecting a legitimate program and then posting it, without warning, to a bulletin board system. "Trojanizing" of normal software or malicious invasion of systems is certainly happening in some areas, but it is not needed in the current computing situation. Although there is debate over the relative contribution of "natural spread" and virus exchange to the current virus problem, it is known that code made available only as openly published material does eventually infect machines in the normal computing environment. The term vx does not, therefore, require any imputation of sinister motives or hidden activity for the purposes of this discussion.)

There are some gray areas between these two poles. As stated previously, some people have both written antiviral software *and* contributed to viral spread. Given, however, that one could expect a continuum of opinion, those in the middle are remarkably few. Either you are for virus exchange, or against it.

One other, separate, group should be noted. Viral programs are often cited as an example of "artificial life," and the research community in that field, both professional and amateur, has a legitimate interest in viral programming. Work in the "a-life" field, however, does not justify unregulated code and source exchange. For one thing, current viral programs in the wild (those found in normal home and business computers, as opposed to those that exist only in a research or laboratory environment) have only the most tenuous claim to artificial life. Common viral programs are simplistic snippets of code without anything like the complexity of the simplest known natural life-forms. In addition, those who really do work in the artificial life area will be well aware that it does carry possible dangers and that research should be subject to controls similar to those imposed on biological and genetic study.

The most common argument for virus writing tends to boil down to, "You can't stop me." Many promote virus writing on the grounds of freedom of speech, a rather curious position in light of the incoherence of the arguments. (The most vocal of these tend to be Americans, who frequently cite "First Amendment Rights." This refers to the first amendment to the U.S. Constitution, which Americans tend to see as some universal law, rather than an arbitrary political document, however desirable.)

Rights, though, carry with them a weight of responsibility. As is often quoted, your "right" to swing your fist ceases at the end of my nose. You have a "right" to free speech—so long as you are responsible and do not perpetrate fraud. You have a "right" to study whatever you like—so long as you are responsible enough not to carry out experiments in poison with human subjects. No PC is an island—at least, not where viral programs are concerned. Therefore, your "right" to study, write, and distribute viral programs carries the responsibility to ensure that your creations do not—ever—run on machines where they are not authorized.

One of the most confusing aspects of the exchange/no exchange debate is the concept of the good virus. There is nothing inherently evil in the concept of reproduction. (Dangerous, yes.) In fact, the very earliest experiment with self-reproducing programs was the Xerox worm of Shoch and Hupp. This was designed to spawn segments of the central program on other machines in the network, thus bringing the power of many processors to bear on a single problem. Thus, in theory, viral programming could represent the same level of advanced technology in software that parallel processing represents in hardware.

That's the theory. And it is promoted by no less eminent a researcher than Dr. Fred Cohen, who did seminal work on the security-breaking class of viral programs in a thesis, in 1984, and dissertation, in 1986. Unfortunately, the theory founders on some rather hard facts.

The earliest attempt to write reproductive programs was by Shoch and Hupp and was meant for productive purposes. Cohen is interested in the use of such programs to handle computer maintenance and management tasks. Many such tasks are simple, but repetitive—ideal candidates for the use of viral programs. The concept of beneficial viral programs is not, therefore, unthinkable. It is, however, problematic. Some consider that future advances in technology and more careful programming will avoid the kind of trap that befell Shoch and Hupp's infamous Xerox worm. Others believe that the problems are too great to be overcome.

There are three questions to ask of a new, inherently dangerous, technology. Has it a useful application? Can it fulfill that application better than current technologies? And can the danger, either inherently or effectively, be controlled?

To date, no one has answered those three questions. Although a variety of uses has been proposed for viral programs, there are none that are not effectively being done by other means. No viral programs have, indeed, been seen to be as effective as normal systems. Operating-system upgrades could not guarantee universal coverage. Network management tasks could not promise reliable feedback. Automated utilities would confuse novice-level users, who never run utilities anyway. The most useful function is still that proposed by Shoch and Hupp—and their programs were not, strictly speaking, viral.

(Vesselin Bontchev's examination of this question in "Are 'Good' Viruses Still a Bad Idea?", published in the Proceedings of the EICAR 1994 Conference, is the most detailed to date and is required reading for all who want to join the debate. His proposals, while demonstrating good ideas for safety and control, are still primarily an advanced automated distribution system. The necessity for viral functions in this regard is still unproven.)

Some pitfalls are inherent in the viral function. While a reproductive program does not have to cause trouble, the fact that such an entity spreads into new situations, changing them, means that viral code must be programmed with extreme care simply to avoid damage. As evidence, I cite the fact that most viral programs found in the wild do not appear to have been written with the intention of causing harm. The

majority of the problems generated by the most common viral programs are due to programming errors or oversights. Michelangelo has
killed many more systems by creating boot problems due to a conflict
with the Stoned virus than by overwriting disks on the March 6 trigger
date.

Other problems arise from the current computing environment
and the existence of "bad" viral programs. It is hard enough—impossible in any complete way—to tell whether a program is a virus. To
then have to determine whether a given virus is good or bad would be
completely out of the question. Thus, to release supposedly beneficial
viral programs into the current maelstrom without first having brought
the virus problem under some semblance of control would be terribly
irresponsible.

In relation to all of this, it has been suggested that viral programs
should be written to get rid of viral programs. This has been tried. Den
Zuk was intended to eliminate the BRAIN virus. Two observations: it
hasn't, and, in most cases, the cure has been worse than the disease.
Den Zuk is generally more dangerous than BRAIN.

Those in the vx camp will point to two current viral programs that,
they say, do have useful functions. One of these programs produces
compressed executable files, thus saving disk space, while the other
performs encryption on files. However, both of these functions are provided by other programs—from which, indeed, code was stolen for
those two "good" virals. Neither of the viral programs are as easy to use
or control as the original programs, and both have bugs that must place
them firmly in the malware grouping, for nuisance value, if nothing
else.

Currently, therefore, the utility of viral programs is very much unproven. This would mean, though, mean only that they are neutral,
were it not for the lack of any demonstrable control. Methods of control
have been discussed primarily by Fred Cohen, but even he remains
unconvincing. The mechanisms generally are limited to environmental
checks that can either fail or be easily cut out of the program.

(Cohen frequently cites viral "programs which have been running
since 1986 with no ill effects" and speaks of a VCE—a viral computing
environment. There are two points to be noted here. One is that Cohen
has not yet described his viral programs in anything like the detail he
put into his earlier work, so there can be no independent assessment
of his claims. The second point is that the very term, VCE, implies that
a viral computing environment is substantially different, and should
be kept separate, from the "normal" computing environment as it is

currently known. A VCE may very well be a powerful entity, but it is still an unknown and unproven concept.)

Computer viral programs have an inherent danger: that of reproduction and spread. If you study explosives and pass along that knowledge, you also have to pass along the materials before there is any risk of a blast. Even then, the materials do not multiply themselves: when exhausted, another supply must be found. The same is *not* true of viral programs. These entities are *designed* to reproduce. And, unlike the study of dangerous animals, or even germ warfare, viral programs are built to reproduce, multiply, and spread without the aid of a skilled, or even aware, operator. If you are careless with a deadly animal or weapon, it is still only a single danger in a localized area. If you are careless with a computer virus, it can spread worldwide.

We do not use computers because they are smart. Computers *aren't* smart. Sometimes we use them because they can do calculations very quickly, but even this is only a special case of the real value of computers. Computers always do the same thing in the same way. They are repeatable. They are, in this manner, reliable. Even a computer error can be useful to us—so long as it always happens the same way.

Consider, then, the computer virus. To reproduce without the informed assistance of the user, the virus must be, in the computer sense, transparent. It must operate without alerting the operator, or interfering with the operator's interaction with the computer. If the virus even posts a notice ("Hi! I am infecting object X!"), it has a nuisance value and is, therefore, not good. (Vesselin Bontchev notes that even such a notice, by possibly delaying a process, may have grave consequences far beyond annoyance.)

If, however, the virus does *not* notify the operator, then the operator is not aware of some additional code in the machine. This extra code will have an unknown, and inherently unknowable, effect on the computer. The operations of the computer are, therefore, no longer repeatable. This is a Bad Thing (™).

Some will protest that I have overblown the danger of both the notification messages and the possibility of conflicts. The point that I am trying to make is that you cannot predict the harm that may arise from interference either with the operator or the programs. Software is digital and is subject to catastrophic collapse without prior warning. For those without a background in computer risk assessment, an excellent overview for the nonprofessional is found in Lauren Wiener's *Digital Woes*. An intriguing compilation of the types of things that can go wrong is to be found in Peter Neumann's *Computer-Related Risks* (again, see the book review section). At the very least, as Sarah Gordon points out, the virus is an autonomous agent, making decisions and carrying out activities according to its own internal constructs and the intention of its programmer. This is very likely not in correspondence with your own intention and is therefore an invasion of privacy.

A number of virus writers will object that their creations simply are not harmful. Not only is it impossible to guarantee that your virus will not conflict with existing systems, you also cannot guarantee that a given system will not conflict with your virus. Almost all file-infecting viral programs will interfere with applications that have an internal integrity checksum or a nonstandard loader and will cause those applications to fail. (An example of this is that Windows programs infected with DOS viral programs always fail to load.) The "Ohio" virus (a prior version of Den Zuk) was not intended to carry any destructive payload, but an unusual interaction with a certain network operating system caused fatal disk corruption.

Historically, and statistically, virus-exchange people have been careless and incompetent programmers. Remember that we are talking vx, here, and those viral programs that have been released into the wild. There may be, carefully hidden in the desk of a virus writer, the "perfect" and harmless virus. If so, we haven't seen it yet. The majority have obvious bugs, sloppy coding, and derivative programming. Less than 1 percent are interesting for *any* reason; only a handful have unique styles of algorithms. And even these last have programming pathologies.

Two other reasons are often given to justify virus exchange. The first is generally described as experimentation and education. The second is described as antiviral research or, more commonly, assessment of antiviral programs. These arguments *do* have some validity and should be examined. Ultimately, though, the reality fails to support the claim.

The call for experimentation is somewhat tied to the argument for a good virus. Current viral technology may be crude and ridiculous, but how can it be improved if there isn't any work or sharing of results? Quite true. People in the vx community, however, have obviously not read or noted any programming journals or texts. Discussions of programming and algorithms are supported by well-annotated code fragments. You don't present a whole program to discuss a specific function any more than you send an entire car with a manual on auto repair. You certainly don't use encoded or "DEBUG script" object code: that has no explanatory value at all.

And I have yet to see, in the vx materials, any discussion of legitimate and positive uses for viral technology, any discussion of control technology, or any discussion directed at ensuring that viral programs do not create conflicts.

In regard to education, it is true that a study of viral programs is related to a knowledge of operating system internals, as well as assembly-language programming. However, viral study *requires* such knowledge, rather than providing it. Giving someone a virus and expecting the person to learn from it is akin to "teaching" a surgeon by handing him or her a scalpel and pointing at a patient. Even the vx old guard is beginning to realize this. Viral programs use normal computer functions. If you understand computers, a virus is trivial. If you don't, well . . .

As far as virus-exchange tutorials go, well, let me put it this way. I am a teacher. I also review technical books on a daily basis. Some are great, enough are good, many are bad, and some are just plain awful. Only a few are worse, in terms of tutorial effectiveness, than vx "zines" (electronic periodicals).

Recently, someone who makes his living pushing virus source code promoted a collection of viral programs by suggesting you could test antiviral programs with it. This, superficially, sounds like a good idea—if you don't know what *real* software testing is like. What do we know about the quality of this "zoo" (set of virus samples)? What do we know about the structure, organization, documentation, and so forth? How many duplicates are there? Of course, we *do* want duplicates in some cases; we want every possible variation on polymorphs. (For Tremor, that works out to almost six billion files.) But then, this collection was on a CD-ROM. What a pity. The most successful viral programs are boot sector infectors, and you need to have real, infected disks to truly test for them. At a minimum, you'd want all seven "common" disk formats, in both system and nonsystem versions. That's 14 disks—for *each* BSI.

For all the length of this section, it is still only an overview. And, for all its length, it probably hasn't convinced anyone who thinks virus exchange is a good idea to change his or her mind. Ethics education (it used to be called "values education"), in whatever form and however presented, has very little to show that it works. There are various theories and models of moral training, the most sophisticated probably being Lawrence Kohlberg's "Moral Development" schema. All, though, basically boil down to sitting around talking about ethical dilemmas. They may develop debating skills and rhetorical sophistry, but there is no evidence to suggest that any of these programs leads to any significant change in behavior. Discussions about computer ethics tend to be very pessimistic for just this reason.

Probably the major reason for this is that modern society has no fundamental moral foundation. The most widely cited (and Johnson gives an excellent critique of it) is utilitarianism—"the greatest good for the greatest number." Leaving aside the difficulties of assessing such a measure, utilitarianism, along with all the other modern "humanistic" philosophies, has nothing to support itself. Why is "the greatest good for the greatest number" to be chosen over "what *I* want"? An alternative is deontology, ethical principles derived from the concept of duty. (Ironically, this philosophy, although arguably superior to utilitarianism, is limited to Kohlberg's stage four almost by definition.) Again, however, there is no underpinning to the concept of duty itself.

Ironically, the much-maligned "Judeo-Christian Ethic" did have such a foundation for moral standards—God. The theistic universe may yet have the last laugh over the mechanical universe of B. F. Skinner's *Beyond Freedom and Dignity*.

None of which, unfortunately, looks likely to reduce the virus problem any time soon.

TRUST

In the wake of the Internet/Morris/UNIX Worm of 1988, the statement was made that this kind of activity was very damaging to the computer networks and networking applications that were being built up. The damage was not of a technical nature. The real tragedy was the destruction of trust.

The Internet is a unique and superlative creation. Millions of people are given access to amazing resources, at a fraction of the cost that billing functions alone would consume if it were a strictly commercial enterprise. I am not a starry-eyed visionary seeing a noncommercial utopia here: there is plenty of business conducted on the net already, and it will certainly be a boost to industry and commerce in the coming years. However, it has developed along cooperative lines, with most of the software necessary for its operation being made freely available. The real value of the Internet, though, is not the programming. The material that makes it all worthwhile, that is driving a rush to gain access to the net, is the information. The generation of this information involves literally hundreds of millions of hours of volunteer activity every week, enough to create 50 books' worth of information every day. The Internet can, in a sense, be seen as the largest volunteer organization in the world, after the Christian church. All based on the trust that other users will write other interesting and useful materials.

In the novel *Terminal Compromise* one character makes an impassioned speech about our relationship to the computer. We have a profoundly dichotomous view of information technology. On the one hand, the computer is the scapegoat for every problem that we have. Is a delivery late? The computer is down. Is an order wrong? The computer must have made an error. Are we frustrated by a salesclerk's indifference to our needs or a massive corporate inflexibility? The computer can't cause all that.

On the other hand, our reliance on the computer has become so total that we no longer see the absurdity of some of our beliefs. Do the accounting figures show a loss, although we are clearly doing a booming business? It must be so: the computer calculated it. Do we dislike the candidate of a leading party? We might as well vote for him or her: the computer said that party will win, and we don't want to be unrepresented. A recent stock market crash was traced not to a crop failure, not to a resource exhaustion, not to a destruction of industrial capacity, but to the fact that preprogrammed trading software triggered a massive sell-off. The computer said the stock would crash, so it did.

Society is built on trust. We must trust, to a certain extent, to get anything done. We trust that the person with the large knife is going to chop up the steak for our dinner, rather than eviscerate us. We trust that the person with the gun is only going to give us a speeding ticket, not shoot us. We trust that the person with the club is going to hit the small white ball, not us (as much as they may wish to when they miss the small white ball).

Trust is not as widely available, in some places, as it once was. We now lock our doors, and probably our windows, too. We spend extra time ensuring that our protective devices are engaged and working. We spend extra resources acquiring protective devices. We do this in the name of "security," because we no longer trust that our persons or goods are safe from those around us.

Security is a chimera, though. As public figures have found, in tragic situations, no one, regardless of stature or protection, is truly secure. Even a president, surrounded by armed guards, is a target for a nut with a gun.

And *that's* when you can trust the guards.

The cracker community derides all talk of security. They talk of having the right to access systems simply because they can. We, the security community, are fools who cannot protect our own systems. Therefore, they do us the favor of trailing through our ill-protected systems, possibly erasing a few files to let us know that they've been by.

Ray Kaplan is famous (in some circles, infamous in others) for his teleconferences where data-security specialists are invited to converse with actual crackers and phone phreaks—to "meet the enemy." At one such session, the "enemy" was presented with a scenario.

"Suppose," he was asked, "you opened your door one day to find someone cracking the lock on your door. Would you accept his right to do that?"

"Certainly," said the enemy—taking the high moral ground of a constant seeker after knowledge, he would ask to see how it was done.

The scenario escalated through better locks, bars on windows, and so forth, until I took the microphone.

"Suppose," I said, "I find this person working on the lock. I am interested in how it is done. My wife, however, is not. In fact, she is decidedly nervous of strangers. I explain this to him and ask that he refrain. Am I within my rights to expect him to do so?"

There was a pause, and then, somewhat reluctantly it seemed, a "Yes."

As contrived as this may sound, I believe that to be a hopeful sign. There is, ultimately, some common ground, and therefore a basis for trust. We have, however, a long way to go to get there.

At the same meeting, another interesting point was raised. A systems administrator from NASA addressed the enemy and was greeted as the keeper of a "big playground" for those of the cracking persuasion. This happened shortly after a much-publicized break-in of the NASA computers. It was at a time when NASA was in great difficulty over a number of issues. Because of all of the problems, NASA's budget had eroded over time, and there was no possibility of looking at new projects: indeed, some of the old ones had to be scrapped or shelved. In all likelihood, that break-in cost the agency many millions of dollars in lost budget allocations, quite apart from any loss, damage, or increased security expenditures it may have directly caused.

More recently, there has been a considerable amount of media coverage given to pornographic materials being carried by bulletin boards and networks and the use of computer messaging by pedophiles to make contact with children. These items create a public sensation out of all proportion to their prevalence, but point out the fact that all these abuses of trust have a larger effect: a change in the public perception.

The crackers' actions are not simply an isolated battle between themselves and the security specialists. The public does not understand the technical niceties of poking around in computers. To the public, primarily non computer-using, a break-in is a violation. The existence of people who routinely break into computers and thereafter boast about it is evidence of a host of brilliant, but lawless, fiends and, therefore, proves that computers cannot be trusted. NASA relies on computers; computers cannot be trusted; ergo, by extension, NASA and all its projects are suspect. Science relies upon computers; computers cannot be trusted; ergo, how can we rely on any information, whether about pollution, fish stocks, medicine, or magic crystals?

Ken Thompson's by now famous lecture, "Reflections on Trusting Trust," has been reprinted many times and is frequently referred to in security articles. In it, he describes how he rewrote a C language compiler program. The new compiler, when compiling the UNIX login program, would produce a login program that would behave normally, except that it would also allow access to any account, with a password of Thompson's choice. In addition, the modified compiler could be used to compile a "normal" version of the source code, but still produce a "modified" compiler. This meant that all overt traces of the modification (that is, the change of the source code) could be removed, but still leave the modification—the "back door" into all accounts—intact.

What Thompson described was not a virus. The trap door could only be implanted in operating or security systems that were compiled by a "modified" compiler. However, it does describe a security weakness that (a) can be propagated and (b) gives no trace of its origin. Identical "normal" source code when compiled with a "normal" compiler gives an exact copy of the "normal" compiler, and when compiled with a "modified" compiler, gives an exact copy of the "modified" compiler. Only an exhaustive and detailed examination of the object (machine) code itself will indicate which version has the problem. Maybe.

The concept of the "trusted source" is an important one in data security. It has an exact and central application in dealing with viral programs. When a virus infection is suspected, you are always told to boot clean with a known clean system disk. The reason for this is that if the virus has used some form of stealth technology to subvert the operating system, then you cannot believe the reports that the system gives you—and that are necessary to determine whether a virus is present.

The concept of the trusted source has another application in virus protection. The virus-protection software, itself, has to be known to be clean, uncontaminated, and uncorrupted. As has been noted, commercial software and "shrink-wrap" are no protection against infection. Authors and distributors of shareware, however, are more sensitive to the issue and are examining various ways to ensure that software can either be guaranteed against tampering or authenticated to be free of any changes.

Finally, there is the most important lesson from Thompson's essay. Particularly in dealing with viral programs, it is important to know that the people with whom you share disks and programs not only bear you no malice, but that they also are capable of defending themselves. That is, after all, one of the key points of the viral program: it uses your system to reproduce and spread without your consent or knowledge. Goodwill, programming skills, resentment of imputations, and even business standing all count for nothing. What matters is, are these people clean?

To close, I would like to address those charged with the responsibility of drawing up guidelines and procedures for antiviral protection within a company. Many companies have established policies stating that an employee found to have brought an infection into business premises is to be fired. This really has the situation backwards. Do you trust your employees? At least, do you trust them to be working *for* you, rather than against you? A dismissal policy shows an extraordinary faith in the ability of an employee to know when he or she has been infected, but an appalling lack of faith in their goodwill. I put it to you that your employees are much more likely to be mistaken than to be malicious. Your policy should reflect caution about abilities, but show trust in your people.

After all, if you mistrust your employees, you have a lot more to worry about than viral infections.

SCOPE

How bad is the situation? Should you be worried at all? How much risk is there?

The truth is, nobody knows.

There are some rough indicators out there, and some studies have been done. There are even the beginnings of mathematical models of viral spread. However, it is almost impossible to get an accurate picture.

For one thing, the picture is constantly changing. The virus situation changes faster than any other computer-related technology, with the possible exception of the Internet. Generations of operating systems, applications software, and computer hardware seem to be on 18- to 24-month cycles. New versions of antiviral software are released quarterly or even sooner. While the explosive, exponential growth in the numbers of new viral strains has seemed to lessen, there are still hundreds of new strains being seen every month.

Primarily, though, the problem lies in getting the information.

Studies of the problem rely on self-reporting by those infected. Most studies are conducted by companies producing antiviral software. Their contacts tend to be customers. Therefore, the number of infections detected tend to be from "protected" environments. Even when "public" studies are done, the results are highly suspect. Most business people see computer viral infections almost as a moral failing. The computer virus carries, unfairly, the taint of pirate software. Therefore, few companies are willing to report realistic numbers. In 1990, the Auditor General of Canada released a report on computer security failings in the federal government. For the nine months covered by the study, there were 29 virus infections in government computers. I happened to be working in a federal government office at the time, and judging by the number of infections that I dealt with personally, the number should have been on the order of 1,500 per month.

Some very rough figures, based upon the best available studies, indicate that the problem is still growing. Although more companies are becoming aware of the problem, consistent antiviral measures are relatively rare. A business can expect to see about one virus incident per month per hundred computers. Infection incidents usually affect multiple machines before being detected. A 1993 study indicates that recovery of each infected machine costs about $200. If you use a computer, you are at some risk, and the level of risk in terms of both varieties and total number of viral programs is still growing.

Here are some very broad and general statements about the levels of risk in different situations. Please assume all the disclaimers you have ever read, especially, "Your mileage may vary."

The level of risk increases with the number of systems in use. This is mostly in terms of the number of strains produced. The number of strains produced is likely to be affected by the cost and therefore, accessibility of a system, the number of competent programmers for a given system, and the desirability of a given platform as a viral target.

As of this writing, there are likely 7,000 different viral strains for MS-DOS. By the time you read this, that will probably be at least 8,000.

The number of Macintosh viral programs is very much lower, still fewer than 100. Unprotected Macintosh shops, however, are at very much greater risks, with infection rates approaching 100 percent in most cases.

The situation with Ataris and Amigas has been slightly different. There has been a very active virus-exchange community among users of these two systems almost from the very beginning. Sharing of viral programs has been common even among normally legitimate user groups.

In 1991 only 10 percent of computers had antiviral protection. In 1992 only about a quarter had some kind of protection. By 1994 the number climbed to just over half. However, this study is based upon reports of all forms of virus protection. Very few business computers have effective multilayered protection in place. Of those many forms of virus prevention in place, too many are not used regularly at all. Most are out of date. Almost no companies have established effective policies and procedures in regard to viral programs.

The virus situation is not tied to any one computer or operating system. Viral programs are impossible to detect and eliminate with 100 percent accuracy. As new systems become popular, old viral programs will die out—and new ones will be written.

The amount of risk increases with the number of disks handled, as well as with the number of users and the number of programs. The stereotypical high-risk situation is that of a school or college computer lab. Interestingly, many lab administrators consider their systems "safe" if they can recover them at the end of the week. The risk to users and students seems to be neglected.

In the Western world, by and large, we live longer and healthier lives than those in developing countries, or even than our own ancestors a few centuries back. Is it because of heart/lung machines? Kidney transplants? CAT scans? None of the above. It is because of soap operas.

Soap companies wanted to sell more product. (They still do.) So they launched massive advertising vehicles to convince people to wash more things more often. This has resulted in a very limited number of disease carriers in our society and, therefore, a greatly reduced level of infections and disease, with consequently longer life spans. This comment about soap operas is, of course, facetious. But the effect is real, with public health care workers due the lion's share of the credit.

Hygiene sets up a cycle that feeds back on itself. Because there are fewer disease vectors and carriers, there are fewer new cases of disease. Because there are fewer cases of disease, there are fewer carriers. Smallpox has been eradicated because of a determined effort on the part of public health officials around the world. Even before that, however, it was almost unknown in the Western world. Typhus, cholera, and other former scourges are still tragic when they strike, but an outbreak is now major news, rather than a daily occurrence.

It is ironic that the pinnacle of Western civilization's technology is subject to hygiene levels more suited to the most backward cultures on earth, but that is the case. Only recently have a bare majority of computers been subject to any form of virus protection. In most cases that protection bears more resemblance to a semiannual bath than to a daily grooming. The many un-, or ill-protected systems are subject to many virus attacks. Once infected, and in most cases they *are* infected by first exposure, they become carriers and vectors themselves, sending out copies of infected programs and disks. These files and disks in turn create new carriers, which spread the infection farther and, incidentally, stand a good chance of reinfecting one of the earlier vectors, should it happen to have been discovered and cleaned. It is especially true in the virus area that if you are not part of the solution, you are part of the problem.

In this situation, you are potentially under attack not only from those who bear you malice, but also from any of your friends who are not competent enough to protect themselves. Disease carriers are not always skulking, wild-eyed anarchists; the most successful are happy bonhomous sorts who have no idea of the illness they are spreading. Therefore, it behooves you to educate those around you and to try, as far as possible, to assist with their protection. As I say at the end of my virus seminars, this makes another dozen or so people I can safely exchange disks with.

Viral programs can carry destructive payloads. Any kind of damage that can be done by software can be done by a virus. (No, not blowing up the hardware. We've already covered that.) Yet few of them carry real trouble with them. Most are just a nuisance. Why?

Viral technologies have developed a number of ways of avoiding detection. Yet at the same time, many viral programs carry messages of some type. Not only are the messages themselves a giveaway, but even the superfluous text strings buried in code carry a cost paid for in the size of the virus. And that is just for the text, not for the animation, graphic displays, and even songs that are sometimes carried. Why?

When you get right down to it, why write a virus at all?

Well, why do people write on bathroom walls?

(Did you ever notice that no one writes on the bathroom walls at home? Or even at work?)

Everyone wants their promised Warholian 15 minutes of fame, and preferably sooner rather than later. Some are born to it; some achieve it. Some write on walls. Some write viral programs. Some of the early viral programs were outright advertising (BRAIN, MacMag, and Den

Zuk). Others were coy about it, but virus writers tend to "sign" programs with a nickname, even today. (Ah, isn't it wonderful how brave you can be behind a mask?) There are those who campaign for a cause, like the authors of Stoned and Groen Links. Then, there are those who don't give any clues to their identity, content with the fact that their digital child is out there, creating havoc.

Creating a virus is easy, especially if you just take someone else's and change the text strings or modify the code by throwing NOP codes into it. A fairly cheap route to fame. Or infamy.

Then there are those who see viral programs as pranks. Most in the vx community seem to see themselves in this vein, although it is hard to justify such a position in light of the level of nuisance (and worse) that viral programs create. It is even harder to see any humor in the unimaginative outpourings of most of these crews. (I must admit, I would have a hard time keeping a straight face over the Spanish Cookie virus . . . unless I had just lost some files to it.)

FALSE ALERTS

The major computer virus "event" of 1994–95 was the enormous number of false alerts. A false alert is not the same as a false-positive result from antiviral software, but is an announcement of a virus resulting from either a genuine misunderstanding or a deliberate hoax. In either case, a false alert tends to take on a life of its own as well-meaning, but naive, users try to warn friends and net acquaintances of the new danger.

False alerts arguably do more damage than all malicious software combined. (Of course, if there were no malicious software, there couldn't be any false alerts.)

Be careful out there—but don't be paranoid. In the very early days, Jeffrey Mogul proposed the "metavirus." The advantage, he said, was that you could make one without having to write a line of code—just some text. His offering was:

> **WARNING!** *A serious virus is on the loose. It was hidden in the program called 1987TAXFORM that was on this bboard last year. This virus does several nasty things:*
>
> 1. *Copies itself into several important system programs so that it will propagate to other disks*

2. *Copies itself into your own data files so that it can infect system programs on other systems*
3. *Keeps track of the files you encrypt and mails copies of the cleartext to a bboard in Iowa and a computer at the NSA*
4. *Randomly garbles files so that you don't necessarily know they are damaged*

By now, it is possible that your system is infected even if you didn't download this program, since you could easily have been infected indirectly.

The only safe way to protect yourself against this virus is to print all your files onto paper, erase all the disks on your system with a demagnetizer, buy fresh software disks from the manufacturer, and type in all your data again. But FIRST! send this message to everyone you know, so that they will also follow these steps to protect themselves.

The work involved in that last paragraph is, of course, more than you would face if you were infected with even the most malign of viral programs.

The most famous of the recent false alerts is the "Good Times" announcement. There is some controversy over the identity of the originators of the message, but all indications are that it was a sincere, if misguided, attempt to warn others.

It seems most likely that the Good Times alert was started by a group or an individual who had seen a computer failure without understanding the cause and associated it with an email message that had "Good Times" in the subject line. The announcement states that there was a message, identified by the title of "Good Times," which, when read, would crash your computer. The message was said to be a virus, even though there was nothing viral about that sort of activity (even if it *were* possible).

Other parts of this book discuss the possibility of ANSI bombs and other text-based malicious software. Suffice it to say that the possibility of such a message is remote. The fact that the warning contained almost no details at all should have been an indication that the message wasn't quite right. There was no information on how to detect, avoid, or get rid of the "virus," except not to read messages with "Good Times" in the subject line. (The irony of the fact that all the warnings contained these words seems to have escaped most people.)

Despite the total lack of any facts behind the warning, copies of the Good Times alert are still being distributed almost a year after it was first published. This false alert has been extremely resistant to eradication. In the spring of 1995, a FAQ was prepared exposing the falsity of the warning, but the echoes of Good Times will likely carry on for a while yet.

(In a rather pathetic, and distressingly common, attempt at infamy, a member of the vx community has produced a Good Times virus. Like the virus named after the older Proto-T hoax, the new Good Times is a simplistic and uninteresting specimen, unlikely to produce any significant result besides confusion and having nothing in common with the original alert.)

The JPEG virus hoax is a straightforward prank, released on April 1 of both 1994 and 1995. The announcement was rather carefully crafted of technobabble that recalled, for example, the data overrun bug in sendmail that was used by the Internet Worm. The warning was said to be the result of research by "Dr. Charles Forbin." Charles Forbin is the main character in the science-fiction book *Colossus* and the movie *The Forbin Project*. (The story is along the usual computer-takes-over-the-world line.)

Although the announcement of the JPEG virus was an obvious hoax, the concept of a virus hidden in a graphics file is a complex one. In general, the data in a graphics file would never be executed as a program and therefore would be of no use as a viral vector. During 1994, however, a GIF (Graphics Interchange Format) file caused much alarm when posted to a Usenet newsgroup. The file header contained a very odd section of data, with suspicious text references. Those who examined it ultimately decided that the file was harmless, and that this was possibly a hoax aimed at a select and suspicious few on the nets.

Few outside of Canada will have heard of the "Budget virus" of 1995, but it is still receiving mention in general, technical, and business periodicals within the country. When the Federal Budget is introduced, copies are sent to all major financial institutions, along with explanatory and background material. In February 1995, this material was to be distributed on diskette, rather than in printed form. The Finance Department apparently checked the master disk for viral infection with two different scanners (the identity of which have not been made public). The floppy was then sent to a duplication house, for a run of more than 5,000 copies. The duplication house itself, seemingly *after* the copies had been made, checked the disk with ThunderByte Scan—and was warned of a "suspect virus" on it.

I am not sure who first broke the story, but neither the duplication house nor the Canadian agent for ThunderByte was reticent in talking to the press. Senior management in accounting firms pontificated on the disaster that could have overtaken the economic structure of the nation, with this virus paralyzing all of its financial institutions.

The specific damage the virus could have done was left unstated. In fact, the virus was only identified as being "unknown," the clear implication being that it was new and that only the advanced technology of one particular scanner was able to find it. Further, the virus never *has* been identified. Given that any halfway competent virus researcher can tell you a number of things about a virus within hours, and that the "virus" is still unknown after half a year (as of this writing), it is clear that there never was any virus.

You want to be informed of new viral programs. You also want to inform your friends and community. But you do *not* want to spread false alerts, which make people waste time and resources protecting against dangers that weren't there. Yet false alerts can often, to the nonexpert, look like the real thing. How can you tell?

The quickest way to check a report is to know who it came from. Unless you follow *VIRUS-L/comp.virus*, though, you won't be able to identify trustworthy people. There are some items you should always find in a real alert. Detail is one: what objects are affected, the specific increase in the size of program files, text or search strings in the infectious portion, amount of memory taken by resident programs. All valid alerts should state how an infected program or disk can be identified *before* it is run, not just the effects of the virus on the computer. The report should also state which scanners (and which specific versions) have been tested against the new virus, and what they report. (Most of the time, the better scanners will report *something*, even with a new virus.) Finally, a valid alert will identify virus researchers and antiviral developers to whom samples have been sent.

FUTURE TRENDS

Predicting the future in any technological field is a mug's game. The more so in the virus field, where change happens so extraordinarily quickly. I will content myself, therefore, with a few observations on current trends, and some speculations on possibilities that may never come to pass.

The virus problem continues to grow. Both numbers of infections and numbers of new strains are increasing rapidly. Although the rates are higher than they have ever been, the exponential curve of the growth is beginning to flatten. This is possibly due to a saturation in the vx community, in that almost as many people are leaving it, as they mature, as are joining at the bottom end. There is, as yet, no evidence of any reduction in numbers.

Operating systems do not appear to present any barriers to viral growth. We are, as of this writing, on somewhat of a cusp in the desktop market, with OS/2, Windows, NT, UNIX, and some systems still under development vying for the position that MS-DOS has held for roughly the last decade. Whatever standard emerges, be it a single operating system or an open-systems environment that works across platforms, will be the new major target for viral programs. The specific weaknesses of current operating systems may be eliminated, thus killing off viral programs using those methods of attack. New patterns of use, however, will give rise to new methods of attack. The problem will remain.

Those who study data security will know of the U.S. government security standards referred to as the "Orange Book." I neither want nor need to go into detail on the levels of security specified. One item, however, deserves scrutiny here—the concept of "mandatory" versus "discretionary" security controls. Discretionary controls are those over which a user or, at least, a system administrator, has control. With discretionary controls, the person can control access, changes to the system, operations, and so forth. Mandatory controls, however, remove this ability from the user or administrator. Mandatory controls are fixed, and they limit how the system may be used.

The same concept, in a slightly different form, has been used in discussions of virus protection. The reason that computers are vulnerable to viral attacks is that they use what is technically referred to as von Neumann architecture. What this means is that there is no difference, to the computer, between the programs and the data. Programs are simply data that it executes and since programs are data files, they can be manipulated in the same way as any other data files. It is possible, however, to design a computer that does not work this way: a computer that would not allow any manipulation of the programs. This type of architecture would be safe from viral infection. Unfortunately, it would be very much less useful than current computers. The machines would be hard-wired in the same manner as terminals, automated teller machines, game machines, and dedicated word processors. The price of safety is a great reduction in the utility of the machine.

In comparison to previous levels, the past few years have seen significant increases in protection for computers—but only in relative terms. In absolute terms, protection levels are almost nonexistent. Slightly over half of computers surveyed showed some form of virus protection in place. (Remember, that means that almost half of all computers have no protection at all.) Consider that of those with access to protection, a majority do not use it regularly; of those that use protection, a majority use only a single product or type; of those with multilayered protection, a majority have installed it by default and without regard to local requirements; and of those who have attempted appropriate installations, a majority do not have any form of policy regarding antiviral protection. The remainder constitute a minority so small as to be statistically insignificant. The vast majority of systems, therefore, are potential breeding grounds of greater or lesser fertility.

The antiviral market is constantly in motion, but there are a significant number of adequate products available. Unfortunately, studies indicate that inferior products are predominant. Reviews of antiviral products are rare. Some magazines refuse to consider reviews of antiviral programs because of fear of lawsuits. Some of the most widely distributed reviews are very suspect.

The level of knowledge of the viral situation is very low among both the general populace and the majority of computer users. No popular computer periodicals carry any regular information; those articles that get published are technically suspect. Two antivirus journals are well established, but their distribution remains relatively low. Aside from new product announcements, serious articles on the virus situation seldom appear in the trade press. Two technical training companies have attempted to present computer virus seminars; both attempts were canceled after very short runs, the companies citing lack of attendance.

It is very hard to predict what the next advance in virus technology will be. The various techniques that have arisen have been both completely obvious in retrospect and a complete surprise when they happened.

There are a number of techniques that could be used to obtain more space for viral programs on disks without detection by normal utilities. So far, only one appears to have been explored, and that, only by a single virus. It is unlikely that these avenues will be explored by virus writers because such techniques require too much research and dedication to task. However, if one should be used in a single successful virus, it will undoubtedly be copied by many others.

GUI (graphical user interface) systems are rife with insecurities. In general, GUI users do not check the structure and characteristics of their file systems, and many changes can go undetected. In addition, applications run under GUI operating systems tend to have very large program files, a great number of program and ancillary files for each application, and odd or arbitrary directory and file structures. All of this vitiates against the detection of viral infections.

These current considerations aside, however, there are a number of potential vulnerabilities in graphic systems that would allow for the invocation of viral programs in ways that would not be obvious to the casual user. The very heavy processing load that GUIs place on a system would serve to hide a great deal of viral overhead. The trend to open systems is one that is pushing the development of interfaces to allow operations and functions to be invoked in a common manner, regardless of the underlying platform. This desirable cross-platform functionality will also allow viral programs wider range. So far, this possibility has been realized in only one case, but the likelihood will increase as the ability and supporting systems grow.

I want you to bear two things in mind. One is that from here on in, this section gets pretty "blue sky." This is speculation, not prediction. There is some technical validity to the possibilities I want to outline, but there is nothing to say that they *will* happen just because they can.

The second is that this is not a suggestion list for the vx community. These ideas are based on concepts that we have already seen. You can be quite sure that virus writers have already thought of them. The intention here is to let the security community, as well as those computer users interested in protecting themselves, think about what might lie ahead.

I have already touched on the concept of open systems. Very likely this will involve some form of underlying operating-system kernel and a commonly used language, scripting capability, or set of utilities overlaying the different platforms. Although most current viral programs have been written with very low level languages, it is not necessary that they always are. The **CHRISTMA EXEC** was written with a high-level language and was extremely successful.

We have already seen one example, in the Scores virus, of a program designed to target specific software or systems. (It is not isolated:

the AntiCAD and dbase viral programs are examples in the MS-DOS world.) This can be expanded or modified in a number of ways. Is it likely, though, that virus writers will make any real efforts in this direction, aside from the attacks made on antiviral software? While certain products and companies have been targeted by various viral programs, only one case shows deliberate malice toward a program or manufacturer. This type of thing is, however, quite possible.

A targeted virus would not hunt down a specific system, as such. Rather, using the broadcast distribution under which viral programs operate, the program would check each system it arrived on. If the system was not a target, then the virus would simply proceed to reproduce and attempt to evade detection. If the target was detected, then the virus payload would trigger. Thus a targeted virus would exist, quietly, on many more nontarget systems than on targets.

A targeted virus, like any other, would be quickly identified and added to the scanner arsenal. However, with current very low levels of protection, it could do extensive damage to the target systems. It is sheer speculation to try to assess the reaction to such a virus. Very likely the mere existence of such an entity, aside from any direct damage it did, could cost a large corporation millions of dollars in lost or delayed sales. On the other hand, a company so stung might be a major factor in promoting better virus awareness.

A specific company's software or systems need not be the only target for a virus. Specific individual systems could be targets as well.

Spread would be random, in the shotgun pattern seen with any virus. Detecting a specific system might be quite tricky and would require some knowledge of the target, but not necessarily a lot. The size of targeted viral programs would be a hindrance to their spread, since they would have to carry the necessary intelligence to identify the chosen system, as well as the payload.

Consider the stereotypical cracker. He (well, they generally are male) sits in front of his PC or terminal, with a modem, electronically kicking doors. He may have a "demon dialer" or other utility programs to speed the search for doors to kick, but is essentially limited simply because of the fact that he is only one person with one (or very few) terminal, modem, and phone line.

What, on the other hand, if the cracker could clone himself? And clone his system, modem, and phone lines? He might then be able to kick two doors at once. Or ten. A hundred. Thousands. This, of course, is precisely what viral programs do. This binary hydra may start with a single system, but as it spreads, the infected machines become part of the distribution system. The virus may use disks, programs, network links, or other resources to spread, but if you have any of these, the virus can use them. You, unknowingly, become part of the attack.

Once the target system is reached and identified, the payload can be activated. Here the possibilities are limited only by the imagination and by the fact that viral survival decreases as the program size grows. The payload could be a simple message. Or the standard destructive payload that erases files or disks. The payload could, however, be much more subtle.

The programming could be designed to subvert, once an initial penetration of the system had been made, the security of the computer from the inside. The virus could be designed simply to identify the system. As one researcher theorized, you could go a long way to identifying an unknown system just by crashing it and then watching for the support team to be dispatched. Alternatively, the virus could be designed to collect internal information (a password file, say?), bundle the package of info into itself, and rebroadcast itself, to slowly work its way home.

A question was posed on the *RISKS-FORUM Digest* regarding antiviral protection applied to data obtained from the Search for Extra Terrestrial Intelligence (SETI) program. On the face of it, this is absurd. If there are intelligent aliens out there who have the technology to contact us, they are unlikely to have Macs or MS-DOS. Yet, as with the Desert Storm viral myth and related rumors about viral programs interfering with missiles, there are some slender threads of fact involved—just enough to make the rumor resistant to elimination.

The original poster mentioned the "fact" that all computers are based on Turing machines and that all Turing machines are able to emulate each other. This statement is then used to propose that an advanced alien intelligence would be able to devise a program that would be able to infect all computers, and, by extension, a program that would be able to crash all of earth's computers. There are several problems with this concept.

The first is the extreme misunderstanding of what a Turing machine is. While a Turing machine can be described in physical terms, and while a limited Turing machine can be built, the Turing machine is properly a mathematical concept. It can be used to determine whether a program can be written to solve a certain class of problem and, if such a program *can* be written, whether the program will ever give you a useful answer. The determinations of a Turing machine are independent of specifics of hardware, architecture, or physical limits. It is only in this way that the Turing machine is said to be a universal computer. Real, physical, existing computers can run models of Turing machines, but do not otherwise emulate Turing machines. Turing machines do not emulate other computers: you cannot run Windows on a Turing machine, although a Turing machine might be able to tell you if you could ever write a utility that might keep Windows from crashing so often.

Although data from the SETI project is massaged in computers, it is still just that—data. In discussing the ability of viral programs to travel through vectors that are normally assumed to be data, it is emphasized again and again that computers don't distinguish between programs and data: a program is data that a computer has been told to execute. In the case of SETI, however, the distinction is abundantly clear. It makes as much sense to run SETI data as it does to read the object file from your favorite computer game.

Even given all of the above, there is still the possibility of error and software malfunction. The famous Internet Worm took advantage of a software loophole that allowed the end of a data overrun to be entered as an executable command. It is not beyond the bounds of possibility that an unknown bug in the programs examining SETI data will somehow allow the computer to attempt execution of a random part of that data as code. That "random" is important, though. Who knows what a random sequence of bytes might do? Cohen's calculations put the mean time between totally random occurrences of viral programs in the order of hundreds of thousands of years. Given the relatively few computers involved in SETI research, our Sun will likely die before our computers do. (Or, to put it another way, we are at staggeringly greater risk of catching the ultimate virus from the actions of teenage mutant copyright breakers scanning in pictures from *Playboy* than we are from SETI data.)

Ah, you say, but that is only if this is all random. What if the aliens are deliberately programming viruses and trojans into the data stream? Well, assuming for the moment that there *are* aliens, and assuming that they, for some completely inexplicable reason, want to shut down our computers, trying to embed trojans in the data stream would be a particularly stupid way to go about it. Like supposed NSA types trying to include a mythical virus in a purported PC's printer that is going to some random country in, say, the Middle East, the aliens would have to know more about our computers than we do. Our computer architectures are not the only ones possible. Even at the most basic level of digital electronics, who is to say that alien computers use binary logic? It could be trinary (or *n*-ary). And even if some superintelligent race somewhere had written a virus that could infect CP/M, UNIX, VMS, MacOS, MVS, and MS-DOS, have you any idea of what the code would look like after umpteen million years between galaxies?

It'd be easier to go around in a flying saucer handing out packages that you said were upgrades to "Mortal Kombat III." In both disk sizes.

This is also, in a sense, the ultimate answer to the question of the military use of viral programs. If you have enough information about enemy computers and procedures to have half a chance of designing a good virus, you have enough information to do more direct sabotage in other ways.

Memoirs of a (Cross-Border) Virus Researcher

There isn't any budget for my reviews of antiviral products. I do not charge developers for reviewing their products, and I don't receive any payment from users. Developers send free copies of their product, and my only outlay is for the occasional mailing to request antiviral materials, software, and products. Plus my time.

At least, that's the theory.

Bear with me while I digress into politics for the moment. Since I started all this the "Chin-That-Walks-Like-a-PM" foisted upon us something called the "Free Trade Agreement." This is supposed to make cross-border dealing much easier. In fact, just recently the government has extended this deal to become the "North American Free Trade Agreement," covering more ground, don'cha know. This means that importing and customs are going to be much easier to deal with, as well as cheaper.

At least, that's the theory.

So how come this has recently become so very much more difficult and costly?

Most courier services seemed to be able to handle customs, although the good old national mail service was often the best bet. All the developer or publisher had to do was write "evaluation copy, no commerical value" on the package, and all was well. I got the software, and the reviews went forth. Then we got the GST, and in spite of there being no commerical value, a "service value" had to be charged. (What "service value"? I'm the one providing the service here, and I'm not charging anyone.) So a fictional (low) service value has to be put on it, generally reflecting the price of the blank disks.

No longer. I have here a package from a software developer. Via U.S. mail and then Canada Post. He has been very careful. The package has a customs declaration. The material is described as "two diskettes and printed material." It is described internally as an "evaluation copy, not for resale or use." A value of $2 is declared. I had to pay $7.98 to receive it. $2.98 is the GST. GST is 7 percent. Seven percent of $2 is $0.14. Ah, but the value for tax is not the $2 declared. The value for tax is $42.53. Where did they get $42.53 from? I have no idea. Even so, there is still $5 unaccounted for. Ah, no, here we are. $5 "handling fee." "Handling fee?" This is the post office! They are supposed to handle mail! Or maybe it's the $2.98 GST that they are charging $5 to handle. In that case, I didn't ask them to handle it. If Revenue Canada wants them to handle the GST, let Revenue Canada pay the $5 handling fee to collect the $2.98. Or, since the $2.98 is a result of "mishandling," the $0.14 that they should be handling.

So much for "free trade." But then, like the man said, be grateful you don't get all the government you pay for.

APPENDIX A

FREQUENTLY ASKED QUESTIONS

What is a computer virus?

A computer virus, or a viral program, is one that will use your computer, and what you normally do with it, to copy and spread itself. Many people use the term loosely to cover any sort of program that tries to hide its function and tries to spread onto as many computers as possible. Be aware that what constitutes a "program" that a virus can infect may include a lot more than is at first obvious—don't assume too much about what a virus can or can't do!

However, viral programs are not "magic." They are written by ordinary (although perhaps twisted) people, and they have to be run on your computer in order to work.

Computer viral programs are a serious problem, and one that not enough people are doing anything about yet. The steps to protect yourself against them are not hard, but first you have to be willing to learn some of the basics of how viral programs work.

What are the symptoms and indications of a virus infection?

There isn't any *one* kind of symptom. In fact—although there are all kinds of symptoms that virus authors have written into their programs, such as messages, music, and graphic displays—often viral authors try to *avoid* symptoms, so that the virus can spread undetected.

The main indications of infection are changes in file sizes and contents, changes of interrupt vectors, or the reassignment of other system resources. The unaccounted use of RAM, or a reduction in the amount known to be in the machine, are important indicators. The examination of the boot sector is valuable to the trained eye, but the novice can generally spot the gross differences between those boot sectors known to be valid and those that are infected. Unfortunately, these symptoms, along with longer disk activity and strange behavior from the hardware, can also be caused by genuine software, by harmless "prank" programs, or by hardware faults.

Pay close attention to your system. Look particularly for any change in the memory map or configuration as soon as you start the computer. For users of MS-DOS 5.0 and up, the MEM program with the /C switch is very handy for this. You don't have to know what all the numbers mean, only that they

205

shouldn't change. Mac users have "info" options that give some indication of memory use, but they may need ResEdit for more detail.

Can viruses spread from one type of computer to another?

The simple answer is that no currently known viruses can do that. Although the disk formats may be the same (e.g., Atari ST and DOS), the different machines interpret the code differently. For example, the Stoned virus cannot infect an Atari ST because the ST cannot execute the virus code in the boot sector. The Stoned virus contains instructions for the 80x86 family of CPUs that the 680x0–family CPU (Atari ST) can't understand or execute.

The more general answer is that such viruses are possible, but unlikely. Such a virus would be quite a bit larger than current viruses and might well be easier to find. Additionally, the low incidence of cross-machine sharing of software means that any such virus would be unlikely to spread—it would be a poor environment for virus growth.

Could mainframe computers be susceptible to computer viral programs?

Yes. Numerous experiments have shown that computer viruses spread very quickly and effectively on mainframe systems. However, no one has ever seen a "PC type" computer virus on mainframe systems except in these tests.

While some say that they do not fit the most limited definition of a computer virus, the CHRISTMA EXEC of 1987, the Internet Worm of 1988, and the WANK worm of 1989 all affected mainframe computer networks, and all had viral properties.

I haven't lost any files yet—I can't have a virus. (Can I?)

Oh, yes you can.

Not all viral programs deliberately erase files. Not all viral programs carry a "dangerous" payload. At least, not on purpose. Many viral programs, probably most of them, seem to be written only to spread.

However, the authors may not be as smart as they would like to think. Almost all of the viral programs ever found have some kind of problem and may eventually do some kind of mischief.

What is a trojan horse?

A trojan horse is a program that does something undocumented that the programmer intended, but that the user would not approve of if he or she knew about it. According to some people, a virus is a particular case of a trojan horse, namely one that is able to spread to other programs (i.e., it turns other programs into trojans, too). According to others, a virus that does not do any deliberate damage (other than merely replicating) is not a trojan. Finally, despite the definitions, many people use the term 'trojan' to refer only to a *non-replicating* malicious program, so that the set of trojans and the set of viruses are separate.

What is an ANSI bomb?

The ANSI.SYS program is a program that provides standard screen control, generally used to emulate an ANSI terminal. It can also be used to redefine keys on the keyboard. This latter use is not as well known, although it is used by some to provide keyboard macros or to remap specialized keyboard layouts.

ANSI bombs are not viral, in that they do not reproduce. They may be considered as trojans or logic bombs. An ANSI bomb is a sequence of characters that is interpreted by ANSI.SYS as redefining a key or keys on the keyboard. Thereafter, these keys will send not the normally assigned characters, but the redefined string. This string may contain any ASCII characters, including <RE-TURN> and multiple commands. Therefore, the space bar, for example, can be redefined to:

```
DEL *.*<cr>Y<cr>
```

This sequence would, in MS-DOS, delete all files in the current directory.

ANSI bombs are stored in normal text files or messages. They are triggered by "porting" the text to the "console" device while ANSI emulation is active. What this normally means is that they are triggered when a user employs the "TYPE" command to read the text of a file.

What are the main types of viruses?

Generally, there are two main classes of viruses. The first class consists of the file or program infectors, which attach themselves to program files. These usually infect arbitrary COM and/or EXE programs in the PC, and code resources on the Mac. File infectors can be either direct action or resident. A direct-action virus infects programs each time the program that contains it is executed. A resident virus hides itself somewhere in memory the first time an infected program is executed, and thereafter infects other programs when they are run, "opened," or even, in some cases, just "looked at."

The second category is boot sector infectors (BSIs). These viruses infect code in certain areas on a disk that are not ordinary files. On DOS systems, there are ordinary boot sector viruses, which infect only the DOS boot sector, and MBR viruses, which infect the master boot record on fixed disks and the DOS boot sector on diskettes. Examples include Brain, Stoned, and Michelangelo. Such viruses are always resident viruses. Finally, a few viruses are able to infect both files and boot sectors. These are called "multipartite" viruses.

Can boot sector viruses like Stoned infect nonbootable floppy disks?

Yes. Any diskette that has been properly formatted contains an executable program in the boot sector. If the diskette is not bootable, all that boot sector does is print a message like "Nonsystem disk or disk error; replace and strike any key when ready," but the diskette is still executable and still vulnerable to infection. If you accidentally turn your machine on with a nonbootable diskette in the drive and see that message, it means that any boot virus that may have been on that diskette *has* run and has had the chance to infect your hard drive, or whatever. So when thinking about viruses, the word "bootable" (or "nonbootable") is really misleading. All formatted diskettes are capable of carrying a virus.

What steps should be taken in diagnosing and identifying viruses?

Most of the time, a virus scanner program will take care of that for you. (Remember, though, that scanning programs must be kept up-to-date. Also remember that different scanner authors may call the same virus by different names. If you want to identify a virus in order to ask for help, it is best to run at least two scanners on it and, when asking, to say which scanners, and what versions, gave the names.) To help identify problems early, run it when you use new programs and diskettes, when an integrity checker reports a mismatch, when a generic monitor program sounds an alarm, or when you receive an updated version of a scanner (or a different scanner than the one you have been using).

If you run into an alarm that the scanner doesn't identify, or doesn't properly clean up for you, first verify that the version you are using is the most recent, and then submit a suspect virus to recognized experts for analysis. We will get back to you with suggestions on how to clean up your system. (This helps not only you, but others as well: we will be using the new virus to test antiviral software and ensure it can keep you safe.)

I think I have detected a new virus. What do I do?

Whenever there is doubt over a virus, you should obtain the latest versions of several (not just one) major virus scanners. Some scanning programs now use "heuristic" methods (F-PROT, TBSCAN, CHECKOUT, and SCANBOOT are examples), and "activity-monitoring" programs can report a disk or file as being possibly infected, when it is, in fact perfectly safe (odd, perhaps, but not infected). If no string-matching scan finds a virus, but a heuristic program does (or there are other reasons to suspect the file, e.g., change in size of file), then it is possible that you have found a new virus, although the chances are probably greater that it is an odd-but-okay disk or file.

Whichever is the case, send a copy of the infected file to recognized experts, and we will get it to the antiviral authors in order to ensure that either this new virus gets caught or (if it turns out to be a false alarm) that they fix the false alarm.

What is the best protection for my computer?

There is no "best" antivirus program. In fact, there is no program that can magically protect you against all viruses. But you can design an antivirus protection strategy and build layers of defense. There are three main kinds of antiviral software (and many "combos"):

1. ACTIVITY MONITORS. These try to catch viral type activity, such as attempts to write to an executable file, reformatting the disk, and so on.
2. SCANNERS. Most look for known virus "signature strings" (patterns known to occur in viruses, but not in good software), but some use AI (artificial intelligence) techniques to recognize viral code. They usually also include virus removers.
3. CHANGE DETECTORS. These compute a "checksum" for files when they are presumably uninfected, and then compare newly calculated values with the original ones to see if the files have been modified.

How often should I upgrade my antivirus tools to minimize software and labor costs and to maximize my protection?

This is a difficult question to answer. Antiviral software is a kind of insurance, and insurance calculations are difficult.

There are two things to watch out for here: the general "style" of the software, and the signatures that scanners use to identify viruses. Scanners should be updated more frequently than other software, and it is probably a good idea to update your set of signatures at least once every two months.

Some antiviral software looks for changes to programs or specific types of viral "activity," and these programs generally claim to be good for "all current and future viral programs." However, even these programs cannot guarantee to protect against all future viruses and should probably be upgraded once per year.

Of course, not every antivirus product is effective against all (or any!) viruses, even if upgraded regularly. Thus, do *not* depend on the fact that you have upgraded your product recently as a guarantee that your system is free of viruses!

Could an antiviral program itself be infected?

Yes, so it is important to obtain this software from good sources and to trust results only after running scanners from a "clean" system. But there *are* situations where a scanner appears to be infected when it isn't.

Most antiviral programs try very hard to identify only viral infections, but sometimes they give false alarms. A scanner contains "signature strings" to identify viral infections. If the strings are not "encrypted," then they will be identified as a virus by another scanner. Also, if the scanner does not remove the strings from memory after they are run, then another scanner may detect the virus string "in memory."

Some change-detection antiviral programs add a bit of code or data to a program when "protecting" it. This might be discerned by another change detector as a modification to a program, and therefore suspicious.

It is good practice to use more than one antiviral program. Do be aware, however, that antiviral programs, by their nature, may confuse each other.

Is it possible to protect a computer system using only software?

Not perfectly. However, software defenses can significantly reduce your risk of being affected by viruses WHEN APPLIED APPROPRIATELY. All virus defense systems are tools—each with its own capabilities and limitations. Learn how your system works and be sure to work within its limitations.

A very high level of protection/detection can be achieved with only software, using a combination approach.

You can use a scanner on all new (and "returned") disks and programs to reduce the risk of a virus entering your system, but you have to remember to do this all the time. You can use change detectors to tell you when something odd is happening, but you have to remember that some programs do change themselves. You can use an activity monitor to prevent deletions and formatting, but it may prevent you from formatting a new disk or getting rid of an old file.

As each layer is added, invasion without detection becomes more difficult. However, complete protection against any possible attack cannot be provided without seriously restricting the type of work the computer can do. As the examples above show, viral programs use only ordinary computer functions, albeit in an unwanted fashion. In other words, if the computer is useful, it is at risk.

Is it possible to write-protect the hard disk using only software?

The answer is no. There are several programs that claim to do that, but *all* of them can be bypassed using only techniques that are known to be employed by current viruses. Therefore you should *never* rely on such programs *alone*.

Will setting DOS file attributes to "read only" protect them from viruses?

No. While the MS-DOS "Read Only" attribute will protect your files from a few viruses, most viruses simply override it and infect the files as they would normally do. So, while setting executable files to "Read Only" is not a bad idea, it is certainly not a thorough protection against viruses!

Will a write-protect tab on a floppy disk stop viruses?

It will stop a virus (and anything else) from getting onto the diskette. The write protection on IBM PC (and compatible) and Macintosh floppy disk drives is implemented in hardware, not software, so viruses cannot infect a diskette when the write-protection mechanism is functioning properly.

However, a write-protect tab will also prevent you from putting anything else onto the diskette, and as soon as you take the tab off, the disk is vulnerable.

Also remember:

1. A computer may have a faulty write-protect system (this happens!)—you can test it by trying to copy a file to a (presumably) write-protected diskette.
2. Someone may have removed the tab at some point, allowing a virus on.
3. The files may have been infected before the disk was protected. Even some diskettes "straight from the factory" have been known to be infected in the production process.
4. Transparent write-protect tabs (e.g., Scotch tape and its equivalents) don't work.

So, it is worthwhile to scan even write-protected disks for viruses.

Can I avoid viruses by avoiding shareware/free software/games?

No. There are many documented instances in which even commercial "shrink-wrap" software was inadvertently distributed containing viruses. Avoiding shareware, freeware, games, and such software only isolates you from a vast collection of software (some of it very good, some of it very bad, most of it somewhere in between . . .).

In fact, much of the best *antiviral* software is shareware.

The important thing is not to avoid a certain type of software, but to be cautious of ANY AND ALL newly acquired software. Simply scanning all new software media for known viruses would be rather effective at preventing virus infections, especially when combined with some other prevention/detection strategy, such as integrity management of programs.

Can I avoid viruses by avoiding BBS systems?

The answer is a very definite *NO!*

In the first place, electronic bulletin boards and networks are about the only places to get any kind of reasonable information about viral programs.

In the second place, most sysops take far more care than the average computer user to "stay clean."

As proof, all studies have shown that boot sector infectors, although there are fewer of them, are more successful in terms of the number of infections they make. Boot sector viral programs do not infect files and therefore cannot be spread by file transfers from a bulletin board. (There are exceptions to this rule, but they are so rare that I have never seen one.)

What is the best way to remove a virus?

Do the minimum that you must to restore the system to a normal state, starting with booting the system from a clean diskette. It is very unlikely that you need to "low-level reformat" the hard disk since no virus seen to date requires this action!

If backups of the infected files are available and appropriate care was taken when making the backups (this means mainly that in the case of *executable* files, one should depend on the *original* copy), this is the safest solution, even though it requires much more work if many files are involved.

More commonly, a disinfecting program is used. If the virus is a boot sector infector, you can continue using the computer with relative safety if you boot it from a clean system diskette. But it is wise to go through all your diskettes removing infection, since sooner or later you may be careless and leave a diskette in the machine when it reboots. Boot sector infections on PCs can be cured by the two-step approach of replacing the MBR (on the hard disk), either by using a backup or by the FDISK/MBR command (DOS 5 and up), and then using the SYS command to replace the DOS boot sector.

Can a virus hide in a PC's battery-backed CMOS memory?

No.

For one thing, the CMOS RAM in which system information is stored and backed up by batteries is too small to store much of anything except system information.

More importantly, however, CMOS is not "normal" memory. It is referred to as "ported" memory. This means that in order to get anything out, you use I/O commands. So anything stored there is not sitting directly in memory. Nothing in a normal machine loads the data from that area and executes it, so a virus that "hid" in the CMOS RAM would still have to infect an executable object of some kind in order to load and execute whatever it had written to CMOS.

A malicious virus can, of course, *alter* values in the CMOS as part of its payload, but it can't spread through, or "hide" itself in, the CMOS.

Can a virus infect data files?

Some viruses (Frodo, Cinderella) modify nonexecutable files. However, in order to spread, the virus must be executed. Therefore the "infected" data files cannot be sources of infection.

However, note that it is not always possible to make a sharp distinction between executable and nonexecutable files. One person's code is another person's data and vice versa. Some files that are not directly executable contain code or data that can under some conditions be executed or interpreted.

Some examples from the IBM PC world are source files for any compiler or interpreter, macro files for some packages like MS Word and Lotus 1-2-3, and many others. Currently there are viruses that infect boot sectors, master boot records, COM files, EXE files, BAT files, and device drivers, although any of the objects mentioned above can theoretically be used as an infection carrier. PostScript files can also be used to carry a virus, although no currently known virus does that.

What does the <insert name here> virus do?

If an antivirus program has detected a virus on your computer, don't rush to post a question asking what it does. First, it might be a false-positive alert (especially if the virus is found only in one file), and second, some viruses are extremely common, so the question, "What does the Stoned virus do?" or "What does the Jerusalem virus do?" is asked repeatedly. In any case, if you really *need* to know what a particular virus does (as opposed to knowing enough to get rid of it), you will need a longer treatise than could reasonably be given to you, and one that is likely to be more technical than most of the readers would want.

Therefore, it is better if you first try to answer your question yourself. There are several sources of information (see following question) about the known computer viruses, so please consult one of them before requesting information publicly. Chances are that your virus is rather well known and that it is already described in detail in at least one of these sources.

There is another major problem: if you ask for technical details on one virus, and you actually have another, using that "little knowledge" could be a very dangerous thing. Trying to correct the Stoned virus, when you actually have the Stoned-16, will create more damage than the virus itself caused.

Where can I find out about a specific virus?

This depends a lot on what system you use and on how accurate and timely you want the information to be. Probably the biggest source is Patricia Hoffman's VSUM database. It describes only MS-DOS viruses, but almost all of them. Unfortunately, it tends to be too verbose and is regarded by many in the field as being inaccurate, so we do not advise people to rely solely on it.

Another is the *Computer Virus Catalog*, published by the Virus Test Center in Hamburg. It contains a highly technical description of computer viruses for several platforms: MS-DOS, Mac, Amiga, Atari ST, UNIX. Unfortunately, the MS-DOS section is somewhat incomplete.

There are also two print journals: the monthly *Virus Bulletin* (published by Sophos in the U.K., but U.S. subscriptions can be obtained by calling [203] 431-8720) and the monthly *Virus News International* (published by S&S International). Unfortunately both are *very* expensive (the subscription may be $250 per year).

The best source of information available on Apple Macintosh viruses is the on-line documentation provided with the freeware Disinfectant program by John Norstad. This is available at most Mac archive sites.

Where can I get more information on viruses in general?

The "V.I.R.U.S. Weekly" service, available via mail or fax, should keep you up-to-date on the latest antivirals, as well as new and possibly dangerous viral programs to look out for. The "Slade's Journal" column is intended to be an ongoing course in computer viral programs: you will find a lot of your questions answered if you read the back issues of it.

Note the book review section of these appendices, but there are also three excellent texts on computer viruses available that should cover most of the technical questions you might have:

Rogue Programs: Viruses, Worms and Trojan Horses, edited by Lance J. Hoffman, Van Nostrand Reinhold, 1990.
A Pathology of Computer Viruses, by David Ferbrache, Springer-Verlag, 1992.
A Short Course on Computer Viruses, by Dr. Fred B. Cohen, Wiley & Sons, 1994.

What are "stealth" viruses?

A "stealth" virus is one that hides the modifications it has made in the file or boot record, usually by monitoring the system functions used by programs to read files or physical blocks from storage media and by forging the results of such system functions so that programs that try to read these areas see the original uninfected form of the file instead of the actual infected form. Thus the viral modifications go undetected by antiviral programs. However, in order to do this, the virus must be resident in memory when the antiviral program is executed.

A "clean" system is needed so that no virus is present to distort the results. Therefore, it is a good idea to prepare, now, before you need it, a bootable "system" disk. Write-protect this disk, and keep it safe so that you can "boot clean" when you want to check your system. Original bootable MS-DOS disks from the manufacturer should provide such a clean system if the disks are unwritable.

What are "polymorphic" viruses?

In order to eradicate a virus infection, all copies of the particular virus in various places (program files, boot records, and so on) have to be found and identified. A program that accomplishes this task is called a virus scanner. A "polymorphic" virus is one that tries to escape virus scanners by producing copies of itself that act the same but "look different" to a scanner. One method is self-encryption with a variable key; however, these viruses (e.g., Cascade) are not termed "polymorphic," as their decryption code is always the same and thus can be used as a virus signature.

One type of polymorphic virus will choose among a variety of different encryption routines. Only one would be plainly visible in any copy of the virus. A virus scanner would have to exploit several signatures (one for each possible encryption method) to reliably identify a virus of this kind.

A more sophisticated polymorphic virus will vary the sequence of instructions in its copies by interspersing it with "noise" instructions (e.g., a "No Operation" instruction), by interchanging instructions, or even by using various instruction sequences with the same result. The most sophisticated form of polymorphism discovered so far is the MtE Mutation Engine written by the Bulgarian virus writer who calls himself the "Dark Avenger."

What are "companion" viruses?

A companion (or spawning) virus is one that, instead of modifying an existing file, creates a new one that (unknown to the user) gets executed before some normal program. The only way this has been done so far is by creating an infected COM file with the same name as an existing EXE file. The purpose of creating such files is to fool integrity checkers that look only for *modifications* in *existing* files.

What are "false positives" and "false negatives"?

A "false-positive" error is one in which the antiviral software claims that a given file is infected by a virus when in reality the file is clean. A "false-negative" error is one in which the software fails to indicate that an infected file is infected. Clearly, false negatives are more serious than false positives, although both are undesirable.

It has been proven by Dr. Fred Cohen that every virus detector must have either false positives or false negatives, or both.

In the case of virus scanners, false positives are rare, but they can arise if the scan string chosen for a given virus is also present in some benign programs (because the string was not well chosen). False negatives are more common with virus scanners because scanners will miss a completely new or a heavily modified virus.

One other serious problem could occur: a "positive" that is misdiagnosed. As mentioned, if you have one virus and try to "disinfect" another, you can create problems. This is one reason we always recommend using more than one antiviral program.

APPENDIX B

QUICK REFERENCE ANTIVIRAL REVIEW CHART

This listing is intended to give a quick overview guide to the comparative features and effectiveness of many different antiviral products.

Key

Type: S = scanner, D = disinfection (restoration of state), R = resident, I = integrity checking, M = activity monitor, O = operation restricting, E = encryption

UI (user interface): C = command line, G = menu or GUI

(The following are based on a 1 = poor, 4 = excellent scale)
Doc = documentation
Ease: I = Installation, U = use
Ovrl: Overall rating for general use

Sites

VTC = ftp.informatik.uni-hamburg.de (134.100.4.42)
cert = virus materials now moved to cs.ucr.edu
eugene = eugene.utmb.edu (129.109.9.21)
garbo = garbo.uwasa.fi (128.214.87.1)
nwu = ftp.acns.nwu.edu (129.105.113.52)
risc = risc.ua.edu (130.160.4.7)
simtel = mirrored at oak.oakland.edu among other places
urvax = urvax.urich.edu (141.166.36.6)

For more detailed reviews, see /pub/virus-l/docs/reviews at cert.
For general virus info see *virus-l* FAQ (Frequently Asked Questions list) at various sites.

Please send updated versions of antivirals to Rob Slade at 3118 Baird Road, North Vancouver, BC, Canada V7K 2G6. Publishers shipping from outside of Canada are advised to label the materials as samples per GST section 215(1), without value and not subject to GST.

Amiga

Product	Ver	Type (SDRIMOE)	UI (CG)	Doc (1–4)	Ease (I)	(U)	Ovrl (1–4)	Price	Comments
BootX (discontinued) amiga.physik.unizh.ch, ux1.cso.uiuc.edu or wuarchive.wustl.edu /mirrors2/amiga.physik.unizh.ch /util/virus	5.23	SDRM	G					Free	
Computer Malware Base VTC, cert	9508	info		4			4	Free	
LDV	1.73								
VirusChecker	6.26							Free	
amiga.physik.unizh.ch, uxl.cso.uiuc.edu or wuarchive.wustl.edu									
VirusZ	3.06								
Virus Tracker	2.45								
ZeroVirus									

Atari

Name	Version	Type			Price
Chasseur II atari.archive.umich.edu		D			
FCHECK atari.archive.umich.edu	25	I			
Protect6 atari.archive.umich.edu larserio@ifi.uio.no		DR			
Sagrotan atari.archive.umich.edu	4.12	S			
VIRUSDIE atari.archive.umich.edu		S			
Computer Malware Base VTC, cert	9508	info	4	4	
VKILLER woodside@ttidca.com atari.archive.umich.edu /atari/Utilities/Virus	3.84	SD			Free

Mac

Product	Version	Type (SDRIMOE)	UI (CG)	Doc (1-4)	Ease (I) (U)	Overall (1-4)	Price	Comments
Computer Malware Base VTC, cert	9508	info		4		4	Free	
Disinfectant nwu, sumex-aim.stanford.edu mac.archive.umich.edu	3.6	SDR					Free	
Gatekeeper Chris Johnson	1.3	R MO					Free	(no longer supported)
Rival Microseeds Publishing								
SAM Symantec/Norton	5	SD M					$99	
Virex (see MS-DOS, product not by same author)	4.5.5							
VirusDetective Jeff Shulman	5.10.5							

MS-DOS

Product / Vendor	Version	Features						Price	Notes
AntiViral ToolKit KAMI, various agents	2.2	SDRI						$59.95	
Antivirus (IRIS) Fink Enterprises		SDR M	C	2	2	4	2	$49	
Antivirus-Plus Trend Micro		SDR M	C	2	2	4	2	$99	
AVAST! ALWIL Software	7.0	SDRIMO	CG	3	3	2	3		
Computer Malware Base VTC, cert	9508	info		4			4	Free	(note also CAERObase and Computer Virus Catalog)
Data Physician + Digital Dispatch	4.0B	SDRIM	C	2	2	2	2		
DISKSECURE risc, urvax, eugene	2.42	IM	C	2	3	3	4		BSIs only (cf. also FixMBR, Fix-UTIL, SafeMBR)
Dr. Sol. AVToolkit S&S International Ltd. support@sands.co.uk, Ontrack	7.10	SDRIMO	CG	3	2	3	4		

Product	Version	Type (SDRIMOE)	UI (CG)	Doc (1-4)	Ease (I)	Ease (U)	Overall (1-4)	Price	Comments
F-PROT frisk@complex.is, risc, urvax, eugene, garbo	2.19	SDR	CG	3	3	3	4	home-free; bus. $1/CPU	
F-PROT Professional Data Fellows Command Software	2.19	SDRI	CG	3	3	3	4		
Hoffman Summary risc, urvax, eugene	501	info	G	3	3		3	$35	
HS Stroem System Soft	3.58	I	C	2	2	2	3	$15	
HyperACCESS/5 Higraeve		S	C	2	1	2	2		terminal program with scanner
IBM AntiVirus/DOS local IBM rep	2.2	SRDI	CG	2	2	2	3	$35	

Product / Company	Version								Price	Notes
ImmuneII Higher Ground Diagnostics	4.1	SD M	CG	1	1	3	2		$40	(see also PC-Cillin)
Integrity Master risc, urvax, eugene	2.51	S I	CG	4	3	3	3		$28	
LANProtect Intel	1.1	S	CG	1	2	2	2			
Norton AntiVirus Symantec	3.0	SDRI	G	2	3	2	3		$130	
PC-Cillin Trend Micro	2.95L	SDRIM	G	3	3	3	2		$139	
Rising Anti-Virus Rising Science and Technology Inc.		M	C	1	2	2	2			
SafeWord Virus-Safe Enigma Logic	1.12	I	C	2	3	4	3			
SIX (also BRECT) DriftNet BBS +1-506-325-9002	3.08	I	C	2	3	2	2		Free	
ThunderByte Utility risc, urvax, eugene, garbo	6.35	SDRIMOE	C	2	2	3	3		$29	
VACCINE (WWS) The Davidsohn Group	5.00	SD IMO	C	2	1	2	2			
VACCINE (Sophos)	9111	S I	CG	2	2	2	3			
Untouchable	1.1	SDRIM	CG	2	2	2	2			

Product	Version	Type (SDRIMOE)	UI (CG)	Doc (1–4)	Ease (I)	Ease (U)	Overall (1–4)	Price	Comments
VDS risc, urvax, eugene	2.10T	I	CG	2	2	3	2		
VET Cybec	8.2	SDRIM	CG	3	3	3	3		
Victor Charlie Delta Base Enterprises	5.0	IM	C	3	2	3	3	$99	
Virex-PC Datawatch (VIRx now assumed under this product)	2.94	SDRIM	G	4	2	4	4	$49	
Virus0Buster Leprechaun Software (70451.3621@compuserve.com)	3.75	SDRIMO	CG	3	3	3	4		
VIRUSCAN Suite risc, urvax, SIMTEL, garbo, mcafee.com	2.22	SDRIM	C	2	2	2	3	~$25/module	

Product / Source	Version								Price / Notes
VirusNet PC SafetyNet		SDRI	CG	3	3	3	3		(See also F-PROT)
VirusSafe (LAN) EliaShim Micro	4.01	SDRI O	CG	2	2	2	2		
VI-Spy RG Software Systems	10.0	SDR M	CG	2	2	3	3		$150

OS/2

Product / Source	Version								Price / Notes
HyperACCESS/5 Higraeve		S	C	2	1	2	2		terminal program with scanner
IBM AntiVirus/OS/2 local IBM rep	2.2	SRDI	CG	2	2	2	3		$35
SCAN/OS/2 Suite risc, urvax, SIMTEL, garbo, mcafee.com	2.20	SDRIM	C	2	2	2	3		~$35/module

UNIX

Product / Source	Version								Price / Notes
Computer Malware Base VTC, cert	9508	info		4	4	4	4		Free
Tripwire ftp.cs.purdue.edu pub/spaf/COAST/Tripwire		I							Free

APPENDIX C

REVIEWS OF ANTIVIRAL PRODUCTS

Introduction to the Antiviral Reviews

Antiviral software generally brings out new releases faster than any other type of application. Therefore, in one sense, almost all of these reviews are out of date.

On the other hand, a great many releases contain only incremental changes, and so do not affect the overall operation of the program. Nor, interestingly, do antiviral programs tend to change effectiveness very much over time in relation to other programs. Over the four years that I have been reviewing and testing programs, most have tended to stay the same in comparison to whatever else is available.

Hopefully, then, this may be of use to you. However, please use this only as a guide to choose products that you do, then, evaluate yourself.

Activity Monitors

Techmar Computer Products
AntiVirus-Plus ("AI vaccine")

Activity monitor with resident and nonresident scanners

Ratings (1 = poor, 4 = very good)

Installation	2
Ease of use	4
Help systems	1
Compatibility	2
Company stability	3
Documentation	2
Hardware required	2
Performance	2
Availability	2
Local support	1

227

General Description

CURE is a manual scanning program with disinfection features. IMMUNE2 is a resident scanner that checks files as they are loaded, disks when accessed, and memory when the program is first loaded. PREVENT1 is a resident vaccine program.

Recommended only for situations using the computer in fairly limited and standard fashion, where automated attendance is a primary concern.

Protection against major known viral programs and some viral-type activites from new or unknown viral programs. Easy setup with no requirement for user decisions, but strong possibility of interference with normal computer operations. If used, it is recommended that experienced viral specialists be available to handle infections identified. Not recommended for systems with frequent changes in software or configuration.

Comparison of Features and Specifications

Installation AntiVirus-Plus appears to require installation from the *A:* drive onto a hard disk. It is possible to install onto a floppy disk, and it is possible to install from a drive other than *A:*, but the program will continue to request a "write-able" disk in *A:*.

The documentation states that removal from the hard drive requires "de-installation," but this does not appear to be the case.

Installation is almost completely automated. Modification of AUTO-EXEC.BAT is not sophisticated, but did not cause problems in testing.

Ease of use IMMUNE2 and PREVENT1 are automatic, background processes that function without operator attention. When the programs "identify" a process, they do not do so either by virus name, or by identity of infected program. The user is requested (by IMMUNE2) to run CURE, but no parameters are given. (See also "Compatibility" regarding false alarms.)

Help systems None provided.

Compatibility Both CURE and IMMUNE2 identify common and well-known viral programs, although not always by the "standard" names. Jerusalem-B is identified as "Black Friday #1," for example. All AntiVirus-Plus programs are fairly noisy about their detection of a virus, vis the message that appears when IMMUNE2 is invoked while a virus is present in memory:

```
                                        +===========================+
                                        " Warning !!                "
Fri  1-18-1991 13:02:09.49"                You are using  an       "
A>antvirus\immune2                      "   infected disk(ette).    "
!! A Virus is present in y"                                         "
!! Removing the virus now " Use ANTI VIRUS "cure"                   "
!! A Virus is present in y" program to remove virus.                "
!! Removing the virus now "                                         "
!! A Virus is present in y" Hit any key to continue                 "
!! Removing the virus now +===========================+
!! A Virus is present in your computer memory !!
!! Removing the virus now !!
!! A Virus is present in your computer memory !!
!! Removing the virus now !!
!! A Virus is present in your computer memory !!
!! Removing the virus now !!
The ANTI-VIRUS immunity program is now resident.
```

The same window, without quite so much "background noise," appears when any disk, infected with a known boot sector virus, is accessed, even by a directory request. It also appears when an infected program is run and states that the program has been disinfected. The program is *not* disinfected on disk, but the virus appears to be barred from memory. (Note that the virus in memory, which triggered the display above, was not removed from memory, but was rendered inactive.)

The PREVENT1 program, however, fairs rather worse. It does not appear to prevent any change to the boot sector, and therefore it seems that new boot sector viral programs will be undetectable by the program, unless they are very crude. This problem, however, pales in comparison with the problems PREVENT1 will cause with normal, uninfected, programs.

If you use a program (such as a word processor) to delete or modify a program file, PREVENT1 will halt program execution. This may not seem like a big deal: after all, how many people use (as I do) WordPerfect as a disk manager? However, some programs, WordPerfect among them, make changes to the program itself when you change some part of the configuration, and PREVENT1 will stop this as well, telling you:

```
                              Set-up Menu

 0 - End Set-up and enter WP

 1 - Set Directories or Drives for Dictionary and Thesa
 2 - Set Initial Settings
 3 - Set Screen and Beep Options
 4 - Set Backup Options       +===========================+
                              " Warning !!                "
Selection: 0                  "  You have been running    "
                              "  an infected program.     "
Press Cancel to ignore cha"                               "
                              " PREVENT1 has removed the   "
                              "  memory infection !        "
                              "                            "
                              " Hit any key to continue    "
                              +===========================+
```

It is, therefore, inadvisable to use AntiVirus-Plus on a system that undergoes frequent changes in this manner.

PREVENT1 is not completely consistent here. WordPerfect is halted when trying to delete a program file, PCTOOLS is not. It's quite possible that some viral programs may slip past this protection.

Company stability Techmar is the distributor of AntiVirus-Plus and other IRIS products in the United States. Fink Enterprises, which distributes IRIS products in Canada, will not carry AntiVirus-Plus.

Company support Help-line support was not used in testing. Techmar shipped very quickly but did not properly identify the package, which created problems at the border.

Documentation Documentation is provided solely on disk. The directions are clear and readable, but very little information is provided beyond the most basic installation. Some points in the documentation are not consistent with program operation, but not to the point of preventing installation or operation.

Hardware requirements Documentation states hard disk required, but this can be avoided. Disk "wants" to be installed from *A:* drive.

Performance IMMUNE2 and CURE will identify many common viral programs. They fail to identify the AIDS virus, which is interesting in that, while AIDS infections are not common, the virus source code is available and widely known to researchers. (CURE was the first scanning program tested that was not able to identify the virus.)

PREVENT1 will prevent some disk-writes to program files, but allows others to pass, including the deletion of program files. It apparently does not check any writes to disk boot sectors or "bad" sectors.

Local support None stated or found.

Support requirements Alarms will likely require intervention by experienced personnel.

Cheyenne Software
InocuLAN

Menu front end and LAN additions for IRIS AntiVirus

Ratings (1 = poor, 4 = very good)

Installation	3
Ease of use	3
Help systems	2

Compatibility	2
Company stability	2
Company support	2
Documentation	2
Hardware required	3
Performance	2
Availability	2
Local support	1

General Description

A repackaging of IRIS AntiVirus with a menu interface and NetWare messaging, logging, and Netware Loadable Module (NLM) features. Recent ads show inclusion of the VirAway scanner, which was not included in the version sent for testing.

Comparison of Features and Specifications

Installation The package is shipped on two unprotected 1.44M or 1.2M floppies. Installation as an NLM is available only in automated form; installation on a workstation or server is available in either automated or manual form. Automated installation will create entries in the AUTOEXEC.BAT for PREVENT, IMMUNE, and EXAMINE. Optionally, a recovery disk may be created that backs up system areas and files from the hard disk.

Ease of use Operation of the IRIS files is automated through the InocuLAN menu. There are few options in any case, so use should not be difficult regardless of circumstances.

Help systems On-screen help is available.

Compatibility The LAN features are for NetWare only. In testing, PREVENT has been fairly intrusive in regard to fairly normal applications use.

Company stability Cheyenne has recently been showing a much stronger presence in the market.

Company support The usual.

Documentation A *Supervisor Guide and Reference*, several copies of a *User Guide*, and several copies of a "Quick Reference Card" are included in the package. The *Supervisor Guide* is the master reference, with the others being subsets of it. The text is quite simple, with several sections being essentially repeated up to three times with very minor differences. There is little in the package that should present any difficulties, but there is little in the manual to help if they arise. A section on general virus information starts with a clear statement of what a virus is, and how it infects . . . and ends in less than a page.

Hardware requirements NetWare 2.x or 3.x.

Performance InocuLAN is basically a LAN version, and menu front end, for the IRIS AntiVirus product. Besides the LAN features and menu, additional items are the ability to scan Macintosh files on the server and the preparation of a recovery disk, with hard disk and system information. (Note that the manual initially suggested saving system info to the hard disk itself: This is of limited use in recovering a deleted hard disk.)

Local support None provided.

Support requirements The package has limited options, so support requirements should not be high.

Higher Ground Diagnostics, Inc.
Immune II

Scanner and activity monitor
$40

Ratings (1 = poor, 4 = very good)

Installation	1
Ease of use	3
Help systems	2
Compatibility	2
Company stability	1
Company support	2
Documentation	1
Hardware required	3
Performance	1
Availability	1
Local support	1

General Description

This appears to be a shareware distribution of the PC-Rx (nonhardware) version of PC-Cillin, formerly produced by Trend Micro Devices. There are modules for scanning, activity monitoring, and Windows display functions.

Comparison of Features and Specifications

Installation As received, the package was in an archive within an archive within encoded email. Potential users would need MIME64 and ZIP format extractors.

Installation is not well documented. There are notes dealing with various conflicts and incompatibilities. Users likely will need to check and change a number of settings and will need to read all the assorted text files to find out what those might be.

REVIEWS OF ANTIVIRAL PRODUCTS

An INSTALL.EXE file was contained within the innermost archive file. It was corrupted.

Ease of use A graphical front end is provided.

Once a scan has been started, it cannot be terminated. An attempt to terminate a lengthy scan crashed the test computer hard.

Help systems Invocation of some modules without correct command-line switches gives a list of switches.

Compatibility Numerous incompatibilities with various programs are listed in one of the text files.

Company stability This is going to require a bit of background.

My first introduction to this incarnation of the product was in a posting on a virus discussion group infamous for the posting of virus code. The subject had a "get-rich-quick" flavor to it, and I at first assumed that it was simply another spam message. I was surprised to find that it actually did seem to refer to an antiviral product. Subsequent email indicated that the party doing the posting was either the author of a "get-rich-quick" book or the producer of an infomercial seminar. The author of the antiviral program was said to have asked for help with direct sales, and the marketer was purported to be so impressed with the product that a deal was struck for distribution rights.

However experienced the sales company is in the world of TV and mail order, it obviously has a few things to learn about life on-line. When the promised "free trial version" arrived, it did so as an 800K MIME (base64) encoded email message. The person doing the mailing, now identified as John Luke, made contemptuous remarks to the effect that the Internet "doesn't work." (It can be safely assumed that Mr. Luke is as unfamiliar with Internet tools as he is with Internet marketing: not only was MIME used instead of the arguably more accessible uuencode, but a subsequent copy, said to fix various bugs, would not extract.)

Extraction of the base64 file produced a self-extracting ZIP format archive, which, in turn, contained another self-extracting archive. These were accompanied by buggy installation batch files and unhelpful, all uppercase, difficult-to-read text files containing such gems as "BE SURE TO THEN READ, UNDERSTAND AND AGREE TO THE LICENSE THEREIN ENTITLED BY THE FILE NAME FREELICE.TXT."

Benefit Sales, and John Luke, appear to be selling on a pyramid construction, as indicated by the advice "MAIL A CHECK OR MONEY ORDER FOR $40 TO BECOME A REGISTERED DISTRIBUTOR. YOU WILL RECEIVE $5 FOR EACH $40 IMMUNR [sic] II SALE YOU GENERATE AND YOU WILL BE GIVEN PERMISSION TO DISTRIBUTE THIS FREE TRIAL VERSION TO INTRODUCE IMMUNE II" in one of the text files and his email address (mmn stands for "Making Money Now"). Other text files buried deeper inside the archive seem to indicate that the developer/producer of the program is Higher

Ground Diagnostics. Careful examination of the programs, and some text files, reveals the names PC-Cillin and Trend.

Trend Micro Devices produced and marketed PC-Cillin in 1991. At that time it had a change-detection component that used a hardware storage device connected to the parallel port of the computer. Later Trend produced a software-only version called PC-Rx. It sporadically produced a newsletter for customers. I have removed the review of PC-Cillin from this edition of the book because I am no longer at all certain the company still exists.

On the face of it, Trend has either folded or dropped this particular product. It may have reverted to the original programmer. However, the careless preparation, including comments such as "Confusing Section. . . . . . .!!!" in the documentation, allow a more sinister construction of the facts.

In short, I have no idea who any of these people are, and I certainly wouldn't trust them with the security of *my* computer.

Company support One comment in a text file indicates support is by mail and phone from Higher Ground Diagnostics at the Ohio address.

Documentation The documentation is careless, inconsistent, and incomplete. There are references within the program to check the Immune II manual—and one reference in one text file that says a manual is available once you register.

Hardware requirements One of the text files states that almost two megabytes of disk space is required for use. In testing, slightly over one megabyte was used.

Performance The package is slow enough that at times I thought the test machine had locked up. Number of viruses detected is below par for current scanners.

Scanning of file archives compressed with the ZIP format is said to be supported, but in tests failed utterly.

A bug in PCSCAN will recursively check directories that do not exist but that are all reported to have the same contents as the current directory. This appears to go on without limit.

Previous concerns with the performance of PC-Cillin in activity monitoring do not appear to have been addressed.

Local support None provided.

Support requirements In its current form it is unlikely that novice users could install or intermediate users could get much out of this program.

Change Detectors

A. Padgett Peterson
DISKSECURE version 2.4

Low-level hard-disk protection
Free for noncommercial use

Ratings (1 = poor, 4 = very good)

Installation	4
Ease of use	4
Help systems	3
Compatibility	3
Company stability	4
Company support	3
Documentation	2
Hardware required	3
Performance	4
Availability	2
Local support	2

General Description

DISKSECURE replaces the partition table of the hard disk with code that performs load-time checking, prevents access to the hard disk if booted from a floppy, and offers software write protection to the system areas of the disk.

I should state a bias here. DISKSECURE is a very powerful protective system and, unlike many others of similar function, is completely confident in telling you what is being done. In reviewing antiviral and security software, I have come to the point where I am positively afraid of running some of these systems: much more so than I am of any viral programs. DISKSECURE has, however, saved my hard disk a number of times from the predations of these other security programs, and for this I am profoundly grateful.

Comparison of Features and Specifications

Installation Default installation is simple and can be accomplished through a supplied batch file. A "quick start" reference is provided along with the regular documentation. For protection of the hard disk, only DISKSEC2 need be run, although this limits the possibilities for recovery.

Novice users may not be sufficiently aware of the dangers inherent in this process, and it is highly recommended that the entire documentation be read. The program is replacing the partition table of the hard disk, and, if it fails, all information that the computer requires to access the disk and information will be lost, even if the information is not physically erased. Although the possibility of this is very small, a backup of the partition boot record prior to installation would be a good idea. This is, in fact, one of the options of the program and should be accepted.

Despite its power, DISKSECURE has caused very few problems over the years. The greatest number of problems occur with those users who know just enough to realize the potential problems of this type of program and who are afraid of it. I have, on several occasions, had people worry that it might have been a trojan program. These are the users who have not read the documentation for the program.

Ease of use Operation of the programs is simple. DISKSEC provides ample prompting and opportunity for the user to stop at any point. The program now has even more options and can fully control all aspects that used to require some manual intervention by the user.

DSRPART can be used to recover the hard disk from boot-sector-infecting viral programs of the type that overwrite the master boot record of the hard disk. (On floppy disks, the first physical sector on the disk is the boot sector. On hard disks the first physical sector is the master boot record, or MBR, which contains a short section of code followed by a description of the size and attributes of the disk called the partition table. Because of the limited number of floppy disk formats, the same thing is accomplished on floppies with only one media-descriptor byte. Thus, while using the SYS command can wipe out any BSI on a floppy disk, some BSIs cannot be so eliminated on a hard disk if they infect the MBR rather than the boot sector.)

Help systems None provided. DISKSEC is well prompted, and the other programs have no options.

Compatibility The original program, since it was so intimately tied to the low-level hardware and disk structure, would not work with nonstandard disk formats. Padgett has worked very diligently over the years, and the more recent versions will even work with such oddities as dedicated Novell network servers and Windows 32BitDiskAccess. The program even has the option of moving the TSR portion to avoid conflicts. The author warns against using DISK-SECURE with QEMM in stealth mode.

Company stability Padgett Peterson has demonstrated, over a number of years, a dedication to the development of antiviral software purely for the safety of computer users. He is to be commended, the more so since this endeavor has been largely unremunerated.

Company support Padgett is well known as a contributor to *VIRUS-L / comp.virus* and is also a member of the GEnie "Virus and Security Round-Table."

Documentation The documentation is quite clear to anyone familiar with MS-DOS operations. Occasionally certain points may not be clear to novice users (for example, the fact that "removal" of DISKSECURE is done via the DSRPART program).

Hardware requirements None specified, but a hard disk and at least one floppy disk (which can be used to boot from) would appear to be minimum requirements.

Performance The program is able to detect all known boot sector infectors, even some recent ones that use new stealth methods and little-known interrupt hooking. Most infections can be removed by the program automatically. Boot infectors that modify the MBR can be removed through the use of the recovery information stored by the program upon installation.

The program indulges in some "stealth" technology of its own: The partition boot record appears unchanged after installation.

Local support Padgett is available via the Internet and GEnie.

Support requirements DISKSECURE is simple enough for a novice user to run and should provide significant protection with minimal risk. Recovery is quick and easy, as long as the user remembers the importance of DSRPART.COM. Intermediate users should note the difficulties in running system-optimizing software.

General Notes

This program should be a part of the DOS operating system. It has, in fact, been offered to three manufacturers of DOS: all three have rejected the opportunity.

DISKSECURE was originally shareware. Very few people registered the program. In spite of this, Padgett has continued to improve the program and has now released it as freeware for noncommercial use. This is very much to his credit, and not particularly to the credit of the shareware-using community. I definitely recommend that all MS-DOS users get and use this program, and that companies license its use.

Stroem System Soft
HS 3.58

Boot virus change detection
$15, licensing available, free for noncommercial use

Ratings (1 = poor, 4 = very good)

Installation	2
Ease of use	2
Help systems	2
Compatibility	3
Company stability	2

Company support	2
Documentation	2
Hardware required	3
Performance	3
Availability	1
Local support	1

General Description

HS is a change-detection system specifically targeted at boot sector infectors and other boot sequence corruption problems. It can be installed in either the CONFIG.SYS (by preference) or AUTOEXEC.BAT files to check the system at boot time. (A commercial version is also available.)

Comparison of Features and Specifications

Installation The package is distributed as shareware and must be installed manually. The instructions are clear but require a first run to produce a "clean state" database and then modification of the CONFIG.SYS or AUTOEXEC.BAT files for automated checking. (HS can be run from the command line for manual checking.) The installation instructions assume a clean machine.

Ease of use Once installation is complete, protection should be automatic.

Help systems The command-line program has a "/?" switch for a brief help message.

Compatibility The program is targeted at boot sector infectors only. Compatibility problems with Novell/DR-DOS and QEMM are addressed in the documentation.

Company stability The program has been developed over a period of some time. It has been quite stable over the past year.

Company support Support is available only by post or Internet email.

Documentation The documentation is quite brief, but clear enough in regard to program operation.

Hardware requirements DOS 3.2 or higher. HS will only run under DOS, but it can be installed on OS/2 and Windows NT multiboot systems.

Performance HS will automatically detect and remove boot sector infectors. The invocation of the program in the CONFIG.SYS or AUTOEXEC.BAT files is fairly late in the boot sequence and therefore potentially subject to stealth avoidance. HS has, however, attempted to address a number of stealth technologies.

Local support None provided.

Support requirements Novice users would likely require some help with the program.

Stiller Research
Integrity Master

Change-detection program with built-in signature scanner
$32.50, licensing available

Ratings (1 = poor, 4 = very good)

Installation	3
Ease of use	3
Help systems	4
Compatibility	3
Company stability	3
Company support	3
Documentation	4
Hardware required	4
Performance	3
Availability	2
Local support	2

General Description

IM is a change-detection program with built-in scanner. SETUPIM is an installation and tutorial program. (A Windows installation program is included that will set up a program group for commonly used functions.) Also included are a file viewer, printer scheduler, and utilities to check the efficacy of the system.

Comparison of Features and Specifications

Installation Integrity Master is sold directly from Stiller Research and agents. A fully functional version is distributed as shareware, and Stiller Research is a member of the Association of Shareware Professionals. The shareware distribution archives for Integrity Master are full of files, a large number of which relate primarily to the distribution and description of the program. The number of files is somewhat daunting, as is the size of the README.DOC file. The file does, however, start with the suggestion that the novice simply run the SETUPIM program, and this is worthwhile advice to follow.

I received also a version on disk from the developer on a 1.44M unwritable diskette. If a shareware author can do this, there is no excuse for the commercial operations.

Calling SETUPIM an installation program is misleading. It is less than an installation program—and much, much more. For the novice user, SETUPIM has some of the most "user-friendly" features of any product yet reviewed. It certainly has the best explanations of the antiviral process and the options for security of any installation program.

Although the program and system, overall, is well designed and has advanced in respect of virus-detection technology, I was quite surprised to note that the installation procedure has not fixed some earlier bugs.

While there is provision for installation to a drive other than *C:*, there is no option to change the default installation directory.

The programs (both IM and SETUPIM) have a command-line switch that "forces" monochrome mode with a monochrome monitor on a "color" adapter. This is important, since some of the menu "highlighting" is invisible on a monochrome monitor. The programs *can* change to monochrome in "midsession," so it should not be difficult to add a short "screen test" for the completely novice user, rather than making them use the command-line option. (This applies only to SETUPIM: a proper installation will tell IM which video mode to use.)

(If IM is invoked before SETUPIM is run to create the parameter file, IM will refuse to run. Three options are presented, including "Abort," which is described, with an unusual lack of clarity, as "Quit and return.")

The SETUPIM program prepares a parameter file for use by IM (which sets up the various options for running the integrity checks) and produces a suggested procedure for completing the installation, but it does not actually do the copying and placement of files, or the invocation of the initial "signature" calculations. While readily admitting the value of having a "cold boot" before this is done, it should be possible to do some more of this for the novice user before turning him or her loose with a (softcopy) instruction set. Alternately, the installation program could strongly suggest that a "cold boot" and other security measures are desirable, but offer to proceed with installation if the user desired, on the clear understanding that this is "second best." (This approach is taken with some of the options during the setup.)

This is not to say that the instructions in the IMPROC.TXT (the suggested installation procedure document file produced by SETUPIM) are in any way inadequate. The instructions are clear and straightforward. The file is displayed to the user at the end of the SETUPIM part of the installation process, and the user is given the command to invoke the IMVIEW file viewer in order to review the file later, or the IMPRINT batch file in order to print it in hardcopy. (The IMPROC.TXT is unclear at one point, the one where almost everyone seems to fall down. The document contains the injunction to "cold-boot" the computer, and it is probably not clear to the novice user that this does not mean to do it "right now.")

The SETUPIM program also contains a tutorial. Both the operation of the program and the conceptual aspects of virus protection, data loss, and security measures are covered. This is extremely useful, and the only problem I have with it is to wish that more of the material from the documentation could be included.

The installation procedure does not address installation of IM in the AUTOEXEC.BAT file, although use of scheduling software is mentioned in places. The installation process does, however, suggest the preparation of a bootable disk with IM files on it for recovery purposes. If the installation process is interrupted, a screen message suggests the option of installing via the Windows program, IMWIN. While this does set up a Windows program group, one of the items in the group must then be chosen in order to complete installation.

Ease of use The screens, menus, and options are well laid out, and labels are well chosen with a view to clarity of meaning. The SETUPIM program is amazingly well designed with the novice user in mind.

At a couple of points during installation the user can be left staring at a screen and possibly wondering if he or she did something wrong. (The amount of time this takes, however, varies widely depending upon the speed of the machine.) The program noted that there was no boot sector on my boot drive, since it reads the sector with an interrupt that conflicts with LANtastic server software. At times, the program is stepped (or "timed") through a sequence that begins to suggest the possibility of an infinite loop. (The "timed" stepping is probably a good idea here; some users may give up before it reaches the conclusion.) The tutorial, at certain points, requests specific keystrokes but accepts anything, not a pedagogically sound design. Some minor keystroke "trapping" and a "please press the arrow key, you can practice later" message would improve it.

The GUI, windows, and menus are here used as they are meant to be in order to make the program useful and quick to operate. Not only is the label and option wording well chosen, but each item, as it is selected, pops out a window with extra explanation about what it does. Often the window will contain a brief, but clear, discussion of the pros and cons of using this particular option.

Help systems Help is only partially context sensitive. The help key, however, brings up options for help with the operation of the program, the screen display, or a help index. (If the index is chosen, the currently "open" menu is "selected.")

However, the explanatory "window" beside each selected item seems to largely obviate the need for any kind of help system. (On items where the explanation could be confusing, for example the "Files to iNitialize" options, the help index is of little assistance, and one would need recourse to the manual. The index is, however, very extensive, even covering what the AUTOEXEC.BAT file is, although with less detail than a novice would need in order to automate checking.)

Compatibility The documentation notes possible problems with file locking under LANs, Windows, and OS/2. Potential problems with LANs are noted, and recommendations are made for specific operating systems.

Company stability Both the change-detection and scanner components of the product are mature and stable. The scanner, although the secondary part of the package, ranks quite well in scanner tests and has been consistently maintained over the years.

Company support Support is available via fax, phone, and email as well as through a pay-per-call third-party number. Registered users may call direct for support, and it is available through at least two BBSes. (Note that ASG, the pay-per-call number, is completely independent of Stiller Research. Stiller Research does not receive any of the charges for support provided through ASG.)

Documentation Integrity Master's documentation is a massive text file, which begins with a section intriguingly titled "Don't Read This." This is, in fact, a suggestion to novice users that they skip the first section, on the workings of IM, and just use the installation program. It also suggests that they *do* read the second section, which is a general treatment of viral programs and the various other types of data disasters that commonly occur.

The documentation as a whole has a "technical" flavor, but is clear and unambiguous. The intermediate user should have no problem with the first section, but might be well advised to read section two first, to have a clear grasp of the reasons for the various options IM offers.

Section two's overview of viral programs and other risks to data contains excellent information. It could form the basis of a very useful primer on data integrity as a whole.

Hardware requirements A minimum of 260K memory and DOS 2.x or higher is required. Refreshingly, a hard disk is not. It appears that IM can be installed on any disk that has room for the programs and files. In fact, IM can be installed on a hard disk, and then the IM.EXE and IM.PRM files copied to a floppy and used anywhere. IM does not "demand" the presence of the equipment it was originally installed on.

Performance Installation and calculation of signatures for the full hard disk were faster than for other tested change detectors. IM states that its "quick check" looks only for changes to the file date and size. It is likely that the "turbo" modes of other change detectors do the same, without being as honest about it.

(With all the information presented on-screen each time an option is selected, it is remarkable that IM is extremely responsive.)

The storage of "signatures" is a matter of much debate. IM stores them in each directory checked. There is, however, provision for storage of the signature files on an "off-line" diskette, which adds a security factor.

IM's virus scanning picked up all common viral programs tested against it, and a good many that were less so. Some new viri were detected on the basis of similarity to known code.

Local support None provided.

Support requirements As with any change-detection program, assignment of causes to different types of alterations may be problematic. However, the program itself should provide ample explanation to any reasonably intelligent person, regardless of the level of "computer" background. The integrated virus scanner should be of great assistance with identifying the most commonly seen viral programs.

General Notes
Recommended as the change-detection component of virus detection or protection for all levels of computer users.

Enigma Logic, Inc.
SafeWord Virus-Safe version 1.12 (900831)
Change-detection software

Ratings (1 = poor, 4 = very good)
Installation	3
Ease of use	4
Help systems	3
Compatibility	3
Company stability	3
Company support	2
Documentation	2
Hardware required	4
Performance	3
Availability	2

General Description
SafeWord (R) Virus-Safe 1.12 is a manual or TSR program-file checking package based upon signatures that the program calculates when installed. Signature algorithms can include a DES- or MAC-based calculation. Enigma Logic makes similar programs for various mini and mainframe operating systems. As suggested by this association and the documentation, Safeword is best used in a managed environment. The package is, however, simple enough to give significant protection to a naive user.

Comparison of Features and Specifications
Installation The disk received was not write-protected.

The installation procedure first specifies the creation of a "sterile kernel diskette" and warns you not to execute any programs that might be infected while this diskette is in the drive. However, the procedure, as specified in the *SafeWord Virus-Safe User Guide* (Release 1.0, July 1989) does not give any indication as to how you might be able to deal with any existing viral infection. The procedure does warn against using the "sterile kernel diskette" for any other purpose, but does not mention write-protecting it. The procedure also indicates that the sterile diskette should be prepared before installation onto the system. This would seem to indicate that the sterile diskette will be using the check signatures stored on the system, and not "off-line."

Preparation of the sterile diskette is not part of the automated installation, although the directions given do not indicate why it could not be. Automated installation is suggested to be invoked from the A: drive but can be performed from, and to, any drive, including floppy diskettes. The installation process is fairly standard, creating a subdirectory and copying files. At one point it asks for a "seed phrase" in order to ensure that check signatures differ for each machine that the program is installed on. Given the sophistication of the signature generation contained in the package, this may seem to be overkill, but it does provide an additional measure of security. Default automated installation should not take more than ten minutes on any machine.

Although the installation program is stated to deal with the CONFIG.SYS and AUTOEXEC.BAT files, when installing onto a floppy boot disk system it will not. Nor does it check or create signatures for the system areas.

A brief manual installation procedure is listed that will allow nonstandard installations, but it still does not provide security to the system areas of floppy diskettes.

SafeWord starts, by default, in "Learn" mode, which means that minimal installation can be performed. Once the SafeWord package is installed and operating, it will query each "new" program the first time it is invoked.

(The package also contains a batch file for removal or de-installation of the program, and this is simply, elegantly, and thoughtfully designed.)

Ease of use Default installation and operation is extremely easy, and almost any user should be able to perform installation without introduction or even reference to the manual. The "Learn" mode is very self-explanatory and even gives some direction on the choice of the security level (in terms of the trade-off between sophistication of checking and time required for analysis). Of all programs evaluated so far, SafeWord offers the best on-screen information regarding the problems detected and the options available to the user.

The command-line switches, which allow for a greater variety of security checking, are not prompted for or accessible aside from the command line, but would generally be used by more experienced personnel in any case.

Help systems There are no help systems per se, but the menus and prompts should be very clear to the user.

Compatibility The program requires minimal hardware. In testing, it did not conflict with any other resident programs, although the documentation does suggest running SWVSAFE.COM after all other device drivers in the CONFIG.SYS file, if invoked from CONFIG.SYS. Interestingly, invoking the SWVEDIT program while the Jerusalem-B virus is resident in memory caused a "divide overflow" error (invoking SWVSAFE with Jerusalem resident did not).

If a change in a program is detected on invocation, SafeWord will not arbitrarily shut operation down, as do many other programs, but explains the change detected and presents the various options that could have caused the change. It also allows the option to update the checklist file. This feature makes SafeWord much more compatible with programs like WordPerfect that make changes to their own program code when making configuration changes and with "active" computer environments where configuration changes are frequent.

As the program relies on change detection only, protection against stealth viral programs would be problematic. The ability of the program to check files either at boot time or on invocation would allow the inspection of an assortment of files and give some probability of detecting the infection before the stealth virus had a chance to become resident and circumvent the checking. In the case of infection of the boot sector or infected programs run before SWVSAFE was invoked, the package would not provide any protection.

Tests against spawning viral activity (the renaming of a small COM file to the same filename as a larger EXE file and marking it as hidden) show that an aware user would have indications of a problem. The first time the EXE file is "infected," SWVSAFE.COM will bring up the alert screen stating that the COM program is not registered. On subsequent runs, the small "checking" window will show up twice as both the COM and EXE file are run. (This is only if the self-check alert window has not been "turned off." It also depends upon the alertness of the user: I am certain that most people can bring to mind users to whom this phenomenon would not seem the least bit bothersome.)

Company stability Unknown, but the production of programs for multiple platforms indicates a good presence in the market.

Company support The address and phone number for the company is listed in the documentation, and Bob Bosen was a contributor to the *VIRUS-L / comp.virus* list. He has not, however, been active for some time now.

The package received did not contain any means of registering the program, nor did I receive any direct notice of the update that was announced by Bob Bosen on *VIRUS-L* during the evaluation period.

Documentation The only piece of documentation that was received with the package was the *SafeWord Virus-Safe User Guide* (Release 1.0, July 1989). A README.TXT file included on the disk was dated January 30, 1990, although the program files were dated August 31, 1990. The README.TXT file did not refer to any version number or date, but a file called SWVSVERS, created when the program was installed, identifies it as version 1.12. The documentation also refers to SafeWord PC-Safe and *PC-Safe II User and Supervisor Guides*, although this appears to be data-encryption software (the documentation is not completely clear).

The indications are that the program is intended to be used in a managed environment and that the structure of the manual is written with this in mind.

Sections 1 and 2 deal with an overview of the program and background information on viral programs and file image signatures. As the manual is quite small, these sections do not contain much significant information, but they would be of interest to a computer user at the supervisory or support level.

They would not, however, be of much interest to a naive user. Given the ease of use and the standard installation, a reordering of the contents to place section 3.2 (Automated Installation) at the beginning would make this package suitable for a much wider market. The manual is, otherwise, fairly clear and would not be threatening to a novice. The one area of concern, as mentioned earlier, is the procedure for the making of a "sterile" diskette, and this could be noted as an area best left for support staff or knowledgeable users.

Hardware requirements Does not require special hardware, but does not make provisions for the protection of system areas of floppy diskettes.

Performance There does not seem to be a "linear" measure of how fast a file is checked. Checking of a 28K COM file takes about 10 seconds while a 30K EXE takes 20 seconds (on a 10 MHz PC). An analysis of WordPerfect 4.2 (WP.EXE, 267K), at the highest security level (ANSI X9.9/DES) took more than a minute, while the delay in invoking the program subsequently was about twice that (this on a program that takes 30 seconds to load).

Because the program does not check the system areas of floppy diskettes, there is no protection against boot sector viral programs on floppy-drive-only systems.

Local support None specified.

Support requirements The package could, unsupported, provide significant protection to any user. With more experience, or a greater level of support, further protection can be realized.

General Notes

In its current state, the program provides strong protection against viral infections of program files and nonstealth boot sector infections of hard disk systems. Used in conjunction with other types of antiviral programs, it would provide significant protection in all types of computing environments and for all levels of computer users.

Provision for checking the system areas of floppy disks, and possibly checking of system memory configuration, use, and interrupts would likely strengthen the product.

Zen Works
SIX, BRECT

System and memory change detection
Free for noncommercial, nongovernmental use

Ratings (1 = poor, 4 = very good)

Installation	3
Ease of use	2
Help systems	1
Compatibility	3
Company stability	3
Company support	2
Documentation	2
Hardware required	4
Performance	2
Availability	2
Local support	1

General Description

SIX is a small and specialized change-detection program designed to check system and memory after the boot process has completed. It will detect changes to itself, memory, and certain interrupts. (BRECT is an advanced utility to patch floppy diskettes in order to remove infections.)

Comparison of Features and Specifications

Installation SIX is distributed as shareware. The program is a single small file. Installation could be as simple as copying the SIX.COM file to an appropriate place on the disk and adding the program to the end of the AUTOEXEC.BAT file. SIX will take a snapshot of memory on first invocation and check it on each invocation thereafter.

Ease of use SIX and BRECT are meant as simple, single-purpose tools. They require an understanding of what you are doing but have no complexities in operation.

Help systems None provided.

Compatibility SIX may report and alert if run after programs that make significant changes to memory or interrupts. It should be easily network compatible, but only if used from the same station each time.

BRECT will write a nonbootable boot sector to floppy disks and so will remove the boot capability if used on bootable disks.

Company stability Wallace Hale is a nice guy with interesting ideas, but if he goes under a bus you can kiss your support good-bye. Also, if the programs mess you up (or, more likely, you mess up), the warranty is limited to what you paid. (See above.)

Company support Postal, email, or BBS only.

Documentation The text files clearly explain the operation of the programs, but assume you are familiar with viral operations and do not go into tutorial details.

Hardware requirements Basically, anything that runs DOS.

Performance Within the limits, good.

Local support None provided.

Support requirements SIX would be a good add-on to a supported environment. As the author states, it is not intended as a full antiviral package, but only as an additional, quick level of checking.

Sophos Ltd.
Vaccine 4.28, Sweep 2.41, and D-Fence 2.01
Change-detection, scanning, and "quarantine" software
Vaccine £99.50; Sweep £295/yr.; D-Fence £195/10 units

Ratings (1 = poor, 4 = very good)

Installation	2
Ease of use	2
Help systems	1
Compatibility	2
Company stability	3
Company support	1
Documentation	2
Hardware required	2
Performance	3
Availability	2
Local support	2

General Description
The three products are each sold separately. Vaccine is a change-detection program, and when purchased separately comes with Sweep for an initial check of the system. Sweep is a scanner. (A version that runs under VMS and will check MS-DOS files on a VAX fileserver is also available.) D-Fence is a program that renders disks used within a specific workgroup unusable outside that group and vice versa. The packages are reviewed here together rather than in separate reviews since Vaccine is the major product and the others appear to be adjunct to it.

Comparison of Features and Specifications
Installation The Sophos Vaccine package is shipped on nonwritable disks, both 5¼" and 3½" low-density media.

After having reviewed so many antiviral programs that demand you trust them with your hard disk (Trust us!), it was refreshing to see that Sophos actually suggests that you install the program onto a floppy disk! Unfortunately, this means nothing, as the installation program refuses to install the package unless a hard disk is present. In fact, none of the programs except SWEEP will work on a floppy-only system.

The documentation does give detailed instructions for manual installation.

Ease of use Basic functions of the programs can be accessed reasonably easily. However, specification of some of the command-line options and lists of items to check would definitely be beyond the grasp of novice users and likely beyond intermediate users as well.

Help systems Some on-line help systems are provided, but they do not contribute much assistance.

Compatibility No problems were evident in testing.

Company stability Sophos is a fairly major player in the system-security field, in minicomputer and communications systems as well as micro software. It is also the publisher of the *Virus Bulletin* periodical (and convener of that publication's conference).

Company support Only the address, phone, and fax numbers are given: no mention is made of support. (If SWEEP detects a virus, a message instructs the user to call Sophos "for advice.") The company is available on the Internet. Although I have never called about a specific problem with the product, the company has never returned a phone call or email message in two years.

It is noteworthy that my first review copy arrived with a note saying that the D-Fence program would be dispatched "next week." In spite of waiting eight months before committing the review to paper, the program never did arrive for the first round of testing.

Documentation The manuals are much changed from the first version. The *Quick Start Manual, Vaccine User Manual, Using Vaccine in a Large Organisation*, and *Sophos Utilities User Manual* are included with the Vaccine package; the others have much smaller manuals. The *Data Security Reference Guide*, which was primarily a catalog of other products available from Sophos, is no longer included.

The user manuals are definitely technical reference level. There is a great deal of information regarding the use of the program for the experienced user. There is also information regarding the limitations of the program, or best means of use, but this is often very brief, and one has almost to be looking for it to find it.

The general description of viral programs is limited. Some of the points are plainly incorrect. For example, the description of viral programs states that "[a]fter some time, all programs on the hard disk will be infected," thus implying that all viral programs are file infectors, and it then goes on to list a number of viral programs, the first three of which are boot sector infectors. Among the "rules" for avoiding viral programs are the same tired "avoid BBSes, avoid shareware, buy commercial" themes. The manual also appears to claim that a change-detection system can prevent damage by trojan horse programs and logic bombs.

Hardware requirements None of the programs except SWEEP will work on a floppy-only system.

Performance The documentation admits, albeit briefly and unwillingly, to the weaknesses of change detection, and even specifically mentions that stealth-type viral programs will not be detected if the virus is active. The ability to "snapshot" areas of memory, the interrupt table, and specific (system and/or sector) areas of the hard disk is a valuable plus.

The SWEEP program functions quite well against common viral programs, with the exception that it tends to "find" more than one virus in an infected file (up to eight in the case of a single Jerusalem infection). Users should note that a scan of memory is a separate option with SWEEP. Unlike most other scanners, which scan memory by default but allow you to turn off the memory scan, with SWEEP you must specify a memory scan if you want one.

Local support None provided.

Support requirements A novice user, installing this on a system after all other software had been installed, would likely be provided with good protection against viral programs. However, it is probable that use of this product in any normal business operation would require the support of personnel expert in computer use as well as viral operation.

General Notes

One would have to say that Vaccine is a product for the use of experts. The package seems tacitly to admit this with the additional section in the manual for use in a large concern. As a tool for serious support personnel, the product does provide very significant utilities for protection of computer systems.

Scanners

KAMI Ltd./Central Command Inc. Antiviral Toolkit Pro (AVP)

Resident and nonresident scanner and utilities
$59.95 to $200 for single copy, site licensing available

Ratings (1 = poor, 4 = very good)

Installation	2
Ease of use	3
Help systems	3
Compatibility	3
Company stability	3
Company support	2
Documentation	1
Hardware required	4
Performance	4
Availability	2
Local support	2

General Description

AVP is a nonresident virus scanner with significant strength in dealing with polymorphic and other viral programs using advanced techniques. The package also features a resident portion, heuristic scanning, and utilities.

Comparison of Features and Specifications

Installation AVP now has a commercial system of distribution through agents. I received a copy of the English version from Central Command on two 1.44M disks. Unfortunately, although there is an installation program, there is no manual. There are, in fact, two setup programs, one to install an original version of the package, and another to update it. The installation process consists of copying and decompressing of files, although the system startup files, CONFIG.SYS and AUTOEXEC.BAT, are analyzed and can be amended during the procedure, and the update process can find the original directory.

Ease of use The programs are easy to run with a not quite standard CUA interface. For some reason the program attempts to use as a swap file a directory that is not likely to exist on most systems, but the error message dialogue box allows users to specify another. The /TMP command-line switch can be used to circumvent this, but the explanation in the English documentation is in error at this point.

Help systems Context-sensitive help is available. An interesting feature is the demonstration of sound or video effects of various viruses.

Compatibility The program is particularly strong in detecting polymorphic viruses.

Company stability AVP is a stable product.

Company support The author is an active participant in the *VIRUS-L* discussion list. Some sites may have difficulty in sending messages to his Internet address.

Response, however, is very good. Distribution through national agents is significant. Agents may not support or supply all components of the full package.

Documentation The lack of a printed manual, especially after more than a year has passed, is disappointing. Even a card listing the installation steps would be an improvement. After installation a USERGUID.DOC file appears. This contains a lot of technical detail on the program, especially the virus database structure, but no general discussion of the virus problem.

Hardware requirements DOS 3.3 or higher, 580K free memory, and 16 file handles are stated to be the minimum requirements in the documentation. In testing, the program ran on a machine with as little as 498K free memory.

Performance AVP scores very highly in comparisons of variants detected, but is particularly strong in detecting viral programs with polymorphic or other advanced features. The program also has special functions for detecting infections in compressed files or archives.

    Both installation and operation are very slow, particularly on older machines. On one XT it took over two hours to check 157 programs, 6 megabytes of a 20-megabyte hard drive. On a turbo XT it took 13 minutes to check a floppy disk. A 486 with a 350M hard drive took 19 minutes to scan. The same machine took 36 seconds with TBScan and 99 seconds with F-PROT. The cost in speed is a result of the extremely thorough scanning. No option for a reduced scan is available.

Local support None provided, but Internet response from various agents is good.

Support requirements Once installed, AVP is accessible to any level of user. Intermediate users should be able to handle installation. The program has features that require advanced knowledge to obtain full benefit.

General Notes

AVP is, unfortunately, still not widely known or available despite increased distribution. The recent commercial distribution has restricted the availability of the shareware version, but both older releases and a newer "AVPLite" can be found at various sites. For those serious about virus protection, the package is worth the trouble taken to find it.

Fridrik Skulason
Frisk Software International
F-PROT 2.xx Virus detection/protection/disinfection

Scanner, resident scanner, and disinfector
Free for noncommercial personal use, site license $1(U.S.) per computer (minimum $20), 25 percent educational discount. (See also Safetynet, Data Fellows, and Command Software for commercial versions.)

Ratings (1 = poor, 4 = very good)

Installation	3
Ease of use	4
Help systems	3
Compatibility	3
Company stability	3
Company support	3
Documentation	3
Hardware required	4
Performance	4
Availability	3
Local support	2

General Description

Scanning, resident scanning, and disinfection capabilities. The informational utilities present in the earlier (1.xx) versions have been replaced by heuristic analysis scanning. Change-detection and operation-restricting utilities have been removed and not replaced. Highly recommended for any situation. Best "value for cost" of any package reviewed to date.

Comparison of Features and Specifications

Installation Installation is now added as a feature in the main program. Manual installation is still an option and is likely the one most used by those familiar with the program. Since the program is shareware, and since installation is little more than copying of files, unless VIRSTOP is installed, it is unlikely to present any problems.

In the automated installation, VIRSTOP is installed to be invoked from AUTOEXEC.BAT. Those wishing to invoke it from CONFIG.SYS must do the installation manually.

Ease of use Except for resident scanning, F-PROT is now invoked from a single program. The user, by default, is presented with a graphical interface, but command-line switches are an option for those wanting more speed, or a standard invocation for a large group of users.

There is no "help" key, but the options are fairly simple and explained in text boxes where necessary.

Help systems There is no help per se, although a listing of command-line switches is available.

Compatibility F-PROT consistently maintains the highest ratings in all independent tests of scanning of known viral programs, including my own. In terms of disinfection capability, only Alan Solomon's Anti-Virus Toolkit and now KAMI's Anti Viral Toolkit Pro has similar ratings.

Because of an external language file, F-PROT is available in at least six languages and can be readily translated into others.

The heuristic analysis portion of the program occasionally generates a "false-positive" alert about a program that is not, in fact, infected. This is to be expected from this type of scanning, and the incidence is much reduced from when this function was first included with the program. The heuristic analysis feature has been generally effective in identifying new and "unknown" viral strains, but is not perfect. (Perfection is, of course, inherently unattainable in this type of program.) Indeed, the documentation for this feature states that it is still to be considered experimental, and is very conservative in its claims. Programs known to cause false positives are listed.

F-PROT may be run under Windows, but is not a Windows program. This is planned to be addressed in future, as are improvements for VIRSTOP to make it run with Windows and to check files as they are copied, to check floppy disks as accessed, and to use EMS memory.

Company stability F-PROT was originally a sideline developed by Fridrik Skulason while he was still employed by the university. The acceptance of F-PROT as a highly accurate scanner and effective disinfector have allowed the growth of Frisk Software to a leading position in antiviral software. The basic technology is licensed by at least three other companies. The most recent addition to the company is Vesselin Bontchev, long considered one of the top independent antiviral researchers.

Three commercial versions are available. One, produced by Safetynet and sold under the name VirusNet PC, is the closest to the shareware version with the addition of a change-detection program. Two others, both called F-PROT Professional, are sold by Data Fellows and Command Software. (See the separate review for F-PROT Professional.)

Company support Fridrik Skulason is available through the Internet, and replies to queries can be expected within a week or less. As the program has become much more popular with the general public, numerous people have requested his Fidonet address. Unfortunately, he is not active on either Fidonet or VirNet. Users of the commercial version can obtain the *F-PROT Update Bulletin* from Data Fellows and may also be able to get text file copies from better antiviral archives.

Documentation Being shareware, the package has no printed documentation. The text files included with the programs are very clear and thorough and provide an excellent primer on virus functions and protection, as it relates to scanning and disinfection. The large single USAGE.TXT file has been broken into smaller "chapter" files, which allows for quicker access to a particular function or feature.

As some of the other virus detection and prevention capabilities have been dropped from the package, so the very excellent discussions of the different types of antiviral software, and their strengths and weaknesses, have been dropped from the documentation. It is recommended that interested parties obtain old (1.xx) versions of F-PROT for this material.

The virus information files previously contained in separate text files have been included as a virus information feature within the main program.

Hardware requirements No special hardware is required.

Performance During testing, F-PROT has consistently identified more viral programs than the "current release" of any other product. F-PROT is generally slower at scanning because of the multiple signatures being used to check for each virus, but is not the slowest scanner tested.

The user is in control of F-PROT at all times, with the exception that VIRSTOP will not allow the boot sequence to continue in the case of a boot sector infection at startup.

F-PROT, in seven years of my testing, has not given a false-positive alarm on any normal program, nor has it interfered with any normal program operation. Users have, from time to time, reported false positives but these are generally with less well known programs and are often fixed within a week.

The various functions and utilities that have been dropped from the 2.xx version programs still have significant value. Serious virus researchers and consultants would do well to obtain copies of older (1.xx) versions. These have been retained, and are available, at better antiviral source sites.

Local support Since F-PROT is shareware, there are no local dealers from which to obtain support; however, knowledgeable users are fairly common.

F-PROT is also available as a commercially distributed product or as part of other security products.

Support requirements Very little support should be needed for this program. On occasion assistance may be needed in disinfection, or in positively identifying a new viral strain, but no product tested deals with this situation better than F-PROT.

General Notes

Because of its "shareware" distribution, F-PROT is best compared against McAfee's Associates SCAN program. F-PROT is kept up-to-date with regular additions to the signature file and constant improvements to the program. SCAN versions are released at approximately the same frequency as F-PROT, but in two and a half years F-PROT releases consistently identified more viri, and with greater accuracy, than did the "same-level" releases of SCAN. SCAN also needs to release far more "bug fix" versions than does F-PROT. Fridrik Skulason publishes fewer signatures of new viruses on the *VIRUS-L/comp.virus* distribution lists than he used to, but some others are supplying appropriate signature strings in his format. F-PROT is significantly cheaper than the SCAN suite as well, and is complete in one package, although the SCAN suite in total now offers some edge in utility.

I am personally sorry to see that the former utilities are not included in the current package. However, it is unarguably simpler for novice users to install and use the newer package, free from the confusion of the multiplicity of files contained in the previous version.

Data Fellows Ltd (also Command Software) F-PROT Professional 2.17

Resident and manual scanning, change detection
$50 and up (varies)

Ratings (1 = poor, 4 = very good)

Installation	3
Ease of use	4
Help systems	3
Compatibility	3
Company stability	3
Company support	3
Documentation	3
Hardware required	4
Performance	4
Availability	3
Local support	2

General Description

Scanning, resident scanning, and disinfection capabilities. A commercial version of the shareware F-PROT package, it also contains change-detection software. DOS and Windows software, plus a specific Windows "resident" scanner (Gatekeeper). OS/2 and NetWare versions are available separately. (A package from Command software is similar, but has no Windows resident component, OS/2, or NetWare versions.)

Comparison of Features and Specifications

Installation The product is shipped on three writable but protected 1.44M disks. There is separate installation for each of the DOS, Windows, and Gatekeeper programs.

In the automated installation, VIRSTOP is installed to be invoked from AUTOEXEC.BAT. Those wishing to invoke it from CONFIG.SYS must do the installation manually.

Ease of use While the individual modules of the package are easy to use, tighter integration between them would help improve the product.

Help systems On-line help is available.

Compatibility Same as for F-PROT.

Company stability Fridrik Skulason now has an established company. F-PROT is being included in commercial programs and is now sold in these commercial versions. Frisk has, however, committed to continuing to support the shareware version. Data Fellows has been the European agent for F-PROT for some years, but is also actively involved in the antiviral research community, and is genuinely "adding value" to the product. Command Software has been less active, but recently hired Sarah Gordon who has done major work in the reviewing of antiviral software and significant research into the virus-exchange and computer "cracking" community.

Company support Data Fellows is available on the Internet and has some presence on Fidonet as well. Data Fellows provides an excellent *F-PROT Update* publication, which covers not only new features but also general news on the virus scene.

Data Fellows and Command Software have an agreement to support the F-PROT Professional product, regardless of the source.

Documentation The manual from Data Fellows is very complete and contains some excellent general background. However, Gatekeeper, Windows, and Windows Administration are essentially separate manuals contained in the same binder, and this can be confusing. The Gatekeeper manual does need some clarification in the network area.

The documention from Command Software is more basic.

Hardware requirements No special hardware is required. The DOS programs can be run from floppy disk.

Performance See as for F-PROT.

Local support The popularity of the shareware version makes it likely that local users can give you assistance. Data Fellows has an extensive VAR network in the countries they distribute to.

Support requirements Very little support should be needed for this program, although additional help may be required for full functionality in network situations. On occasion assistance may be needed in disinfection, or in positively identifying a new viral strain, but no product tested deals with this situation better than F-PROT.

IBM Corporation
IBM AntiVirus/DOS 2.1 (also IBM AntiVirus/2)

Scanner and change detector
$29.95 (U.S.) $37.95 (Canada)

Ratings (1 = poor, 4 = very good)

Installation	3
Ease of use	3
Help systems	3
Compatibility	3
Company stability	4
Company support	2
Documentation	2
Hardware required	4
Performance	3
Availability	2
Local support	2

General Description

An integrated change-detection and scanning system with a GUI (graphical user interface) for manual operation. Provision for operation under either DOS or Windows (OS/2 version available separately). Recommended as a basic protection system for most users. Now bundled with PC-DOS, and a definite reason to prefer PC-DOS to the MS-DOS versions. This is the retail version: a "site license" version is also available with additional features and information.

Comparison of Features and Specifications

Installation IBM Antivirus/DOS is shipped on three 720K or six 360K writable but protected diskettes. Two install programs are provided (for DOS and for Windows), with no provision for manual installation. The Windows installation program is a bit odd in places, giving an impression of completing a few times before it actually does. If a previous version of the program is detected, it will be updated.

The user is in charge of the operation at every point, but not always given much information. There is, for example, the option to install for either DOS only or DOS and Windows operation. It is not clear from the documentation whether the Windows installation also installs the DOS files (it does).

The earlier VIRSCAN did not suggest installation on the hard drive at all. In opposition, Antivirus/DOS must be installed on a hard disk, and only one operation is stated to work in the absence of a hard disk. This does allow for "off-line" signature scanning. There is also a set of files for a "stand-alone" scanner.

Ease of use The user interface is generally clearly laid out. Using the DOS program with a monochrome monitor, though, the menu item selected is almost impossible to distinguish.

While the documentation talks of "fuzzy" and "heuristic" systems, details of operation and options are not given. This does prevent "false alarms" being presented to the user, but may allow viral changes as well. This is good in that it does not require much in the way of knowledge from the user, but there is no option to provide the information for those more capable.

Help systems Help is available via the F1 key. The Windows version has a version of the manual on-line and a fairly abbreviated set of virus descriptions.

Compatibility The structure of the signature file is no longer outlined in the manual.

Company stability These guys are Warped. Really Warped.

Company support Those on the Internet and Usenet who receive *VIRUS-L/ comp.virus* will have access to David Chess's postings and email address. IBM also sells a support package that includes a variety of antiviral assistance.

Whether from faulty diskettes or damage in shipping, my own copy had defective gates on two of the three 720K disks. This was not evident until I tried to remove the diskettes from the drive, when they jammed. This could cause a trip to the shop to get the diskette removed, or, at worst, damage to the disk drive.

Documentation The level of the documentation is uneven. At some points, such as installation, it seems to be written with the novice as the primary audience, and the experienced user may find it frustrating. At other points, in regard to some of the options that can increase the level of protection, the reader had better be used to fighting with technical manuals and lists of switch settings. The program is definitely easy enough to use without the manual, but customization is not explained as well as in other products.

The material provided is generally accurate, and very well written. New contents provide better general background to the virus situation, but still show some minor errors, such as the date of the first known virus.

Hardware requirements DOS 3.3 +, Windows 3.1 + (for the Windows portion), memory required is variously stated as 640K, 450K, 400K, and 480K, disk space of 1.6 or 2.6 megabytes (for DOS and Windows, respectively).

Performance Speed and general detection and protection capabilities are still neither the best nor the worst tested, but should be acceptable in most situations. The basic "system" check that is performed deals with change detection first. Only if a change is detected is scanning brought to bear. (This is obviously not the case with diskette scanning, and the system can be made to scan everything by default if desired by the user.)

The package will now scan PKZip and LZEXE format compressed files.

Local support Local support from IBM staff is, in my experience, becoming more dependable.

Support requirements The program should be suitable for any user.

General Notes

This product is a basic antiviral tool, but one that will offer substantial protection to the normal user. Users in a "high-risk" environment may want slightly more protection than the package has to offer.

Intel Corp.
LANProtect 1.0

Netware scanner with scheduling utility

Ratings (1 = poor, 4 = very good)

Installation	2
Ease of use	2
Help systems	1
Compatibility	2
Company stability	3
Company support	3
Documentation	1
Hardware required	2
Performance	2
Availability	2
Local support	1

General Description

Detect-only scanner with scheduling provisions. Server-based within a network.

Comparison of Features and Specifications

Installation Shipped unprotected on writable media, both 720K and 360K disks.

The product received is identified as a "30 day test drive version." This may account for the fact that it doesn't work.

An installation program is provided. There is no provision for manual installation. You must install with "SUPERVISOR" rights. Therefore, you must have an expendable Netware system to test this product.

Ease of use The product uses the standard Novell menuing system interface and should not be difficult to use. However, the product appears to have much the same options as Novell security in general, and therefore a thorough grounding in Novell security would seem to be a prerequisite.

Help systems None provided.

Compatibility A special Michelangelo disinfector is provided. The documentation for it states that it will overlay an infected boot sector with a "standard" boot sector. This it does. Bootable disks will thus become unbootable. As it only overlays the boot sector, it is ineffective against Michelangelo infections on hard disks—probably a good thing. You wouldn't want to lose your partition table.

Company stability Intel? Surely you jest.

Company support A number of options for communicating with Intel's Net-Direct system are listed. Registered users receive signature updates for a year.

Note that the "800" numbers for the United States and Canada do, indeed, work from Canada.

As with everyone else, Intel received a copy of the initial evaluation for their own review. I received a telephone call from one of their service people who asked about some of the points raised. He seemed to be quite genuinely interested in these points and asked about other antiviral software that addresses the shortcomings of the LANProtect product. He also stated that the "current" version is now 1.5, and that it does contain some disinfection capability.

Documentation The documentation is extremely short. It gives directions on the invocation of the program and some of the options in terms of when to scan, who to report the results to, and so forth.

There is a READ.ME file on disk that contains errata. It also suggests that "Detailed information on viruses can be obtained through a product such as:" and then presents a promotional blurb for the Hoffman *Virus Summary List*.

Probably a good thing. The "What Is a Computer Virus?" section is terse to the point of being useless. I'll bet you didn't know that a BSI could "spread via the network cabling." Or that a TSR virus "infect[s] all files as they are run." And, of course, we have the obligatory mention of the modem as a source of infection.

Hardware requirements Novell Network.

Performance The manual lists endorsements from both Novell and the NCSA: the NCSA has slightly more cautious wording.

Note that no disinfection capability is mentioned for this product.

Local support None provided.

Support requirements Probably requires thorough knowledge of Novell security provisions.

General Notes

Although LANProtect is currently a "single layer" of protection, the server-based approach to scanning and protection is another layer that should be added to "complete" the picture in future. Intel appears to be concerned to make this product a more complete and viable package in future.

Techmar Computer Products (TCP)
VirAway 1.46 scanner (dated 910128)

Nonresident scanner
$49

Ratings (1 = poor, 4 = very good)

Installation	2
Ease of use	3
Help systems	1
Compatibility	2
Company stability	3
Company support	2
Documentation	1
Hardware required	4
Performance	2
Availability	2
Local support	1

General Description

VirAway is identical to the CURE program shipped with AntiVirus-Plus from
Techmar. The program is recommended only to "backstop" other systems and
should not be depended upon as the only means of antivirus protection in its
current form.

Comparison of Features and Specifications

Installation VirAway, as shipped to me, comes completely unprotected. This
may not be the usual form, as the disk documentation contains a README
file that states that no changes have been made to the documentation—and I
received no documentation with the package.

An installation program is provided that will only install from drive *A:* to
the *C:* drive in a directory called \VIRAWAY. However, as installation consists
solely of copying three files (and one "start-up" batch file to the root directory),
it is not difficult for the intermediate user to perform a "custom" installation.

Ease of use Although VirAway came with no documentation, it responds to the
same command-line switches as does CURE. (Not terribly surprising: not only
are the files identical in size, but CURE, when run, also identifies itself as version 1.46 of VirAway.) Again, if no switches are used, the program will present
a menu of options.

However, command-line switches seem to be able only to "add" to the
default options. (For example, one cannot turn off the display of final statistics
from the command-line invocation.)

There is an annoying bug in the program when allowed to disinfect: it
appears to count both the infection detected and the cleaning process as an
infection. The final statistics will indicate that one file virus was found, and one

cleaned, but will show the virus named as having caused two infections. (If two files are, in fact, infected, the display shows only two infections.)

Help systems None provided.

Compatibility As stated in the review of AntiVirus-Plus, VirAway will find most common viral programs, but will not find the AIDS virus.

VirAway will find viral programs active in memory, and, in testing, rendered them inactive. However, sufficient traces remained in memory to set off alarms from other virus scanners.

Company stability Techmar is the distributor of IRIS products (from Israel) in the United States.

Company support The evaluation copy of AntiVirus-Plus was shipped in good time, although Techmar had not properly filled in the customs declaration. The copy of VirAway came unsolicited, which seems to indicate an active marketing group if nothing else.

Documentation Not supplied.

Hardware requirements MS-DOS 2.0 or higher, 256K memory. The promotional material states that a dual floppy system is necessary, which conflicts with the installation batch file.

Performance Detection of viral programs appears to be sufficient for most situations. Disinfection of memory appears effective, with the proviso noted above about false alarms from other scanners. (According to memory-mapping utilities, the memory is also still "reserved.") Disinfection of boot sector viral programs appears to be effective. Disinfection of program files appears effective as to the virus removal, but may leave programs damaged.

During testing, the memory was infected with the Jerusalem-B virus (which VirAway reports as Black Friday #1). When VirAway was run, the virus was rendered inactive in memory, but it had already infected the VirAway program file. VirAway then disinfected itself, but increased in size from 81,835 to 81,840 bytes on disk. Subsequent runs with the program against test sets of viral programs showed some odd behavior and an inability to identify all previously identified viral programs. Also, subsequent runs of VirAway showed a lack of ability to remove infections from memory.

Local support None provided.

Support requirements The program, while fairly simple to run, would not necessarily be suitable for novice users. Disinfection of viral infections is probably best left to experienced staff (and possibly other programs).

General Notes

As it stands, the program cannot be highly recommended. The number of viral programs detected is low even by the standards of other (admittedly more expensive) programs. The disinfection ability is somewhat questionable and therefore undependable.

RG Software Systems, Inc.
Vi-Spy 9.0 Professional Edition

Scanner, disinfection, and operation monitoring
$150, site licensing available (starting at $40/unit, min. 25 units)

Ratings (1 = poor, 4 = very good)

Installation	2
Ease of use	3
Help systems	1
Compatibility	2
Company stability	3
Company support	3
Documentation	2
Hardware required	4
Performance	3
Availability	2

General Description

Virus scanning and disinfection, both resident and nonresident. Also some recovery and operation monitoring. Recommended for intermediate users. Provision is made for Windows operation. Automatic-scheduler utility.

Comparison of Features and Specifications

Installation Vi-Spy was shipped to me on writable but protected media, low density 3½" and high density 5¼", but I have been informed by Ray Glath that this is only for review copies: ordinarily the product is shipped on nonwritable disks. An installation program is provided, as are instructions for manual installation. The automatic installation seems to consist merely of copying and decompressing files, although it does check for viral infection before proceeding and will refuse to proceed if infection is present. Installation to Windows is a part of the package, but in testing this was found not to work effectively. (An addition was made to the WIN.INI file, but no icon was entered into the Windows system. Ray Glath contests this: there is supposed to be an additional step that the user is directed to take. I ran the installation three times and reached the same result each time.)

Ease of use The various programs are easy to use, although the plethora of command-line options recommends careful study of the manual. The on-screen messages are quite clear and contain good explanations of the options and possible situations.

Help systems The VSMENU program allows on-line reading of the documentation and also provides for additional material to be added by the user. However, it would be difficult to call it a "help system" as such. The on-screen display is simply a visual editor. One would hope, for example, to be able to "search" the list of viral programs—one cannot.

Compatibility No problems were found in testing. The primary test machine reserves an extensive area at the top of memory. In testing, this was identified as a possible viral-type activity. The potential danger, as well as other possible causes, were listed, but there was an option to proceed, rather than merely reboot.

Company stability RG Software Systems is one of the oldest commercial (non-shareware) makers of antiviral software.

Company support The company lists phone, fax, and BBS numbers for support. This is the first time I have received a tech-support callback before I received the software for review. Two days before I received the package, Ray Glath called to apologize for an unsatisfactory support call in which the caller had intimated he was me. (I am by no means making fun of RG Software here. It should be noted that Ray Glath is one of the only producers of antiviral software who has bothered to take advantage of my offer to "review the review" before I posted it to the net. Ray Glath responded in writing and in depth. He also offered to provide the names of a number of referees as to the support RG Software provides.)

Only one mention, strangely for a scanning program, is made of the need for updates. However, the mention is that return of the warranty registration provides the user with free quarterly upgrades for one year. (Ray Glath subsequently informed me that the user is informed at the end of the year and offered the option of continuing with update maintenance.)

The accompanying promotional material received with the package made strong representation regarding support. It stressed that many commercial antiviral packages have been bought, rather than developed, by the distributors. It is good to see that RG is bucking this disturbing trend. It also made much of the written material, including a white paper and the *Primer* (see below). The white paper was a fairly straightforward presentation of observations with regard to the viral situation and a list of policy recommendations heavily weighted toward "only buy commercial software." (To be fair, BBSes are not portrayed as universally evil.)

Documentation There are two booklets that come with the package, as well as a number of files on disk. One of the books is a *Guide to Operations*—the actual manual for the program. The documentation is quite clear as to the installation and operation. However, the layout gives a feeling of clutter and presents something of an imposing front. While there is a single sheet inserted into the front of the booklet that provides for quick installation, more effective protection requires a thorough reading of the guide. This should not be a problem for any intermediate user as the documentation is less than 50 pages.

The second manual is a *Computer Virus Primer and Troubleshooting Guide*. Accompanying forms and promotional materials allow you to order additional copies of this booklet "as an educational/training tool." While there is much material of merit in the booklet, in the end it is simply more documentation for the Vi-Spy program. (There is, for example, no attempt to deal with viral infections other than with an antiviral tool.) It is, however, considerably simpler to read than the *Guide to Operations*.

Hardware requirements The only requirement listed is for DOS 2.0 or higher and at least 150K of memory.

Performance In tests the program performed well and speedily. Messages, and particularly identification of viral programs, were quite clear.

The package appears to be very concerned with boot sector infectors, a very good thing in the current climate.

Local support None provided.

Support requirements The intermediate user should be able to operate this program very effectively, provided time is taken to read the manuals. The novice should be able to obtain a good measure of protection from the automatic installation, but will likely require assistance in obtaining full advantage from the program.

General Notes

Recommended for intermediate users. Adjunct change-detection software might also be desirable. (In reaction to the review, Ray Glath informed me that change detection is due in the next release of the product.)

Multilayered Software

ALWIL Software
AVAST! antiviral

Multilayered DOS/Windows package

Ratings (1 = poor, 4 = very good)

Installation	3
Ease of use	2

REVIEWS OF ANTIVIRAL PRODUCTS

Help systems	2
Compatibility	3
Company stability	3
Company support	2
Documentation	3
Hardware required	2
Performance	3
Availability	2
Local support	1

General Description

Multilayered scanning, activity-monitoring, and change-detection software. Separate functions in multiple program files. DOS and Windows versions included.

Comparison of Features and Specifications

Installation The programs are shipped on a single, writable but protected, 1.44M diskette. Installation procedure recommends "booting clean" prior to installation. An interesting feature is a test to check for the ability to write to write-protected diskettes. The installation is in two stages: first, copying all the necessary files under DOS and, then, setting up Windows.

Two features deserve special note. The changes made to the AUTO-EXEC.BAT file are stored in a file called AVAST!.NEW. This requires that the file be renamed to replace the original, but it shows a welcome respect for the user. The other is a de-installation procedure for removing the Windows programs.

A query regarding installation of the Windows components of the package is possibly misleading: you still have to run AVINST in order to have the Windows portion of the program run properly. The only change made to my AUTOEXEC.BAT file was to add the AVAST directory to my PATH. (Twice.) The resident programs were neither added to the AUTOEXEC file nor to any Windows groups, including "Start Up." Initialization of the Windows portions seemed to create some difficulty with invoking Windows in enhanced mode, and the Windows programs would not load and execute, requesting more memory on an 8 meg system. (According to the authors, this should not be the case.) The "de-installation" function of AVINST appeared to work perfectly.

Ease of use The interface is generally easy enough to figure out. Additional features of the program, such as scanning a floppy disk, must be first entered into the "Command Line" menu, and only then invoked with the function under the "Run" menu. Some procedures, such as the actual invocation of the installation process itself, are confusing, but can be determined by an intermediate-level user.

Help systems Help is available as a command-line switch for the DOS programs, and on-screen for the Windows versions.

Compatibility The software can detect a significant number of viral programs, although disinfection is more limited. My tests noted a few misses, but caught some rare species. One scan identified a single Stoned infection as two different variants. The modular nature of the package makes it very flexible. While not network software as such, there is provision for testing and reporting on a Novell network.

Company stability I had not heard of the company until this year, but the software is copyright 1988 to 1995. The program structure is thoughtful and shows mature development.

Company support The manual gives contact information by telephone, fax, email, and BBS. An "AVS" support package provides monthly updates and a quarterly magazine, for an additional charge.

Documentation The manual is quite well written for a product developed in a country where English is not the primary language. The text is generally grammatical, though sometimes awkwardly worded. (The "Avast" name comes from "AntiVirus Advanced SeT.") In spite of occasional hiccups in wording, the content is solid, honest, and realistic.

Hardware requirements Only MS-DOS 3.3 or higher and 256K of RAM are stated. The program takes nearly a megabyte of disk space and seems to require substantial Windows memory.

Performance The product is primarily concerned with speed, and making the least impact on the user. The default operation has some loopholes, but these are not serious and could be addressed in a high-risk environment by a more rigorous setup of the program. Program operation itself is not among the faster packages.

Scanning detection does not rank with the best available software (although is not far behind) and disinfection is limited to the most commonly found viral programs. The scanner can detect internally infected compressed executables, but does not check inside archives.

Local support None provided.

Support requirements Basic scanning should be accessible to the novice. Overall, though, installation and setup probably require a supported environment.

Digital Dispatch, Inc.
Data Physician Plus! 4.0B

Resident and nonresident scanning, disinfection, activity monitoring, change detection

Ratings (1 = poor, 4 = very good)

Installation	2
Ease of use	2
Help systems	1
Compatibility	3
Company stability	2
Company support	2
Documentation	2
Hardware required	4
Performance	2
Availability	2
Local support	1

General Description

VIRHUNT is a nonresident scanner, change detector, and disinfector (with "generic" disinfection). RESSCAN is a resident scanning program (with a Windows compatible component WIN-RS and a network component, RS-NET). VIRALERT is an activity monitor (with a Windows component, WIN-VA). ANTIGEN adds a change-detection module onto executable files, which can also disinfect unknown viral programs that do not change original code and can add password protection to programs to prevent unauthorized use. Two other (file viewing and "Disk Killer" recovery) utilities are included. Also notable is the fact that the installation program will save copies of the CMOS and "boot records" of the hard drive.

Comparison of Features and Specifications

Installation Data Physician Plus! is shipped on three writable and unprotected 360K diskettes. (Each used to be clearly stamped with the serial number in very large, clear digits. I assume this is still the case with regular copies, although mine were simply stamped "DEMO COPY." The serial number is not always an easy item to find on any software.)

A "Quick Start" sheet, separate from the manual, suggests that you simply run RESSCAN and then use VIRHUNT if a virus is discovered. (RESSCAN, by default, does a full scan of the disk when invoked and then remains resident.)

The manual is fairly imposing and technically oriented at first glance. (It is unbound, printed on one side, and three-hole punched.) Page 10 is the first mention of installation and suggests that you might wish to run the INSTALL program in order to install VIRHUNT alone.

INSTALL is a "menued" program, but it is hard to say that it is very useful. It does describe the programs, but does so in language that a novice would likely not be comfortable with. The description is not very long, but is followed by the full list of command-line options for the program. You can now choose which ones you want and then have them all installed at once. (ANTIGEN is not included in the installation options.) Entries can now be made in your AUTOEXEC.BAT file.

INSTALL does have two interesting features. One is the "Recovery" function, which allows the CMOS and boot sector (and presumably the MBR, although this is not explicitly stated) to be stored off-line, and restored if necessary to recover a "damaged" disk. (This function is shared by VIRHUNT.)

The other is the ability to create batch files for running the various programs. A "fill in the blanks" form is presented, and a batch file is created that will run the specified program with the specified options. (The F1 key is stated to give "information": this turns out to be simply the program descriptions.) A major deficiency in this function is that the default filename for the batch files is always the same. At first I thought that this meant one batch file could be created in order to run all the programs, but this is not so. Each batch file overwrites the previous one: if a filename exists, the user is not warned that the previous file will be lost. (With this in mind, the option to "pause" the batch file if a virus is found becomes somewhat ridiculous.) Do *NOT* use this on AUTOEXEC.BAT. (After installation of a program, there is a similar function to update AUTOEXEC.BAT. It will install RESSCAN and RS-NET in AUTOEXEC. It allows the user the option to back up AUTOEXEC.BAT before changing it.)

Ease of use   The interface, while not overly difficult, is not particularly easy or consistent. A user familiar with a variety of interfaces will likely be able to figure out how it works by trial and error, but a novice may get stuck in certain places.

A number of the options are difficult to figure out. Partially this is simply a matter of the complexity of a "useful" system. (Data Physician has a large number of options, which could be helpful in a wide variety of situations.) However, in a number of cases the difficulty is caused by poorly chosen wording or a lack of information. For example, ANTIGEN cannot be used from a write-protected disk, even when it is protecting files on another, since it creates temporary work files in its own area. However, the error message is extremely terse and gives no indication of the real problem. As another example, once a list of files for ANTIGEN to protect has been selected, the command to proceed is "Quit." Even having read the manual thoroughly, and after having gotten VIRHUNT to create a signature file for change detection, it took me three runs, by trial and error, to find the correct setting to have VIRHUNT use the signature file to "generically remove" a new virus.

A number of option combinations give odd results. For example, in order to use the "generic disinfection," one must "turn off" virus checking. However, if virus checking is turned off while scanning to *create* the change-detection signature files, a file with no signatures is created. (To make matters worse, if you specify creation of the signature file, any previous file is overwritten without warning.)

Help systems   Little provided. A list of viral programs and their "characteristics" is provided in VIRHUNT: it is extremely terse and of very little use.

Compatibility Data Physician appears to be very compatible with a variety of hardware, networks, and Windows.

Company stability Digital Dispatch's antiviral programs have been on the market for many years, although not widely publicized. Other products by the company are unknown.

Company support Nothing is mentioned about support, specifically, except that if you get a copy of a new virus to DDI, they will get a fix out by the next day. However, you have to hunt around a bit in order to find the address and phone number. (In fact, the printed address only ever mentions the five-digit Zip code. The "5 + 4" code is found in the "About DDI" section of the VIRHUNT program.) In suggesting that you send a copy of a virus to them, mention is made of sending it by modem—but no BBS number is listed anywhere.

Documentation The documentation is not necessarily poorly written, but is extremely technical in nature. As the technical reference sections appear, the writing becomes more confident. The type of document DDI is used to producing is very obvious. There is little general discussion of viral programs, nor of the strengths and weaknesses of various portions of the program.

There are now two substantial READ.ME files on the disk. In fact it is likely that the third disk would not be needed were it not for the fact that the entire documentation for the program exists not only in a text file, but also in an MS-Word–format document. Actually, having the softcopy version is very helpful for searching via text editor, as the table of contents isn't very useful. However, the documentation for the virus description language (for specifying newly found, or your "own," viral programs) is still almost entirely on the disk file CIL.DOC—which no longer exists. (It is still referred to in the documentation, so presumably the capability still exists.)

Hardware requirements At least one disk drive, 384K, and MS-DOS 2.x or higher. All of the programs will run on a single-floppy system.

Performance Virus scanning is relatively slow, in comparison to other current products. Most common viral programs are detected, but not all. Identification of some new viral programs that are similar to older ones is not particularly good.

Change detection is effective with VIRHUNT, as is the generic disinfection. ANTIGEN, however, is much less so. On one test, it did not detect the presence of an infection, although the "protective" code seemed to go through the checking cycle twice. (That test also allowed the infection of other files.) In another test, the infection was caught and successfully removed, but only after infection of another file had occurred. ANTIGEN was never able to stop the infection operation, be it direct action or memory infection.

ANTIGEN will conflict with programs having internal loaders or nonstandard headers.

Local support None provided.

Support requirements It is unlikely that the novice would be comfortable with the program at all. The intermediate user may be able to obtain some protection through the program, but is unlikely to be able to utilize it to the fullest extent. Advanced support personnel should be responsible for the installation and configuration of the program.

General Notes

This is definitely a program for the advanced technical user with a good background in antiviral protection. The package contains a number of protective layers and options and can perform in a great many situations. The configuration and command-line options allow for many different kinds of protection in different environments.

It is, however, not a product for the average user. It can certainly be installed on a novice's system by advanced technical support and contains a number of options for doing exactly that in a large corporate environment. The ability to specify notices to users in the event of infection as well as the configuration files for "group" installations are two examples of advanced options.

The product would also be of use to the serious virus researcher supporting a user population. The CIL virus specification language is extremely detailed and much more effective, in this case, than simple string-searching capabilities of other scanners.

The program is recommended for the technical user with advanced knowledge of computer viral programs, in a large user population with centralized responsibility for security.

S&S International plc.
Dr. Solomon's Anti-Virus Toolkit (AVT) 7.10

Multilayered detection and disinfection system, strong scanning and disinfection components, intended for advanced use

Ratings (1 = poor, 4 = very good)

Installation	2
Ease of use	3
Help systems	3
Compatibility	4
Company stability	3
Company support	3
Documentation	3
Hardware required	4
Performance	4
Availability	2
Local support	3

General Description

Menu-driven (TOOLKIT) activity-monitoring (VirusGUARD, GUARDMEM), change-detection (ViVerify, Certify), scanning (FINDVIRU), disinfection and operation-restricting (Author, NOFLOPPY, NOHARD) suite of programs. Also contains additional utilities (SHRED, TKUTIL, DEFERBAT, DEFERKEY).

Comparison of Features and Specifications

Installation The program is shipped on nonwritable 1.44M disks, two for DOS and one additional one for Windows. (Other disk formats can be requested.) There are two installation programs, both of which run from DOS. Windows installation will install all of the DOS software as well. The installation program will, at the user's discretion, also add the resident portion of the package to the AUTOEXEC.BAT file; however, it does not affect the PATH statement, and therefore all virus checking must either start from within the TOOLKIT directory (or whichever one the user creates) or be invoked with a full pathname. A handy feature is the inclusion of a card of installation instructions actually packed with the disks, but these are not quite enough for the novice. The instructions call for using the FINDVIRU program to check for infections before doing the installation (which is good) but don't say which disk it is on. (The file actually resides on the Toolkit DOS disk #2, so it is not intuitively obvious.)

I have recommended the manual installation. The installation program provided is simple and quick, and I can see no problem with using it. However, the full advantage of this product is not, and probably cannot be, provided with an automated installation.

Ease of use The TOOLKIT program provides a clear and uncluttered menuing system to access the various parts of the package. The screen messages and displays are intelligible and there is little chance for confusion.

There are a number of command-line options for use with the various programs when not using the TOOLKIT interface. The defaults are well chosen and should be appropriate for most situations and for novice users.

For situations where client support is available, the message generated by VirusGuard on detection of a virus can be customized to direct the user to the local security-support person.

Help systems On-line help is available. The Windows version contains the *VIRUS-L* FAQ document. (Careful readers will note that the FAQ is the 1992 version, but that was current at the time of testing.) The "Virus Encyclopedia" is also available on-line. Note that on-line help is currently the only source of information about the American offices.

Compatibility No conflicts were encountered in testing.

Company stability S&S International is an established presence in the antiviral software field. For some years it published *Virus News International* (now *Secure Computing*).

Company support The manual no longer lists provision for support through distributors, but the on-line help (choose Index, then Distributors) lists a truly impressive array of agents. The earlier version I reviewed came from OnTrack in the United States, and I have been extremely impressed with the regularity of updates that they shipped. The current package appeared to come from the S&S office in Massachusetts, but no American address is given in the manual: you have to look it up in the on-line help. (I am told that an "American" edition is in process.)

Documentation The documentation is an excellent study work for those just entering the computer virus field and wanting an introductory work. The explanation of how viral programs work is one of the best general treatments of the subject, even including suggestions for companies wishing to set up policies and procedures for in-house data recovery teams. Even before the table of contents, there are sections detailing "Quick Virus Check," "Quick Repair," and "Quick Install" for the novice. The *Virus Encyclopedia*, an excellent reference to known MS-DOS viral programs, is now a separate manual, but still included with the package.

Hardware requirements The Toolkit now requires 330K of memory and 2.5 to 4 megabytes of disk space to install (for DOS and Windows versions, respectively). The FINDVIRU scanner can still be run from a floppy disk.

Performance This package is consistently cited as being one of the two most accurate scanners for virus identification, and also one of the two best in terms of disinfection.

The package now has the ability to scan "inside" archived and compressed files, although this is not enabled by default.

NetWare and OS/2 versions are also available. Mac, NT, and Windows 95 versions are in development.

The TKUTIL program can remove references to CPAV, MSAV, and NAV in start-up files. Normally I would deplore a hostile action against a competing antiviral product, but I'm not sure that principle applies here. The action is not taken by default, and the user must find the refernce in the manual and specifically request the action. Also, these products have given such a high rate of false alerts that many antiviral researchers recommend against their use.

Local support The company seems to have become more responsive on the Internet, and from a call on *VIRUS-L* for review programs was the first to arrive. In addition, the East Coast office in the United States provides both a World Wide Web site (http://www.sands.com) and ftp (ftp://ftp.sands.com).

Support requirements The package is easy to use, particularly in the areas of scanning and disinfection, and should not require any additional assistance in detection of known viral programs. However, the package has very strong and sophisticated protection components that would give fullest advantage when installed by knowledgeable support personnel.

The ongoing upgrade programs provided should be very strongly considered in the case of this package.

General Notes

This package provides very strong antivirus protection to the advanced user, and very strong virus scanning capability for all users.

Therefore, this package is highly recommended for use by advanced users, who are willing to make the commitment to study the material provided. The package is recommended for novice users where local support is available.

Fridrik Skulason
F-PROT 1.xx

Virus utilities

Note: This is an older generation than the current versions of F-PROT. It is not likely to be widely available, and, of course, the scanner component will be outdated. It is, however, included because of the excellent suite of utilities it contained, which are no longer available in the current version.

Ratings (1 = poor, 4 = very good)

Installation	2
Ease of use	3
Help systems	2
Compatibility	4
Company stability	2
Company support	3
Documentation	2
Hardware required	4
Performance	3
Availability	3

General Description

Of the five classes of antiviral systems, the only one that F-PROT does not provide for is encryption. It provides vaccine (F-LOCK), change-detection (F-OSCHK, F-XLOCK), operation-restricting (F-DLOCK, F-XCHK), and scanning (F-DRIVER.SYS, F-FCHK, F-DISINF, F-SYSCHK) protection. The package also includes various system information utilities.

Comparison of Features and Specifications

Installation The installation of F-PROT is not a one-step process, since the package contains a number of different programs for various protective purposes. The user must decide which programs to select, and therefore the installation must be done in stages.

There is no installation program, but the documentation does have a separate installation file. This file states that the user should have a knowledge of MS-DOS, and that is probably necessary. The installation process, however, is described clearly and is quite complete.

The package is distributed as "shareware," and therefore any user who obtains it is likely to have the necessary skills for its installation.

The installation procedure does "allow" one possible point of infection—if the computer is infected when the program is installed. But the program will immediately detect the infection unless it is not found in the signature file. Since the program is "posted" in archived format, the user should be able to clear the infection and start with fresh files.

Ease of use All the functions of F-PROT are found in different programs, and all are invoked from the command line, so when a user knows what function is desired, it is a simple matter to obtain it. Only two of the programs have any switches other than file or path specification.

Help systems As all packages are invoked from the command line for a single function, there is no need for on-line help. When programs are called without necessary file or path specifications, a message explaining what is needed appears.

Compatibility The various programs have been tested on a wide range of computers and have not created any problems with hardware, even on systems that have serious problems with TSR programs.

The documentation lists a number of "contra-indicated" software packages and systems that may conflict with program operations. However, in four years of testing, no normal character-based program or TSR has been found to conflict with any F-PROT program.

Company stability See F-PROT version 2.xx.

Company support No problems have been encountered with the program so far. Fridrik Skulason is available through the Internet, and replies to queries can be expected within a week or less.

Documentation Being shareware, the package has no printed documentation. The text files included with the programs are very clear and thorough and provide an excellent primer on virus functions and protection. Novice users may, however, find the USAGE.TXT document to be daunting. Fortunately, only the INSTALL.TXT document is required in order to use the product. The virus listings are comprehensive as to the number of viral programs, if somewhat less technical and detailed than the Brunnstein and Hoffman listings.

Hardware requirements No special hardware is required.

Performance During testing, F-PROT has consistently identified more viral programs than the "current release" of any other product. It has occasionally given a false positive, but only in the case of identifying a definite virus with two different names, or when scanning another virus scanning product. F-PROT is generally slower at scanning, and the separate signature file renders it slower still, but the separate file also allows new signatures to be added without waiting for a product upgrade.

The user is in control of F-PROT at all times, with the exception that F-DRIVER.SYS will not allow the boot sequence to continue in the case of a boot sector infection at start-up.

F-PROT, in four years of testing, has not given a false-positive alarm on any normal program, nor has it interfered with any normal program operation on my system.

Local support Since F-PROT is shareware, there are no local dealers to obtain support from. F-PROT has fewer users of this older version in North America than SCAN, and so local help may be harder to obtain, but the documentation should make up for any deficiencies.

Support requirements In a situation where technical support is available for the user base, installation may best be performed by the support group. A corporate environment will probably wish to have security policies, and support for the package in addition to installation would best be coordinated by this group.

Symantec
Norton AntiVirus 3

Manual and TSR virus scanning, as well as change detection
$130 (U.S.), $69 (U.S.) $79 (Canada) for annual update service

Ratings (1 = poor, 4 = very good)

Installation	3
Ease of use	2
Help systems	2
Compatibility	3
Company stability	3
Company support	2
Documentation	2
Hardware required	2
Performance	2
Availability	4
Local support	1

General Description

The NAV.EXE program has the ability to scan memory, boot sectors, and files for the presence of known viral programs, and to "inoculate" programs to detect change. It can also recover some damage to programs and boot sectors.

Comparison of Features and Specifications

Installation The program is shipped on three 1.44M "read-only" disks, therefore cannot be infected at the user's site without active intervention.

Network installation assistance is provided in the installation program.

Ease of use The program is "menu driven," but use without a mouse is not necessarily intuitive, nor do all menus work consistently. Ten pages of the manual are devoted to the use of the interface. The menus are, however, generally clear and readable.

The "Advanced scan" and "Auto-inoculate" features of the system are simply variations on checksumming and change detection, but are set up and explained in a manner that appears to be unnecessarily confusing. The options available in the "Options/Configuration" menu allow for a considerable degree of customization, but reasons for choosing certain options are not clearly explained in the initial installation section of the manual. Some options do not appear to work: I did not choose to "Disable scan Cancel *button*" (*b* being the letter used to access this option), but the "cancel scan" option was disabled on my program anyway.

If a virus is detected in memory at the beginning of a scan, the program will refuse to scan further. This is an advantage in that it prevents infection by viri that infect each file as it is open, but there is no "discretion" on this feature, and it activates even when boot sector viri are found. The program does not terminate, but will not perform (in terms of scanning). No help is given at this point: the user is referred to a section of the manual.

Help systems The program contains an extensive help file. Personally, I did not find the on-screen help to be very useful, generally having to go to the manual if I could not figure out the operation from the menus.

Compatibility Although not stated in the manual, many functions no longer work for CPUs lower than a 286 level.

Company stability Symantec and Peter Norton have both been solid companies in their respective environments. Symantec has also purchased Zortech, Certus, and Fifth Generation, all of which have been marketing antiviral software and recently merged with Central Point, which had been following a similar pattern.

Company support The company appears to have removed both a technical-support line and a "Virus Newsline" for update information on new viral signatures.

The distribution of updated signature files has been problematic. Initially they were available only from the Symantec BBS or on CompuServe, where Symantec runs a support forum. Offers of space on other systems were turned down. Subsequently, a Symantec representative stated that update files could be distributed via BBSes, at the same time that other agents were saying that this was a violation of copyright. At one point a demo version of the program was stated to be available on "hundreds of bulletin boards worldwide." This was later found to refer to the Symantec BBS and CompuServe only. Most recently permission has been granted to distribute the update files from ftp sites on the Internet. However, no announcements of availability were made and the future of this distribution is completely unknown.

It should be noted that although the initial program was promised to the reviewer, it required 11 return phone calls to five different offices to finally have it delivered over three months later. Other shipping was similar, although most recently the package was the fourth to arrive after a general call for review materials.

The series of acquisitions by both Symantec and Central Point means the company has absorbed a significant group of antiviral software vendors. This represents more than a dozen products that have been removed from the market or have had support withdrawn. The buyouts appear to have been done solely to gain market share. Less than a month after the company had been purchased, callers were being told that the product support for Fifth Generation products had been discontinued, and were offered "upgrades" to NAV. To date, only one of the technologies of the "orphaned" products has been added to the Norton AntiVirus.

Documentation The documentation is much improved from earlier versions, but still refers only to program operation and has little general discussion of viral programs.

Hardware requirements A 286 or above is required for many functions.

Performance The TSR scanner is invoked from CONFIG.SYS. While it cannot prevent infection of the system from a "boot sector" infected diskette, it does not detect the presence of such a virus in memory, and it neither prevents infection of diskettes, nor alerts the user to the use of an infected diskette or the operation of infecting.

Repair of viral programs appeared to be effective on those few for which this is an option. However, the major option tends to be deletion.

Local support Although local sales offices of Symantec/Peter Norton are widely available, support is only provided through central technical support.

Support requirements In its current form, the product is suitable for novice users, but installation and actions when a virus is found may require more expert support.

General Notes

Statements from former employees indicate serious problems within the Norton AntiVirus product development group, possibly with regard to management. Normally, this would simply fall within the realm of mere gossip, but the almost complete lack of development of the product over the past year tends to add credence to the rumor.

McAfee Associates
Scan suite

Scanning, disinfection, and resident scanning modular suite
$25–$35 per program

Ratings (1 = poor, 4 = very good)

Installation	2
Ease of use	3
Help systems	2
Compatibility	2
Company stability	3
Compant support	3
Documentation	2
Hardware required	3
Performance	2
Availability	3
Local support	1

General Description

SCAN is a boot sector, memory, and file scanning program, with some disinfection and change-detection capabilities. Disinfection is now accomplished by a switch in the SCAN program. VSHIELD and SENTRY are resident file-infection-checking and activity-checking programs. A Windows interface is also available.

FSHIELD, Sentry, and VCOPY have been discontinued and are no longer supported.

Comparison of Features and Specifications

Installation SCAN does not require installation as such. All programs, however, are distributed in .ZIP format and use PKUNZIP version 2.04G for unpacking with authenticity verification.

VSHIELD is distributed in two, mutually exclusive, versions. One version requires the use of SCAN's /AV or /AF option, which adds an authentication CRC check onto programs. A second level of protection is added in one version with file infection checking for known viral programs. The programs can also be used to prevent the running of unauthorized programs. VSHIELD must be installed "manually" by the user in the AUTOEXEC.BAT file with all desired options and switches. (Installation utilities are separately available from certain dealers.)

The distribution of SCAN as shareware has led to the "release" of many "trojan" versions of SCAN. McAfee Associates has attempted to deal with the security problem in two ways: the use of the "authentic verification" envelope on ZIP archives, and the VALIDATE program produced by McAfee Associates itself. Unfortunately, both methods have problems. The "-AV" codes have been "spoofed" by copies of PKZIP that will add a code, not necessarily that of McAfee Associates. More recently, the security of the PKZIP "-AV" codes has been broken: it is now possible to duplicate any code. The VALIDATE code is more secure (although it has been cracked) but requires a knowledge of the validation code from a "trusted source."

Ease of use The SCAN program is fairly simple to execute, but provides for a very large number of options in the form of software "switches." These can complicate the use of the program, but probably will not be used by most users. The base scanning function is simple to operate, and novice users will probably not use any other functions. (The one major exception is the /AV option. If used on a program that is already "self-checking," it will likely cause the program to terminate, and so must be identified and removed. The program has therefore added an /AF option that will store the change-detection information to a file rather than appending to the program.)

Help systems If SCAN is invoked with no specifications, it gives three "screens" of a listing of the "command-line switches." This can also be obtained with the /?, /H, or /HELP switches.

Compatibility SCAN and the other programs in the suite are updated frequently, and the latest version should be able to handle almost all viruses that a user would encounter.

Unfortunately, recent versions have seen a major decrease in the accuracy of virus identification. A number of scan strings have become "generic" and will identify a number of viral strains. Some of these have been so identified (as "Gen "): a number still report the name of a specific virus regardless of the actual strain found. Along with this, there has been a corresponding decline in the ability of /CLEAN to disinfect programs and disks.

Company stability McAfee Associates has been producing versions of SCAN for a number of years, updating on a frequent but somewhat irregular basis. SCAN is probably the most widely used virus scanner in North America at present. The company has recently "gone public" to expand into the shareware utilities market and is buying programs from other shareware authors.

In the past year there have been major changes to both the corporate and support structure of the company. McAfee Associates now appears to be concentrating on a position as a leading provider of network and corporate utilities.

Company Support The company appears to be trying to promote support through CompuServe rather than other sources.

Documentation The directions for use of the programs are restricted to listings of the "command-line switches." They are clear in all cases, if somewhat concise. Novice users will find little conceptual information about viruses, or specific information about the various viral programs that SCAN will deal with. The list of viral programs, VIRLIST.TXT, is no longer included in the archive.

The documentation, while not quite alarmist, certainly strongly suggests that the user, if any virus is ever found, should retain the services of McAfee Associates or an authorized agent. Also, outside sources (such as the Hoffman virus list) often state that viri can be dealt with by, for example, using the "SCAN /D" option, without warning that this merely deletes and overwrites the existing file.

Hardware requirements The only stated requirement is DOS 3 or higher.

Performance SCAN now ranks as one of the slower scanners reviewed. Note also the loss of some accuracy in identifying individual viral strains.

Note that /CLEAN has come under increasing criticism for its performance in removing infections, particularly in the area of BSI and MBR viral strains. Versions of the earlier CLEAN program tested (and MDISK) have, in my own experience, occasionally left the computer or disk in a worse state than the virus.

Local support Because of the very wide use, local support of SCAN is more generally available. The available version, however, is not always the latest, as many users, in my experience, tend to use the one version they obtain for at least a year before seeking another.

There are also a number of shareware products that "enhance" the use of SCAN, such as menuing "front ends" or programs to assist in checking archived files.

Support requirements If at all possible, it would be best if knowledgeable users assisted with the use of SCAN. The programs are simple enough to be operated by a novice user, and no harm should result, but best results will be obtained with the program if someone aware and informed of virus operation is involved.

General Notes

Version numbering, which has been problematic in the past, is now standardized and explained in a file in the distribution archive.

ESaSS B.V.
ThunderByte Utilities

Scanning, disinfection, change detection, operation restriction, encryption
$35

Ratings (1 = poor, 4 = very good)

Installation	2
Ease of use	3
Help systems	3
Compatibility	2
Company stability	3
Company support	2
Documentation	2
Hardware required	3
Performance	2
Availability	2
Local support	1

General Description

An extension of the earlier ThunderByte Rescue and ThunderByte Scan programs. These programs are still contained in the set, but are supported by a disinfector with two "generic" disinfection modes (TBCLEAN), a change detector (TBCHECK), an "overwriting" delete (TBDEL), operation-restricting programs (TBDISK, TBFILE and TBMEM), a menuing interface (TBAV), and standardized TSR handling for compatibility with Windows and Novell Netware.

(Associated, though not separately reviewed, is a "quarantine" component called TBfence, which is similar to the D-Fence program by Sophos.)

Comparison of Features and Specifications

Installation Installation is a matter of copying the programs to disk and deciding how to run them. The documentation, while clear enough as to use, does not supply much in the way of direction for installation. With the new, larger set of utilities, there is a section on installation in the documentation file.

Although an intermediate or experienced user will be able to determine how best to use these programs fairly easily, novice users may not have sufficient information for installation. Intermediate users may also have difficulty in deciding how best to use the programs, as weaknesses and shortcomings of the various modules are not noted.

Ease of use The programs are very easy to use. The command-line switches should not be strictly necessary for effective use, but can provide significant extra information or use for the expert.

Help systems Because of the newer programs that do not require command-line switches, an "empty" invocation does not bring up a list of command-line options. However, an invocation of any program with a "?" or "help" argument will.

Compatibility Incompatibilities with specific programs or networks are noted in the .DOC files with suggestions for workarounds.

Company stability The company has been supporting this product, with regular updates, for quite some time now. An "agent network" has been established. An earlier announcement of a commercial product based on the technology does not seem to have led to any actual product.

Company support Contacts with the company have been sketchy so far. Some of the agents, particularly Jeff Cook of the United States, have been very active in promoting the product on Fidonet.

Documentation The documentation has been substantially improved in the matter of grammar and errors. However, there is still little coverage of viral concepts in general, and the shortcomings and weaknesses of the program modules in particular. A section of the documentation entitled "Anti-Virus Strategy" contains no general discussion, policies, or procedures, but simply refers to the use of specific modules of the package. Installation of the program overall still needs work.

Hardware requirements None stated.

Performance The ThunderByte Scan program has always been one of the fastest scanners available. Even with heuristic scanning implemented, it still shows startling speed. A test run on a 386 machine with a "normally" loaded 75 meg hard drive completed in under half a minute. A test on a 486/33 with a full 350 meg drive took 36 seconds.

The "price" of this speed is debatable. Most scanners no longer scan the entire length of a program, but only the "top and tail," where most viral programs must attach in order to function. Although such programs will detect most viral programs, it will not find those that can insert themselves anywhere, such as the "Commander Bomber." Some of those connected with Thunder-Byte, most recently one of the agents, have stated that this is one of the means to speed up the program. Franz Veldman, who should know, strongly objects to this statement. However, it is extremely unlikely that TBSCAN does scan the whole file.

TBSCAN does report some changes to files, but a test run on a directory of antiviral programs showed that numerous updated programs were ignored.

The operation-restricting programs operate as advertised, although such programs always operate under the proviso that whatever software can protect, software can circumvent. Interestingly, the Thunderbyte programs are not automatically exempt from interference: an attempt to disinfect a program with the TBFILE program resident resulted in a warning. (Another interesting point is that an attempt to infect one file, while stopped, was allowed to change the file creation date. This is used by this particular virus as an infection marker.)

The most attractive part of this new package is the second "generic" disinfection mode. Most generic disinfectors use a "return to state" algorithm, much like the hamming code used for error correction in memory or communications systems. This relies on the calculation of an "image" identity of the original, uninfected file and is of no use "after the fact." TBCLEAN uses this, but also has a "heuristic" cleaning mode, which does not rely on any "prior knowledge" of either the infecting virus or the original file.

A success rate of 80 percent is claimed for the heuristic cleaning mode. However, there are two factors to be considered. The second is the ability to clean files infected with an unknown virus. The first comes to us from Hippocrates' injunction to physicians, "First, do no harm." Therefore, TBCLEAN was tested against some uninfected files. Of the six files tested, the four COM files were not harmed, but both EXE files were damaged, and thereafter useless.

Subsequent tests of disinfection of infected COM files were successful and restored files to their original state.

In attempting to use the "checksum" method of disinfection, I found that the TBSETUP program *cannot* be used to find an infected file. Running TBSETUP after an infection will void the ability to recover. (This is mentioned in the documentation, but given the difference between this and other programs, it bears repeating.) However, this disinfection mode otherwise works well.

Local support As noted above, it is difficult to get in touch with the principals via the posted email addresses, but the agents, particularly Jeff Cook, are active on the Fidonet virus-related echoes. Unfortunately, this activity does not seem to extend to *VIRUS-L/comp.virus* where there have been few postings from anyone related to the company. Franz Veldman has recently been active in private virus discussion groups, but this provides little support to the average user.

Support requirements On a "scan-only" basis, the program is simple to use. Invocation of any of the various modules is also quite simple. Installation will require more expert assistance.

General Notes

ThunderByte was, for a time, one of the fastest developing programs and is a very good set of utilities. However, the principals and agents of the company have been very averse to any and all reviews. The distribution archive, in fact, contains an editorial directed against the scanner tests included in the Hoffman VSUM list. The American agent conducted a vendetta against one reviewer that resulted in a flame war on Fidonet lasting more than a year, and the cancellation of that series of reviews. That same test of the product sparked the comment, from Franz Veldman, that no test or review should be released unless it could be proven to be absolutely without flaw. Unfortunately, this same standard does not seem to apply to the ThunderByte product. This attitude, and the lack of development over the past year, do not bode well for the future of the product.

Cybec
VET antiviral 8.2

Scanner, two-option resident scanner, activity monitor, disinfector, change detector, and utilities
$90.00 (Australia) for 1-year license, updates posted quarterly

Ratings (1 = poor, 4 = very good)

Installation	3
Ease of use	3
Help systems	2
Compatibility	3
Company stability	3
Company support	3
Documentation	3
Hardware required	4
Performance	3
Availability	2
Local support	2

General Description

VET is a fairly standard scanner/disinfector with a strong emphasis on boot sector infectors. VET_RES is a resident scanning system with various options. Utilities included are VCRC, for change detection; HUNT, a "baiting" change detector; and VET_TRAP, which saves MBR, boot sector, and "top of memory" data for evaluation of suspect new virus. A Windows interface is available, and a NetWare NLM is in final test and should be available when this review sees print.

Comparison of Features and Specifications

Installation The program is shipped on a writable but protected 720K diskette, with another for the Windows interface. The installation program is very well prompted and explains the choices the user has to make. Two or three sentences of rationale are given as the user cycles through the options presented. Standard installation, although somewhat more complicated than some other products, is quite reasonable and should give the novice no problem. (Ironically, a possible exception is the installation of the Windows interface. The interface uses the VET program, but is separate from it. Installation of VET adds to the PATH command in the AUTOEXEC.BAT file, but if the Windows interface is installed immediately following, without an intermediate reboot, VETWIN won't be able to find VET.) Custom installation, however, should only be attempted by intermediate or advanced users, and that only after all of Chapter 1 has been read. The manual is somewhat technical, but computer support personnel should feel right at home. (Given VET's origin in college computer labs, this orientation is quite reasonable.)

Having said that, technical-support staff will find a number of helpful functions for customizing installation, and for aiding installation in sites with many PCs. Both "Master" and "Network" options assist in initiating the program on multiple PCs in a corporate environment.

The installation process is very "careful" and should ensure that no virus contaminates the program.

Installation is possible on systems with no hard drive, but some of the installation functions, such as modification of AUTOEXEC.BAT, are not performed.

Ease of use Most of the VET programs are command line, rather than menu, driven, but the default usage should be easy enough for most novice users. Users are told very plainly about problems, as well as possible, and recommended, courses of action. Novice users will find that standard usage gives them a fairly solid measure of protection. The only important part of the package that is difficult to use is the change-detection component. Intermediate and expert users will find various options that can increase the level of security or avoid conflicts in specialized environments.

Help systems A list of command-line options can be obtained with the "?" switch.

Compatibility No problems were found in testing. A Windows interface for the VET program is available. The VET_RES programs will sound an audible alarm running under Windows, but will not display the warning screen. Suggestions are made to allow coexistence with various networks.

Company stability Cybec has a significant presence on *VIRUS-L*, as well as other research groups. It is now to be considered among the top international virus research companies.

Company support The usual. In addition, Cybec is fairly active on *VIRUS-L/ comp.virus* and is reachable through the Internet. The product is updated quarterly for those with a valid license. Updated documentation on disk makes this look almost like a shareware package. A newsletter called *Cyclops*, available to customers, is not as detailed as the *F-PROT Update Bulletin*, but is a lot funnier.

Documentation The documentation is now excellent in terms of program operation. The removal of the primer material and the humor is disappointing. Introductory-level explanations are, however, inegrated throughout.

Hardware requirements No special hardware is needed. The program will work with MS-DOS 2.x or higher and can be run from a floppy disk if needed.

Performance There is a very strong emphasis on boot sector protection in the package, not surprising, in that it started life as a defense against Stoned and produced the "Man who named Michelangelo." Data bases, detectors, and recovery tools are included for analysis of the boot sector and master boot record. VET_RES checks the boot sector every time it monitors a change in a floppy disk in the drive, and checks for a disk in the drive when <Ctrl><Alt><Del> is pressed.

Scanning is among the fastest reviewed and ranks with ThunderByte and Virex-PC.

Unfortunately, the program has not been included in many of the most widely distributed independent scanner trials. My own tests do not indicate any shortcomings in the scanning coverage of the program.

Local Support The company is reachable via the Internet.

Support requirements VET is suitable for all user levels, but is particularly recommended for supported sites.

General Notes

An improvement in the change-detection component would contribute to the full multilayered defense. VET is, however, a significant package, and well worth serious consideration, particularly in large environments.

Datawatch Corporation
Virex for the PC version 2.8

Scanning, change detection, and activity monitoring
$49

Ratings (1 = poor, 4 = very good)

Installation	3
Ease of use	4
Help systems	2
Compatibility	3
Company stability	4
Company support	3
Documentation	4
Hardware required	4
Performance	3
Availability	4
Local support	?

General Description

VPCSCAN is a virus detection and disinfection product. It will remove some viral programs from files or optionally delete files that cannot be disinfected. Disinfection or deletion is at user control. Two "levels" of TSR protection are available: VIREX is a resident scanner and change detector; VIREXPRO has, in addition to those features, activity-monitoring capability. VPCSCAN is one of the the fastest scanning products reviewed. Virex for the PC vaccine is customizable with multiple options and allows "protection" of specified files, as well as alerts on "formatting" and "program modification," and is recommended for "expert" users. Documentation is an excellent overview of viral and PC operations.

Ross Greenberg was the original author of Virex-PC and one of the first to produce an antiviral product, Flu-Shot. Microcom/Datawatch's Virex product for the Macintosh is also well established. VIRx, is an associated file available on electronic bulletin board systems. It was formerly a scan-only demonstration product, but is now a shareware distribution of the program, missing VIREXPRO and registration data.

Comparison of Features and Specifications

Installation Disks shipped writable, but protected.

In earlier versions, effective installation was impossible without reading the documentation and understanding the concepts and system configuration thoroughly. This has been improved. The documentation is complete and quite clear, but naive users may find the number of functions and features, and the explanations, daunting to tackle.

Ease of use Once installed, the system operates without intervention, unless viral activity is detected. The alert screens are clear and informative. The decisions necessary and the usefulness or "hindrance" of the system depends largely on the installation, which should be "matched" to the experience of the user.

VPCSCAN's screen display shows the files checked individually, but continues to display the directories checked until the screen is full, so that a number of directories can be seen at once. This is much clearer than the practice of other programs, which only display one file at a time, or only the directories checked, especially given the speed of VPCSCAN's operation.

Help systems Alert screens contain somewhat esoteric but very complete information on the activity taking place. This will be very helpful to expert users, but even novices will find it easier to make an informed decision on whether or not to allow an operation.

Compatibility VPCSCAN has substantially improved its position with regard to identification of viral programs. Current versions are roughly equal to the performance of the SCAN program, although identification is more accurate than SCAN.

Company stability Microcom is a stable and diversified company, if somewhat smaller than a Lotus or Microsoft. Virex for the Mac has been around for some time, although it is not one of the current leaders among Mac antivirals. Ross Greenberg was one of the first to write an antiviral program for MS-DOS (Flu-Shot), and it is still a viable program. The Virex-PC program has been recently purchased by Datawatch.

Company support The support provisions have increased since Datawatch purchased the product. Support is available through the sources listed above, and also on AppleLink, America Online, and GEnie by contacting DATAWATCH. The manual states that updates are made quarterly and that registered users will receive "notification" of updates. The price of updates has been reduced to $15 from $25 each, or you may receive a year's "subscription" for $50 as opposed to $75. Updates may be downloaded free for two years from the date of purchase by calling the company's bulletin board directly. At the time of my first review, update notices were delayed, but this has improved since.

Documentation Very good (clear, concise) section on general virus information.

The installation procedure, which previously could have resulted in an infected working copy, has been improved.

The installation prompts are no better or worse than others reviewed, but the documentation explains all options very clearly, both in terms of what is available, and the reasons behind certain functions.

Hardware requirements There are no special hardware requirements.

Performance VPCSCAN is amazingly fast. File checking is at least twice as fast as either F-PROT or SCAN across all platforms tested.

Virex for the PC has more options than other vaccine-type programs, as well as change-detection capabilities. An earlier weakness in detecting Stoned infections in memory and Stoned infection activity has been corrected. Although Virex for the PC will make a checksum of disk or diskette boot sectors, it does not checksum partition boot records.

Local support No provisions.

Support requirements The installation and operation of Virex for the PC and VPCSCAN should not be beyond the average intelligent user who is willing to spend time with the manual before installation. However, in supported environments, it would be best to have the support staff perform installation.

General Notes

A very solid product with an excellent scanner. Of the multilayered commercial antivirals, this one may still have some weaknesses in the matter of unknown boot sector infectors. However, it will give superior defense against the currently common viral programs.

Leprechaun Software Pty Ltd.
Virus Buster version 3.75

Very complete range of antiviral protection programs, including change detection, resident and nonresident scanning, activity monitor, and operation restriction

Ratings (1 = poor, 4 = very good)

Installation	3
Ease of use	3
Help systems	3
Compatibility	3
Company stability	3
Company support	2
Documentation	3
Hardware required	4
Performance	3
Availability	2

General Description

Virus Buster offers a very wide variety of antiviral protection and is suitable for both novice and experienced users. BUSTER and WATCHDOG/PROTECT are nonresident and resident change-detection software, respectively. In addition, WATCHDOG provides activity monitoring and operation restriction. FIDO/Phideaux allows WATCHDOG to run under Windows. DOCTOR and VBSHIELD provide nonresident and resident signature scanning. DISKLOK provides access restriction to the hard disk and detection/disinfection of boot-sector viral programs. KEYLOK restricts access to the computer if it is left unattended. VBCOPY checks files for viral signatures during copy operations. VBSAVER provides other Virus Buster programs with the ability to detect stealth viral programs. A file browser, LIST, and a task scheduler, ONCEADAY, are also included.

Comparison of Features and Specifications

Installation The package is shipped on dual media. Both sets of disks are writable, but protected. The manual is dauntingly thick, but the first page provides information on installation and clearly outlines the "Standard" and "Default" methods for installation.

Installation is quite intelligent. Time to install will vary greatly, depending upon the options chosen. As is indicated in the manual, default installation can be quite lengthy.

Ease of use Most of the programs run with a mouse-sensitive menuing interface, but there is also an option to use command-line switches for those more familiar with the system who wish faster and more direct control.

Menu and mouse use is well explained in the manual and should present no difficulty to anyone. It is, however, not quite standard for those used to a CUA (Common User Application) interface.

Help systems A number of help systems are available, and help for menu items is context-sensitive. It is, however, fairly brief in most cases.

A very nice feature is the fact that some characteristic information is given about any virus detected, rather than merely a name.

Compatibility The programs appear to be well behaved. Provision has been made for the WATCHDOG TSR to work under Windows.

The PROTECT program is one that adds information to program files in order to detect any changes made to the files. As has been noted with other similar programs in the past, this practice may conflict with programs that already have internal self-checks. However, a number of such programs, modified by PROTECT, showed no problem in subsequent runs.

Company stability The company has apparently enjoyed sufficient success to open an office in the United States and is enjoying well-deserved success in Australia.

Company support The documentation lists numbers for voice, fax, and BBS in Australia, and the manual stresses the use of the BBS for support. A small window in the lower right-hand corner of the screen continually scrolls through the phone and fax numbers for the North American office (which I received my copy from), as well as the serial number—a nice feature when calling for support.

Documentation Although the printed documentation is the size of a significant novel, the arrangement of the material is thoughtful and well presented. Chapter 1 is a single page that explains how to install the program. Subsequent chapters explain how the manual works, how the program works, how the interface works, how installation works, and so forth. (If I may be permitted a small "peeve," the typeface is still awful.) Much information is duplicated in different chapters as many of the programs have common options.

Chapter 18 is a good description of the virus situation—with the one proviso that it overemphasizes the value of "buy only commercial" as a defense against viral programs. The statement that "no professional software house releases viral programs . . ." may be syntactically correct, but is misleading in terms of the actual safety of commercial software.

Hardware requirements None stated.

Performance The description of VBSAVER's operation is very short, although perhaps understandably so, in view of the battle for security technology between virus writers and antiviral developers. The documentation seems to imply that VBSAVER is ineffective until invoked, and in tests it was unable to assist in identification of stealth boot viral programs, although the DOCTOR program did state that a stealth virus might be operating and recommended rebooting.

DISKLOK is unusual among hard-disk access-restriction programs in that it stores copies of the original system areas and restores them if any change is detected, thus defeating most boot sector viral programs including Stoned. DISKLOK can be bypassed, but the manual is quite clear about possible dangers and what to do about them.

WATCHDOG was effective in preventing writing to disks during testing. Any attempt to write to a protected area generates an alert window. The menu lets the user allow or disallow the operation, and optionally provides information on the action detected.

Local support None provided.

Support requirements Virus Buster can be almost fully utilized by a novice user. Expert help in installation should provide a very high level of protection.

General Notes

Virus Buster provides one of the most complete defenses against viral attack yet reviewed, ranking with pre-version 2.00 F-PROT in the range of protection provided. The help systems, interface, and manual should allow it to provide a high level of protection to even naive users. A weakness in the area of detection of memory-resident viral programs should be addressed, but the combination of defenses does not seriously weaken the overall protection delivered by the package.

Leprechaun Software also has a new companion product called C:CURE, a hardware "write-protect" for IDE hard drives. I have discussed this with the U.S. office, but have not seen the product yet.

General Security Software

Leprechaun Software International
Network Security Organizer (NSO) version 1.0

NetWare security assessment and antiviral manager

Ratings (1 = poor, 4 = very good)

Installation	3
Ease of use	3
Help systems	2
Compatibility	2
Company stability	3

Company support	2
Documentation	2
Hardware required	3
Performance	2
Availability	2
Local support	1

General Description

Reports on various aspects of NetWare security and vulnerabilities; manages updating of antiviral software, as well as messaging and logging.

Comparison of Features and Specifications

Installation Installation is automated insofar as the copying of files is concerned. Access rights must be granted manually. Some features, such as a number of functions of the security check, are immediately available. Others appear to require activation the next time the individual users, on various workstations, log on to the network. There is no provision for manual installation, nor are the specialized operations described in much detail.

Ease of use Once fully installed, the operation and use of NSO itself is quite simple. The interface is CUA compliant and, like the Virus Buster interface, well designed and clearly laid out.

Help systems Help is available at all times in the NSO program. Assistance with installation of the program is very limited.

Compatibility Operates only with the Novell NetWare operating system. The system is stated to perform updates with a number of antiviral packages.

Company stability Doing well.

Company support The normal routes.

Documentation The manual is very small, and obviously intended to portray the program as simple to install and use. Unfortunately, it goes a bit overboard in this direction. While the implications of the reports NSO gives you are perhaps best left to a specialized worker in network security, the lack of background in the manual may leave some users or administrators with a false sense of protection. On the other hand, the warnings NSO gives are quite detailed and specific, so perhaps additional material is unnecessary.

However, there are some definite gaps in the information about the program itself. Content about certain aspects of the installation is very scanty. Some material is obviously missing: the program is said to be able to check for, and update, a wide range of antiviral programs. Of those listed, MSAV, F-PROT, FindVirus, and Sweep have no entries in the set of command line switches needed to do this.

Included is a much-reduced version of the Virus Buster manual. This covers the basics of installation and operation without the additional background of the full manual. For system administrators wanting a quick reference, it would be a handy guide.

Performance NSO's ability to manage and report on vulnerabilities for a specific network is long overdue. Some of the functions, such as the ability to check status on different machines, or update virus software, can be obtained through the use of utilities and script files if the administrator wishes to take the time to do it. Others, such as the virus risk analysis, would be very tedious and time consuming, as well as difficult to automate. For those without a specific background in security, this is a fairly effective one-stop source for virus and security analysis and control on the network.

Local support None provided.

Support requirements Minimal.

Mergent (formerly Pyramid Development Corp.) PC/DACS

General PC security program, very rich in features
$249.00

Ratings (1 = poor, 4 = very good)

Installation	2
Ease of use	3
Help systems	2
Compatibility	2
Company stability	3
Company support	3
Documentation	2
Hardware required	3
Performance	3
Availability	3
Local support	2

General Description

From a lot of perspectives, this is the Cadillac of PC security programs. Just about every security function that you could want is part of the package. Virus protection can be achieved via boot protection, file write protection, and restriction of access to floppy drives. At the same time, if you are interested strictly in virus protection, this may be more than you want.

Comparison of Features and Specifications

Installation Once again, another program that adds the security of a multiuser operating system to DOS. And, once again, a package that seems to think that installation is complete once the files are in place, and the program is running. Actually, PC/DACS does a bit better in this regard than others tested. Chapter 1 of the installation guide suggests a minimal installation, but Chapter 2 includes a table with security goals and some direction on how to achieve them. However, given the extensive feature set of the product, this chart is quite terse. Antivirus protection is said to be achieved with "Virus Prevention Attributes," and the fact that you can write-protect files to prevent infection. There is no discussion of the complexity of this task.

A tutorial is included, but again this is of little use in terms of security concepts, and deals strictly with the program interface. There are, indeed, a couple of weaknesses. In Lesson 1, an ID is created, complete with suggested password. The ID is deleted in Chapter 6, but a bored administrator might not make it all the way, and so leave a vulnerability in the system. (Check out PC/DACS installations around you. Is there an account LOCAL1 with password, TUTORIAL1? You now have "local administrator" privileges.) Lesson 2 tells you to check Lesson 5 if you don't see "Administrative Maintenance" on the Main Menu: Lesson 5 has nothing to say on the subject.

Ease of use The interface is easy to use, and the "screen flow" is understandable. Options that are used less frequently have extra explanatory detail. As noted, some functions may require additional explanation in terms of the implications of certain choices.

The ability to predefine groups and application "views" makes administration less of a chore.

Help systems Help is available for most screens.

Compatibility Specifically designed to interfere with, or limit the use of, some utility software. May hamper or preclude recovery efforts in the event of disk problems.

Note that the suggested settings for rights access preclude proper operation of SETVER and other programs that alter their own executable files.

Boot protection *cannot* be used if there are non-DOS partitions.

Company stability Aside from name changes, quite stable.

Company support Primarily phone and fax. (Apparently there are internal arguments regarding email.)

Documentation Of the documentation stated to be a part of the package, only the *Installation Guide* and *Administrator Reference Manual* were included with the review package. The manuals are well laid out. Some entries could be clearer: in a number of cases, you will have little idea of the operation and functions until you run the program. Again, note that the documentation refers to the program operation only—security implications are not dealt with.

System requirements DOS 3.x or higher (there is an error in the manual), 640K memory, and 1 to 2 megs of hard disk space, depending upon options and features desired.

Performance In comparison with other PC security products, PC/DACS contains a wealth of features. For the experienced security officer, many of the desired features of multiuser operating systems are contained within.

The password-choice functions are a good example. Minimum password lengths can be imposed. The password can optionally be prevented from being identical, or an anagram, to the user name. There can be restrictions on the format of the password, and a history of up to 12 previous passwords can be disallowed. On the other hand, there appears to be nothing against the altering of a single character in the password when changing it.

Virus protection appears to be limited to write protection, boot protection, and encryption.

There are indications of certain areas of vulnerability. The system can be recovered with only a boot disk and the original program disks. This means that the hard disk *is* accessible through software means. The "Time Out" feature is meant to disable access from the keyboard if the workstation is left for a period of time, but apparently will not work if any processing is taking place at the time. Therefore a PC running a communications session, or doing processing-intensive computing, will be left vulnerable. (Such processes can be started in such a way as to disallow any keyboard access, but this is not always feasible.)

Local support There is an 800 number (which even works from Canada).

Support requirements A thorough background in data-security concepts would be required to take full advantage of the package. Knowledge of the operations of various programs and the DOS operating system is highly recommended.

Johnson Computer Systems, Inc.
PC-Vault (formerly PC-Lock)

Very simple general security program
PC-Vault $35; PC-Vault Plus $90

Ratings (1 = poor, 4 = very good)

Installation	3
Ease of use	3
Help systems	1
Compatibility	2
Company stability	2

Company support	2
Documentation	2
Hardware required	3
Performance	1
Availability	2
Local support	1

General Description
A minimal set of security features for MS-DOS systems.

Comparison of Features and Specifications
Installation PC-Vault and PC-Vault Plus are shipped on unprotected 1.2M diskettes (one for each). The installation process is two-phased, with a preparatory step to configure the program and then the installation itself. There are extensive reminders to read the documentation on disk.

Ease of use The functions of PC-Vault are much simpler than most other general security products and are consequently much simpler to use.

Help systems On-line help is not available.

Compatibility There are extensive warnings about compatibility problems with various utilities. Use of PC-Vault to protect the MBR and boot sector may conflict with other antiviral software.

Company stability Unknown.

Company support Unknown.

Documentation The documentation is quite short and refers strictly to program operation.

System requirements None stated.

Performance PC-Vault is intended to provide some password protection for access to PCs, as well as optional directory restrictions. The protection should be adequate for most users up to an intermediate level of skill but may not be effective against a determined attack. Recovery after infection by a boot sector infector may present problems.

Local support None provided.

Support requirements Installation and operation are fairly simple and should require a minimum of support.

Micronyx, Inc.
SAFE (Secure Access Facility for the Enterprise) version 3.5

Encryption and operation restriction system, primarily directed at restriction
of access rather than protection
$295

Ratings (1 = poor, 4 = very good)

Installation	2
Ease of use	1
Help systems	1
Compatibility	2
Company stability	3
Company support	3
Documentation	1
Hardware required	1
Performance	2
Availability	1
Local support	1

General Description

SAFE is a security system primarily directed toward restriction of access. This
does provide some protection against modification of program files, but the
system is not an antiviral package per se. It is reviewed here in the interest of
completeness. Because of this, numerous "failings" are reported here that have
no bearing on the suitability of the package in its intended role.

Comparison of Features and Specifications

Installation The product is shipped on unprotected 3½" (720K) disks. Reference
is made in the installation manual to a "token reader," but this was not included
with the evaluation unit.

Automated installation is the only option. Installation instructions are
given in both the *Installation Guide* and the *Quick Installation* pamphlet. One
of these *must* be read. Failure to read the instructions may result in an improperly installed system, and one that may impair operation.

This is odd, given that the installation process is so highly automated. For
example, the computer is rebooted twice during the installation process. The
first time is handled completely by the installation program. The computer is
rebooted and continues with the installation. This requires no operator intervention. The second time, however, the user is instructed, very tersely, that the
system is *not* installed, and to follow the "next" step in the installation process.
Study of the installation guides reveals this to be the running of the security
setup, which installs user accounts. Given that the system comes with default
accounts, and that the "Quick Installation" suggests that you use them, the
system should be able to proceed to that point and prompt the user for a choice.

If the user does not take this further step, the system is, in fact, partially installed, contrary to what has been said. In addition, at this point the program will not remove itself through the "Remove" option on the menu. It gives the terse, and as it turns out erroneous, message that the path to the SAFE directory is incorrect. There is a RECOVERY batch file that can be used at this point. A further reboot and run of the CLEANUP batch file are needed in order to fully restore the system to normal operation.

Ease of use In common with most security systems, SAFE requires a lot of thought. The program interface is not hard to figure out, but the setup of access rules is not going to be an easy task.

Help systems None provided.

Compatibility SAFE requires removal of all other antiviral security before installation. All TSRs must also be removed and added to the system after installation. An exception to this appears to be mouse driver software.

SAFE requires that disk maintenance and repair utilities not be used once the system is installed. There may also be conflicts with memory managers and programs requiring certain keystrokes.

Company stability Unknown.

Company support Unknown.

Documentation The documentation is extremely daunting, even for those familiar with installation and administration manuals on midrange computers. I was, for a time, unsure as to whether I did, in fact, have an MS-DOS version of the product for evaluation. A *Quick Installation* pamphlet is provided, which does guide the user through the steps for installation. In fact, the main documentation recommends that "software evaluators" use the quick installation without reference to the other documentation. While it is true that this will perform a successful installation, it by no means provides sufficient information for an informed review of the product.

In addition to the *Quick Installation* and some other reference cards, there are three manuals in the documentation. The *Installation Guide* lists the installation requirements, the steps necessary to install the program, and some options for customization. The *User Guide* describes installation and use of SAFE on a stand-alone machine or network, while the *Administrator Guide* deals with security at a "corporate" level.

It is unlikely that even the advanced user will fully appreciate the ramifications of the *Installation Guide* unless the other manuals are read as well. Although the directions for installation are explicit and clear, there is almost no description of what the installation of SAFE does to the computer system.

The *User Guide* contains a section with a general discussion of data-security "concepts." This leads into a short section on SAFE "concepts," but still gives little information regarding the operation of the program itself. There is extensive discussion of access "rules" and of the interface of the program itself.

The *Administrator Guide*, interestingly, is almost a carbon copy of the *User Guide*, except for the added sections dealing with the Global User Setup and Audit programs. No further details are available regarding what it is that SAFE actually does, and how. Assessment of the strengths of the system can therefore only be determined by experimentation. It is obvious that Micronyx believes firmly in security by obscurity.

Hardware requirements An MS-DOS computer with version 3.3 or higher, 640K memory, a floppy disk drive, and a hard disk with 6 megabytes of free space. (Once installation is complete, approximately 2.4 MB of files may be removed.) Note that if only 640K memory is available, SAFE occupies 62K.

Performance The operation-restricting aspects of the system should be able to prevent infection by most file-infecting viral programs. However, the fact that protection is file-based does not seem to help with protection against boot sector infectors. (The hardware requirements of the system prevented full testing of this, but the initial results indicated that infection of the hard disk was not prevented.) Additionally, the system does not appear to protect against FAT (or system) viral programs, nor against companion viral programs.

Local support None available.

Support requirements SAFE is a security system, and the "virus-protection" component is really incidental to that. Setup of the security system will require assistance by those experienced in security matters. This is not a system to be handed to the novice, or even intermediate user.

Command Software Systems Security Guardian

Full-featured PC security program
$250

Ratings (1 = poor, 4 = very good)

Installation	2
Ease of use	3
Help systems	2
Compatibility	2
Company stability	2
Company support	3
Documentation	2
Hardware required	3
Performance	3

Availability   2
Local support   2

General Description
Midrange-functionality security package.

Comparison of Features and Specifications
Installation The program is shipped on two unprotected 720K diskettes. As is usual with general security programs, installation is taken to mean only copying the files to the hard disk. However, the configuration is menu-driven and relatively straightforward.

Ease of use Menu-driven.

Help systems On-line help is available. You may also build help screens for your own menu items.

Compatibility As usual for an operation-restricting program.

Company stability Unknown.

Company support The company is accessible via the usual channels, plus Internet access and an 800 number that works even from Canada. My experience with them has been amicable, but has indicated some problems with shipping.

Documentation The documentation is reasonably clear in terms of the operation of the program itself, but fails to fully explain some of the program functions. For example, the system is intended to run as an extendable menu front-end to DOS. While the operations of the edit menu itself are fairly clear, the creation of new menus is less so.

Again, as with many security products, there is no general discussion of security. The full value of the system may not be achieved without further study.

Hardware requirements No special hardware is required. The serial and parallel ports may be secured, as well as the floppy disks.

Performance Security of the system is not absolute, but a careful setup should be adequate for most purposes. The program has most features one would want and is good value at the price.

The system does not provide protection against boot sector viral programs.

Local support Internet access and an 800 number.

Support requirements A security background would be helpful in order to take full advantage of the package.

Fischer International Systems Corporation
Watchdog version 7

Operation-restriction, change-detection, and encryption software

Ratings (1 = poor, 4 = very good)

Installation	3
Ease of use	3
Help systems	2
Compatibility	3
Company stability	3
Company support	3
Documentation	3
Hardware required	4
Performance	3
Availability	2
Local support	2

General Description

Watchdog is a general security product for a PC, and therefore it is difficult to compare it with the bulk of virus security products. Please note in the following that this is one of the few products providing general security for the PC, and therefore the comments regarding some of the difficulty of use apply only to those who are looking strictly for virus protection. Those wishing to compare it to other overall security products should compare it with SAFE and DISK-SECURE. (Please note that the other generic security package, Advanced Security, is no longer supported.)

Between versions 6 and 7, extensive efforts were made to provide ease of use and improved explanations of the operation of the program. Watchdog now enjoys a fairly clear advantage over other general PC security programs.

Comparison of Features and Specifications

Installation Since Watchdog is primarily concerned with access and operation restriction, the longest part of the installation is going to involve the decisions you make regarding access. The *Installation Guide* says that you need to answer some questions, and that preparing your answers ahead of time will speed the installation process. Superb understatement. What you essentially are doing is adding the multiuser security access of a mainframe, minicomputer, or LAN to MS-DOS. Therefore, expect to dedicate the same time and attention to the installation that you would give to the system administration of a similarly sized minicomputer. Indeed, one of the first steps in installation is to set up a "System Administrator" account. (If you are the only person to be using the micro, that's you.) You will also have to set up any user accounts.

For each user, you will have to determine on a device (printer, serial port, floppy drive), directory, and sometimes even file-by-file basis, whether or not this user has access to the entity, and which type of access. Much of this may be the same from user to user, but the initial planning will take considerable thought. For example, you may grant certain users access to all the DOS programs and files so that they can use the utilities. But, if they are only running the utilities, they will not need "write" access to the DOS directory, right? Well, if they don't have write access, they can't use SETVER, since it writes to itself each time it is used with a new program. The new documentation does address some of these issues and suggests special attention for the more commonly used programs such as WordPerfect and Lotus 1-2-3.

For the program and package to be at all effective you must plan the access controls very thoroughly and very carefully. It is *not* going to be enough to read *Getting Started*. Since version 6, however, the installation process has been considerably improved, as has the documentation. I would strongly recommend that *all* installers read the *Concepts Guide*. This manual is reasonably short, and reading it should not be an onerous task.

The manuals see installation as being merely the copying of the program onto the hard disk. The actual protection seems to be seen as "management." In this case, however, the job isn't finished until the administration is done. The process has been improved with the new installation and setup procedure. Watchdog now allows "transparent access" to unrestricted areas, so by default you could leave the system unprotected after installation and do your administration at a later date. The setup program also now shows you which areas are unprotected and therefore prompts you for more complete protection.

Ease of use Once the decisions regarding access and control have been made, the actual implementation is quite straightforward. (However, recall that, as with the SETVER example, the terminology regarding the setting of permission and access may sometimes be open to interpretation.) Users should have no problems with a properly setup system unless confronted with unusual new "error" messages. In many cases, Watchdog may aid in ease of use of the computer through the menuing access system.

Again, remember that you are adding multiuser controls to what was formerly a "personal" computer. The additional security of this system comes at a cost of additional administration and support.

Help systems On-screen help is provided on most screens and menus in Watchdog. Note that this is only help on the operation of the program: ultimately the safety of the system rests with you.

Compatibility Depending upon installation, there may be problems with programs that rewrite their own code, or write into "system" directories. Version 7 has made provisions for the operation of Windows as well as multitasking and memory-management utilities.

Company stability Fischer is well established in the security field and has a good reputation in mainframe security.

Company support My experience with the company on other occasions has been very favorable. This program has now been reviewed twice. Fischer responded to my first review and shipped the updated version 7, which addressed many of the criticisms I had of version 6. Note that, although I make every effort to provide an opportunity for a reaction from vendors, commercial software houses have been singularly lacking in responding, and so the reply itself is a point in Fischer's favor.

Documentation Watchdog now comes with eight manuals. Daunting, perhaps, for the neophyte, but it actually reduces the amount of material you have to read. Only one, the *SA Program Guide*, is of any great size. *Getting Started, Setup Guide*, and *Quick Reference* are obviously intended, and generally rightly so, to be the heart of the documentation. *Concepts Guide, Advanced Topics, SA Program Guide, Producing Reports*, and *User Guide* are relegated to a secondary role. I would, however, suggest that the *Concepts Guide* be given prominence. It is not long, and it gives a clear picture of what Watchdog *can* do in the way of security.

I would still suggest a general security handbook, although the *Concepts Guide* does cover many of the basics.

Hardware requirements This system is intended to protect data on the hard drive. It may also manage device access.

Performance Ultimately, Watchdog is far more, and somewhat less, than an antiviral protection package. The necessary administration of the system may not be worth the benefit if virus protection is the only concern. The operation, restriction, and particularly the boot protection of Watchdog can provide protection against the most common of current viral infections. However, that software operation restriction does have an Achilles heel: what software can do, software can undo. If using Watchdog for virus protection, check the change-detection audit frequently. The reports and audits, in fact, are a major strength of Watchdog. SAs should take advantage of the resource.

Fischer also produces a hardware security card, Watchdog Armor, which works in conjunction with Watchdog. (See review in the next section.)

Local support The company has an 800 number (which even works from Canada) and Internet access.

Support requirements For those used to a PC environment, the support requirements will be quite high. Those familiar with security on other platforms will find it much the same.

Miscellaneous

Hilgraeve, Inc.
HyperACCESS/5 version 3.0

Communications software

Ratings (1 = poor, 4 = very good)

Installation	1
Ease of use	2
Help systems	2
Compatibility	3
Company stability	2
Company support	2
Documentation	2
Hardware required	2
Performance	3
Availability	2
Local support	1

General Description

Feature-rich communications and terminal-emulation program, but definitely for the advanced user.

Comparison of Features and Specifications

Installation I was surprised to find, given Hilgraeve's emphasis on virus detection, that the disks, five 360Ks and three 720Ks were shipped unprotected.

Installation, interestingly, is not covered in the manual. Among the ads for CompuServe, Dow-Jones, NewsNet, OAG, and other goodies is a flyer labeled "Quick Install Guide." The only information on the installation is that you run the INSTALL program. (Installation apparently makes no attempt to add to your "path": You are directed to change to the HyperACCESS directory before running the program.) The manual does, however, list the files supplied, and their functions, in Appendix J.

Installation, due to the fact that files are shipped compressed, is a fairly lengthy process, taking 45 minutes on the old XT test machine. It is not very dependable, either, missing some of the options that it specifically asked me about during the process.

The only information about the disk space needed is a comment on the card that you could install it to a 1.2 meg or larger floppy. The INSTALL program at one point gives you the option of a "full" installation taking up 1.1 megs of space, or a 400K minimal installation. Unlike some other programs that allow this kind of customization, you are only offered these two options, with nothing in between. In any case, it turns out to be nonsense. The program will not install if there is less than 1.5 megs of disk space available. I thought this might have been due to decompression needs, but, in fact, this is the size needed for a full install. Therefore, you *cannot*, in contradiction to both the documentation and the INSTALL program, install to a floppy disk. I am not sure what the minimal installation might be after you have deleted extraneous files, but I estimate it to be about 1 meg.

Ease of use While beginners will find HyperACCESS reasonably easy to use, it is likely to be the "Power User" who is really interested in this program. There are a range of fascinating features, such as the ability to use the mouse to choose options from the screen, even on strictly text-based systems. Hilgraeve obviously sees PROCOMM as the competition and has followed, to a certain extent, the "one key command" philosophy. Not entirely—many of the HyperACCESS functions must be chosen from a menu. In certain cases, however, HyperACCESS has chosen a better route. Many of the "one key" commands are more intuitive (Alt-H for help, for instance), and the menu and screen layouts are more comprehensible. Unfortunately, many of the screens and functions are much less intuitive, and the program takes some getting used to.

Once you start getting into the settings for various functions, this is definitely for experienced users only. One example—sending ASCII text. This is a fairly normal function, in that many users will compose a message off-line, and then send it to the BBS, email or text-editing systems they are using on the host computer. Many host systems will present a prompt at the beginning of each line, and it is best to "wait" before sending the next line. HyperACCESS/5 has a feature to do so, and it is unthreateningly called "wait for this character after sending each line." However, the prompt character to wait for must be entered as a hexadecimal representation. (An ASCII character chart is provided. As usual, it covers not only the "proper" 7-bit ASCII characters but the 8-bit IBM PC graphics characters as well.)

The script language, HyperPilot, is extensive and seems to owe much to the C language. The table of contents alone for the language reference chapter is three and a half pages of very dense type. Chapter 11, however, does give a briefer overview of the more basic commands. Once again, this is a compiled-script situation. Scripts that have not been precompiled will be so after the first usage, if the proper files are all available.

Help systems Alt-H is a universal help key, but this is another program where if you don't know the answer already, you are going to have a hard time finding it in the help system.

Compatibility An interesting feature is the ability to import a PROCOMM dialing directory file. The program is also available for OS/2 and, in fact, is shipped with both versions on disk. VT terminal emulation is generally good. File transfer protocols are generally good, although there is a problem with Kermit uploading.

Company stability Hilgraeve and HyperACCESS/5 have been around for a while. They have not obtained a great "presence" in the communications software industry.

Company support The usual.

Documentation The documentation consists of one manual, plus the easily overlooked "Quick Install Guide" flyer. In general, the manual is clear and well laid out. (Small boxed marginal notes are sprinkled throughout the manual and are generally very helpful hints and points.)

However, it is at this point that the package deserts the "Power User." While the general information on how to use the program is all there, the details on many of the more interesting points are lacking. Several times, in reading the manual, I just got to the point where I felt the next few pages would give me an explanation of a particularly intriguing aspect of HyperACCESS/5, only to find that the next page was a new topic or chapter. The intermediate user will easily be able to grasp and use the basic functions of the terminal program; the advanced user is left wondering whether the experimentation necessary is worth the effort to see if a specific advanced feature lives up to its billing.

Hardware requirements Must install to a hard disk. May be able to run from hard-disk floppies if copied over.

Performance HyperACCESS has a number of features not normally associated with terminal-emulation programs. As mentioned previously, some of these, such as the ability to choose menu options on text-only systems with a mouse, are minor but handy.

HyperACCESS/5, like PROCOMM, has a host mode. The menus provided to the caller are not as pretty as those of PROCOMM, but the functionality is all there. Again, since it is built in, there is no need for programming on the part of the HyperACCESS user. The security aspects are also much better on HyperACCESS/5: there are multiple options, which can be allowed or denied. One proviso—the program ships with an "unlimit" password, which, as it implies, allows unlimited access. The "unlimit" password does not require a specific "account" name. I would strongly recommend that all purchasers delete this entry, even if they do not plan to use the "host" option.

The most bizarre of HyperACCESS's features is virus checking. This is intended to catch viral programs, or infected files, as they are being downloaded. Note that there are the same limitations with this virus checker as with any other: compressed or archived files, or files otherwise manipulated for transmission, may "hide" viral infections. (HyperACCESS/5 does implicitly recognize this: another function is the ability to unzip ZIP format archives. This only works with PKZIP 1.1 format archives.) The READ.ME documentation states that HyperACCESS *is* able to find viral infections inside ZIP files, and I was able to generate a virus-detection alarm with some very common infections that had been compressed with the PKZIP 1.1 format. The default, by the way, is that virus checking is off. I strongly suspect that uploading is not checked. (Hilgraeve used to advertise HyperACCESS/5 with a virus-checking "copy" program called HCOPY. This is apparently still available on the Hilgraeve BBS, but I have not seen it on other boards.)

A chapter is devoted to the additional benefits of "HA5 to HA5" communications; in other words, calling another HyperACCESS/5-equipped computer. This is primarily concerned with promoting the proprietary Hyper-Protocol file transfer protocol. Some mention is made of time-delayed and automatic calls, but this can also be done with normal systems and the script language.

Local support None provided.

Support requirements The intermediate user should be able to access the basic features of the program. (Some problems with installation may inhibit initial use.) Even the advanced user will need to devote several hours, and possibly days, to the initial setup and learning more than the most modest features.

Rising Computer Science and Technology Company
Rising Anti-Virus Card (RAVC)

Hardware-based (ISA half-slot card) activity monitor for Intel/BIOS/ISA computers

Ratings (1 = poor, 4 = very good)

Installation	2
Ease of use	2
Help systems	1
Compatibility	3
Company stability	2
Company support	1
Documentation	1
Hardware required	4
Performance	2
Availability	1
Local support	1

General Description

Small form factor ISA card with ROM extensions for activity monitoring and write protection.

Comparison of Features and Specifications

Installation The package, as I received it, had the card, a 1.44M writable but protected disk, and no instructions. Installation should apparently be a simple matter of installing the card. None of the four programs on the disk appear to be necessary either to installation or to operation.

There are four dip switches on the card. The MEMTEST program seems to have provision for determining what the positions of the switches should be, but in my installation it did not give any clear statement, and the positioning that seemed to be indicated was not correct.

On first installation, the card produced a ROM checksum error and denied access to the hard disk. After a number of installation attempts, the card allowed the system to boot normally.

Ease of use When a suspect activity is detected, the user is presented with a box on-screen. In some cases this is a clear direction, such as to reboot the computer from a clean disk; an informational message, such as notice that a suspect program has been removed from memory; or a rather terse menu of choices to reboot, "Yes" (allow the suspect operation), or abort (the program currently running).

Help systems None provided.

Compatibility The program did not produce overt conflicts with programs. Utilities performing disk writes to system areas and modification of programs will generate alerts and may be terminated. Testing with a limited set of viral programs did not uncover any obvious weaknesses in the package. The RAVC was not tested with Windows, but does not appear to have provisions for it. (With other similar packages the alert screen does not appear but the alert beep can be heard.)

Company stability Unknown, but said to be a major vendor in China.

Company support None provided.

Documentation None provided. This makes determination of other factors difficult.

Hardware requirements Stated to be DOS 2.0 or higher. The card will work with any 8- or 16-bit ISA or EISA slot.

Performance The activity monitor appears to check for modification of .COM and .EXE files, but not .BAT or .SYS. Boot sector infectors are prevented from infecting the hard disk. In the case of a boot sector infector, the user is requested to boot from a clean system disk, but this does not appear to be necessary. Attempts to write or copy to .COM files produced irregular alerts, but I was never able to get a virus to successfully infect. System infectors that do not directly write to executable files were also unsuccessful. Companion viral programs were not tested but the creation of new executable files usually prompted an alert.

Copying or updating of software files is subject to numerous alerts, and the RAVC would likely be unsuitable for development environments. It should probably be removed during software upgrades.

Programs provided for the setting and clearing of passwords, and a network program, have no discernible effect on operation.

Local support None provided.

Support requirements

If there are no problems with installation, this could be used unsupported in an environment where programs are not changed.

Fischer International Systems Corporation Watchdog Armor card

Hardware card that enhances the security of Watchdog

Ratings (1 = poor, 4 = very good)

Installation	2
Ease of use	3
Help systems	3
Compatibility	3
Company stability	3
Company support	3
Documentation	3
Hardware required	4
Performance	3
Availability	2
Local support	2

General Description

The Watchdog Armor is a hardware enhancement to the Watchdog general security system. A primary virus control feature is prevention of floppy boot. Although upgradable by software, the system has provision for prevention of corruption by software.

Comparison of Features and Specifications

Installation The package, if ordered as a separate upgrade to the Watchdog PC Data Security product, is shipped with one unprotected 720K diskette. Installation requires the Watchdog software, and I would recommend ordering the whole package at once if you want the hardware protection. Retrofitting is certainly possible, but it is probably easier to set up the whole package than to upgrade the hardware after installing WATCHDOG. The Armor hardware and software is integrated with the PC Security software and some accommodations must be made. As only one example, the software-controlling diskette booting must be turned off before the card is installed.

The installation process must be followed carefully, but it is relatively straightforward for any user who has installed cards in the computer before. The configuration of the card must be set with jumper switches (a program is provided to check for appropriate memory locations), the card itself is installed, the card is verified, and the Watchdog System Administrator program is updated.

Ease of use Control of the hardware setup is quite easy, and the functions are thereafter part of the Watchdog program itself.

Compatibility The functions of the Watchdog Armor card appear to be limited to boot protection and hardware encryption and should not present problems with compatibility.

Company stability Fischer is well established in the security field and has a good reputation in mainframe security.

Company support My experience with the company on other occasions has been very favorable. This program has now been reviewed twice. Fischer responded to my first review, and shipped the updated version 7, which addressed many of the criticisms I had of version 6. Note that although I make every effort to provide an opportunity for a reaction from vendors, commercial software houses have been singularly lacking in responding, and so reply itself is a point in Fischer's favor.

Documentation The documentation refers only to installation and removal of the card, but is clear and well organized.

Hardware requirements Since the operations do not seem to affect disk access (in regard to disk activity monitoring or operation restriction) and the card is not a replacement of or adjunct to disk controller cards, the product can be used with any type of BIOS/Intel machine with an ISA or related bus. (This includes just about anything.)

Performance A concern with software upgradable hardware is that the hardware is subject to attack by software that can mimic the upgrade function. The Armor card is software upgradable. However, the card has a physical switch that must be set in order to perform the upgrade. If the switch is inadvertently left in the writable position, the user is warned at each boot.

Local support The company has an 800 number (which even works from Canada) and Internet access.

Support requirements Use of the card should not add any additional support requirements beyond the use of Watchdog itself.

Atari

A & Z Vidovic
Chasseur II

Boot-sector overwriter
50 FF ($15)

Comparison of Features and Specifications

Installation The files (at least BOOTBASE.DAT) *must* be installed in a directory called CHASSEUR.II or the program will not function.

Ease of use There are only three options on the main menu: check disk, vaccinate, and check memory. These are represented by icons, with no words.

Help systems None provided.

Compatibility Unknown. The vaccinate function, although stated to be irreversible (which, oddly, appears to contradict the documentation), seems not to harm MS-DOS disks. It adds a jump at the beginning and a short message at the end. (MS-DOS "system" disks, of course, will no longer be bootable.)

Company stability Unknown.

Company support None provided.

Documentation A README.VIR file states that they believe the program is simple enough that there is no need for documentation. This is generally true, but it is a pity that there is not more detail on some of the claims made for the program.

Hardware requirements None stated.

Performance Unknown. This seems to be a tool for very technically literate users, aimed at boot sector infectors only.

Local support None provided.

Support requirements It is unlikely that even intermediate users would understand, say, the memory listings generated. However, it should be effective against boot sector infectors even in novice cases. (One should note that *all* of the Atari boot sector overwriting programs may damage certain self-booting disks.)

Roger Lindberg
FLIST and FCHECK

Change-detection software
£5

Comparison of Features and Specifications

Installation FLIST must be run first in order to make a FILELIST.LIS comparison database. Thereafter, FCHECK can be run in the same directory as the database in order to note changes. (FCHECK can be run from the AUTO folder as long as FILELIST.LIS is present as well.)

(A sense of humor! When invoked, the program presents a message box stating, "I am not a wealthy man Please consider a donation," signed Roger Lindberg, 1991. The acknowledgment "button" does not state the normal "OK" but rather "I WILL.")

Ease of use If FILELIST.LIS exists (which it does, in the distribution file), it must be deleted first, or a new name must be chosen. (The documentation states that the name *must* be FILELIST.LIS.) Creating the file is not exactly straightforward: the file must be created, then loaded, and then a new menu selected to add those files to be checked. Files must be selected individually. Then the file must be saved before exiting the FLIST program.

The FCHECK program has no options: it simply checks the file length and checksum against the stored values. It must be watched: if there is some problem, the fact is noted, but the program does not leave the information on-screen before it terminates.

Help systems None provided.

Compatibility Unknown. Generally should not be a problem, but will report changes in programs that alter their own code.

Company stability Unknown.

Company support Unknown.

Documentation Not extensive, but adequate if read carefully.

System requirements None stated.

Performance Reasonably quick operation, once set up. A bit difficult to do the initial installation. No attempt to "diagnose" changes on the disk.

Local support None provided.

Support requirements Probably will require assistance of at least an intermediate user, and someone versed in the potential of viral programs, to alter other program files.

Lars-Erik Osterud
Protect6
Boot sector overwriting disinfection and file-change operation restriction
100NKr ($15)

Comparison of Features and Specifications
Installation The program is small and is to be placed in the AUTO folder to run resident.

Ease of use The user is prompted to overwrite the boot sector if a bootable sector is detected, or to prevent modification if an attempt to alter a file is detected.

Help systems None provided.

Compatibility The program may alarm on programs that alter their own code. Some similar programs have difficulty with bootable MS-DOS disks, but this program is specifically said to be safe with MS-DOS disks.

Company stability Unknown.

Company support Voice, BBS, and Internet contact info is provided.

Documentation Brief, but covers the two functions of the program.

Hardware requirements Atari, unspecified.

Performance Unknown. Note that activity-monitoring/operation-restricting software that uses system calls is subject to bypass by low-level programming.

Local support None provided.

Support requirements Support may be needed for users unfamiliar with whether or not certain programs should be changing their own code.

George R. Woodside
VKILLER version 3.84 (April 1991)
Scanner, disinfector, and utilities
Donation

Comparison of Features and Specifications

Installation No installation information is given, but the program is very simple to install, with only a few related files, all contained in the distribution archive.

Ease of use The program is menu- and icon-driven. Most options are self-explanatory. ("Guard" could be clearer: it is the replacement of the boot sector with either a "message" boot sector to overwrite any boot sector viral programs, or a monitoring program.)

The program will allow you to examine disk sectors, although there does not seem to be any provision for editing.

Help systems None provided as such.

Compatibility Unknown, but VKILLER is currently the most widely recommended Atari antiviral.

Company stability Unknown.

Company support Phone, mail, GEnie, CompuServe, and Internet contacts are given.

Documentation The manual does not cover all of the features of the program in detail, but most can be figured out on screen. The documentation does provide an excellent overview of the Atari disk formats and structure as an exposition of how boot sector viral programs work.

Hardware requirements Medium- or high-resolution monitor.

Performance Unknown, but this is currently the most widely recommended Atari antiviral.

Local support None provided.

Support requirements Unknown. The program appears to be simple enough not to need any support, but advanced users will find additional functions they may find helpful.

Amiga

Peter Stuer
BootX version 5.23

Scanner and disinfector with some operation restriction

Comparison of Features and Specifications

Installation Both automated and manual installation is provided.

Ease of use BootX can be run from either the CLI or the Workbench. Once invoked, it can be made the foreground task by a "hot key" call. The program is menu-driven, with a comprehensive range of actions.

Help systems Can use the AmigaGuide.library function if available.

Compatibility Unknown but unlikely to cause problems. Some problems are noted with Enforcer. Will work with certain compression programs to check compressed executable files.

Company stability Unknown, but this is currently one of the major recommended Amiga antivirals. The program is distributed as freeware.

Company support The author's mail and email addresses are given, as well as contact info for "Safe Hex International."

Documentation Simple but straightforward directions on the installation and running of the program. There is little general discussion of viral programs and operation, but some is mentioned in conjunction with certain features of the program. Unusually for a shareware/freeware package, there is an extensive glossary, which may provide some background. (I learned, for instance, that a "linkvirus" is the term for what is more generally known as a program- or file-infecting virus.)

Hardware requirements 512K RAM or higher and at least one disk drive. KickStart 2.04 and ReqTools.library 38 or higher. Workbench 2.1 or higher to use the language-independence utility and 3.0 or higher to use the Amiga-Guide.library help feature. Various decompression programs may be needed to check compressed executable files.

Performance Unknown at this time due to lack of a test suite. Currently one of the most highly recommended Amiga antivirals.

Local support The author is reachable via Fidonet and Internet mail.

Support requirements Users experienced with shareware should have no problems.

APPENDIX D

ANTIVIRAL VENDORS AND CONTACTS LISTING

This file is a listing of antivirus contacts, primarily those involved in the production of a specific antiviral program, device, or book. There are many others who are contributing to the antiviral arena, but this list concentrates on vendors rather than individual researchers. Major research groups or consortia are also listed. Please send any updates or corrections to roberts@decus.ca.

Companies that operated only as marketing agents, or products that are strictly a repackaging of others, have been removed. Resellers who add modules have been retained.

The information included is as much as I could gather of:

Company:	**vendor company, author/developer, or institute**
Address:	for above
Phone:	for above
Fax:	for above
Sales:	separate phone or distributor information
Support:	if separate from above
Contact:	for this product
Email:	for head office or contact
Other:	BBS, Web site, etc.
Product:	program, hardware device, book, etc., commented if unavailable

Company:	**Abacus**
Address:	5370 52nd St., SE, Grand Rapids, MI 49512
Phone:	+1-800-451-4319, +1-616-698-0330
Fax:	+1-616-698-0325
Product:	*Computer Viruses: A High-Tech Disease*, Burger (out of print), Virus Secure for Windows (no longer available), *Computer Viruses and Data Protection*, Ralf Burger, 1-55755-123-5

Company:	**A. B. Data Sales, Inc.**
Address:	2210 Hanselman Ave, Saskatoon, Sask. S7L 6A4
Phone:	+1-306-665-6633, +1-306-652-7228
Fax:	+1-306-652-1955
Product:	HardDrive Lockup

Company:	**A.C.C Inc.**
Address:	West Orange, New Jersey, 07052, USA
Phone:	+1-201-325-7985, +1-201-736-7109
Fax:	+1-516-378-6124
Contact:	Wendy Schwartz
Product:	V-Phage hard-disk write protect
Company:	**ACM Press**
Address:	11 W. 42nd St., 3rd Floor, New York, NY 10036
Phone:	+1-212-869-7440
Product:	*Computers under Attack*, Peter J. Denning, ed., 0-201-53067-8
Company:	**Aladdin Knowledge Systems**
Address:	India
Sales:	Marketed by Doon Instrument Processors
Product:	"Hasp" security card
Company:	**Henrik Alt**
Address:	Kirgelweg 25, 7160 Gaildorf, Germany, Kto. 6428662, bei KSK Schwäbisch Hall, Blz 622 500 30
Phone:	07971/7996
Product:	Sagrotan (Atari)
Company:	**ALWIL Software**
Address:	Prubezna 76, 100 31 Praha 10, Czech Republic
Phone:	(+42 2) 782 20 50
Fax:	(+42 2) 782 25 53
Sales:	+42-2-782-25-47
Contact:	Pavel Paudis/Michal Kovacic
Email:	baudis@alwil.anet.cz
Other:	BBS: (+42 2) 782 25 50, http://www.anet.cz/alwil/alwil.htm
Product:	AVAST! antiviral
Company:	**Autrec, Inc.**
Address:	4305—40 Enterprise Drive, Suite A, Winston-Salem, NC 27106
Phone:	+1-(919) 759-9493
Fax:	+1-919-759-9489
Product:	PC-SAFE II half-card security board
Company:	**B.R.M. Technologies**
Address:	5 Kiryat Mada St (Luz building), Har Hotzvim, Jerusalem, Israel
Contact:	Gilad Japhet
Email:	gilad@brm.co.il
Product:	V-Analyst checksumming program, UTScan

Company: **Bangkok Security Associates**
Address: 888/32-33 Ploenchit Road, Bangkok 10330, Thailand
Phone: + 662-251-2574
Fax: + 662-253-6868
Sales: Computer Security Associates, + 1-803-796-1935; or Lannatec Associates Inc, 166 Anna Avenue, Ottawa, Ont. K1Z 7V2, + 1-613-724-5978
Other: BBS: 662-255-5981
Product: Victor Charlie 5.0—change detection

Company: **Bantam Books/Doubleday/Dell**
Address: 666 Fifth Ave., New York, NY 10103
Product: *V.I.R.U.S. Protection*, Pamela Kane, 0-553-34799-3

Company: **Bits-N-Bytes Computer Services**
Address: 333 15th St, Brooklyn, NY 11215, USA
Contact: Christopher Mateja
Email: mchlg@cunyvm.cuny.edu
Product: Virus database (product not yet available)

Company: **Black Box Canada Corporation**
Address: 1111 Flint Road, Unit 13, North York, Ontario M3J 3C7
Phone: + 1-800-268-9262, + 1-416-736-8011
Fax: + 1-800-268-4221
Product: PC Security Board

Company: **NCC Blackwell**
Address: 1001 Fries Mill Road, Blackwood, NJ 08012
Phone: + 1-800-257-7341, + 1-609-629-0700
Product: Viruses, Bugs and Star Wars, Geoff Simons (1989), 0-85012-777-7

Company: **Brightwork Development, Inc. (cf. McAfee)**
Address: 766 Shrewsbury Ave., Jerral Center West, Tinton Falls, NJ 07724
Phone: + 1-908-530-0440, + 1-800-552-9876 (US only), + 1-201-530-0440
Fax: + 1-908-530-0622
Product: Sitelock, Novell add-on operation-restricting software ($495)

Company: **Business One Irwin**
Address: Homewood, IL 60430 (Publisher One, Baltimore, Maryland?)
Product: *The Computer Virus Desk Reference* (1992)

Company: **Canadian System Security Centre/Communication Security Establishment**
Phone: + 1-613-991-7331

Fax:	+1-(613-991-7323
Contact:	Aaron Cohen
Email:	acohen@cse.dnd.ca
Other:	ftp site manitou.cse.dnd.ca
Company:	**Carmel Software Engineering**
Address:	EPG International, Hans-Stiessberger-Strasse 3, D-8013 Haar by Muenchen (head office Israel?)
Product:	Turbo Anti-Virus Set (basis for MSAV)
Company:	**CE Software**
Address:	1854 Fuller Road, PO Box 65580, West Des Moines, IA 50265
Contact:	Don Brown
Product:	Vaccine (Mac)
Company:	**Certus International (cf. Symantec/Norton)**
Company:	**Cheyenne Software**
Address:	55 Bryant Avenue, Roslyn, NY 11576
Phone:	+1-800-243-9462, +1-516-484-5110
Fax:	+1-516-484-3493
Product:	InocuLAN
Company:	**CMG Computer Products**
Address:	P.O. Box 160310, Austin, TX
Phone:	+1-512-329-8220
Product:	APO disk access restriction
Company:	**COAST Project and Laboratory**
Address:	Dept. of Computer Sciences, Purdue University, W. Lafayette IN 47907-1398
Phone:	+1-317-494-6010
Fax:	+1-317-494-0739
Contact:	Professor Gene Spafford
Email:	coast-request@cs.purdue.edu
Other:	http://www.cs.purdue.edu/coast/
Product:	Tripwire integrity monitor for Unix and security archive
Company:	**Command Software Systems**
Address:	1061 E. Indiantown Road, Suite 500, Jupiter, FL 33477
Phone:	+1-407-575-3200, +1-800-423-9147
Fax:	+1-407-575-3026
Contact:	Lance McKay, Sarah Gordon
Email:	lmckay@commandcom.com, sales@commandcom.com, support@commandcom.com, sgordon@commandcom.com, 463-2858@mcimail.com
Other:	BBS +1-407-575-1281
Product:	F-PROT Professional (cf. Frisk)

Company:	**Commcrypt, Inc.**
Address:	10000 Virginia Manor Road, Suite 300, Beltsville, MD 20705-2500
Phone:	+1-301-470-2503, +1-301-470-2500, +1-800-334-8338
Fax:	+1-301-470-2507
Other:	BBS: +1-301-470-2510
Product:	Detect Plus, ACCESSGuard, CRYPTOLock
Company:	**Computer Antivirus Research Organization (CARO)**
Phone:	+49 721 376422
Fax:	+49 721 32550
Company:	**Computer Emergency Response Team (CERT)**
Address:	Software Engineering Institute, Carnegie Mellon University, Pittsburgh, PA 15213-3890
Phone:	+1-412-268-7090 (CERT 24-hour hotline)
Company:	**Computer Integrity Corporation**
Address:	P.O. Box 17721, Boulder, CO 80308
Product:	Vaccinate
Company:	**Computer Security Engineers LTD (CSE)**
Address:	St. James House, New St. James Place, St. Helier, Jersey JE4 8WH, Channel Islands
Phone:	+44 534 500 400
Fax:	+44 534 500 450
Sales:	(see also Computer Virus Research Lab Wiesbaden)
Support:	P.O.Box 85502, 2508CE Den Haag, Netherlands, Tel.: +31 70 36 52 269, Fax: +31 70 36 52 286, BBS: +31 70 38 98 822
Contact:	Niels-Jorgen Bjergstrom, Commercial Director; Righard Zwienenberg, programmer
Email:	njb@csehost.knoware.nl
Product:	PC Vaccine Professional
Company:	**Computer Security Institute (CSI)/Miller Freeman**
Address:	600 Harrison Street, San Francisco, CA 94107
Phone:	+1-415-397-1881, +1-415-905-2470
Product:	*Computer Security Handbook, CSI Black Book, The PC Virus Control Handbook,* Jacobson (1990)
Company:	**Computer Virus Office**
Address:	The Ministry of International Trade and Industry, IPA(Information-Technology Promotion Agency, Japan), 3-1-38, Shibakoen, Minato-ku, Tokyo, 105 Japan
Phone:	03-3437-2301
Fax:	03-3437-5386
Company:	**Computer Virus Research Lab Wiesbaden (also Network Security Center)**

Address:	Howard Fuhs Elektronik, Rheingaustr. 152, 65203 Wiesbaden-Biebrich, Germany
Phone:	+49 611 67713
Fax:	+49 611 603789
Contact:	Howard Fuhs
Email:	100120.503@CompuServe.com
Other:	FIDO:2:244/2120.7
Product:	PC Vaccine Professional (see CSE), AVP (see KAMI), "Computerviren und ihre Vermeidung" 3-528-05319-4

Company:	**Contemporary Books**
Address:	3250 South Western Avenue, Chicago, IL 60608
Phone:	+1-312-782-9181
Sales:	Beaverbooks Ltd., 195 Allstate Parkway, Markham, Ontario L3R 4T8
Product:	*Virus!: The Secret World of Computer Invaders That Breed and Destroy*, Allen Lundell (1989)

Company:	**Cordant, Inc.**
Address:	11400 Commerce Park Drive, Reston, VA 22091-1506
Phone:	+1-703-758-7303
Contact:	Bryan Dorsey
Product:	Assure HW/SW antiviral

Company:	**COSMI, Inc.**
Address:	431 N. Figueroa Street, Wilmington, CA 90744
Phone:	+1-310-835-9687
Product:	Virus Terminator

Company:	**Cybec**
Address:	P.O. Box 205, Suite 3, 350 Hampton Street, Hampton, Victoria 3188, Australia
Phone:	+61 3 9521 0655, +44-6-0683-6780, +353-5-138-3650, +605-281-2757, +649-378-9790
Fax:	+61 3 9521 0727
Contact:	Nichols Engleman, Roger Riordan
Email:	support@cybec.com.au, sales@cybec.com.au
Product:	VET antiviral, *Viruses and Your PC*

Company:	**CyberSoft, Inc.**
Address:	1508 Butler Pike, Conshohocken, PA 19428
Phone:	+1-610-825-4748
Fax:	+1-610-825-6785
Contact:	Peter V. Radatti, President
Email:	radatti@cyber.com, info@cyber.com
Product:	VFIND UNIX and NT antiviral

Company:	**Cylink Corporation**
Address:	910 Hermosa Court, Sunnyvale, CA 94086

Phone:	+ 1-408-735-5800, + 1-800-533-3958
Fax:	+ 1-408-720-8294
Product:	SecurePC—half-card DES encryptor

Company:	**Data Fellows Ltd**
Address:	Paivantaite 8, FIN-02210 ESPOO, FINLAND
Phone:	+ 358-0-478 444
Fax:	+ 358-0-4784 4599
Email:	f-prot@datafellows.fi
Other:	BBS: + 358-0-4784 4500, http://www.datafellows.fi/
Product:	F-PROT Professional (cf. Frisk)

Company:	**Datamedia Corporation**
Address:	20 Trafalger Square, Nashua, NH 03063
Phone:	+ 1-603-886-1570
Fax:	+ 1-603-886-1782
Sales:	One Woodlands Court, Ash Ridge Road, Almondsbury, Bristol BS12 4LB, + 454 201515, FAX: + 454 616367
Product:	SECUREcard for PC

Company:	**Datawatch Corporation**
Address:	Triangle Software Division, P. O. Box 51489, Durham, NC 27717
Phone:	+ 1-919-490-1277, + 1-800-822-8224
Support:	(see also Software Concepts Design)
Contact:	Mary Golden-Hughes
Other:	BBS: + 1-919-419-1602
Product:	Virex-PC, also Virex for Mac—scanner

Company:	**George Davidsohn and Son Inc./The Davidsohn Group**
Address:	20 Exchange Place, 27th Floor, New York, NY 10005
Phone:	+ 1-212-422-4100, + 1-800-999-6031
Fax:	+ 1-212-422-1953
Sales:	PR—Howard J. Rubenstein Assoc. Inc.
Support:	+ 1-212-363-3201
Contact:	212-489-6900—Laurie N. Terry
Email:	warren@worlds.com
Product:	Vaccine 5.00 antiviral

Company:	**DialogueScience, Inc.**
Address:	Computing Center of the Russian Academy of Sciences, Room No 103a, House No 40, Vavilova Street, 117967, GSP-1, Moscow, Russia
Phone:	+ 7-095-137-0150, 135-6253
Fax:	+ 7-095-938-2970, 938-2855
Contact:	Sergei Antimonov, General Director
Email:	lyu@dials.msk.su, bob@dials.msk.su, loz@dials.msk.su
Other:	BBS: + 7-095-938-2856, Fidonet 2:5020/69

Product:	Aidstest virus scanner/disinfector primarily for Russian viruses, Doctor Web, ADinf
Company:	**Digital Dispatch, Inc.**
Address:	9725 Pleasant Avenue South, Suite 2L, Bloomington, MN 55420
Phone:	+1-612-884-9914, +1-800-221-8091
Fax:	+1-612-884-9916
Product:	Antigen, Data Physician, Novirus-Anti-viral software
Company:	**Digital Enterprises**
Address:	Gaithersburg, MD
Product:	V-Card
Company:	**Director Technologies, Inc.**
Address:	906 University Place, Evanston, IL 60201
Product:	Disk Defender—half-slot virus write-interrupt device
Company:	**Diversified Computer Products and Services**
Phone:	+1-617-592-9001
Fax:	+1-617-776-1515 (answered by switchboard, though)
Product:	PC Doctor antiviral
Company:	**EliaShim Microcomputers Ltd.**
Address:	5 Haganim St., Haifa 35022, Israel
Phone:	+972-4-516111, +972-3-5628620
Fax:	+972-4-528613
Support:	+972-3-5628618
Contact:	Jonathon Stotter
Email:	info@eliashim.co.il
Other:	BBS +972-4-516113
Product:	ViruSafe antiviral, MasterSafe general security program
Company:	**Elsevier**
Address:	Mayfield House, 256 Banbury Road, Oxford OX2 7DH, England
Sales:	655 Avenue of the Americas, New York, NY 10010, +1-212-989-5800, fax: +1-212-633-3990
Product:	*Computer Virus Handbook*, Harold Joseph Highland (1990), 0-946395-46-2
Company:	**EMD Enterprises**
Address:	7930 Belridge Road—Suite B , Baltimore, MD
Fax:	+1-717-235-1456
Contact:	Alan A. Gilmore, Director of Marketing
Email:	A.GILMORE1@genie.geis.com
Product:	Scanner and hardware device
Company:	**Enigma Logic, Inc.**
Address:	2151 Salvio Street, #301, Concord, CA 94565 USA (94520?)

Phone:	+1-415-827-5707, +1-800-333-4416 (US only)
Fax:	+1-415-827-2593
Contact:	Bob Bosen
Product:	Safeword—change-detection software

Company:	**ESaSS B.V.**
Address:	P.O. Box 1380, 6501 BJ Nijmegen, The Netherlands
Phone:	31-80-787 881
Fax:	31-80-789 186
Sales:	Calmer Software Services, 361 Somerville Rd, Hornsby Heights NSW 2077, Australia, +61 2 4821715; or P.O. Box 527, Dagsboro, DE 19939, +1-302-732-3105, fax +1-302-732-3105
Contact:	Franz Veldman
Email:	Veldman@esass.iaf.nl
Other:	Data: 31—85—212 395, (2:280/200 @fidonet)
Product:	ThunderByte Utilities, ThunderByte card

Company:	**European Institute of Computer Antivirus Research (EICAR)**
Address:	c/o Siemens Nixdorf AG, Otto-Hahn-Ring 6, D-8000 Muenchen 83, Germany
Phone:	+49 089 636 82 660
Fax:	+49 089 636 82 824
Contact:	Dr. Paul Langemeyer

Company:	**Fink Enterprises**
Address:	11 Glen Cameron Road, Unit 11, Thornhill, Ontario L3T 4N3
Phone:	+1-416-764-5648
Fax:	+1-416-764-5649
Product:	IRIS Antivirus (from Israel, cf. Techmar)

Company:	**Fischer International Systems Corporation**
Address:	P.O. Box 9107, 4073 Merchantile Avenue, Naples, FL 33942
Phone:	+1-813-643-1500, +1-800-237-4510
Product:	Watchdog

Company:	**Foley Hi-Tech Systems**
Address:	172 Amber Drive, San Francisco, CA 94131
Phone:	+1-415-826-6084
Fax:	+1-415-826-1706
Other:	BBS +1-415-826-1707
Product:	Safety Disk

Company:	**FoundationWare (cf. Symantec)**

Company:	**Frisk Software International**
Address:	Postholf 7180, IS-127 Reykjavik, Iceland

Phone:	+354-5-617273
Fax:	+354-5-617274
Sales:	See Command Software, Data Fellows, and SafetyNet; German version +49-40-6932033 or percomp@infohh.rmi.de
Contact:	Fridrik Skulason, Vesselin Bontchev
Email:	sales@complex.is, support@complex.is
Product:	F-PROT 2.xx Virus detection/protection/disinfection
Company:	**G4 Software**
Phone:	+1-800-486-9552
Fax:	+1-310-536-9796
Product:	Virotect
Company:	**Ross M. Greenberg**
Address:	P.O. Box 335, New Kingston, NY 12459 (Virus Acres, New Kingston, NY 12459)
Phone:	+1-914-586-1700
Fax:	+1-914-586-2025
Email:	greenber@ramnet.com
Product:	Flu shot+ antiviral/Virex-PC (see also Microcom)
Company:	**Higher Ground Diagnostics, Inc. (cf. Trend Micro Devices)**
Address:	901-F Robinwood Avenue, Columbus, Ohio 43213 or 4061 Riverlook Parkway, Marrietta, GA 30067
Phone:	+1-404-951-9466, +1-614-236-4602, +1-800-741-BRAD (-2723)
Fax:	+1-614-236-4804
Sales:	John Luke, Benefit Sales Inc., PO Box 11825, Daytona Beach, Florida 32114-1825, +1-904-677-9600, fax +1-904-677-0040, mmn@america.com
Product:	Immune II (cf. PC-Cillin)
Company:	**Patricia M. Hoffman**
Address:	3333 Bowers Ave Suite 130, Santa Clara, CA 95054, USA
Phone:	+1-408-988-3773
Fax:	+1-408-988-2438
Sales:	Vacci Virus, 84 Hammond Street, Waltham, MA 02154, +1-617-893-8282, Fax +1-617-969-0385
Email:	75300.3005@compuserve.com
Other:	BBS +1-408-244-0813
Product:	*Virus Summary* document
Company:	**IBM Corporation**
Address:	Long Meadow Road, Sterling Forest, NY 10979
Sales:	+1-800-742-2493
Contact:	Steve Rosenblatt, Brand +1-914-759-4582

Email:	chess@watson.Ibm.Com
Other:	http://www.brs.ibm.com/ibmav.html, gopher://index.almaden.ibm.com
Product:	IBM AntiVirus

Company:	**Information Systems to Increase Profits**
Address:	P.O. Box 4529, Middletown, NY 10940
Phone:	+ 1-800-274-3007
Fax:	+ 1-914-496-3504
Product:	Sys Guard, Sys Guard Security Card, and Virus Guardian VG-303 card

Company:	**Integrity Technologies, Inc.**
Address:	1395 Main Street, Metuchen, NJ 10004
Product:	VirALARM 2000 PC

Company:	**Intel Corp.**
Address:	3065 Bowers Ave., Santa Clara, CA 95051
Phone:	+ 1-503-629-7000
Fax:	+ 1-800-458-6231, + 1-503-629-7580, +44-793-431-166
Sales:	+ 1-800-538-3373, +44-793-431-155
Support:	Pay + 1-900-288-7700 ($30 per call), +44-793-421-777 (French), +44-793-421-333 (German)
Other:	BBS + 1-503-645-6275, +44-793-432-955
Product:	LANDesk Virus Protect (formerly LANProtect)

Company:	**International Microcomputer Software, Inc. (IMSI)**
Address:	1938 Fourth Street, San Rafael, CA 94901
Phone:	+ 1-415-454-7101, + 1-800-833-4674
Other:	BBS 415-454-2893
Product:	VirusCure Plus

Company:	**IRIS Software (I. S. Software and Computers Ltd.)**
Address:	6 Haodem Street, Petach Tikva, Israel
Phone:	+972-3-9221280
Fax:	+972-3-9228060
Contact:	Donny Gillor, Development Manager
Email:	DONNY@iris.co.il
Product:	AntiVirus-Plus

Company:	**Isolation Systems**
Address:	26 Six Point Road (Willowdale, Ontario?)
Phone:	+ 1-416-231-1248
Contact:	Patrick Bird, President
Email:	heuman@mtnlake.com, heuman@user.rose.com
Product:	PC, Mac security board

Company:	**Jitec**
Phone:	+ 1-514-462-3132

Contact:	Benoit Laliberte
Product:	Vectoria "virus proof" PCs

Company:	**Johnson Computer Systems, Inc.**
Address:	20 Dinwiddie Place, Newport News, VA 23602
Phone:	+1-804-872-9583
Fax:	+1-804-874-8090
Other:	BBS: 804-877-6261
Product:	PC-Vault software write protection (formerly PC-Lock)

Company:	**Chris Johnson**
Product:	Gatekeeper and Gatekeeper Aid (Mac)

Company:	**KAMI Ltd.**
Address:	109052 Nizhegorodskaya st. 29, Moscow, Russia (until Jan. 1996)
Address:	123364 Geroev Panfilovtcev str., 10, Moscow, Russia
Phone:	+7 (095) 262-1294, 923-0261
Fax:	+7 (095) 278-9418, +7 (501) 882-8628
Sales:	ALEX International Inc.&Co., Credit Suisse, ch-8070 Zurich, Paradeplatz, 8, Postfach 590G134; MC3162@mclink.it; Central Command Inc., P.O. Box 856 Brunswick, Ohio 44212, +1-216-273-2820, sales@command-hq.com; pierrev@ibm.net; roger@sydney.dialix.oz.au; vac@uucp.polbox.com.pl; mannig@world-net.sct.fr; prokon@gtc11.gtc.net; avp-support@metro-net.ch; 100120.503@compuserve.com
Contact:	Eugene Kaspersky
Email:	eugene@kamis.msk.su, avp-support@icomm.rnd.su
Other:	BBS: +7 (095) 278-9949, FidoNet:2:5020/156, http://www.icomm.rnd.su/, ftp://ftp.command-hq.com/pub/command/avp, ftp://ftp.icomm.rnd.su, http://www.command-hq.com/command
Product:	Antiviral Toolkit Pro (AVP)

Company:	**Kensington Microware Ltd.**
Address:	2855 Campus Drive, San Mateo, CA 94403
Phone:	+1-415-572-2700
Product:	Passproof (Mac)

Company:	**Key Concepts**
Address:	316 South Eddy St., South Bend, IN 46617
Phone:	+1-219-234-4207, +1-800-526-6753
Fax:	+1-219-234-6414
Product:	SureKey/2

Company:	**KWARE, Inc.**
Address:	2952 Timberwood Way, Herndon, VA 22071
Phone:	+1-703-560-2076
Sales:	Dist. by REB Management Consultants Inc., 8518 Spartan Road, Fairfax, VA 22031
Product:	SEER (MS-DOS)

Company:	**Laboratory of Computer Virology**
Address:	Bulgarian Academy of Science, Bulgaria, Sofia 1113
Phone:	+359-2-719212
Contact:	Eugene Nikolov
Email:	eugene@virbus.bg
Other:	BBS: +359-2-737484 (9600bps), FidoNet 2:359/110

Company:	**Lassen Software, Inc.**
Address:	5923 Clark Road, Suite F, P. O. Box 2319, Paradise, CA 95967-2319
Phone:	+1-800-338-2126, +1-916-877-0408, +1-916-877-0512
Fax:	+1-916-877-1164
Product:	Trusted Access

Company:	**LeeMah DataCom Security Corp.**
Address:	3948 Trust Way, Hayward, CA 94545
Phone:	+1-415-786-0790

Company:	**Leprechaun Software Pty Ltd.**
Address:	P.O. Box 134, Lutwyche Queensland 4003, Australia
Phone:	+61 7 2524037
Sales:	Leprechaun International, 2284 Pine Warbler Way, Marietta Georgia 30062 USA, +1-404 971 8900, +1-800-521-8849, fax +1-404 971 8988
Contact:	Roger Thompson (res.) +1-404-509-7314
Product:	Virus Buster antiviral

Company:	**Levin and Associates**
Address:	P.O. Box 14546, Philadelphia, PA 19115
Phone:	+1-215-333-8274
Product:	Checkup change detection (MS-DOS)

Company:	**Roger Lindberg**
Address:	Cyklonvagen 3, 451 60 Uddevalla, Sweden
Product:	FLIST and FCHECK (Atari)

Company:	**Magna**
Phone:	+1-800-755-MAGNA (not from Canada), +1-408-433-5467
Product:	Empower (Mac)

Company:	**Mainstay**
Address:	5311-B Derry Avenue, Agoura Hills, CA 91301
Product:	Antitoxin (Mac)
Company:	**Maze Computer Group**
Address:	P.O. Box 515, Lenon Hill Station, (New York, NY 10021?)
Product:	V*Screen
Company:	**McAfee Associates**
Address:	2710 Walsh Avenue, Suite 200, Santa Clara, California, 95051-0963
Phone:	+1-408-988-3832
Fax:	+1-408-970-9727
Email:	mcafee@aol.com, mcafee@netcom.com, support@mcafee.com, scott_gordon@cc.mcafee.com
Other:	BBS +1-408-988-4004, mcafee.com is IP 192.187.128.1
Product:	Viruscan suite of programs plus other utility software
Company:	**McGraw-Hill Ryerson/Osborne**
Address:	2600 Tenth St., Berkeley, CA 94710
Phone:	+1-415-548-2805, +1-800-227-0900
Sales:	300 Water Street, Whitby, Ontario L1N 9B6, +1-416-430-5000, fax: +1-416-430-5020
Product:	*The Computer Virus Handbook*, Richard Levin (1990), 0-07-881647-5
Company:	**Mergent (formerly Pyramid Development Corp.)**
Address:	70 Inwood Rd, Rocky Hill, CT 06067-3441
Phone:	+1-203-953-9832, +1-800-759-3000, +1-800-688-DACS (3227)
Fax:	+1-203-953-3435
Product:	PC/DACS (retail $249.00)
Company:	**Micronyx, Inc.**
Address:	1901 N. Central Expressway, Suite 400, Richardson, TX 75080
Phone:	+1-800-634-8786, +1-214-690-0595
Fax:	+1-fax: 214-690-1733
Sales:	7 Canon Harnett Court, Warren Farm Office Village, Stratford Road, Wolverton Mill, Milton Keynes, England MK12 5NF, 0908-221247, Fax: 0908-223416
Support:	+1-214-644-1344
Product:	SAFE (Secure Access For the Enterprise), TriSpan
Company:	**Microseeds Publishing, Inc.**
Address:	2 Dorset Ln, #A, Williston, VT 05495-9758
Contact:	authors Frederic Miserey and Jean-Michel Decombe from France
Product:	Rival antiviral (Mac)

Company:	**National Computer Security Assn (NCSA)**
Address:	10 South Courthouse Avenue, Carlisle, PA 17013
Phone:	+1-717-258-1816
Fax:	+1-717-243-8642
Sales:	P.O. Box 509 Westmount, Montreal, Quebec H3Z 2T6, +1-514-931-6187, fax +1-514-931-0878
Contact:	Bob Bales, Peter Tippett, Michel Kabay, Richard Ford
Email:	rford@ncsa.com, bbales@ncsa.com, ptippett@ncsa.com, mkabay@ncsa.com
Other:	http://www.ncsa.com
Product:	Conference

Company:	**National Institute of Standards and Technology (NIST)**
Address:	Computer Security Division, A-216 Technology, Gaithersburg, MD 20899
Phone:	+1-301-975-33282
Fax:	+1-301-948-0279
Contact:	Bob Bagwill webmaster@csrc.nist.gov, rbagwill@nist.gov
Email:	csrc@nist.gov
Other:	BBS (WWW dialin): +1-301-948-5717, http://csrc.nist.gov/virus/, ftp://csrc.nist.gov/virus/, gopher://csrc.nist.gov/virus/

Company:	**Nemesis**
Address:	Am Rain 8b, D-7512 Rheinstetten 2, Karlsruhe, Germany, Sparkasse, Ettlingen, BLZ 660 512 20, Kto. 135 66 33
Contact:	Sysop: Robert Hoerner
Other:	BBS +49-721-821355, Fido 2:2476/8
Product:	Nemesis activity monitor

Company:	**Network-1, Inc.**
Address:	P.O. Box 8370, L.I.C., NY 11101
Phone:	+1-800-NETWRK1, +1-718-932-7599
Fax:	+1-718-545-3754
Product:	Check-4-Virus for VMS ($495)

Company:	**NetZ Computing Ltd. (see also NSE Software)**
Address:	Israel
Sales:	Marketed in the US by Vine Computer Industry
Contact:	Zvi Netiv
Product:	InVircible antiviral

Company:	**Nighthawk Electronics Ltd.**
Address:	P.O. Box 44, Saffron Walden, Essex CB11 3ND, UK
Phone:	(0799) 40881
Fax:	(0799) 41713

Company:	**Norman Defense Data Systems Inc.** (formerly International Computer Security Association [ICSA] and National Computer Security Association [NCSA])
Address:	2775-B Hartland Road, Falls Church, VA 22043
Phone:	+1-703-573-8802
Fax:	+1-703-573-3919
Contact:	David Stang
Email:	norman@digex.com, 75300.2673@CompuServe.COM
Other:	BBS: 703-573-8990
Product:	ViruSchool and V-Base programs

Company:	**John Norstad**
Address:	Academic Computing and Network Services, Northwestern University, 2129 Sheridan Road, Evanston, IL 60208 USA
Email:	j-norstad@nwu.edu
Other:	Archived at ftp.acns.nwu.edu (129.105.113.52)
Product:	Disinfectant for Mac

Company:	**Northbank Corporation**
Address:	Richmond, VA
Product:	Guard Card

Company:	**NSE Software** (see also NetZ Computing)
Address:	7 Abba Hillel St., Ramat-Gan 52522, Israel
Phone:	+972-3-575 6324
Fax:	+972-3-575 7434
Contact:	Amir Netiv
Other:	BBS: +972-3-575 8585 (9:9721/120)
Product:	V-CARE, V-GUARD, ViGUARD Generic Anti-Virus.

Company:	**Orion Microsystems**
Address:	P.O. Box 128, Pierrefords, Quebec H9H 4K8
Phone:	+1-514-626-9234
Product:	Ntivirus

Company:	**Lars-Erik 0sterud**
Address:	0kriveien 39, N-1349 Rykkinn, Norway
Phone:	+47-2-131571
Other:	ABK-BBS +47-2-132659
Product:	Protect6 (Atari)

Company:	**Panda Systems**
Address:	801 Wilson Road, Wilmington, DE 19803
Phone:	+1-800-727-2632, +1-302-764-4722
Email:	PSKane@Dockmaster.ncsc.mil or 0003607248@mcimail.com
Product:	Dr. Panda Utilities, BEARTRAP, Panda Pro

Company: **PanSoft Software & Support**
Address: P.O. Box 12-292, Christchurch, NEW ZEALAND or 52A
                Dyers Pass Road, Christchurch, 2, NEW ZEALAND
Phone: (064) 3 3322-727
Contact: Peter Johnson
Product: IMMUNISE & SCANBOOT

Company: **PC Dynamics, Inc.**
Address: 31332 Via Colinas, Suite 102, Westlake Village, CA 91362
Phone: +1-818-889-1741, +1-800-888-1741
Product: Total Security

Company: **PC Guardian Security Products**
Address: 1133 E. Francisco Blvd., Suite D, San Rafael, CA 94901-
                5427
Phone: +1-800-288-8126, +1-415-459-0190
Fax: +1-415-459-1162
Contact: Noah Groth, President; Brett Fhuere 800-882-7766
Product: Data Security Plus, Encryption Plus

Company: **Penn State Virus Committee**
Address: Penn State University
Phone: +1-814-863-7896
Contact: Chair—Gerry Santoro

Company: **Personal Computer Card Corp.**
Address: 5151 S. Lakeland Dr., #16, Lakeland, FL 33813
Phone: +1-813-644-5026
Product: PCSS

Company: **A. Padgett Peterson**
Address: POB 1203, Windermere, FL, 34786
Phone: +1-407-352-6007
Fax: +1-407-352-6027
Email: padgett@tccslr.dnet.mmc.com
Product: DISKSECURE, SafeMBR, FixMBR

Company: **Pittsburgh Computer Virus Specialists**
Address: P.O. Box 19026, Pittsburgh, PA 15213
Phone: +1-412/481-3505
Fax: +1-412/481-8568
Other: BBS: 412/481-5302
Product: AntiVirus consultation services, Subscription FAX ser-
                vice

Company: **Jonathan Potter**
Address: P.O. Box 289, Goodwood, SA 5034, Australia

Phone:	(08) 2932788
Product:	ZeroVirus for Amiga

Company:	**Prentice-Hall, Inc./Brady**
Address:	One Lake St., Upper Saddle River, NJ 07458
Phone:	+1-201-236-7139, +1-800-428-5331
Fax:	+1-201-236-7131
Contact:	Beth Mullen-Hespe
Email:	beth_hespe@prenhall.com
Product:	*Computer Viruses and Anti-Virus Warfare*, Hruska (1990)

Company:	**RG Software Systems, Inc.**
Address:	6900 East Camelback Road, Suite 630, Scottsdale, AZ 85251
Phone:	+1-602-423-8000
Fax:	+1-602-423-8389
Contact:	Ray Glath
Email:	76304.1407@CompuServe.COM
Other:	BBS: +1-602-970-6901
Product:	Vi-Spy, Virus Bulletin subscriptions (PC Tracker)

Company:	**Rising Computer Science and Technology Company**
Address:	Level 3, North Block, Yi Bin Fan Dian, Hai Dian District, Beijing 100080, P. R. China
Phone:	256-7073
Fax:	256-4934
Contact:	Alex Lau
Email:	alau@sirius.com
Product:	Rising Anti-Virus Card (RAVC)

Company:	**S&S International Ltd.**
Address:	Alton House, Gatehouse Way, Aylesbury, Bucks HP19 3XU, England
Phone:	+44 1296 318700
Fax:	+44 1296 318777
Sales:	+44 1296 318800, Sales Fax: +44 1296 318888, S&S Software International, Inc., 17 New England Executive Park, Burlington, MA 01803, +1-617-273-7412, fax: +1-617-273-7474
Support:	support@sands.co.uk, support@sands.com
Other:	BBS: +44 1296 318810, http://www.sands.com, ftp://ftp.sands.com
Product:	Dr. Solomon's Anti-Virus Toolkit (AVT) 7.0, *Dr. Solomon's Virus Encyclopedia*, *Secure Computing* magazine

Company:	**SafetyNet, Inc.**
Address:	140 Mountain Ave, Springfield, NJ 07081

Phone:	+1-201-467-1024, 1-800-OS2-SAFE
Fax:	+1-201-467-1611
Email:	support@safe.net, safety@gti.net
Other:	BBS: +1-201-467-1581, http://www.safe.net/safety/, ftp://ftp.safe.net/pub/safetynet/
Product:	StopLight ELS, StopLight LAN, StopLight for OS/2, VirusNet PC, VirusNet LAN (contains F-PROT, cf. Frisk)
Company:	**St. Martin's Press**
Address:	175 Fifth Ave., New York, NY 10010
Product:	*Computer Viruses, Worms, Data Diddlers, Killer Programs and Other Threats to Your System: What They Are, How They Work and How to Defend Your PC, Mac or Mainframe,* John McAfee and Colin Hayes (1989), 0-312-02889-X
Company:	**SECTRA**
Address:	Teknikringen 2, S-583 30 Linkoping, SWEDEN
Phone:	+46 13 235214, +46 13 235200
Fax:	+46 13 212185
Contact:	Tommy Pedersen
Email:	tcp@sectra.se
Product:	TCell unix change checker
Company:	**Secure Systems**
Phone:	+1-813-392-4821, +1-404-475-8787
Fax:	+1-404-740-8050
Email:	sharonwebb@delphi.com
Other:	BBS: 404-475-0833
Product:	<LOCK>
Company:	**Securkey Systems, Inc.**
Address:	1674 Eglington Ave. West, Toronto, Ontario M6E 2H3
Phone:	+1-416-784-2883
Fax:	+1-416-784-0338
Product:	Telecommunications encryption interface, DES/MAC keys
Company:	**Alexander Shehovtsov**
Phone:	(044) 266-70-28 (9:00—18:00 Kiev, Ukraine) voice
Other:	Fidonet 2:463/30.5 or 2:463/34.4
Product:	RLOCK software write protection
Company:	**Jeffrey S. Shulman**
Product:	VirusBlockade, VirusDetective (Mac)

Company: **Silver Oak Systems**
Product: IronClad

Company: **Softhansa GmbH**
Product: AntiVirus 1.0E (Mac)

Company: **Software Systems**
Address: 2300 Computer Avenue, Suite 15, Willow Grove, PA
                19090
Product: Disk Watcher

Company: **Solinfo Ltda.**
Address: Calle 71 No. 10-48 Ofc. 501, Bogota, Colombia
Phone: +571-211-4469, +571-212-2174
Fax: +571-211-5750
Contact: Luis Bernardo Chicaiza Sandoval
Email: solinfo@uniandes.edu.co
Product: Compucilina antiviral (review copies not available)

Company: **Sophco**
Address: P.O. Box 7430, Boulder, CO 80306
Product: Vaccinate-Anti-Viral Software

Company: **Sophos Plc/Virus Bulletin Ltd.**
Address: 21 The Quadrant, Abingdon Science Park, Abingdon, Ox-
                fordshire OX14 3YS, UK
Phone: +44-235-559933, +44-235-555139
Fax: +44-235-559935
Email: enquires@sophos.com, virusbtn@vax.ox.ac.uk
Other: http://www.sophos.com
Product: Vaccine, Sweep and D-Fence antivirals, Virus Bulletin
                periodical, *Survivor's Guide to Computer Viruses* (1993),
                0-9522114-0-8, UK£19.95

Company: **Springer-Verlag**
Address: 175 Fifth Ave., New York, NY 10010
Phone: +1-212-460-1500, +1-800-777-4643
Fax: +1-212-473-6272
Sales: Heidelberger Platz 3, D-14197 Berlin, +49-30-82071
Email: orders@springer-ny.com
Product: *A Pathology of Computer Viruses* by David Ferbrache of
                the UK Defense Research Agency (1992), 0-387-19610-2/
                3-540-19610-2, $49.00; *PC Viruses: Detection, Analysis
                and Cure*, Alan Solomon (1991); *Robert Slade's Guide to
                Computer Viruses*, Second Edition (1996), 0-387-94663-2

Company: **Star Technologies (UK) Ltd**
Address: Passfield Enterprise Centre, Liphook, Hants, GU30 7SB

Phone:	+44-428 751091
Fax:	+44-428 751117
Contact:	Greg Watson
Email:	gw@startech.demon.co.uk
Product:	UNIX virus checker (Intel/BIOS BSIs only?)
Company:	**Stiller Research**
Address:	2625 Ridgeway St., Tallahassee, FL 32310-5169
Phone:	+1-904-575-0920
Fax:	+1-904-575-7884
Email:	74777.3004@compuserve.com
Other:	http://delta.com/stiller/stiller.htm
Product:	Integrity Master change-detection software
Company:	**Stroem System Soft**
Address:	Husebyveien 58c, 7078 Saupstad, Trondheim, Norway
Contact:	Henrik Stroem
Email:	hstroem@ed.unit.no, hstroem@pvv.unit.no
Product:	HS 3.58
Company:	**Peter Stuer**
Address:	Kauwlei 21, B-2550 Kontich, Belgium
Email:	Peter.Stuer@p7.f603.n292.z2.FidoNet.Org
Product:	BootX (Amiga)
Company:	**Swarthmore Software Systems**
Address:	526 Walnut Lane, Swarthmore, PA 19081
Product:	Bombsquad, Check-4-Bomb Anti-Trojan software
Company:	**Symantec**
Address:	10201 Torre Avenue, Cupertino, CA 95014
Phone:	+1-408-253-9600, +1-800-441-7234, +1-416-923-1033
Fax:	+1-503-334-7400
Support:	Cust. Serv. +1-408-252-3570, Technical Support: +1-503-465-8450
Other:	BBS: +1-503-484-6669, Retrieval Fax: +1-503-984-2490
Product:	Norton AntiVirus and Utilities, SAM (Symantec Anti-Virus for Macintosh)
Company:	**Tacoma Software Systems**
Address:	7526 John Dower Road W., Tacoma, WA 98467
Product:	VIRSTOP 1.05
Company:	**T.C.P. Techmar Computer Products**
Address:	98-11 Queens Boulevard (Suite 2-C), Rego Park, NY 11374
Phone:	+1-800-922-0015 (US only), +1-718-275-6800

Fax:	+ 1-718-520-0170
Product:	IRIS Antivirus (cf. Fink), Antivirus-Plus, VirAway scanner, COMLOCK

Company:	**Steve Tibbett**
Phone:	+ 1-613-731-5316
Email:	s.tibbett on BIX
Other:	BBS + 1-613-731-3419
Product:	VirusX for Amiga

Company:	**Thompson Network Software**
Address:	P.O. Box 669306, Marietta Georgia 30062 USA
Phone:	+ 1-404 971 8900, + 1-800-521-8849
Fax:	+ 1-404 971 8988
Contact:	Roger Thompson (res.) 404-509-7314
Email:	support@thomnet.com, roger@thomnet.com
Product:	Network Security Organizer

Company:	**Thuna Technologies (Upgrades, Etc.?)**
Address:	2432-A Palma Drive, Ventura, CA 93003-5732
Phone:	+ 1-800-955-3527
Fax:	+ 1-805-650-6515
Sales:	+ 1-805-650-2030
Support:	+ 1-805-650-2044, + 1-805-650-2042
Product:	MR. BIOS

Company:	**Tomauri, Inc.**
Address:	30 West Beaver Creek Road, Unit 13, Richmond Hill, Ontario L4B 3K1
Phone:	+ 1-416-886-8122
Fax:	+ 1-905-886-6452
Product:	PC Guard—password protection board, also for Mac

Company:	**Transfinite Systems Company, Inc.**
Address:	P.O. Box N, MIT Post Office, Cambridge, MA 02139
Phone:	+ 1-617-969-9570
Product:	Ft. Knox (Mac)

Company:	**Trend Micro Devices, Inc. (cf. Higher Ground Diagnostics)**
Address:	2421 W. 205th St., #D-100, Torrance, CA 90501
Phone:	+ 1-310-782-8190, + 1-800-228-5651
Fax:	+ 1-310-328-5892
Other:	BBS: 310-320-2523
Product:	PC-Cillin—change-detection hardware/software

Company:	**University of Cincinnati**
Address:	Dept. of Computer Engineering, Mail Loc. 30—898 Rhodes Hall, Cincinnati, OH 45221-0030
Product:	Cryptographic Checksum-Anti-Viral software
Company:	**usrEZ**
Address:	18881 Von Karman Ave., Suite 1270, Irvine, CA 92715
Phone:	+ 1-714-573-2548
Product:	ultraSECURE for Mac
Company:	**Van Nostrand Reinhold**
Address:	115 Fifth Ave., New York, NY 10003
Product:	*The Computer Virus Crisis*, Fites/Johston/Kratz (1989), 0-442-28532-9; *Rogue Programs*, edited Lance Hoffman (1990), ISBN 0-442-00454-0
Company:	**Vancouver Institute for Research into User Security**
Address:	3118 Baird Road, North Vancouver, B. C. V7K 2G6
Contact:	Robert Slade (res.) + 1-604-984-4067
Email:	roberts@decus.ca, Rob.Slade@f733.n153.z1.fidonet.org
Product:	Seminars, vendor contact list, product reviews, *V.I.R.U.S. Weekly/Monthly*
Company:	**VDS Advanced Research Group**
Address:	P.O. Box 9393, Baltimore, MD 21228
Phone:	+ 1-717-846-2343
Fax:	+ 1-717-846-2533
Contact:	Tarkan Yetiser
Email:	tyetiser@yrkpa.kias.com
Other:	BBS + 1-717-846-3873
Product:	VDS change detector and scanner
Company:	**John Veldthuis**
Address:	21 Ngatai Street, Manaia, Taranaki, 4851, New Zealand
Phone:	+ 64-6-274-8409
Email:	johnv@tower.actrix.gen.nz
Other:	FIDO 3:775/40.0, archived at ab20.larc.nasa.gov
Product:	Virus_Checker for Amiga
Company:	**A. & Z. Vidovic**
Address:	Tour Panoramique, Duchere, 69009 Lyon, France
Product:	Chasseur II (Atari)
Company:	**Villa Crespo Software**
Address:	1725 McGovern Street, Highland Park, IL 60035
Phone:	+ 1-708-433-0500
Fax:	+ 1-708-433-1485
Product:	Failsafe Computer Guardian

Company:	**Secure Computing (formerly Virus News International) (cf. S&S Int'l)**
Address:	William Knox House, Britannic Way, Llandarcy, Swansea, SA10 6NL, England
Phone:	+44 (0) 792-324000
Fax:	+44 (0) 792-324001
Product:	Security periodical

Company:	**Virus Test Center, University of Hamburg**
Address:	Fachbereich Informatik—AGN, Vogt-Koelln-Strasse 30, rm. 107 C, 22527 Hamburg, Germany
Phone:	+49-40-4123-4158 (KB), -4175 (SFH), -4162 (ML)
Contact:	Margit Leuschner (VTC, secretary), Prof. Dr. Klaus Brunnstein, Simone Fischer-Huebner
Email:	brunnstein@rz.informatik.uni-hamburg.dbp.de
Product:	*Computer Virus Catalog* (MS-DOS, OS/2, UNIX, Mac, Amiga and Atari)

Company:	**Virus Test Laboratory**
Address:	Computer Science Department, University of Tampere, Finland
Fax:	+358 31 2156070
Contact:	Marko Helenius
Email:	cshema@uta.fi

Company:	**VIRUS-L/comp.virus**
Contact:	Nick FitzGerald
Email:	VIRUS-L@Lehigh.Edu, (n.fitzgerald@csc.canterbury.ac.nz for FAQ submissions)
Other:	news://comp.virus, ftp://cs.ucr.edu/pub/virus-l
Product:	*VIRUS-L* FAQ

Company:	**Vision Fund**
Address:	10 Spruce Lane, Ithaca, NY 14850
Contact:	Robert Woodhead
Product:	Interferon (Mac)

Company:	**George R. Woodside**
Address:	1590 Lombardy Road, Gardnerville, NV 89410-5633
Phone:	+1-702-782-4816
Fax:	+1-702-782-9527
Email:	76537.1342@compuserve.com
Product:	VKILLER for Atari ST

Company:	**Woodside Technologies**
Address:	474 Potrero Ave., Sunnyvale, CA 94086

Phone:	+ 1-408-733-9503
Product:	Fortress UNIX antiviral
Company:	**XTree Co. (cf. Symantec)**
Company:	**Zen Works**
Address:	P. O. Box 528, Houlton, ME 04730
Contact:	R. Wallace Hale
Email:	halew@nbnet.nb.ca
Other:	BBS + 1-506-325-9002
Product:	SIX, BRECT
Company:	**Zortech, Inc. (cf. Symantec)**

APPENDIX E

ANTIVIRAL BOOKSHELF

Virus

Computer Viruses and Data Protection, Ralph Burger (1991)

ISBN 1-55755-123-5
($19.95)
Abacus
5370 52nd Street SE
Grand Rapids, MI 49512
USA

A most telling quote is to be found on page 31 of this book. In answer to the question, "What do you think about the publication of information about computer viruses?" Burger quotes a "highly knowledgeable" although "secret" source as saying:

> *I feel that it's the people who know the least about it that talk the most. You tend to hear little from people who actually understand something about computer viruses. . . . You don't have to include instructions on how to use computer viruses.*

The quote is telling on three counts:

1. Burger tends to go on at great length (350 pages) without giving out much information.
2. There is little hard information in the book that would be of use to the average home or corporate user concerned about protection against viral programs.
3. Burger's fancy for publishing viral source code seems to have no purpose except to build notoriety.

You are left with the feeling that Burger has gathered a great volume of information and is publishing it without truly understanding it. A section is devoted to the work of Fred Cohen. A subsection refers to "Cohen's Contradictory Virus." It seems to be related to Cohen's proof, by contradiction, that the problem of identification of any given program as "viral" or "nonviral" is undecidable. In Burger's book, however, there is no proof, little logic, and only patches of pseudocode that really don't demonstrate anything.

Burger's writing style is very difficult. Even with section headings and marginal annotations, it is extremely difficult to follow the discussion. There is very little structure to the flow of arguments, and there are occasional bizarre changes of subject. At one point, Burger reproduces a letter that he sent to various corporations and then complains that the poor response he got indicates that the companies did not understand the gravity of the virus situation. While I can agree with Burger on his repeated assertion that too few people are "virus literate," I can certainly sympathize with the companies. They probably couldn't understand his letter.

It is hard to understand why certain information was included and why other material was not. The chapter on specific viral programs spends five pages listing eight viral programs: it also spends five pages giving the names of 30 "trojan" programs, which presumably could be renamed at will. The Lehigh virus, generally thought to be almost extinct in the wild, is described. Stoned and Michelangelo are notable by their absence. (While Brain is one of the viral programs described, the book nowhere deals with the functions of boot sector viral programs.) No Mac viral programs are described or listed, although there is one example each from the Atari and Amiga environments.

The chapter on protection strategies, while it does have some useful points, also places heavy emphasis on such bizarre suggestions as writing custom software for all applications, or running everything from EPROMs. (It also suggests the use of CD-ROM for software media, apparently unaware of the fact that CD-ROMs have already been shipped with infected software.) A section on an "EDP High Security Complex" may prevent people from contaminating a keyboard with spilled coffee, but it won't do much to prevent viral infections.

Errors are legion. Some mistakes are understandable and unimportant, such as referring to the Jerusalem virus as the Israeli PC and TSR virus (p. 68). Others might have more significance, such as the statement that the Israeli PC virus makes all infected files into TSRs (p. 68). In some places the book contradicts itself, warning against BBSes and shareware (p. 129) and yet saying that the danger of receiving viral programs from data transfer is no higher than through other means (p. 292). Still other statements are flatly impossible, such as the assertion that the DEFENDER trojan "[writes] to ROM BIOS" (p. 110). Chapter 5 is supposed to give examples of viral programs. (In fact, most of the chapter is occupied by reprints of the McAfee VIRLIST.TXT and an early version of Jan Terpstra's virus signature list.) Of the virus description material that Burger wrote, the only entries that do not contain errors are those that contain no information.

Burger's stated purpose in publishing the viral source (Preface, p. viii) is to show how easy it is to write a virus. In this aim, he must be said to fail miserably. Although the assembly listings in the book will hold no terrors for those with a significant background in low-level programming in the MS-DOS environment, those people wouldn't need any direction on how to build a virus. A "batch" virus, which would be easily within the range of the intermediate user, turns out to use DEBUG in order to build some small but vital components, with completely unexplained parameters. Those who are familiar with the architecture know that building a virus is trivial: those who aren't will not find here a convincing demonstration of ease.

Another excuse for including the code is to "illustrate the weak points in your computer system" (p. 315). Again, this rationale is unconvincing. Few readers, outside of those familiar with assembly programming, would be either able or willing to compile and test the code provided. (Indeed, Burger, only five paragraphs beyond the previous statement, warns readers *not* to "proceed with risky tests of virus programs.") Certainly, the code itself proves nothing in terms of the strengths and weaknesses of any computer system. More extensive case histories of either viral infestations or specific viral programs would have been far more convincing.

Burger's attitude to this business of virus source code is strangely inconsistent. Although there is source code listed in the book, Burger specifically states that he will not publish the source for his VIRDEM.COM program. Although he doesn't publish the source, a copy of the VIRDEM program is supposed to be on the companion disk for the book.

For those who are completely new to the field, this book is too untrustworthy to recommend as a primer. Neither will it be very useful to those looking for direction on protecting either home or corporate systems. For those having done some serious study of viral programs or data security, the book raises interesting points for discussion, although the specifics asserted may have to be tested and challenged. For those who are interested in writing their own viral programs—fortunately, this book is *not* going to be a big help.

A Short Course on Computer Viruses, Fred Cohen (1994)

ISBN 0-471-00768-4
($34.95)
Wiley & Sons
5353 Dundas Street West, 4th floor
Etobicoke, Ontario
CANADA M9B 6H8
tel: 416-236-4433
fax: 416-236-4448
jdemarra@wiley.com
aponnamm@jwiley.com

This book is fun. I mean, it starts out with the statement, "I would like to start with a formal definition," followed by about a paragraph's worth of symbolic logic, followed by, "So much for that!" I assume that the surface joke is accessible to all: for those who know of the troubles Dr. Cohen has had over the years with those who insist on an informal translation of his work, it is doubly funny. From that beginning right through to Appendix A (a joke), the light tone is maintained throughout, and it makes for a thoroughly enjoyable read.

Besides being fun, though, the book is solid material. Possibly one could raise quibbles over certain terms or minor details, but over almost nothing of substance. The only halfway controversial point in the book is Dr. Cohen's continued crusade on behalf of "benevolent" viral programs. While I agree that the concept is worth further study, Dr. Cohen has not yet applied the rigor of his earlier work to proofs that such programming can be guaranteed safe or that benevolent viral programs are the best way to accomplish his proposed examples.

The material in the book will be accessible to any intelligent reader, regardless of the level of computer knowledge. The most benefit, however, will be to those planning data-security or antiviral policies and procedures. They will find here a thoughtful, provoking, and insightful analysis.

Computers under Attack: Intruders, Worms and Viruses, Peter J. Denning, ed.

ISBN 0-201-53067-8
ACM Press
11 W. 42nd St., 3rd floor
New York, NY 10036
USA
tel: 212-869-7440

This book is a very readable, enjoyable, and valuable resource for anyone interested in the computer world. The papers are interesting and sometimes seminal works. Some are classics, such as Ken Thompson's "Reflections on Trusting Trust" and Shoch and Hupp's "The Worm Programs." Others are less well known but just as good, such as the excellent computer virus primer by Spafford, Heaphy, and Ferbrache.

The book is divided into six sections. The first two deal with networks and network intrusions, the next two with worms and viral programs, and the last two with cultural, ethical, and legal issues. While all of the topics have connections to data security, there are some significant absences. (There is, for example, no discussion of the protection of data against operational damage, as in accidental deletions and failure to lock records under multiple access.)

In addition to shortages of certain fields of study within data security, the treatment of individual topics shows imbalances as well. The division on worm programs contains seven essays. Six of these deal with the Internet/Morris/UNIX Worm. The seventh is the unquestionably important Shoch and Hupp work, but it is odd that there is so much material on the Internet/Morris/UNIX Worm and nothing on, say, the CHRISTMA EXEC.

What, then, is the book? It is not a data-security manual: the technical details are not sufficient to be of direct help to someone who is responsible for securing a system. At the same time, a number of the essays raise points that would undoubtedly lead the average system administrator to consider security loopholes that could otherwise go unnoticed.

Is it a textbook? While it would be a valuable resource for any data-security course, the missing topics make it unsuitable as the sole reference for a course. The breadth of scope and the quality of the compositions make it very appealing, as does the inclusion of the large social component.

While the book won't have the popular appeal of a *Cuckoo's Egg*, it is nevertheless a good read even for the nontechnical reader. The section on international networks is particularly appropriate as society is becoming more interested in both email and cyberspace. The overview it gives on related issues would benefit a great many writers who seem to have a lot of "profile," but little understanding.

My initial reason for reviewing the book was primarily as a resource for those seeking an understanding of computer viral programs. As such, there are definite shortcomings in the coverage, although what is there is of very high quality. The additional topics, far from detracting from the viral field or clouding the issue, contribute to a fuller understanding of the place of viral programs in the scheme of computers and technology as a whole. Therefore, while it would be difficult to recommend this work as a "how-to" for keeping a company (or home) safe from viral programs, it should be required reading for anyone seriously interested in studying the field.

Computers under Attack is a realistic overview of the current state of thinking in information technology and the problems facing society as a whole. Far from the "gee whiz" of the futurist, and equally distanced from the sometimes dangerous "CH3CK 1T 0UT, D00DZ!" of the cyberpunk, Denning's collection of essays is important not only for the concerned computer user, but also for anyone concerned with the future of our increasingly technically driven society.

A Pathology of Computer Viruses, David Ferbrache (1992)

ISBN 0-387-19610-2
($49.00)
Springer-Verlag
175 Fifth Avenue
New York, NY 10010
USA
tel: 212-460-1500
    800-777-4643

This book is a broadly based and technical compendium of research and information relevant to computer virus research on a number of platforms. For those seriously interested in the study of viral programs, this is an excellent introduction.

Chapter 2 is a linear chronology of viral and related research, events, and activities from the 1960s up through 1990. Chapter 3 is an introduction to major research and theory. Chapters 4 through 8 cover technical items and functions of viral programs on PCs, Macs, mainframes (particularly UNIX), and networks.

A series of appendices gives background information on the boot sequence, record and file structure, disk structure, and other related technical details for PCs, Macs, and UNIX. In addition, there are contact lists and references for further research and information.

This book is not for the home user, or even for the IT manager for a small business. The material will require some dedicated study. However, the cross-platform references and the serious security perspectives on policy and procedures will be of considerable value to the larger corporation as well as the virus researcher.

The Computer Virus Desk Reference, Chris Feudo (1992)

ISBN 1-55623-755-3
Business One Irwin
Homewood, IL 60430
USA

The work is structured as a small "book" with a lot of large appendices. The "book" part, unfortunately, is somewhat confused. There are items that, if they are not perhaps in outright error, definitely mislead the naive reader. For example, the definitions at the beginning of the book tell us that a trojan horse "can easily implant itself in any normal program." The absolute distinction between a trojan horse and a viral program may not always be clear. A program infected with a virus may be seen as a type of trojan horse since it carries an undesired payload. However, most researchers would agree that a trojan horse is the combination of carrier and payload, and that the distinction between a trojan and a virus is that the trojan does *not* have the ability to "implant itself" in another program. Reproduction is the domain of the viral program.

Feudo also makes reference (p. 34) to "replacement" viral programs. These he describes as programs that "recode" (and, presumably, recompile) other programs to include themselves. While this kind of activity is occasionally discussed by the research community, no such viral programs have ever been seen. The closest is "p1" in the fictional work, *The Adolescence of P-1*, by Thomas J. Ryan.

It is difficult to see why other parts of the book, while interesting, are included in a computer virus reference. For example, there are three pages dedicated to the technology and vendors of wireless LANs. While the network spread of viral programs is a concern, there is no distinction at all between wired or wireless LANs in this regard.

The book overall is somewhat unstructured. Chapter 2, entitled "Viral Attacks," turns very quickly into an extremely technical overview of the disk and program structure of MS-DOS computers. It then goes on to give a number of case studies of Mac-specific viral programs. Two of these are repeated in Chapter 4, "Viral Program Analysis," in which most of the MS-DOS case studies are given.

As previously mentioned, most of the "contributed" material is in appendices. This is not, however, the case with the Hoffman *Virus Summary List*, the bulk of which comprises Chapter 5. (Interestingly, although the VTC/CARO *Computer Virus Catalog* is mentioned in the acknowledgments, it is *not* reproduced in the book at all.)

The contributed reference material may be very helpful to those who have no access to computer network archives and sources. However, it should be noted that much of this is very dated. Although the book has a copyright date of 1992, and I received a copy early in 1993, the Hoffman *Virus Summary List* is dated August 1991. If I recall correctly, the last of the reviews I sent to Chris Feudo were slightly before that. The contact info listed for me is even older: so old that all of the email addresses listed were invalid by the summer of 1991.

Aside from the dating of the material, there is much here that is not available in other printed works, or to those who do not have net access. However, this is primarily a reference work and should be supplemented by more accurate conceptual material on viral operations and prevention. This is particularly true for beginning computer users, since much of the work is either highly technical, or requires additional background material as an aid to understanding.

The Computer Virus Crisis, 2nd ed., Fites, Johnston, and Kratz (1992)

ISBN 0442-00649-7
Van Nostrand Reinhold
c/o Nelson Canada
1120 Birchmont Road
Scarborough Ontario
CANADA M1K 5G4
tel: 416-752-9100
fax: 416-752-9646

Despite its professional appearance and impressive credentials, this work is an unfortunately sloppy and undisciplined approach to the problem. The looseness of the book starts with the definition of a virus: it really doesn't give one. There is a section of the introduction entitled "What is a computer virus?" but although they state that they prefer the Cohen or Adleman definitions (without quoting them), quote the Podell/Abrams definition, and meander around related terms such as worms and trojans, no definition is ever finalized.

The book tends to read in a schizoid fashion. It often contradicts itself, again starting with the definition of a virus, where a "buggy" program that submitted jobs to the queue too frequently is first used as an example of a virus, and then is said to contradict the definition of a virus. Page 10 gets points for stating that downloaded software is probably safe; page 60 loses them all again by stating that "bulletin boards present the greatest exposure to computer viruses"; and the very next sentence on page 60 states that bulletin boards are less risky than other means of obtaining software. Page 62 mentions the rumor that a virus was spread via email, dismisses CHRISTMA EXEC and the Internet Worm as nonviral, and then pooh-poohs the concept.

A mainframe, and corporate, bias is quite evident in the work. Mainframe professionals are said to know what viral programs are and to be "ethical." (The more corporate of the computer and data-processing associations are also given credit for the lack of mainframe viral programs.) However, this bias seems to preclude an accurate knowledge of personal and microcomputers. DOS (obviously referring to MS-DOS) is said to have "completely overwhelmed CP/M in the late 1970's" in spite of the fact that the PC wasn't marketed until 1981. Apple Corporation is credited with the invention of the GUI (and the Mac Toolbox is credited with the success of Mac viral programs, in spite of the fact that the Toolbox is primarily concerned with the user interface).

A number of myths are presented as fact. The recommended procedure for virus cleanup is a low-level format of the disk. "Physical damage" is listed as one of the symptoms of a virus. A very odd list of nonviral computer attacks contains the "salami scam" (siphoning off fractions of a penny) urban legend.

As with the Feudo book (see review in this section), almost half of the pages in this work are a reprint of the Hoffman *Virus Summary List* (in this case "dated" January 1991, but "copyright" 1990). Graphics are used to take up additional space: a number of the figures are used several times over.

Computer Virus Handbook, Harold Joseph Highland (1990)

ISBN 0-946395-46-2
Elsevier
Mayfield House
256 Banbury Road
Oxford OX2 7DH
ENGLAND
OR
655 Avenue of the Americas
New York, NY 10010
USA
tel: 212-989-5800
fax: 212-633-3990

When Dr. Highland first offered to send me a copy of this work, late in 1992, he indicated that it was outdated. In some respects this is true. Some of the precautions suggested in a few of the essays that Dr. Highland did not write tend to sound quaint. As one example, with the advantage of hindsight, Jon David's ten-page antiviral review checklist contains items of little use and has a number of important gaps. However, for the "general" rather than "specialist" audience, this work has much to recommend it. The coverage is both broad and practical, and the information, although not quite up-to-date, is complete and accurate as far as it goes.

The book starts with, as the title has it, "Basic Definitions and Other Fundamentals." Dr. Highland has collected definitions from a number of sources here, which makes a refreshing change from some of the dogmatic assertions in other works. The fact that the reader is left to make his or her own final decision as to a working definition might be frustrating to some, but is likely reasonable given that the argument over the definition of a virus is still raging. With the changes that are still taking place in terms of new "forms" of viral programs, it is unlikely that this debate will be settled any time soon.

Chapter 1 also contains important background information on the operation of the PC and the structure of MS-DOS format disks. The one shortcoming might be that so much of the book deals with MS-DOS machines that readers dealing with other systems may fail to note the generic concepts contained therein.

Chapter 2 is a concise but encompassing overview of the viral situation by William Hugh Murray. Using epidemiology as a model, he covers the broad outline of viral functions within a computing environment and examines some theoretical guidelines to direct the building of policy and procedures for prevention of viral infection. The article is broadly helpful without ever pushing the relation between computer viral and human epidemiology too far.

Chapter 3 deals with history and examples of specific viral programs. This section is an extremely valuable resource. While other works reviewed have contained similar sections, the quality of this segment in Highland's tome is impressive. Mention must be made of the reports by Bill Kenny of Digital Dispatch who provides detailed and accurate descriptions of the operations of a number of viral programs that are, unfortunately, all still too common. (Chapter 4 is similar, containing three reports of viral programs from other sources.)

Large sections of the handbook deal with the evaluation and review of antiviral software. (I must say that I had great sympathy with that part of the preface that dealt with some experiences encountered when trying to test various packages.) Chapter 5 gives an evaluation protocol and test methodology. The detail here may lead some to skip over it, but it is helpful to those who wish to determine how thoroughly the testing was conducted. Chapter 6, an article by Jon David as mentioned earlier, is a suggested procedure and checklist for testing antiviral software. This chapter is unfortunately weak, and although there is some valuable direction, one comes away with the impression that the important thing to test is whether the program runs on a VGA monitor and has a bound manual. Antiviral testing was then in its infancy, and Mr. David's article reflects the general tone of those times. Chapter 7 is concerned with specific product evaluations and, as most lists of its type do, shows its age. Of the 20 products listed, I recognize only 7 as still being in existence; of those that do, 4 have changed substantially in the intervening three years.

Chapter 8 is an essay by Harry de Maio entitled, "Viruses—A Management Issue," and it must be considered one of the forgotten gems of virus literature. It debunks a number of myths and raises a number of issues seldom discussed in corporate security and virus management. Chapter 9 is similar, being Dr. Highland's suggested procedures for reducing the risk of computer virus infection.

Chapter 10 is a collection of essays on theoretical aspects of computer virus research and defense. Fred Cohen is heavily represented here, of course, but not as singularly as in, for example, Hoffman's *Rogue Programs*.

Dated as the book may be in some respects, it is still a valuable overview for those wishing to study viral programs or the defense against them, particularly in a corporate environment. While some may find the book to be academic in tone, it never launches into "blue sky" speculations: all of the material here is realistic. The aging of the product reviews makes it difficult to consider it still a reference handbook or a "how-to" resource, but Dr. Highland's work is by no means to be discarded yet.

Rogue Programs: Viruses, Worms, and Trojan Horses, Lance J. Hoffman, ed. (1990)

ISBN 0-442-00454-0
Van Nostrand Reinhold
c/o Nelson Canada
1120 Birchmont Road
Scarborough, Ontario
CANADA M1K 5G4
tel: 416-752-9100
fax: 416-752-9646

Reading the list of contributors to this work was rather like being at "old home week" at *VIRUS-L*. The introduction states that the book arose from Hoffman's frustration over the lack of a suitable text for a virus seminar and that the seminar participants compiled the material from available sources. One of the seminar participants, Chris Feudo, has recently released a computer virus desk reference (see review this section).

The essays contained in the book are grouped into five sections. The distinctions between the sections are somewhat clearer than in Denning's *Computers under Attack*. The overall design of the book makes a lot of sense as a textbook (its primary purpose, after all), but may be less lucid to home or business users looking for specific direction on how to protect their systems.

The first section contains papers that attempt to look at the broad overview of viral-type programs. Although this book is primarily intended as a text in computer-security courses (presumably at the university level), one still feels the lack of an initial concise and clear statement of what viral programs are today. This desire may be unfair: the majority of the works contained in the book were prepared, at least in initial form, prior to 1990. By the time the book was published, however, a larger view of the virus situation should have been possible. Still, as introduction and background material within the context of a virus-related course, these papers are all of significant value.

The second part of the book relates to social and legal topics. The current state of (U.S.) law figures heavily in this section. The discussion of ethics is quite limited. Karen Forcht's article on the subject is very terse, seemingly being only a report of various surveys. (The most interesting point I found in it was the contention, by CEOs, that ethics should be taught in the classroom rather than on the job, which displays either a surprising confidence in the school system, or a definite unwillingness to face the issue themselves.)

Parts three and four separate the study of viral programs into the realms of personal (micro) computers and network situations. This distinction is important, and it is heartening to see it made here. The opening essay in the micro section, by Hoffman and Brad Stubbs, attempts to walk the line between giving information to the user who needs it without giving too much assistance to virus-writer-wannabes. In my own view, it falls somewhat short in this, being perhaps more technical than an introductory article warrants. However, it is a good compilation of the technical background to viral programs in the MS-DOS environment. (The micro section closes on a slightly worse note, with the *PC Magazine* reviews that are starting to become somewhat infamous in the virus research community.)

The section on the network virus contains the two major "dissections" of the Internet Worm. Surprisingly, however, none of the other major network incidents, such as the CHRISTMA EXEC and the WANK worm, are mentioned. Some of the other papers in this section might have more general application to the virus problem overall, such as studies into cryptographic authentication. Others, such as an exploration of viral programs in electronic warfare seem to be "blue sky" excursions with very little relation to reality.

The final section is entitled "Emerging Theory of Computer Viruses." It contains two articles by Fred Cohen and one by Leonard Adleman reporting Cohen's findings. With all due respect to Dr. Cohen, there might be room for works by other theoreticians here.

As a textbook, this tome contains a diverse range of material well suited to a seminar on viral programs. While some of the material is becoming dated and some of the points of view are oversimplified, I have not yet found another book as well suited for raising topics for discussion. The one major flaw is the lack of balance and of opposition to some of the wilder flights of fancy. It would be well to have someone point out that the human immune system cannot fully be used as an analogy of computer virus defense, or to point out the difficulties involved in transmitting a virus from a radio to a fighter aircraft to a military command center. In the classroom, of course, this job belongs to the instructor.

Those looking for a reference for protection against viral programs may find this book to be unsuitable. It does, however, have a place as background material for those large firms in the process of planning overall corporate data-security strategy. Again, it should be used to generate discussion on some issues that other "how-to" books do not yet address.

Computer Viruses and Anti-Virus Warfare, Jan Hruska (1992)

ISBN 0-13-036377-4
Prentice-Hall/Ellis Horwood/Simon and Schuster
Market Cross House
Cooper Street

Chichester, West Sussex PO19 1EB
ENGLAND
OR
113 Sylvan Avenue
Englewood Cliffs, NJ 07632
tel: 515-284-6751
fax: 515-284-2607

Given the relationship between Hruska, Sophos, and *Virus Bulletin*, the similarity of material, which also appears in *The Survivor's Guide to Computer Viruses*, is not terribly surprising. We have the identical *Virus Bulletin* virus reports (frequency of total reports), the same interest in the AIDS Information diskette scam, the same vendor list (also without product information), the same insistence on calling the virus everyone else knows as Stoned by the term "New Zealand," and the same MS-DOS–only emphasis.

There is no statement as to the intended audience for the book, but it seems to be directed at that very small segment of the population who are interested in computer virus research. Unfortunately, and very oddly, much of the material in this book is of as much use to the virus writer as to the antiviral researcher. There are no full virus samples in the book, but there are handy snippets such as a simple encryption scheme, a master boot record extractor, and a chunk of the dBASE virus, with full instructions for turning it into a disk killer.

Those lowly souls who wish merely to protect their own systems may not be lost by this book, but will very probably be bemused by it all. There is a short but helpful (to the virus writer) section on disassembly of a virus. Two paragraphs are devoted to explaining how to use the DEBUG program to write your own code to extract the master boot record for examination. There follows the offhand comment that the same thing can be done with common utility programs. The hygiene rules for reducing the risk of virus infection include the usual lame points regarding BBSes, shareware, and public domain programs. Recommended is a setup to quarantine a workgroup from outside disks (surprise, surprise: Sophos makes software to support this) and change-detection antiviral software (surprise, surprise: Sophos makes such a program).

The book is good at the basic technical explanations. How viral programs function and how antiviral programs function are clearly set forth in basic terms. Most of the illustrations and figures are helpful, although some are extremely puzzling. (The inclusion of the full text of a virus-source-code opening comment seems to have no justification, nor does the highlighting of portions thereof.) An examination of Novell operations and testing against viral programs is probably a useful inclusion. As long as Hruska sticks with technical details, he's fine.

Given the names mentioned in the acknowledgments, parts of the commentary are very odd in their departure from the general consensus in the research community. Hruska speaks of the recent rise of "network aware" viral programs. (I can recall, and he gives as an example, only one.) There is mention of a media sensation over the Brain virus in 1986; I don't recall any such thing.

Early viral programs from 1987 are contrasted with more recent, destructive, viral programs; both Lehigh and Jerusalem caused erasure of materials. The "ABC News" report of the mythical Desert Storm/Iraqi printer virus is mentioned as barely believable, even though the story had been utterly debunked months before the book was written.

Chapter 5, "Who Writes Viruses," is astonishing. Hackers are defined as being "analogous to drug addicts." Then there are freaks, who have "serious social adjustment problems." University students are linked to software piracy. Employees are mentioned, even though employee "attacks" usually utilize insider knowledge that viral programs don't need. Computer clubs are mentioned (I get the impression Hruska is *not* a joiner), as are terrorist organizations. All of these profiles are caricatures, if not outright fabrications. Ultimately, this entire section is not only useless, but promotes misunderstanding of the situation by fostering false images. Virus writers tend to be self-important and irresponsible—but they aren't freaks (and they generally grow out of it).

For those with antiviral policies and procedures already in place, this work has a position in ongoing study and development.

The PC Virus Control Handbook, Robert Jacobson (1990)

ISBN 0-87930-194-5
($24.95)
Miller Freeman Publications, Inc.
International Security Technology, Inc.
99 Park Ave., 11th floor
New York, NY 10016

As well as being dated, this is a very uneven book. Significant portions are concerned primarily with promoting certain products; others seem to have been added quickly in order to round out the text. Still, it does have some good points, even today.

Chapter 1 is purported to be an overview of virus technology. Starting with a definition that includes only file-infecting viral programs, it then launches into a very lengthy, and very technical, discussion of the boot process, boot sector, and partition boot record. There are indications that the material for this second edition wasn't edited very carefully when it was updated from the first. An example is the promise to define four types of viral programs—followed by outlines of *five* types. Chapter 2 is basically a listing of viral programs, but the identification checklists, based upon symptoms, may be helpful. Again, there are indications that International Security Technologies (IST) was primarily concerned with file infectors and added the boot sector material as an afterthought. (Having denigrated virus-naming conventions in favor of the IST numbering scheme earlier in the book, the boot sector virus IDs seem to be listed in a remarkably "alphabetical" order.)

Chapter 3 is probably the best part of the book. This is a step-by-step guide for investigating and disinfecting a suspected virus infection. It relies very heavily on the Virus-Pro and McAfee programs, but if you can understand the generic types of these specific programs, the guide is very detailed and useful. It is, however, amusing to note that the book makes much of "stealth" viral technology, but fails to use the "self-cleaning" feature of such programs.

Chapter 4 is a sample policy and procedures document. Unfortunately, without additional discussion and background, readers may not be able to make the necessary modifications to fit their own situations. Sadly, the closing bibliography is out of date (and heavily biased).

While the price may seem a bit high for the sake of one chapter, the detailed disinfection procedure in Chapter 3 may be worth it. Certainly, those with a major responsibility for corporate protection may wish to use this material in building their own guides.

PC Security and Virus Protection Handbook, Pam Kane (1994)

ISBN 1-55851-390-6
($34.95/$49.95 CDN)
MIS Press/M & T Books/Henry Holt
115 West 18th Street
New York, NY 10011
USA
tel: 212-886-9378
fax: 212-633-0748

Kane's book is an attractive and easily read overview of the virus situation in the MS-DOS world. The text is friendly and aimed at a nontechnical audience, while the content is accurate and helpful.

Chapter 1 defines not only what a computer virus is, but also much of the current related jargon. A brief history of some infections is given in Chapter 2, with myths exposed in Chapter 3 (including Sara Gordon's interview with the legendary Dark Avenger). Chapters 4 through 8 are discussions of general security assessment, hardware risks, software risks, privacy, and so forth. The overview of a computer's inner workings in Chapter 9 may not seem to be strictly related to security, but it is a nice introduction for those who want to delve deeper. Chapter 11 covers the various types of antiviral software, and Chapter 12 looks at some of the dangers of "expert" advice.

Given that Kane (with Andy Hopkins) runs Panda Systems, it is not surprising that almost no other antiviral software is specifically mentioned. The Panda Pro change-detection, activity-monitoring, and operation-restricting software is included with the book. Chapter 13 is documentation for these utilities. The only other program mentioned is Microsoft's Anti-Virus, whose shortcomings are exposed in Chapter 10, as well as in the excellent and detailed analysis by Yisrael Radai in Appendix B.

Almost half of the book is taken up with the VIRUS-L Frequently Asked Questions (FAQ) list and the MS-DOS section of the Computer Virus Catalog from the Virus Test Center of the University of Hamburg. This isn't quite the "A-to-Z catalog of all known viruses" promised by the cover, but it is certainly the most accurate in what it does cover.

For those working in the MS-DOS environment, this is an easy and helpful resource for protection.

The Computer Virus Handbook, Richard Levin (1990)

ISBN 0-07-881647-5
McGraw-Hill Ryerson/Osborne
300 Water Street
Whitby, Ontario
CANADA L1N 9B6
tel: 416-430-5000
fax: 416-430-5020
OR
2600 Tenth St.
Berkeley, CA 94710
USA
tel: 415-548-2805
     800-227-0900

Unlike Highland's work by the same name (and, interestingly, published in the same year), this *Computer Virus Handbook* isn't really worthy of the name. The material is quite confused and quite inconsistent in quality. Although there are some good points, they are lost in masses of verbiage that too often are mere hand waving and speculation.

The confusion starts even before the book does. Alfred Glossbrenner's foreword mentions two examples of viral situations—one of which is a trojan and the other, a logic bomb. This lack of precision with nomenclature continues throughout the book, until one wonders whether it is really about viral programs at all. A number of rather spurious definitions are given at times. A "chameleon," as defined, sounds no different from a trojan, but the example given is for the "salami" (fractional pennies)-scam urban legend. "Rabbit" programs are those that use up memory or disk space. There is a specific confusion of the boot sector with the master boot record. Some of the other terminology is recognizable, but quite different from that used generally: "multipurpose" for multipartite, "insertion" for overwriting, "redirectors" for system viral programs, and "viral shell" for stealth.

(Levin also must be counted as one of those who include virus source code. Fortunately the "batch" language virus that he includes is an extremely crude virus. Infectious, in a sense, but easily detected and more messy than destructive.)

Levin seems at once very optimistic and pessimistic. He states that local virus experts are widely available and easily found. (I suppose I would have to accept this as true—with the proviso that I, personally, would trust very few local "experts" to know what they are doing.) At the same time, he issues what seems to amount to a blanket condemnation of all antiviral software. (Excepting his own: the book "Contains Money-Saving Coupons for [his] Outstanding

Antivirus Utilities." If they are so outstanding I must admit to a failing in the CONTACTS.LST: until I reviewed this book, I had never heard of them.)

The book does contain some worthwhile material. He does somewhat debunk the "commercial software as protection" myth and mentions that retail and repair outlets can be sources of infection. Chapter 6, "Implementing an Effective Antivirus Policy," generally contains very reasonable and effective guidelines. In particular, he pays attention to the fact that too strict a policy will drive staff to find ways to circumvent it. Some weaknesses: He suggests the use of the read-only attribute as protection and recommends low-level formatting for disinfection.

Levin's writing actually comprises less than a third of the volume. Part Three of the book gives us the C source code for four small utility programs, plus printed documentation for Flu-Shot, SCAN, CLEANUP, and Levin's own CHECKUP. The appendices contain an article on software law, a compilation of all the virus-related newswire stories that appeared in *CompuServe Magazine* from 1987 to 1989, and a copy of the Hoffman *Virus Summary List* from February 1990.

There is unfortunately little here to interest or assist the reader. While the policy guidelines may be helpful, the remaining material is either too vague or error-prone to provide more than additional background to a more authoritative work. While I would not recommend against it, this book should not have much priority in the antivirus library.

The Little Black Book of Computer Viruses, Mark Ludwig

Let us make it clear from the very beginning that this is not a book that is going to help you to protect your computer against viral programs. This book is not really even (as stated in the introduction) *about* viral programs. This book is written to help the person who wants to write a computer virus under MS-DOS.

Excerpt from the cover letter received with the review copy of the book:

> *Please note that most of the official reviews of the book have been either negative or controversial. . . . It seems that for the most part, the computer press is all too ready to take their cues from the self-styled anti-virus experts, who hate the book because it gives away their secrets. This is a classic case of an insider's group trying to control people for their own benefit.*
>
> *I would really like to see a review that was more than just another whitewash—a real attempt to see what people who read the book think of it. Find out why the Writer's Foundation of America named this the best computer book of 1992!"*

Well, Mark, you get your wish. This review certainly isn't going to be any whitewash . . . at least, not of you.

It is very difficult to know where to begin this review. What do you say about a book that has a very important message . . . and says it so very, very badly?

As you can see from the excerpt above, Mark Ludwig might be considered just a tad paranoid. One suspects that he has reason. There are a considerable number of people to whom the very thought of the writing of viral programs is anathema. The one positive contribution of the book is the challenge to consider the possibilities of the benefits of viral programming.

It has not yet been conclusively demonstrated, though, that viral programs can be safely used in an uncontrolled environment. Viral programs *must* change the computing environment in some way. It is inherently impossible to determine in advance what will be safe and what won't. It might be stated that a certain program, whether viral or not, can be safely used in a "standard" computing environment, but anyone who has had anything to do with software development knows that that phrase is meaningless. (As only one example, it is "well known" that MS-DOS is a "single tasking" operating system. I am writing this on a very old MS-DOS machine. There are currently two different TSR programs running, I have "shelled" out of a third "disk manager" in order to use the word processor, and I occasionally "shell" out of the editor in order to look up reference material.)

The major problem with Ludwig's book, however, is not the difficulty of defending his premise that viral programs should be accessible. Both his defense and his book have major shortcomings.

In his introduction, Ludwig attempts to justify his promulgation of viral code. First he states that viral programs are not necessarily destructive. Then he says that viral programs can be used to fight against the elite upper classes. Needless to say, his arguments are not very persuasive.

Most importantly (and probably fortunately so), Ludwig's information just is not that accurate. This is not someone who has been in the mainstream of virus research. (This may account for the frustration of his diatribes against "anti-virus experts.") Even his vocabulary seems a bit odd, using the word "extent" to refer to what everyone else calls filename extensions, and a definition of "worm" that is almost diametrically opposite to that of the mainstream.

There *are* nuggets of information in the book. There are even some premises that, at first glance, seem to have some merit in explaining viral operation. Ultimately, though, the valuable data is available in many other sources and the explanations are only superficial.

To give credit where due, it must be said that the few commented assemblies listed in the book are far superior to those included in Ralph Burger's book. Not only is the code fully and completely commented, but many parts are used as examples in the general discussions. Unfortunately, Ludwig also gives hex dump listings of the programs. It is difficult to see the justification for this, as no skill or understanding is required in order to turn these listings into working viral code (although the typing involved might be tedious).

In the end, though, it appears that Ludwig's book, although controversial, has made little difference to the viral arena. The viral programs he lists cannot be said to be successful. In more than two years, none of them have become widespread in the wild. It may be that everyone who has purchased the book has been responsible for ensuring that the code never "escaped." Since the likelihood of this is very slight, one is forced to the conclusion that the viral code isn't very good.

Naissance d'un Virus, Mark Ludwig (translated by Jean Bernard Condat)

Basically, everything that applies to the *Black Book* applies to this as well. I have only two brief comments to make on the translation.

I note that the promotional material that came with the book states that the original was banned for export from the United States. Even allowing for marketing hyperbole, they must have known that it would give rise to some kind of difficulties. As, indeed, it did: a recent French court challenge has attempted to ban distribution of the book.

The second comment addresses the issue of the educational value of the book. As previously noted, the text sections leave a great deal to be desired in terms of pedagogy. The viral code, however, is intact and unchanged. All the comments are still in English.

Virus!: The Secret World of Computer Invaders That Breed and Destroy, Allen Lundell (1989)

ISBN 0-809-24437-3
($10.95)
Contemporary Books
3250 S. Western Avenue
Chicago, IL 60608
tel: 312-782-9181
OR
Beaverbooks Ltd.
195 Allstate Parkway
Markham, Ontario
CANADA L3R 4T8

My initial reaction to *Virus!* was that it was another "gee whiz!" virus book, long on enthusiasm and informality, and short on facts. However, trying to set that feeling aside, I did find a wealth of research had been done. Given the date of the book (most of it seems to have been written in the fall of 1988, with the final drafting done in early 1989), there is a lot of valuable information contained in it.

The reaction of the knowledgeable reader will probably depend on the level of expectation. Those expecting accurate facts and astute analysis will be disappointed by the many errors and the lack of balance. Those expecting little may be pleasantly surprised by the easy readability and smorgasbord of details and gossip.

Neophyte readers will find Lundell's writing easy to follow and will come away with quite a reasonable set of background information on computer viral programs. The journalistic and storybook style will make spending the two or three hours needed to read it all a very small challenge. This is in sharp contrast to numerous other works reviewed.

However, the book does have serious problems and cannot be recommended as the "final word" by any means. Alongside the valuable factual information, there is a great deal of error, myth, or misinterpretation. For example, while the coverage of the Internet Worm is generally clear and thorough, Lundell seems to have only the most tenuous grasp of the mechanics of the worm itself. (This, in spite of having obvious access to both the Eichin/Rochlis and Spafford papers.) His distinction between a virus and a worm, in the same chapter, is both lucid and accurate, and yet other parts of the book lump bugs, trojans, pranks, and even games together under the viral heading. (Appendix B, a "software bestiary," includes a "Virus Hall of Flame": the only two entries are variations on the mythical "monitor exploding" virus.)

A more serious, and insidious, flaw, though, is the credulous nature of the work. Many times we get only one side of a given story. The extensive digging Lundell has done is sometimes overshadowed by his almost blind acceptance of what he has been told. The careful reader, even without background knowledge, can pick out some of the flaws. Early in the book the discussion of the MacMag/Peace/Brandow virus points out that the standard injunction against shareware and BBSes is rendered almost meaningless in the face of contaminated shrink-wrapped commercial software. Yet that same "buy only commercial" advice is repeated as gospel later in the book.

Despite the numerous flaws, I find it somewhat odd that the book should have been so hard to find, given its readability, information, and precedence. While a good dose of skepticism and a more accurate fact base is needed as an adjunct, it has a place as one of the few books that a naive user could read and still get something out of.

Computer Viruses, Worms, Data Diddlers, Killer Programs, and Other Threats to Your System: What They Are, How They Work, and How to Defend Your PC, Mac or Mainframe, John McAfee and Colin Hayes (1989)

ISBN 0-312-02889-X
($16.95)
St. Martin's Press
175 Fifth Ave.
New York, NY 10010
USA

The first six chapters give the impression of being a loose and somewhat disorganized collection of newspaper articles decrying hackers. Some stories, such as that of the Internet/Morris/Unix Worm, are replayed over and over again in an unnecessary and redundant manner, repetitively rehashing the same topic without bringing any new information forward. (Those having trouble with the preceding sentence will have some idea of the style of the book.)

Chapters 7 to 13 begin to show a bit more structure. The definition of terms, some examples, recovery, prevention, antiviral reviews, and the future are covered. There are also appendices; the aforementioned chronology, some statistics, a glossary, and, interestingly, a piece on how to write antiviral software.

Given what is covered in the book, am I being too hard on it in terms of accuracy? Well, let's allow the book itself to speak at this point.

The errors in the book seem to fall into four main types. The least important is simple confusion. The members of the Chaos Computer Club of Europe are stated to be "arch virus spreaders" (p. 13). The Xerox worm gets confused with the Core Wars game (p. 25). The PDP-11 "cookie" prank program is referred to as "Cookie Monster" and is said to have been inspired by "Sesame Street."

At another level, there are the "little knowledge is a dangerous thing" inaccuracies. These might be the understandable result of a journalist trying to flesh out limited information. The Internet Worm is said to have used a "trapdoor," an interesting description of the sendmail "debug" feature (p. 12). ("Trapdoor" is obviously an all-encompassing term. The Joshua program in the movie *Wargames* is also so described on p. 78.) Conway's "Game of LIFE" is defined as a virus, obviously confusing the self-reproducing nature of "artificial life" and not understanding the boundaries of the programming involved, nor the conceptual nature of Conway's proposal (p. 25). Mac users will be interested to learn that "through much of 1988," they were spreading the MacMag virus, even though it was identified so early that few, if any, ever reached the "target date" of March 2, 1988, and that none of the MacMag viruses in the wild would have survived thereafter (p. 30).

Some of the information is simply wild speculation, such as the contention that terrorists could use microcomputers to spread viral software to mainframes (p. 12). Did you know that because of the Jerusalem virus, some computer users now think it wiser to switch the computer off and go fishing on Friday the 13 (p. 30)? Or that rival MS-DOS and Mac users use viral programs to attack each other's systems (p. 43)? That the days of public bulletin boards and shareware are numbered, and that by the early 1990s, only 7,000 BBSes will remain, with greatly reduced activity (p. 43)? Chapter 13 purports to deal with the possible future outcomes of viral programs, but should be recognizable to anyone as, at best, pulp fiction.

In a sense, I am being too hard on the book. It does contain nuggets of good information, and even some interesting speculation. However, the sheer weight of dross makes it extremely difficult to recommend it. If you are not familiar with the real situation with regard to viral programs, this book can give you a lot of unhelpful, and potentially even harmful, information. If you are familiar with the reality, why bother with it?

Inside the Norton AntiVirus, Norton/Nielsen (1992)

ISBN 0-13-473463-7
($26.95/$33.95 Canada)
Prentice-Hall/Brady
113 Sylvan Avenue
Englewood Cliffs, NJ 07632
USA
tel: 515-284-6751
fax: 515-284-2607

Peter Norton has written a virus book! To most, this would be unsurprising. Longtime virus researchers, however, take gleeful delight in this tacit admission that his diatribes against the "urban legend" of computer viral programs were mistaken. Unfortunately, there isn't much more joy in this book.

This, like the "Michelangelo Special Edition" of the Norton AntiVirus, is an obvious attempt to make hay from the Michelangelo scare of 1992. Guess what virus gets mentioned twice in the first 13 pages alone! (Ironically, 16 pages later, the book takes the media to task for all the hype.) And, unfortunately, it shows the same concern for accuracy and protection that the MSENAV did. The introductory chapter brings in a fair amount of interesting material from a breadth of sources—but little depth of analysis. The reference to "Seventh Son" in one virus must, according to the book, refer to a novel by Orson Scott Card—ignoring the fact that the seventh son of the seventh son has been a reference in Western myth, legend, and superstition for more than a thousand years. The generally disregarded theory that the Jerusalem virus was politically motivated is presented as established fact.

As far as protection goes, the list of viral myths is surprisingly good. Chapter 3, "Strategies for Safe Computing," exhorts you to keep the system clean and off the floor. Useful advice, no doubt, but the most they have to say about viral programs is that it would be best if you didn't get infected. Thanks heaps, guys.

The bulk of the book is, of course, a reprise of the Norton 2.0 documentation. Not many surprises or tips here.

Virus Detection and Elimination, Rune Skardhamar (1996)

ISBN 0-12-647690-X
1300 Boylston Street
Chestnut Hill, MA 02167
Academic Press Professional
tel: 619-699-6362
fax: 619-699-6380
app@acad.com
800-321-5068
publisher@igc.org

Plagiarism is the sincerest form of flattery, so I should, perhaps, be gratified to find that almost the first thing I saw was references to material that I have provided. (I might be forgiven for being less pleased to find sentences copied almost verbatim.) There are a number of common mistakes that Skardhamar does *not* make, and that's good. However . . .

Although he credits some of my writings ("History of Viral Programs By Robert M. Slade Available on computer."), he hasn't read them carefully enough. He gets names, sequences, and technical details wrong. (CMOS RAM is *not* "just normal RAM," the boot sector is not a file, Michelangelo does not "format" the disk, and it's Lehigh University and virus, not "Leigh." Almost every page contains factual errors, some more important than others. He contradicts himself in many places, often within the same paragraph. (Perhaps the author would like to blame this last on his command of English: there are numerous grammatical errors, and a trick is a "ruse," not a "rouge."

My main objection, though, is that Skardhamar, under the "information wants to be free" banner, is distributing virus code. He states that people with the right kind of information make it a policy not to share their knowledge. (This might come as a surprise to Cohen, Denning, Ferbrache, Feudo, Highland, Hoffman, Kane, Solomon, and the whole *VIRUS-L* FAQ team.) Of course he considers the "right kind of information" to be virus code, in spite of the fact (which he even tacitly acknowledges) that for most users such code would do more harm than good. His language, postures, and technical accuracy, are all strongly reminiscent of the vx (virus-exchange) groups and publications.

(To be fair to both the author and Academic Press Professional, I suspect that the code provided would not assemble as it is. On the one hand, I'm glad he isn't spreading working code. On the other, it's too bad he's even trying to fool his vx buddies.)

A disk is included with some snippets of uncommented assembly code, which is supposed to help you disinfect a virus. Few average users would have the resources to produce working code from it. Even fewer would have the time to work through it and make sure that the programs weren't malicious.

In sum this work is badly written, technically inconsistent, and, if it can be relied upon at all, more likely to contribute to virus production and spread than detection and elimination.

Dr. Solomon's Virus Encyclopedia, Alan Solomon (1995)

ISBN 1-897661-00-2
£19.99
S&S International Ltd.
Alton House, Gatehouse Way, Aylesbury, Bucks HP19 3XU, England
+44-1296-318700 +44-1296-318777 +1-617-273-7412
support@sands.co.uk, support@sands.com
Resources for details and reliable information on operations of the thousands of MS-DOS viral programs are rare. The virus listing chapter of *Dr. Solomon's Anti-Virus Toolkit* has often been recommended as a resource for such data. It

has now been published separately from the program documentation and is available from the company.

The general discussion of viral programs is accurate, but fairly terse. There is a quick overview of what a virus is (which contains a very useful list of common false alarms), as well as definitions of the most common terminology. There is a very short history from 1986 to 1994. Technical details are abundant, particularly in the extended discussion of stealth techniques.

The bulk of the book lies in the listings of almost nine hundred viral programs and variants. A very useful and helpful reference, with both a high degree of accuracy and wide coverage of the known viral strains.

For those dealing with MS-DOS viral programs, this should likely be a standard bookshelf fixture.

Be cautious in obtaining the book from sources other than directly from S&S: the ISBN is the same as for the 1992 edition.

PC Viruses: Detection, Analysis, and Cure, Alan Solomon (1991)

($49.00)
Springer-Verlag
175 Fifth Avenue
New York, NY 10010
USA
tel: 212-460-1500
     800-777-4643
OR
Heidelberger Platz 3
D-14197 Berlin
GERMANY
tel: +49-30-82071

Dr. Solomon's Anti-Virus Toolkit, despite the "medicine show" sounding name, is a product that is aimed at the technically literate user and makes little concession to the novice. So, too, in *PC Viruses* the material moves briskly, and the nontechnical or even intermediate reader will likely need to read and reread sections in order to make the necessary connections. Also, while knowledgeable researchers will be pleased with the overall quality of the factual material, certain opinions are stated with a force that makes them seem like gospel truth.

By and large, those opinions have the weight of justification behind them. The book has a very realistic view of the virus situation. It is neither alarmist nor dismissive of the problem. Suggested actions take into account not only the technicalities of the issue, but also human nature and corporate climate.

Chapter 1 is an introduction—to an overview of the field, and also to the author. His statement that he is most familiar with his own software will raise an alert, in the discriminating reader, to watch for bias, although it is not a very formal warning. Still, it is very nice to see at least an acknowledgment of a vested interest, as opposed to so many authors who try to maintain a facade

of impartiality while lauding their own product and savaging their competi-
tors'.

As mentioned, however, the text maintains a very fast "pace," and a reader
who is new to the field may have some difficulty extracting the concepts from
the text. (Very interesting text it is, too.) Moreover, the content is not very well
structured. Chapter 1 is an introduction and presents an overview of the virus
situation, but viral programs are not defined until Chapter 2.

The second chapter does describe what a virus is, and isn't, quite well. It
suffers, though, from the same abandon as the first. After having talked of bugs,
trojans, and worms, there is only one paragraph devoted to a definition of a
virus before the book is off into the esoterica of stealth, memory residence,
interrupts, and self-encryption. Chapter 2 goes on to discuss the detection and
identification of viral programs. While we have been warned that the author
will be referring to his own software, the references to it are quite casual, as if
these tools were a part of DOS. The chapter concludes with an excellent section
on various malfunctions that are not viral in nature, but that generate "false
alarms."

Chapter 3 is a brief summary of viral operation in regard to infection. The
digressions of Chapters 1 and 2 about payloads and detection avoidance are
completely absent here. This makes Chapter 3 much better organized. The material is accurate, but readers should be warned of a somewhat iconoclastic
terminology.

Chapter 4 is the virus-description list that makes Dr. Solomon's Anti-Virus
Toolkit a good buy, even if you don't use the program. Even this 1991 list is
excellent. Some of the more recently important viral programs are not mentioned, but the most common programs are still the older ones, and most of
what you need to know is here. (If you want an update, then buy the program—
if only for the documentation.) A couple of problems: the list is not in alphabetical, or any other, discernable, order. Also, the listings, while highly accurate, are not entirely free of error, or potential misinterpretations. Solomon
repeats the oft-quoted line about Stoned displaying its message "every eighth
infective boot-up." Stoned shows the message based upon a calculation that
has one chance in eight of triggering. It is quite easy to boot more than eight
times in succession without the message being displayed. In addition, the message only displays when booting from a floppy disk. (This is, perhaps, what is
meant by "infective boot-up.")

Chapters 5 and 6 discuss procedures for dealing with viral infections and
some policies for reducing the level of risk of infection and increasing the
chance of detection. Chapter 5, on recovery, is quite good, although short;
Chapter 6, on protection, may be a bit too short.

The book is quite short altogether. There are only 288 pages in total; less
than 70 of these cover viral definitions, overview, history, cure, and prevention.
Most of the rest is made up of the virus listings.

There is a lot to recommend this work. It is much more accurate than most.
It is practical. The virus list is a very valuable resource, and even if this book
is not your primary reference on protection, it should have a place as a refer-

ence for specific infectors. Although the book is dated by time, the material is covered in a manner that avoids, as far as possible, those aspects that go out of date quickly.

Survivor's Guide to Computer Viruses (1993)

ISBN 0-9522114-0-8
(UK £19.95)
Sophos Limited/*Virus Bulletin* Ltd
21 The Quadrant
Abingdon Science Park
Abingdon, Oxfordshire OX14 3YS
UNITED KINGDOM
tel: UK +44-235-559933
          +44-235-555139
fax: +44-235-559935

Overall, the book is a reasonable introduction to the topic . . . of PC viruses. Aside from some review materials of OS/2 programs (which identify DOS virals) there is no attempt to look at other operating systems. Even in this limited context, the book is still somewhat restricted.

Chapter 1 is a history. More accurately, it is a vaguely chronological series of short anecdotes about various viral, and related, happenings. There is much of interest here, but also a most disturbing lack of accuracy. Names are misspelled, events are presented out of order, and some very important occurrences are glossed over while other, relatively trivial, happenings are presented at length. There are annoying technical errors. The book insists on calling Stoned "New Zealand," waits until 1990 to discuss it, and states that it was "the first virus to infect the DOS Boot Sector of the hard drive." A U.K.-centric, as opposed to U.S.-centric, view of the situation is interesting, but shows the same parochialism. (Those who say that this sounds strange coming from an American will be boiled alive in maple syrup.)

Chapter 2 is an overview of viral operations, risk factors, and protective measures. Thankfully, it is more technically accurate than the first chapter. However, it is still very iconoclastic. Most researchers would speak of two distinct types of viral programs, boot sector and file-infecting. (This distinction is technically somewhat arbitrary, but important in terms of the user's perception of a "blank" disk as being safe.) The book insists on five. The additional three result from the breakdown of file infectors into parasitic, companion, and system or FAT virals (which the *Survivor's Guide* calls "link"); the fifth is multipartite, which is simply a combination infector that will attack either boot sectors or files. There are also postulates of such things as an "unscannable" virus, which is interesting in view of the repeated references to Mark Washburn who tried, and failed, to produce such a thing. The risk factors and protective measures are the same we have seen before, with warnings against bulletin boards, and recommendations for diskless workstations.

Chapter 3, although short, is a solid and reasonably thorough introduction to antiviral procedures. Certain sections could use more details; for example, the use of a "quarantine" PC is recommended, but there is no discussion of the problems such a setup can cause—however all of the major points are at least opened for discussion. The heavy emphasis on the use of the FORMAT command for recovery is somewhat questionable, but other options are raised as well.

Dr. Keith Jackson's general advice on evaluating products and reviews, which starts Chapter 4, is very much to the point and raises issues too often ignored. Too bad the book does not follow its own advice more closely. There follow two "ratings" articles, one for DOS and one for OS/2, plus a quick overview of some NLM products.

The choice of viral programs in the chapter on "dissections" is rather odd. The simplistic and relatively rare Batman virus is included, but there is no entry for the ubiquitous Jerusalem, which is not only widespread, but also the "template" used for a number of variants and mutations. It is also interesting to see that original headlines have been kept. Joshi is subtitled "Spreading Like a Forest Fire," even though the original reports of its infectiousness are now known to have been mostly hype.

It is difficult to say whether the remaining materials are chapters or appendices. There is a decent article on virus toolkits by Tim Twaits, a set of rather limited statistics of numbers of reported viral programs from 1991 to mid-1993, a list of vendors (with no indication of product), a rather limited listing of "further information," and a glossary. There is also a "Who's Who." It is amusing to note the introductory quote of Oscar Wilde, "There is only one thing in the world worse than being talked about, and that is not being talked about," given those who are not being talked about. There is no David Chess, no Edwin Cleton, no Paul Ferguson, no Lance Hoffman, no John Norstrad, no Padgett Peterson, no Gene Spafford, no Wolfgang Stiller, no Franz Veldman, no Ken van Wyk (for crying out loud!) . . . and probably no future for me, if I carry on long enough to indicate that I might think I have a complete list.

Related

It's Alive!, Fred Cohen (1994)

ISBN 0-471-00860-5
($39.95)
John Wiley & Sons, Inc.
5353 Dundas Street W. 4th floor
Etobicoke, Ontario
M9B 6H8
CANADA

Other popular works have attempted to address the issue of artificial life and "living" computer programs. None, however, have had the technical depth and background that Cohen brings to this book. The originator of formal computer virus research, he has also been a strong proponent of the use of viral techniques for powerful solutions to common systems problems.

Much of the book deals with the difficulty of defining "life." It is remarkably troublesome to try to build a formula that includes all "living" things, but excludes entities such as crystals, fire, and mud. (A similar difficulty is experienced by those attempting to define computer viral programs, as opposed to utilities and copy programs.) However, like the Creationists who point to gaps in the fossil record and a lack of proof that "special creation" *didn't* happen, Cohen tends to use the definition problem as a negative proof of the vitality of computer programs; we can't prove they *aren't* alive. Chapters 2, 3, 8, and 9 are all, basically, variations on this theme. Interesting, thoughtful, and well-written, but remarkably similar nonetheless.

Chapter 1 introduces the book overall, and Chapter 4 introduces the formalities necessary for defining viral programs. Chapters 5, 6, and 7 deal with real contenders for "living" programs. Conway's "Game of LIFE" is a repetitive, rule-based pattern generator, best explored with computer automation and graphics. Core Wars (or Corewar, as Cohen refers to it) is a venerable programmers' sport of pitting programs against each other to see which can "survive" the longest. (A disk is included with the book, but the text indicates that neither a version of "LIFE" nor "Core Wars" is included. These programs can be found at various program archive sites on the nets.) Chapter 6 explores "living programs"; UNIX shell utilities, which Cohen avoids calling viruses—but which might not be defined as viral, in any case.

While the book is both easy to read and technically solid, the one flaw it has is a lack of breadth. It would have been interesting and, probably, edifying to have examined work in genetic programming, neural network research, or a number of other topics. This work is very good, as far as it goes, but it could have been significantly stronger.

A thought-provoking book. I hope there are subsequent expanded editions. I hope Cohen puts more work into his contention that viruses can be used safely. (And I also hope he includes an MS-DOS formatted disk next time. I can't see my father-in-law giving me permission to extract these files on his computer.)

Computer Crime: A Crimefighter's Handbook, David Icove/ Karl Seger/William VonStorch (1995)

ISBN 1-56592-086-4
$24.95
O'Reilly & Associates, Inc.
103 Morris Street, Suite A
Sebastopol, CA 95472

519-283-6332 800-528-9994 rick.brown@onlinesys.com 800-998-9938
707-829-0515 fax: 707-829-0104 nuts@ora.com

As a guide for law enforcement personnel and systems managers, this provides a good overview and introduction to computer crime and the actions to take against it. Touching on crime, prevention and prosecution, the book is practical and helpful to those needing to get a quick handle on the problem.

It is, however, easily evident that the authors are law enforcement, rather than technical, professionals. It might be possible to argue (rather weakly) for the definitions of viruses, worms, and other malware as described in the book, but the abdication of discussion on encryption is both telling and damaging. The bibliography, though, is of good quality and should make up for the technical shortcomings in this work.

I am delighted to see, for once, not only mention but actual listings of computer laws from outside of the United States. The coverage is still a bit lopsided, with 130 of U.S. federal and state statutes and less than 20 devoted to the rest of the world, but it's a start.

Computer Ethics, Deborah Johnson (1994)

ISBN 0-13-290339-3
Prentice-Hall
113 Sylvan Avenue
Englewood Cliffs, NJ 07632
+ 1-515-284-6751
fax: + 1-515-284-2607
Beth Mullen-Hespe beth_hespe@prenhall.com

Unlike the usual treatment of ethics as proof by exhaustion, Johnson does a complete and reasonable job. Without recourse to mounds of collected work (of dubious merit), the major points of professionalism, property rights, privacy, crime, and responsibility are addressed. Even in this brief space, ethics are studied more rigorously than in more weighty tomes. Not content with the usual reliance on relativism and utilitarianism, Johnson points out the flaws in each.

"Complete" is, I suppose, an overstatement. Although it is difficult to imagine a scenario that the book does not touch upon at some point, ultimately this book is a good primer and discussion starter. Although possibly the definitive work in the field to date, it does not, in the final analysis, get us much closer to a computer ethic.

Recommended. Should be required reading for all computer science students. Exposure wouldn't hurt any number of professionals and executives, either.

Computer-Related Risks, Peter Neumann (1994)

ISBN 0-201-55805-X
£24.75

Addison-Wesley Publishing Company
1 Jacob Way
Reading, MA 01867-9984
+ 1-800-822-6339
+ 1-617-944-3700
fax: + 1-617-944-7273
tiffanym@aw.com

Peter G. Neumann is well known to the members of the Association for Computing Machinery (ACM), but to thousands more he is known as moderator of the *RISKS-FORUM Digest* electronic mailing list (or its Usenet mirror, *comp.risks*). (*RISKS* is notable for the quality and interest of its material and is a recommended mailing list for all newcomers to the Internet, regardless of their areas of interest.) This work is not merely a compilation, but a distillation of the type of material discussed on *RISKS*. The occasional item is not strictly computer related (an ongoing *RISKS* discussion itself), but all demonstrate the variety of ways in which technology may constitute a hazard.

Written primarily in the format of a textbook for an academic environment, the material is not only readable but fascinating for a nontechnical audience. The end notes, challenge questions, and bibliography make it an excellent choice for any course dealing with security, safety, or general systems development issues.

As well as system and software engineering students, this book should have a place on the desk of anyone involved in a technology development project. It *can* happen here.

The New Hacker's Dictionary, Eric Raymond (1993)

ISBN 0-262-68079-3
($14.95)
MIT Press
55 Hayward Street
Cambridge, MA 02142-1399
USA

After Ambrose Bierce's *Devil's Dictionary* and Stan Kelly-Bootle's *Devil's DP Dictionary*, you expect this book to follow the same line. You expect any number of amusing listings, such as Macintrash and messy-DOS. You certainly get these—but a good deal more, besides.

That the book is a source of amusement and entertainment is undeniable. (Indeed, this review almost didn't get written, as I was seduced time and again by the interesting and arcane in its pages.) Raymond and company have, however, compiled substantial material of social, cultural, and historic value for those wishing to understand both the strict hacker culture, and the more diffused genre of technical enthusiasts that surrounds computing and computer networks.

The linguistic analysis of hacker culture is a scholarly work in itself. Whether linguists accept it as such in their own field, this work has done the groundwork and compilation for them. The analysis is incisive: I was quite startled to find the undoubted source for my own discomfort with including punctuation inside quotation marks.

This is not to say the work is without flaws. Originally, the work emphasized mainframe systems, and the current compiler makes much of the foolishness of those early users who saw little value in UNIX. In this work, personal computers are now the object of some fun and are not being taken seriously in terms of computing. No doubt the next edition will take the same stance with regard to Personal Digital Assistants.

(You didn't expect me to get through this without looking up "virus," did you? The book defines "back door," "logic bomb," "mockingbird," "phage," "trojan horse," "virus," and "worm." The virus definition is strictly Cohenesque, and the worm definition refers to "The Shockwave Rider," while ignoring Shoch and Hupp. Generally, though, the definitions contain better information and fewer mistakes than other nonspecialist publications.)

Whether for fun or scholarship, this is a valuable work. I particularly recommend it to the nontechnical manager who needs to understand these unpunctual, unkempt, and ill-mannered nerds—without whom the accounting department can't function.

NetLaw: Your Rights in the Online World, Lance Rose (1995)

ISBN 0-07-882077-4
(U$19.95)
McGraw-Hill
2600 Tenth St.
Berkeley, CA 94710
+1-510-548-2805
+1-800-227-0900
lkissing@osborne.mhs.compuserve.com,
    pmon@osborne.mhs.compuserve.com

Very similar to Rose's earlier *Syslaw*, this is a general guide to various legal aspects of life on-line. The major changes are the broadening of the scope from BBS-level systems to include on-line services and the Internet, and very handy (and interesting) sidebars, which give a thumbnail sketch of the topic under discussion. These usually include a reference to some specific case.

Chapters address the issues of censorship, contracts, commerce, and copyright. Chapter 4, which deals with the responsibility of the system operator in light of on-line dangers, does touch on the topic of malicious software. I was disappointed that this is limited to a not terribly accurate defining of terms, and almost no discussion of the admittedly confused legal situation. Further chapters cover privacy, crime, search and seizure, and a rather disappointing chapter on obscenity. Appendices include some very useful sample contracts, and various U.S. laws.

Given recent developments that have strongly indicated the international nature of the net and international legal ramifications, it is discouraging to see that Rose still presents only a limited and U.S.-centric view. However, the general principles he describes are held in common law, and this book should at least provide guidance for the broader on-line world.

Computer Security Basics, Deborah Russell and G. T. Gangemi Sr. (1991)

ISBN 0-937175-71-4
O'Reilly and Associates, Inc.
103 Morris St., Suite A
Sebastopol, CA 95472-9902
USA
tel: 800-338-6887
fax: 707-829-0104

Computer Security Basics is a pretty accurate name. The book is an overview of many aspects that go into the security of computers and data systems. While not exhaustive, it at least provides a starting point from which to pursue specific topics that require more detailed study. A thorough reading of the book will ensure that those charged with security will not miss certain aspects of the field in a single-minded pursuit of one particular threat.

Having said that, it is difficult to recommend the book as a sole source for information. While it contains a great deal of useful, helpful, and informative material, the quality and accuracy is inconsistent. You would do well to check items with other sources.

The book starts with an introduction of what security is and how to evaluate potential loopholes. The definition points out the useful difference between the problems of confidentiality and availability. (Also defined is the difference between a "hacker" and a "cracker.") The distinction between threats, vulnerabilities, and countermeasures is helpful, but may fail to resolve certain issues. (For example, the discussion does not finally aid in determining whether a manager, too "lazy" to provide good security practices, is just a vulnerability or an actual threat.)

Chapter 2 gives some historical background to the development of modern data security. Chapter 3 looks at access control, Chapter 4 at viral programs and other malware, Chapter 5 at systems and planning, and Chapter 6 at the "Orange Book." Chapters 7 and 8 cover communication, first with encryption and then more generally. Chapter 9 deals with physical and site security, as well as biometrics (for access control), while Chapter 10 deals with the specific physical security of TEMPEST.

There are "Hints" pages scattered throughout the book. These are generally very useful and practical. Not universally: the suggestion (p. 87) that you "vaccinate" programs before running them is seemingly a reference to functions such as (among others) SCAN's "add verification," which has led to problems in the past. Page 97 stresses the importance of never eating or drinking near the terminal: I, in common with most "habitual" users, *constantly* have food or drink near the terminal. In the past 15 years, only once has soda made it into my keyboard, and someone else did that.

I will deal with Chapter 4, "Viruses and Other Wildlife," in detail. The problems of this chapter serve as an illustration of other parts of the book that deal with specialty areas.

The problems actually start on page 7, where an item entitled "Virus Flambé" repeats the popular, but wholly unfounded, myth that some viral programs can cause physical damage. This report again repeats the "flaming monitor" urban legend. (The Jerusalem description, just prior, is not notable for its accuracy either.) Once into Chapter 4, we are told that the difference between a worm and a virus is that a worm is not destructive, whereas a virus always is. The book contradicts itself: we are told both that a worm hides in host programs and that it does not. I was intrigued to learn that Ken Thompson's demonstration of a compiler "trapdoor generator" is a virus, even though it does not pass along its ability to generate insecurities beyond the programs it compiles. A trojan, apparently a "mechanism for disguising a virus or worm," always performs the "advertised" function, as opposed to something referred to as a "trojan mule" (anyone else ever heard this term before?), which does not. "Crabs" are not, as I had thought, prank programs seen on Mac and Atari computers, but a generic term for programs that "attack" the screen display. In the appendix on "Security User Groups," the Computer Virus Industry Association (CVIA) is mentioned, while the Computer Antivirus Research Organization (CARO) and EICAR are not. The International Computer Security Association is not mentioned with the groups, but makes the book list. ("Electronic Groups" mentions Usenet and a rather aging list of newsgroups, but doesn't mention the Internet or any of the "LISTSERVs.")

Other aspects of the book are excellent. The coverage of DES, for example, does not shy away from dealing with the controversy surrounding the standard and is very careful in reporting the research that has been done. The chapter on TEMPEST is interesting. It becomes intriguing when TEMPEST is used as a springboard to discuss the hypothesized health risks of VDTs and states that TEMPEST may be used to shield the user (even though it goes on to say that TEMPEST sometimes involves false "emitters" within the system).

In sum, the book may be a good starting point for beginners who have to deal with computer security at a basic level. While there are shortcomings in the material in the book itself, there are also sufficient resources listed in the appendices to provide a guide for further study by the user.

Digital Woes, Lauren Wiener (1993)

ISBN 0-201-62609-8
($22.95/$29.95 Canada)
Addison-Wesley
P.O. Box 520
26 Prince Andrew Place
Don Mills, Ontario

CANADA M3C 2T8
tel: 416-447-5101
fax: 416-443-0948
OR
1 Jacob Way Reading
Reading, MA 01867-9984
tel: 617-944-3700
800-822-6339
fax: (617) 944-7273

Digital Woes is an accurate, well-researched, and thoroughly engaging treatment of the subject of software risks.

Chapter 1 is a list of specific examples of software failures, large and small. The stories are thoroughly documented and well told. The choice of examples is careful, and useful as well, covering a variety of problems. You could, of course, add to the list. In the virus field, programs are extremely limited in function and rarely exceed 3,000 bytes in length, yet almost every viral strain shows some programming pathology; most of the damage seems to occur by mistake. The user interfaces of antivirals are subject to hot debate, perhaps more importantly than in other systems because of the risks involved in misunderstanding. In regard to decision support, I recall the assumption, on the part of Excel, that everyone wants to use linear forecasting. Everyone involved in technical fields will be able to add other specific examples. For those uninvolved, Wiener's work is quite sufficient and convincing.

Chapter 2 is an explanation of why software contains bugs and why software errors are so deadly. Techies will feel somewhat uncomfortable with the lack of jargon, but they should persevere. Initially, I thought Wiener had missed the point of the difference between analog and digital systems—until I realized I was in the middle of a complete and clear explanation that never had to use the word "analog." (Technopeasants will, of course, appreciate the lack of jargon. Rest assured that the same ease of reading and clarity of language holds throughout the book.)

Chapter 3 examines the various means used to ensure the reliability of software—usually with a depressing lack of success. As with all who have worked in the field, I can relate to the comments regarding the difficulty of testing. At one point, I uncovered a bug in the third minor variant of the fourth major release of the fifth generation of a communications program. Apparently I was the first person on staff who had ever wanted to keep a running log between sessions—and the functions I used combined to completely lock up the computer.

Most *RISKS-FORUM Digest* readers will by now be nodding and muttering, "So what else is new?" However, Wiener here proves herself capable of some valuable and original contributions beyond the pronouncements of those working in the field. Noting that she is familiar with programmers who have never, in 20 years of work, had their code incorporated into a delivered product, she raises the issue of what this type of work environment does to the psyche of the worker. My grandfather carved the wooden decorations in our church, and,

50 years after his death, I can still point that out. However, in a career of analysis, training, and support, I can point to little beyond an amount of Internet bandwidth consumed. (Many would say "wasted.") To the ephemeral nature of the craft, though, you must add the legacy of constant failure. Martin Seligman's *Learned Helplessness* points out the danger quite clearly. A similar thought was voiced some years ago over the impact on developing youth of the then-new video games, and the fact that you could advance through levels, but never, ultimately, win. These children are grown now. You may know them as "Generation X."

Chapter 4 deals with the means to prevent failure. Actually most of the material discusses recovery and—assuming that the system will eventually fail—how to ensure that the failure causes the least damage.

Chapter 5 is entitled "Big Plans" and looks at various proposed new technologies and the risks inherent in them. In this discussion, Wiener warns against those who are overly thrilled with the promises of the new technology. I agree, but I would caution that public debate is also dominated by those strident with fear. The arguments of both sides tend to entrench to defeat the opposition, while the public, itself, sits bemused in the middle without knowing whom to believe. It is a major strength of Wiener's work that the field is explored thoroughly and in an unbiased manner.

Fiction

Shockwave Rider, John Brunner (1976)

A reasonably crafted and amusing diversion. A little slow off the mark for my taste, but the psychodrama cerebrations of the start give way to action by about the one-third point. Good wins out over evil, the nice guys finish first, and "appropriate" technology wins the day.

Enough small talk. What about the virus?

The "tapeworm," as it is referred to in the book, comes in very close to the end. It is a creation of the hero (a computer genius, naturally) used as a tool to end the secrecy and oppression of the ruling elite. The world of the *Shockwave Rider* (the United States of the not-very-distant future) has a universal information network. Audio, video, and data channels are all tied together, and anyone can request information about anything from any terminal. The elite, of course, get the information, the masses get sanitized info and propaganda.

The tapeworm is a security-breaking program. It is not clear, from the text, whether the tapeworm reproduces. There seem to be some reproductive references to multiple "Leads": these might be additional copies of the initiating program. However, unlike programs we think of as viral, the tapeworm does not copy itself and attach to existing files. Instead, the tapeworm adds existing data and programming to itself. This allows it to provide information to requesters and to circumvent the security and privacy measures of the ruling class. (The tapeworm is also incredibly intelligent. It is able to assess and correlate completely dissimilar data points and present them appropriately to the user. Hypermedia to the max.)

References to the tapeworm indicate a size that would preclude reproduction. The authorities are unable to kill it not because of defense mechanisms or numbers of copies; rather, the authorities are prevented from even attempting to kill the tapeworm because the tapeworm has assimilated itself into network programming. To kill the tapeworm is, therefore, to kill the net.

Reasonably good read. Zero information about "real world" viral programs. Interesting conjectures.

When H.A.R.L.I.E. Was One, David Gerrold (1972/1988)

ISBN 0-553-26465-6
($3.95)
Ballantine Books
101 Fifth Avenue
New York, NY 10003
USA
OR
Bantam Doubleday Dell
666 Fifth Avenue
New York, NY 10103
USA

H.A.R.L.I.E. is not a virus. He/it is an experiment in artificial intelligence. For the purposes of the book, the experiment is a success and H.A.R.L.I.E. is alive— H.A.R.L.I.E. is a person. The plot revolves (slowly) around the efforts of corporate management to kill the project (and H.A.R.L.I.E.), and the efforts of the computer (program) and its creators to stave this off. As in most of Gerrold's books, the plot is primarily there to set up dialogues in which he can expound his philosophies.

In both versions, the "virus" is a mere diversion. It has nothing to do with the story at all and is a discussion point between two characters, never referred to again. Indeed, in the first version, the virus is introduced as science fiction, "but the thing had been around a long time before that." Make of this latter statement what you will. My resident science fiction expert can't think of what the prior story might be and ventures that this might be Asimovian self-citation.

Statements have been made that the virus aspect was downplayed in the second version. This is rather ironic. The virus story gets roughly the same amount of ink in both versions, but the early one is definitely superior. H.A.R.L.I.E.-72 gives a fairly simple and straightforward account of a self-propagating program. In fact, aside from the dependence upon dial-up links, the parallels between the H.A.R.L.I.E.-72 virus and the actual CHRISTMA infestation 15 years later are uncanny. Specifics include the use of an information

source for valid contacts and a mutation that loses the self-deletion characteristic.

The H.A.R.L.I.E.-88 discussion is much more convoluted, bringing in ma-
laria, spores, phages, and parasites. There are even two separate invocations of
the worm, one lowercase and one capitalized, both with different definitions.
(One refers to a logic bomb, and the other to a virus directed at a specific target.
Neither definition is so used by anyone else.) The end result is a completely
iconoclastic set of terminology bearing almost no relation to anything seen in
real life.

To further the irony, H.A.R.L.I.E.-88 could have been viral. H.A.R.L.I.E.-
72 could not have been: part of the system is advanced hardware that does not
exist in other computers. Therefore, while H.A.R.L.I.E.-72 has the abilities to
program other computers, such programming could never have resulted in a
reproduction without the additional hardware. H.A.R.L.I.E.-88, however, is
software only. To be sure, the environment includes "2k channel, multi-gated,
soft-lased, hyperstate" processors, roughly a million times more powerful than
the home user's "Mac-9000," but still, as one character has it, just chips.
H.A.R.L.I.E.-88 *could* survive, albeit running more slowly, on other computers.
However, while one character realizes that H.A.R.L.I.E. could be "infectious,"
the discussion dies out without understanding that the primary tension of the
story has just been eliminated.

The Tojo Virus, John D. Randall (1991)

ISBN 0-8217-3436-9
$4.95 (U.S.)/$5.95 (Canada)
Zebra Books, Kensington Publishing Corp.
475 Park Avenue South
New York, NY 10016

What we have, here, is possibly the precursor to *Terminal Compromise*. Published a year before, the plot centers around a diabolical Japanese scheme to
refight Pearl Harbor—only on an electronic battlefield. The Yellow Peril set out
to insert a virus into the computers of the mighty IGC corporation and bring
it to its knees. (Anyone who does not recognize IGC as IBM simply doesn't
know what's happening in the computer world.)

The author, in his end note, makes a lot of silly suggestions about computer
security that basically reduce to the idea that personal computer users will have
to adopt the "mainframe mentality." This advice flatly contradicts the action in
the book, which relies on loopholes in "big iron" security. The bad guys set up
a blackmail sting costing them (ultimately) four million dollars just to get one
password. (Anyone for a little social engineering?) The blackmail operation
serves primarily to introduce (the book's term, here) a "high priced slut" who
provides wild and steamy sex scenes. Fortunately (or unfortunately), depending
upon your taste (or lack thereof), the author has as little imagination in por-
nography as in technology: most of the sex scenes have little more description
than "then wild sex takes place." (This female character, though unsure of what

a "file" or a "disk" is, provides vital plot direction by minutely dissecting the technical security weaknesses in the original plan.)

The plan is to introduce a virus into the (mainframe) email system. I think. (There is an awful lot of extraneous detail.) The email, whether read or not, will encrypt PC hard disks on a given date. (The bad guys somehow think this is safe because it doesn't do anything illegal.) Once the virus hits, no one can access anything, because everyone uses PCs as terminals. Encrypted PCs can't be booted from floppies. The deadly message contained screens full of ones and zeros—obviously "Assembly language" written by REXX hackers! (REXX, boys and girls, is an interpreted language.) While all of this is going on, a single PC with a dialer program is managing to tie up the entire phone system of huge corporate offices.

Ragged plot, inconsistent characters, enough tech to fool those who know even less than Randall.

The Adolescence of P-1, Thomas J. Ryan (1977)

ISBN 0-441-00360-5
($2.25)
Ace Books
360 Park Avenue South
New York, NY 10010
USA

I still like this book of fiction the best. While Ryan is not very good at plotting, his characters, including p1, are very sympathetic. His dialogue is witty, realistic, and engaging; the events, quirky and amusing.

Strictly speaking, p1 is not a virus, but a Shoch-and-Hupp type of worm— a segmented program running on a number of computers. Initially a utility program to steal time on multiple systems, p1 mutates into a living artificial intelligence.

In order to avoid detection, p1 increases the efficiency of programming, storage, and communications of the systems that are subverted. In this way the users do not see excessive processing times, storage allocations, or line charges. Thus, p1 anticipates Fred Cohen's proposal of a compression virus and other beneficial viral programs.

The mechanics of security breaking are not explained and, in any case, would only be applicable to IBM 360 series. The concepts, however, are sound. In one instance, the target system is alert and watching for intrusion. The solution is classic: p1 has subverted IBM, so when a new system disk is requested, a trojan is tagged onto it. Trusted systems and all that. . .

I thoroughly recommend the book. It took me ages to do this review, since I kept getting caught up in it and practically reread the whole book.

Terminal Compromise, Winn Schwartau (1991)

ISBN 0-962087000-5
($19.95/$24.95 Canada)

Inter.Pact Press
11511 Pine Street North
Seminole, FL 34642
USA
tel: 813-393-6600
fax: 813-393-6361

Terminal Compromise was first published in 1991 and was enthusiastically pro-moted by some among the security community as the first fictional work to deal realistically with many aspects of data communications and security. Al-though still available in that form, recently it has been reissued in a softcopy shareware version on the net. (It is available for ftp at such sites as ftp.uu.net, ftp.netsys.com, soda.berkeley.edu, and wuarchive.wustl.edu. Use archie to look for TERMCOMP.) Some new material has been added, and some of the original sections updated. Again, it has been lauded in postings on security-related newsgroups and distribution lists.

Some of you may be old enough to recall that the characters current in *Outland* sprang from a previous Berke Breathed cartoon strip called *Bloom County*. Opus, at one point, held the post of movie reviewer for the "Bloom County Picayune." I remember that one of his reviews started out, "This movie is bad, really bad, abominably bad, bad, bad, bad!" He considers this for a moment, and then adds, "Well, maybe not *that* bad, but Lord! it wasn't good!"

A fairly large audience will probably enjoy it, if such trivialities as language, characterization, and plot can be ignored. For once the "nerds" don't get beat on; indeed, they are the heroes (maybe). The use of computers is much more realistic than in most such works, and many ideas that should have greater currency are presented. The book will also appeal to paranoiacs, especially those who believe the U.S. federal government is out to get them.

A foolish consistency is the hobgoblin of little minds—but it does make for a smoother "read." *Terminal Compromise* would benefit from a run through a style checker . . . and a grammar checker . . . and a spelling checker. On second thought, forget the spelling checker. Most of the words are spelled correctly: they are simply *used* incorrectly. A reference to an "itinerant professional" has nothing to do with traveling. (Maybe the author means "consummate": I couldn't think of a synonym starting with "i.") The "heroine" trade is probably intended to refer to white powder rather than white slavery. There are two automobile "wreaks."

Characterization? There isn't any. The major characters are all supposed to be in their forties: they all, including the president of the United States, speak like unimaginative teenage boys whose vocabulary contains no adjectives other than obscenities. This makes it difficult at times to follow the dialogue, since there are no distinctions between speakers. (The one exception is the president of a software firm who makes a successful, although surprising, translation from "beard" to "suit," and is in the midst of the most moving and forceful speech in the book, dealing with our relationship to computers, when the au-thor has him assassinated.)

The book is particularly hard on women. There are no significant female characters. None. All of the hackers, except some of the Amsterdam crew, are fit, athletic, and extremely attractive to the female of the species. Even among the I-Hack crowd, while there may be some certifiable lunatics, nobody is unkempt or unclean. These urbane sophisticates drink "Glen Fetitch" and "Chevas" while lounging in "Louis Boston" suits on "elegant . . . PVC furniture." Given that the hackers save the day (and ignoring, for the moment, that they caused the trouble in the first place), there seems to be more than a touch of wish fulfillment involved.

(Schwartau tries to reiterate the "hackers aren't evil" point at every turn. However, he throws away opportunities to make any distinctions between different types of activities. Although the different terms of phreaks, hackers, and crackers are sprinkled throughout the story, they are not defined as used by the on-line community. At one point the statement is made that "cracking is taking the machine to its limit." There is no indication of the divisions between phreaks, hackers, and crackers in their various specialties, nor the utter disdain that all three have for virus writers. Cliff Stoll's "Hanover [sic] Hacker," Markus Hess, is described in *Terminal Compromise* as a "well-positioned and seemingly upstanding individual." This doesn't jibe with Stoll's own description in *The Cuckoo's Egg* of a "round-faced, slightly overweight . . . balding . . . chain-smoking" individual who was "never a central figure" in the Chaos Computer Club, and who, with a drug addict and a fast-buck artist for partners, "knew that he'd screwed up and was squirming to escape.")

Leaving literary values aside, let us examine the technical contents. The data-security literate will find here a lot of accurate information. Much of the material is based on undisputed fact; much of the rest brings to light some important controversies. We are presented with a thinly disguised "Windows," a thinly disguised Fred Cohen (maybe two?), a severely twisted Electronic Freedom Foundation, and a heavily mutated John Markoff. However, we are also presented with a great deal of speculation, fabrication, and technical improbabilities. For the technically adept, this would be automatically disregarded. For the masses, however (and this book seems to see itself in an educational light), dividing the wheat from the chaff would be difficult, if not impossible.

We are, at places in the text, given detailed descriptions of the operations of some of the purported viral programs. One hides in "Video RAM." Rather a stupid place to hide, since any extensive video activity will overwrite it. (As I recall, the Proto-T hoax, which was supposed to use this same mechanism, started in 1991. Hmmm.) Another virus erases the disk the first time the computer is turned on, which leads one to wonder how it is supposed to reproduce. (This same program is supposed to be able to burn out the printer port circuitry. Although certain very specific pieces of hardware may fail under certain software instructions, no printer port has ever been numbered among them.) One "hidden file" is supposed to hide itself by looking like a "bad cluster" to the system. "Hidden" is an attribute in MS-DOS and assignable to any file. A "bad cluster" would not be assigned a file name and therefore would never, by itself, be executed by any computer system. In the book, we also have a report of MS-DOS viral programs wiping out a whole town full of Apple computers.

A number of respected security experts have expressed approval of *Terminal Compromise*. This approbation is likely given on the basis that this book is so much better than other fictional works whose authors have obviously had no technical background. As such, the enthusiasm is merited: *Terminal Compromise* raises many important points and issues that are currently lost on the general public.

Snow Crash, Neal Stephenson (1992)

ISBN 0-553-56261-4
($5.99, $6.99 Canada)
Bantam Books
666 Fifth Ave.
New York, NY 10103
USA
OR
1540 Broadway
New York, NY 10036
USA

Snow Crash has been lauded for its accurate portrayal of technology and its contribution to the expanding cyberpunk genre. What most reviewers have neglected to mention, or perhaps didn't notice, is that Stephenson can be very funny when he wants to be. We first meet our hero—or protagonist—Hiro Protagonist in, as the cover blurb has it, "a future America so bizarre, so outrageous . . . you'll recognize it immediately." That future is of ever-expanding strip malls crowded with international franchises and franchise nations, where pizza "deliverators" spend four years at Cosa Nostra Pizza University learning the trade and are then assigned the fastest cars on the road, a bulletproof black uniform and a sidearm that plugs into the cigarette lighter and can take down a telephone pole with one round. This is not an addition to cyberpunk, this is a parody of it.

Well, perhaps not entirely. The punk side gets a good working over, but Stephenson seems to play the technical side pretty straight. In fact, this often seems like two books running in parallel—the lighthearted look at an absurd future and a computer thriller that takes itself very seriously, indeed.

The Snow Crash of the title is—in different forms—drug, virus, and information virus. It is a universal virus, similar to the postulated universal computer virus, which spreads through minds rather than computer systems. As proposed by Stephenson, this virus uses a means of universal communications based upon the underlying structures of the brain. Thus, it can be spread either by a biological vector or an informational one. According to the story, this universality of communication was once a part of the human race, but a factor of it allowed a program to be written to destroy itself (giving rise to a new form of consciousness). The villain of the piece now wishes to return humanity to the former status, after which he will have total control. Hackers are a particular threat to this plan because of their mental discipline, but are also at risk, since their familiarity with machine coding makes them susceptible to a particular graphic display.

Given the extensive research and Stephenson's familiarity with computers, it is odd that when we start getting the explanatory version of Snow Crash, down around Chapter 56, he doesn't draw the obvious analogies to computer viral programs. The "linguistic infrastructure" of our brains could be likened to the processor: The "higher languages" are operating systems. Thus the Stoned virus can infect the hard disk of any Intel/BIOS machine, regardless of whether it is running OS/2, UNIX, or Windows NT. (The transmission of the virus, though, requires the "higher language" of MS-DOS.) Of course, if you do point this out, you have to defend against the criticism that the *real* underlying structure is digital electronics, that digital electronics do not respond to processing, and that not all processors are the same.

Still: this is a good read, with interesting ideas and amusing bits. Some inconsistency in style, and some definite inconsistencies in slang and dialogue, but overall a worthwhile diversion.

APPENDIX F

Sources of Information On-Line

In the first edition, this appendix contained a list of BBSes that carried virus-related discussion groups, antiviral software archives, or were related to antiviral vendors. I'd like to think the fact that I received only one correction to that list was the result of my careful research. A more realistic view, though, would be that it indicated a lack of interest in the list itself. The publication of the first edition coincided with an explosion of interest in the Internet, somewhat to the detriment of local boards.

The ultimate source of information on viral programs is the *VIRUS-L Digest* moderated mailing list. The moderation is fairly informal, and a message is unlikely to be rejected unless it is completely off topic, or contains viral code. However, all messages must still be vetted carefully, and there are often delays in the process. You should see your posting within six weeks, but don't be surprised if it doesn't show up immediately.

If you have access to Usenet news, the simplest method of getting *VIRUS-L* is to subscribe to the *comp.virus* newsgroup. Many people also find this more convenient to work with, since the postings are made as individual messages, rather than in the full digest format.

Anyone who has Internet mail access can subscribe by sending email to LISTSERV@LEHIGH.EDU with the line "SUBSCRIBE VIRUS-L Arthur Dent" in the body of the message. (This is assuming your name is Arthur Dent.) As with all mailing lists, you send subscription and administrative messages to the LISTSERV@LEHIGH.EDU address, and *only* postings that you want the whole world to see to VIRUS-L@LEHIGH.EDU.

The *VIRUS-L* FAQ (Frequently Asked Questions list) is the cooperative effort of a veritable "who's who" of the virus research community. You can get it by sending an email message to mail-server@rtfm.mit.edu with the command:

```
send pub/usenet/comp.virus/VIRUS-L_comp.virus_Frequently_Asked_Questions_(FAQ)
```

in the body of the message. Back issues of the digest are archived at cs.ucr.edu.

Some other Internet lists and groups have limited virus information. *VALERT-L*, available from LISTSERV@LEHIGH.EDU, is a list of new virus and infection reports only. The *comp.security.misc* and *comp.security.announce* newsgroups occasionally carry some virus discussion or alerts.

Suzana Celustka is part of the international virus research community. She became active in research while attending university in Prague, but comes originally from Croatia and is currently resident in Zagreb. In 1994 she started *Alive* magazine, distributed electronically, to examine the relation between computer viral programs and artificial life. *Alive* is available in a number of ways. Subscriptions requests should be sent to mxserver@ubik.demon.co.uk. Back issues are available from ftp://ftp.informatik.uni-hamburg.de/pub/virus/ texts/alive, ftp://ftp.demon.co.uk/pub/antivirus/journal/alive, ftp://ftp.elte.hu/ pub/virnews, ftp://ftp.u.washington.edu/public/Alive, gopher://saturn.felk. cvut.cz, and gopher://ursus.bke.hu. Send your contributions and comments to celustka@sun.felk.cvut.cz.

Local bulletin board systems vary in the coverage of virus topics. Fidonet compatible boards can get the *VIRUS_INFO* and *VIRUS* echoes (discussion groups). There is also a VirNet network, but it has not been active in North America recently. More often, Fidonet BBSes might carry the *WARNINGS* or *DIRTY_DOZEN* echoes. However, Fidonet boards can also now get *VIRUS-L* as a file feed, and this is the best bet.

Virus information areas on commercial systems have a checkered history. Most of them have been run either by one specific vendor, or by people not particularly active in virus research. The best check on a virus topic on a commercial system is to look for an archive of *VIRUS-L Digests*.

As BBS systems change very rapidly we request that you phone these numbers at an appropriate time. Please send notices of updates, corrections, or new systems to Rob Slade.

APPENDIX G

GLOSSARY

activity monitor Antiviral software that checks for signs of suspicious activity, such as attempts to rewrite program files, format disks, and so forth.

ANSI bomb Certain codes, usually embedded in text files or email messages, that remap keys on the keyboard to commands such as "DELETE" or "FORMAT." ANSI (the American National Standards Institute) refers to the ANSI screen-formatting rules. Many early MS-DOS programs relied on these rules and required the use of the ANSI.SYS file, which also allowed keyboard remapping. The use of ANSI.SYS is very rare today.

antiviral Generally used as a short form for antiviral software or antiviral systems of all types.

archive Refers to a file that contains a number of related files, usually in a compressed format in order to reduce file size and transmission (upload or download) time on electronic bulletin boards. Most software that is distributed as shareware is distributed as an archive that contains all related programs, as well as documentation and possibly data files. Archived files, because of the compression, appear to be encrypted and therefore infected files inside archives may not be detected by scanning software. (*see also* compressed executable; self-extracting)

authentication The use of some kind of system to ensure that a file or message that purports to come from a given individual or company actually does. Many authentication systems are now looking toward public key encryption and the calculation of a check based upon the contents of the file or message, as well as a password or key.

AV An abbreviation used to distinguish the antiviral research community (AV) from those who call themselves "virus researchers," but who are primarily interested in writing and exchanging viral programs (vx). (*see also* vx)

backdoor A function built into a program or system that allows unusually high, or even full, access to the system, either without an account or from a normally restricted account. This practice has legitimate uses in program development. The backdoor sometimes remains in a fully developed system either by design or accident. (*see also* trapdoor)

bacterium A specialized form of viral program that does not attach to a specific file. Usage obscure.

bait Usually used in reference to a file, this refers to an infection target of initially known characteristics. In order to trap file infectors that insist on larger files, a string of null characters of arbitrary length is often used. Floppy disks are, of course, used as bait for boot sector viral programs, but the term is not often used in that way. Another name for bait files is "goat" or "sacrificial goat" files.

benign A somewhat careless term often used to describe a viral code that appears not to be intentionally malicious in that it does not carry an obviously damaging "payload" code section. Since viral programs may cause problems simply by the use of system resources or the modification of files, many are of the opinion that a "benign" virus is impossible. (*see also* payload)

BIOS Basic Input/Output System. The initial programming, stored in ROM (read-only memory), that is used to boot the widely used IBM-compatible family of computers based on Intel 80x86 processors. Most of these computers are used with the MS-DOS operating system, but the BIOS programming is sufficient for some viral programs, which can therefore infect machines that do not run MS-DOS.

boot sector Most microcomputers allow booting from a floppy disk, and therefore automatically look for the first sector on a floppy disk and run any program found there. On MS-DOS/BIOS computers with a hard disk, the first physical sector on the hard disk is the master boot record (*see* MBR), and the boot sector is the first sector on the "logical" disk partition.

BRAIN Almost certainly the first virus written in the MS-DOS computing environment that became widespread among normal computer users. An example of a "strict" boot sector infector and the earliest known use of stealth virus programming.

BSI A boot sector infector: a virus that replaces the original boot sector on a floppy disk. A "strict" BSI only infects the boot sector, regardless of whether the target is a hard disk or a floppy diskette. Some viruses always attack the first physical sector of the disk, regardless of disk type; in this case, it attacks the master boot record on hard disks and is known as a BSI of MBR type.

change detection Antiviral software that looks for changes in the computer system. A virus must change something, and it is assumed that program files, disk system areas, and certain areas of memory should not normally change. This software is very often referred to as integrity-checking software, but it does not necessarily protect the integrity of data, nor does it always assess the reasons for a possibly valid change.

checksum In its strictest form, a checksum is a calculation based upon adding up all the bytes in a file or message. This calculation is used in change-detection systems. The term is sometimes carelessly used to refer to all forms of change detection or authentication that rely on some form of calculation based on file contents, such as cyclic redundancy checking. (*see* CRC)

CHRISTMA EXEC A specific example of a viral type of email message. This message was released in December 1987. The user was asked to type "CHRISTMA" in order to generate an electronic Christmas card, but was not told that the program also made, and mailed, copies of itself to other users during the display.

CMOS Stands for complementary metal oxide semiconductor. This is a technology that is used in a form of memory that can be held in the computer, while the main power is off, with low-power battery backup. CMOS memory is used in MS-DOS/BIOS computers to hold small tables of information regarding the basic hardware of the system. Since the memory is maintained while the power is off, there is a myth that viral programs can hide in the CMOS. (CMOS memory is too small and is never executed as a program.) Also, when the battery power fails, the computer is temporarily unusable. This is often attributed, falsely, to viral activity.

code In computer terminology, refers to either human (source) or machine (object) readable programming or fragments thereof. Since viral programs, before they attach to a host program, are not complete programs, they are often referred to as code to distinguish them from programs, which are complete in themselves.

commercial Programs that are sold either directly from the manufacturer or through normal retail channels, as opposed to shareware. Users are often told to "buy only commercial" as a defense against viral infections. In fact, there is very little risk of obtaining viral infections from shareware, and there are many known instances of shrink-wrapped commerical software infected by viral programs. (*see also* freeware; shareware)

companion A viral program that does not actually attach to another program, but which uses a similar name and the rules of program precedence to associate itself with a regular program. Also referred to as a spawning virus.

compressed executable A program file that has been compressed to save disk space and automatically returns to executable form when invoked. Because compression appears to be a form of encryption, programs that are infected before being compressed may hide the infection from scanning software. (*see also* archive; self-extracting)

computer viral program My own invention. In an attempt to avoid the fights over what constitutes a "true" virus, I use the term "viral" to refer to self-reproducing programs regardless of other distinctions. So far, I've gotten away with it.

core wars A computer game in which two or more "programs" attempt to destroy each other inside a simulated computer. Originally played with real programs in the earliest time-sharing computers and inspired by the operations of rogue programs. Often discussed in connection with the "battle" between malicious-software (malware) and protective-software developers. (*see also* malware; rogue)

CPAV/MSAV Central Point Anti-Virus and Microsoft Anti-Virus. Both are essentially the same product. Since the manufacturers won't give us a nice short name to use, we made up our own.

crab Originally "crabs" was a prank program on Macintosh and Atari computers that erased the screen display by having crabs eat it. An obscure usage refers to malicious software (malware) that erases screen displays. There are very few examples of this. (*see also* malware; prank)

CRC Cyclic redundancy check, a version of change detection that performs calculation on the data in a file or message as a matrix. This can detect multiple or subtle changes that ordinary checksum calculations miss. Also used extensively in data communications for ensuring the integrity of file transfers.

DAME Dark Avenger's Mutation Engine. (*see* MtE)

Dark Avenger The pseudonym of a Bulgarian virus writer thought to be responsible for the "Eddie" family of viral programs (among others) and the polymorphic code known as the MtE. (*see also* MtE)

denial of service A form of malicious attack, particularly suited to viral programs, where no data is actually erased or corrupted but where system resources are occupied to the extent that normal service is restricted. The CHRISTMA EXEC did not corrupt data, but occupied mail links to the point where normal transfers could not take place. The Internet Worm did not erase files, but multiple copies of the process eventually meant almost all processing was devoted to the Worm. (*see also* CHRISTMA EXEC; Internet Worm)

encryption A change to a message or file such that the appearance of the data is changed and cannot be recognized as the original without proper processing. Compression does encryption as a side effect of the process; polymorphism is a deliberate version of encryption used in viral programs. (*see also* polymorphism)

false alert A published report alerting users to the presence or activity of a virus that does not actually exist. False alerts may result from false-positive (qv.) or other erroneous results of antiviral software; confusion of viral and normal computer activity on the part of the user; or deliberate hoaxes. False alerts cause people to waste resources protecting against threats that do not exist, or to restrict computer user, and may therefore be seen as a "denial of use" attack. (*see also* metavirus)

false negative There are two types of "false" reports from antiviral software. A false-negative report occurs when an antiviral reports no viral activity or presence, when there is a virus present. References to false negatives are usually only made in technical reports. Most people simply refer to an antiviral "missing" a virus.

false positive The second kind of false report that an antiviral can make is to report the activity or presence of a virus when there is, in fact, no virus. "False positive" has come to be very widely used among those who know about viral and antiviral programs. Very few use the analogous term, "false alarm."

FAT The file allocation table. This is an **MS-DOS**–specific term for the area of system information on the disk that refers to the physical areas of the disk that are taken up by files or portions of files. Certain viral programs are said to take over a file pointer without affecting directory information by manipulating FAT information. This is not quite accurate, and most researchers tend to prefer the use of the term "system" virus or infector.

file infector A virus that attaches itself to, or associates itself with, a file, usually a program file. File infectors most often append or prepend themselves to regular program files, or overwrite program code. The file-infector class is often also used to refer to programs that do not physically attach to files but associate themselves with program filenames. (*see also* companion; system infector)

freeware Freeware is software to which the author or developer still retains copyright (unlike public domain), but for the use of which there is no charge (unlike shareware or commercial software). There are sometimes restrictions on the use or distribution of freeware.

ftp ftp has nothing to do with viral programs or data security at all; it has just come to be such a common term among those who work on the Internet that I have used it in the book a number of times without ever defining it. ftp (almost always written in lowercase) is the "file transfer protocol" of the Internet—the way to copy files between computers. It is often used as a verb, as in, "Where do I find the lastest copy of DISKSECURE?" "Oh, you can ftp it from urvax." A computer set up to provide files for all callers from anywhere on the Internet is known as an "ftp site."

generic Used to refer to various methods that will detect more than one specific virus. Examples are:

- Activity-monitoring and change-detection software, since they look for viral-like activity rather than specific virus signatures, are referred to as generic antivirals. Heuristic scanners are often included since they are a special case of activity monitors.
- A virus signature string that matches more than one virus. The usefulness of generic signatures is sometimes questioned.
- The use of error recovery or heuristic techniques for disinfection.
- Change-detection software, which will alert the user to any modification to a system, whether viral or not.

germ Another term for a viral program that does not directly attach to programs. Usage obscure.

goat *see* bait

heuristic In antiviral terms, the examination of program code for functions known to be associated with viral activity. In most cases this is similar to activity monitoring but without actually executing the program; in other cases, code is run under some type of emulation. There is also, as of this writing, a single case of a "heuristic" disinfection program that attempts to remove viral infections by examination of unknown code.

in the wild A jargon reference to those viral programs that have been released into, and successfully spread in, the normal computer user community and environment. It is used to distinguish those viral programs that are written and tested in a controlled research environment, without escaping, from those that are uncontrolled "in the wild."

integrity checker *see* change detection

Internet Worm Also known as the UNIX Worm after the operating system it used, or the Morris Worm after the author, or, very specifically, the Internet/Morris/UNIX Worm. Launched in November 1988, it spread to some three or four thousand machines connected to the Internet, wasting CPU cycles and clogging mail spools. It affected mail traffic on the Internet as a whole for a few days and is probably the viral program most widely known to the general public.

Jerusalem One of the earliest MS-DOS file infectors known to be in the wild, discovered and probably written in Israel. Originally known as the Israeli virus, it has also been called PLO, Friday the 13th, and 1813. Still one of the most widespread of file-infecting viral programs and frequently used as a template for the development of variant viral strains.

kit Refers to a program that produces viral code from a menu or a list of characteristics. A virus kit requires no skill on the part of the user. Fortunately, most virus kits produce easily identifiable code. Packages of antiviral utilities are sometimes referred to as "tool kits."

Lehigh One of the first MS-DOS viral programs. This virus infected only copies of the COMMAND.COM program. It is thought to have been limited to the campus of Lehigh University where it was discovered, but most researchers and vx boards have copies. The limited use of bootable MS-DOS diskettes makes it unlikely that the virus would successfully spread if rereleased.

link The term link is not used very widely but refers to a variety of objects. Amiga and Atari users talk about a file infector as a link virus. Others use link to refer to "system" or FAT viral programs. (*see also* FAT; system infector)

logic bomb A section of code, preprogrammed into a larger program, that waits for some trigger event in order to perform some damaging function. Logic bombs do not reproduce, and so are not viral, but a virus may contain a logic bomb as a payload. Logic bombs that trigger on time are sometimes known as time bombs. (*see also* payload; time bomb)

MacMag An early Macintosh virus known also as Brandow, after the instigator (the publisher of MacMag), and Peace, after the message payload. MacMag has the dubious distinction of being the first virus known to have infected commercial software.

malicious A virus known to carry an intentionally damaging payload that will erase or corrupt files or data. It is felt by many antiviral researchers that all viral programs carry the potential for unintentional damage since all viral programs change the target environment. (*see also* benign)

malware A general term used to refer to all forms of malicious or damaging software, including viral programs, trojans, logic bombs, and the like.

MBR The master boot record, which, on BIOS/Intel computers running MS-DOS or OS/2 with hard disks, gives information about the hard disk structure and operating system in use. The "physical first" sector on the hard disk, this is a target for a certain class of boot-sector-infecting viral programs. (*see also* BSI)

metavirus The term was first used by Jeffrey Mogul (see Chapter 7) in 1988 to describe the danger of false alerts.

Michelangelo A "descendant" of the Stoned boot sector/MBR virus, this carries a damaging payload that triggers when the computer is booted on March 6, the birthdate of the Renaissance painter and sculptor. First discovered in early 1991, the virus gained notoriety during the Michelangelo scare leading up to March 1992. Although considered by many to have been media hype, the attention generated did disclose many thousands of infections prior to March 6, which were disinfected and therefore never triggered. Michelangelo is still very widespread, in some countries being the most widely reported virus. (*see also* Stoned)

MtE The most widely used abbreviation for the "mutation engine" written by the virus author known as Dark Avenger. Not a virus itself, this is a section of code that can be attached to any virus, giving the virus polymorphic features. Also known, less widely, as DAME. (*see also* Dark Avenger; polymorphism)

multipartite A viral program that will infect both boot sector/MBRs and files.

NAV Norton AntiVirus (made by Symantec).

NLM NetWare loadable module. This system of program invocation is specific to LANs using Novell network operating systems. A number of commercial antiviral systems are including it in their packages. Effectiveness as an antiviral system component is still unknown.

nVIR An early Macintosh virus, the source code for which was inadvertently published electronically. Shortly thereafter, two versions were found in the wild.

payload Used to describe the code in a viral program that is not concerned with reproduction or detection avoidance. The payload is often a message, but is also sometimes code to corrupt or erase data. Reference to "damaging payload" is not to code causing physical destruction of the computer or parts thereof, but to corruption or erasure of files or data.

PGP Pretty Good Privacy, an encryption and authentication system held in high regard by the on-line community. (*see also* authentication; encryption)

phreak Those who are interested in breaking into or otherwise manipulating the telephone system are referred to (and refer to themselves) as "phone phreaks," using the punning variant spelling. This is generally shortened to phreaks in common usage.

polymorphism Techniques that use some system of changing the "form" of the virus on each infection in order to avoid detection by signature scanning software. Less sophisticated systems are referred to as self-encrypting.

prank Software that appears to cause problems or damage, but which, in fact, does not. In a sense the inverse of the trojan horse. Books and programs are now being sold that perform these "stupid computer tricks." May cause heart problems, but no erasure of data. (It is, however, sometimes difficult to draw a hard and fast line between pranks and malware. Pranks generally cause some "denial of service," but usually only for a short time.) (*see also* trojan horse)

public domain A legal term that carries the same meaning in regard to software as it does in the field of literature. Software in the public domain may be used by anyone, for any purpose, in any manner, without restriction. This term is often used carelessly to refer to freeware, which requires no payment, but for which the author still assumes copyright and control, and shareware, which does, in fact, require payment for continued use.

public key encryption An encryption and authentication system that allows at least one "key" to be made publicly available. This allows anyone to read the material with the public key, but does not allow alteration of the message without detection.

rabbit A program that generates multiple copies of itself without attaching to other programs. Generally, this type of attack is a "denial of service" based upon excessive use of disk or memory space or CPU cycles. Usage rare.

resident A program that stays in the memory of the computer while other programs are running, waiting for a specific trigger event. Accessory software is often of this type, as is activity-monitoring and resident scanning software. Viral programs often attempt to "go resident," and so this is one of the functions an activity monitor may check. Also known as "memory resident" and, in MS-DOS circles, TSR.

rogue A program that, because of a bug in programming, interferes with normal system operation. The damage caused by a rogue is unintentional. Used primarily in mainframe circles and now relatively rare.

ROM Read-only memory. A static memory type used to hold programming, regardless of power conditions. Primarily used for the "boot strap" programming for microcomputers. Until recently this memory has been nonwritable in normal operation and so, safe from viral attacks, but this may change with the recent use of "flash" EEPROMs (Electronically Erasable Programmable Read-Only Memory).

salami An apocryphal story of a program that takes advantage of very active systems to make incremental changes. The usual tale is of a banking system that siphons fractions of a penny into the programmer's account. Usage rare.

scanner A program that reads the contents of a file looking for code known to exist in specific viral programs.

Scores A Macintosh virus that seems to have been written with intent to cause problems for a specific company and software program. Because one of the most widely published reports of infection was from an office at NASA, it has also been referred to as the NASA virus.

self-extracting An archive that is stored in program format and that contains the code necessary to do the "de-archiving." Popular with neophyte BBS users because it does not require separate de-archiving programs, it presents a number of potential security vulnerabilities.

shareware Software that is distributed widely, usually on bulletin boards and networks. Users are encouraged to "try before you buy," but those who continue to run the software are supposed to pay for the programs. The honor system of distribution reduces overhead costs, and shareware is generally cheaper than commercial software.

shrink-wrap The plastic film used to protect the packaging of commercial software. "Shrink-wrapped software" is often used as a synonym for commercial software. Many people feel shrink-wrap is some kind of guarantee or warranty. It isn't.

spawning *see* companion

stealth Various technologies used by viral programs to avoid detection on disk. At least one virus has been named "Stealth" by its author, but the term properly refers to the technology, not a particular virus.

Stoned An extremely successful MS-DOS virus, in terms of the number of copies made and systems infected. A BSI of MBR type, it has, like most successful viral programs, been used as a template for numerous other viral strains.

system infector A virus that redirects system pointers and information in order to infect a file without actually changing the infected program file. This is a type of stealth technology. In MS-DOS, often referred to as a "FAT" virus.

time bomb Sometimes used to refer to a logic bomb that triggers on a time event. (*see also* logic bomb)

TOAST This acronym was first used by Padgett Peterson to refer to antiviral software that makes extravagant claims, or where a company spends more on advertising than on development. The origin was a product that advertised itself as, "The Only Antivirus Software That Won't Be Obsolete By The Time You Finish Reading This Ad."

TOM Top of Memory (this is particularly significant in PCs). The amount of RAM is recorded in the computer; viruses may try to tell the software that follows that there is less memory than there really is, so that the virus won't get overwritten.

TPE Trident Polymorphic Engine. Another version of the "mutation engine" type of function, but done by a different group. (*see also* MtE)

trapdoor *see* backdoor

trojan horse A program that either pretends to have, or is described as having, a (beneficial) set of features but that, either instead or in addition, contains a damaging payload. Most frequently the usage is shortened to trojan.

TSR "Terminate and stay resident." (*see* resident)

tunneling Techniques that involved the tracing of the system interrupts to the final programming. Used by both viral and antiviral programs to detect or disable opposing programs.

viral Having the features of a virus, particularly self-reproduction.

virus A final definition has not yet been agreed upon by all researchers. A common definition is

> *a program that modifies other programs in order to contain a possibly altered version of itself.*

This definition is generally attributed to Fred Cohen, although Fred's actual definition is in mathematical form. My own definition is

> *an entity that uses the resources of the host (system or computer) to reproduce itself and spread, without informed operator action.*

I may, of course, be trying too hard.

vx An abbreviated reference to the virus exchange community—those people who consider it proper and right to write, share, and release viral programs, including those with damaging payloads. The term probably originated with

Sara Gordon, who has done extensive studies of the virus-exchange and security-breaking community and who has an aversion to using the SHIFT key.

worm A self-reproducing program that is distinguished from a virus by the fact that it copies itself without being attached to a program file and can spread over computer networks, particularly via email.

zoo Jargon reference to a set of viral programs of known characteristics used to test antiviral software.

APPENDIX H

ANTIVIRAL CHECKLIST

(Just to finish off, and for quick reference)

For each computer

- Directory list of all program files, dates, and sizes
- List of programs run at start-up
- Source code for menus
- Description of boot sector
- Description of partition boot record
- Description of memory map at start-up
- Description of interrupts at start-up
- Backup "originals" of software
- Backup of hard-disk directory structure
- Clean, protected, bootable system diskette

For each office

- Description of current common viruses
- List of local virus information contacts
- List of all hardware and software purchased, suppliers, and serial numbers
- Designated machine for receiving/testing new disks/software
- Log of disks/programs received
- Memory and disk mapping utilities

Regularly

- Back up data
- Monitor disk space, map, memory map
- Monitor program file sizes

At software install/change

- Protect originals

- Install from protected backup
- Trial run on isolated system
- Map memory before and after run
- Offer "bait" files and disks

If infection found

- Send copy to recognized researcher
- Isolate machine and disks
- Perform minimal disinfection

APPENDIX I

ANTIVIRAL FILES ON ACCOMPANYING DISK

In the first edition of the book, I concentrated on antiviral programs for detecting and getting rid of viruses. This time around I have reduced the number of antiviral programs in order to include virus information files.

These files are copyrighted by the original authors, but you may use them without paying license fees.

Programs

UNZIP.EXE (MS-DOS)

This is not an antiviral but a public domain de-archiving utility for the .ZIP files on the disk (all the MS-DOS programs). Zip is a widely used archiving format developed by PKWare for their PKZip set of programs. This utility will only uncompress version 1.1 level Zip files: if you are going to go after updated versions of these files, you will likely need to get the updated version of PKZip (currently 2.04G).

For each of the programs here, you may want to create a separate directory. For example, if you want to extract KILLMONK, create a directory on your hard disk called "KILLMONK" with the command "MKDIR \KILLMONK." Move into that directory (CHDIR KILLMONK) and then copy both UNZIP.EXE and KILLMNK3.ZIP into that directory. Then give the command "UNZIP KILLMNK3" and UNZIP will extract all of the files in the archive. Some of the files will have a .DOC or .TXT extension: please read them with your favorite word processor or copy them to your printer as they are the documentation for the individual programs.

KILLMNK3.ZIP (MS-DOS)

Generally speaking, I don't recommend "single virus" disinfectors. KILLMONK is the one exception. The Monkey virus, mostly in its B variant, is not only extremely widespread but also annoyingly difficult to remove. I forgot to include Tim Martin's excellent program in the first version of the book—and guess what everyone who contacted me wanted?

To use KILLMONK on your computer, place the floppy disk in your *A:* drive and type the following commands at your "C:>" prompt:

```
MKDIR \KILLMONK
CHDIR \KILLMONK
COPY A:UNZIP.EXE
COPY A:KILLMNK3.ZIP
UNZIP KILLMNK3.ZIP
```

Four files will be extracted. KILLMNK3.DOC is the manual, while INT_10.NOT and MONKEY.NOT are technical documents on those two viruses. You can read them with a word processor or you can simply print them all by typing the commands:

```
COPY KILLMNK3.DOC PRN
COPY *.NOT PRN
```

The main program is now ready to use: just type "KILLMONK" and the program will start up. You should read the documentation files to find out more about the program and also to get Tim's address so that you can write and let Tim's boss know what a wonderful and important person Tim is.
Tim Martin
Department of Soil Science
4-42 Earth Sciences Building
University of Alberta
Edmonton, Alberta
Canada   T6G 2E3
martin@ulysses.sis.ualberta.ca

FP-220.ZIP (MS-DOS)

This is the F-PROT virus scanner and disinfector, current at the time of manuscript submission. By the time the book is available (September of 1996), the current version of F-PROT will likely be 2.13 at least. F-PROT tends to be updated about every two months in a major release, and sometimes more often for minor releases (A, B, C, etc.) that add new virus signatures. Updated versions should be available at better BBS systems and antiviral ftp sites. F-PROT is shareware, and an incredible bargain. It is also free for noncommercial use. Full documentation is available in the archive file. Commercial versions of F-PROT are available from other sources.

To use F-PROT on your computer, place the floppy disk in your *A:* drive and type the following commands at the "C:>" prompt:

```
MKDIR \FPROT
CHDIR \FPROT
```

```
COPY A:UNZIP.EXE
COPY A:FP-220.ZIP
UNZIP FP-220.ZIP
```

29 files will be extracted. The ones with the .DOC extension and one called NEW.xxx (with a three-digit extension) are the documentation files. You can read them with a word processor or you can simply print them all by typing the commands:

```
COPY *.DOC PRN
COPY NEW.* PRN
```

(The ones with an .ASC extension are PGP "signatures" for their respective files. If you don't know what **PGP** is, you don't need to worry about these.)

The main program is now ready to use: just type "F-PROT" and the program will start up. Since the files should be updated regularly, and since publishing of books has a long lead time, you will find that when you start it up you will get a warning message on the screen telling you that the program is old and you should get a new one. After that, however, the program will operate normally. It has a menu-driven interface and on-line help. There are, however, other features and functions that you might want to use. You should read the documentation files to find out how to use the resident scanner and other facilities.

If you set the program to scan "all files", F-PROT will detect some, though not all, Word Macro viruses.

Fridrik Skulason
Frisk Software International
Postholf 7180
IS-127 Reykjavik
Iceland
Phone number +354-1-617273
Fax number +354-1-617274
frisk@complex.is

DISINF36.HQX (MAC)

Disinfectant is generally considered to be the best antiviral for the Macintosh. John Norstad has developed and maintained Disinfectant and made it available free of charge, an incredible service to the Mac community. Mac users will need BinHex or a compatible de-archiver to extract the files.

The disk included with this book is an **MS-DOS** formatted disk, so you will need a Macintosh computer with a SuperDrive and Apple File Exchange or similar disk-reading software. A BinHex file contains only text characters, so copy the file to your Mac with either *no* conversion, or a "text-to-text" conversion.

Once you have copied the file onto your Mac, you will need to convert it back to binary form. Recent versions of BinHex or StuffIt should work. Other archiving programs may also have BinHex capability. Once in binary form you will have a "Self-Extracting Archive" (SEA) File. Double-click on it and it will extract itself.

Disinfectant is not intended to detect HyperCard or Word Macro viruses.
John Norstad
Academic Computing and Network Services
Northwestern University
2129 Sheridan Road
Evanston, IL 60208 USA
j-norstad@nwu.edu

DS242.ZIP (MS-DOS)

DISKSECURE is the part that Microsoft, Digital Research, and IBM all left out of DOS. This tiny and elegant specialized change-detection program makes boot sector infectors, the major incidence of infection, obsolete. It can also provide security for the hard disk and help recover from certain types of hard-disk disasters. Earlier shareware versions of DISKSECURE resulted in almost no registrations, so Padgett has now made the program freeware for noncommercial use. (Companies can get custom-made versions.) It would be nice if someone sent Padgett a new Pontiac from time to time. Full documentation is available in the archive: *please* be sure to read it first. You must, for example, install DISKSECURE from floppy disk, and so you will need to copy the files from your hard drive onto a floppy for installation. However, it is important to read the documentation to know what DISKSECURE is doing to your computer. It is one of the safest programs that I know of, but it is extraordinarily powerful, and service people may be very surprised at some of its functions. It is particularly important that you know how to remove the program if you are asked to.

To extract DISKSECURE on your computer, place the floppy disk in your *A:* drive and type the following commands at your "C:>" prompt:

```
MKDIR \DS
CHDIR \DS
COPY A:UNZIP.EXE
COPY A:DS242.ZIP
UNZIP DS242.ZIP
```

23 files will be extracted. The ones with the .DOC extension, one called README.DS and one called WARNING.NOT are the documentation files. You can read them with a word processor or you can simply print them all by typing the commands:

```
COPY *.DOC PRN
COPY README.DS PRN
COPY WARNING.NOT PRN
```

A. Padgett Peterson
Orlando
POB 1203
Windermere, FLA, 34786
(407) 352-6007
Fax: (407) 352-6027
padgett@tccslr.dnet.mmc.com

Virus Information

AMIGAVIR.ZIP, ATARIVIR.ZIP, INDEX.793, MACVIR.*, MSDOSVIR.ZIP, MVSVIR.ZIP, and UNIXVIR.ZIP

For a number of years, the most accurate source of information about specific viral programs has been the *Computer Virus Catalog* (*CVC*) produced by the Virus Test Center (VTC) at the University of Hamburg. This was distributed simply as a series of text files.

These files are the *Computer Virus Catalog*. INDEX.793 is, as the name suggests, an index for the various files. It is in text format and can be read by any word processor on any computer that can read this disk.

MSDOSVIR.ZIP is the archive of MS-DOS information files. To extract the files on an MS-DOS computer, place the floppy disk in your *A:* drive and type the following commands at your "C:>" prompt:

```
MKDIR \CVC
CHDIR \CVC
COPY A:UNZIP.EXE
COPY A:MSDOSVIR.ZIP
UNZIP MSDOSVIR.ZIP
```

In this case 11 files will be extracted. These are all text files with a three-digit extension signifying the date of the file. (For example, MSDOSVIR.793 is the index file for July 1993.) You can read them with a word processor or you can simply print them all by copying them to the printer, as in the preceding example for KILLMONK.

Until sales of the book get big enough to justify the inclusion of a CD-ROM, disk space limits what I can include here. I did, however, want to provide something for the Mac folks in addition to Disinfectant. The five MACVIR files are text files from the *Computer Virus Catalog* describing Macintosh viruses. These can be copied by any Mac with a Superdrive and can be read with your favorite word processor.

For Amiga, Atari, Archimedes, MVS, and UNIX users, my apologies, but all I had space left for were the zipped archives of those parts of the *Computer Virus Catalog* (plus the index, which lists the virus descriptions for all of them). Zip format extractors are available for all those platforms, or you can use an MS-DOS computer to extract the files, and then copy them to your machine. (Apologies to Archimedes users: there wasn't room enough.)

The *CVC* information has been expanded with the addition of the CARO-base material and is now available in a more easily accessible form, the Computer Malware Base. The information is contained in database files, with an access program that runs under MS-DOS. Unfortunately, it is too large a file to include here, but it can be obtained from the VTC site (see below) under the filename CMB30.ZIP.

Virus Test Center (VTC)

University of Hamburg

VTC BBS: + 49 40 54715-235

ftp://ftp.informatik.uni-hamburg.de/pub/virus/progs/

INDEX